OUT OF WEDLOCK

OUT OF WEDLOCK

Causes and Consequences
of Nonmarital Fertility

Lawrence L. Wu and
Barbara Wolfe, Editors

Russell Sage Foundation / New York

The Russell Sage Foundation

The Russell Sage Foundation, one of the oldest of America's general purpose foundations, was established in 1907 by Mrs. Margaret Olivia Sage for "the improvement of social and living conditions in the United States." The Foundation seeks to fulfill this mandate by fostering the development and dissemination of knowledge about the country's political, social, and economic problems. While the Foundation endeavors to assure the accuracy and objectivity of each book it publishes, the conclusions and interpretations in Russell Sage Foundation publications are those of the authors and not of the Foundation, its Trustees, or its staff. Publication by Russell Sage, therefore, does not imply Foundation endorsement.

Library of Congress Cataloging-in-Publication Data

Out of wedlock : causes and consequences of nonmarital fertility / Lawrence Wu and Barbara Wolfe, editors.
      p. cm.
   Includes bibliographical references and index.
   ISBN 0-87154-982-4
      1. Unmarried mothers—Congresses.   2. Unmarried mothers—Services for—Congresses.   I. Wu, Lawrence, 1964–   II. Wolfe, Barbara L.
   HV700.5 .O97 2001
   362.83'928—dc21

2001019331

Text design by Suzanne Nichols

RUSSELL SAGE FOUNDATION
112 East 64th Street, New York, New York 10021
10 9 8 7 6 5 4

Contents

Contributors

LAWRENCE L. WU is professor of sociology at the University of Wisconsin-Madison.

BARBARA WOLFE is professor of economics, preventive medicine, and public affairs at the University of Wisconsin-Madison.

JUDI BARTFELD is assistant professor in the consumer science department and specialist in cooperative extension at the University of Wisconsin-Madison.

LARRY L. BUMPASS is professor emeritus of sociology at the University of Wisconsin-Madison and codirector of the National Survey of Families and Households.

ANDREW J. CHERLIN is Griswold Professor of Public Policy in the department of sociology at Johns Hopkins University.

JOHN ERMISCH is professor of economics at the Institute for Social and Economic Research at the University of Essex and a fellow of the British Academy.

E. MICHAEL FOSTER is associate professor of health policy and administration at Pennsylvania State University.

IRWIN GARFINKEL is M.I. Ginsberg Professor of Contemporary Urban Problems in the School of Social Work at Columbia University.

DEBORAH ROEMPKE GRAEFE is a Family Research Consortium postdoctoral fellow at the Center for Human Development and Family Research in Diverse Contexts at the Pennsylvania State University.

ROBERT HAVEMAN is John Bascom Professor of economics and public affairs at the University of Wisconsin-Madison.

SAUL D. HOFFMAN is professor of economics at the University of Delaware.

THEODORE J. JOYCE is professor of economics in the Zicklin School of Business, Baruch College, City University of New York.

ROBERT KAESTNER is professor in the School of Public Affairs, Baruch College, City University of New York.

KELLEEN S. KAYE is a senior analyst specializing in human services policy at the U.S. Department of Health and Human Services, Office of the Assistant Secretary for Planning and Evaluation.

KATHLEEN KIERNAN is professor of social policy and demography and codirector of the Centre for the Analysis of Social Exclusion at the London School of Economics and Political Science.

SANDERS KORENMAN is professor in the School of Public Affairs, Baruch College, City University of New York.

DANIEL T. LICHTER is Robert F. Lazarus Professor in population studies and professor of sociology at the Ohio State University.

The late LEE A. LILLARD III was professor of economics at the University of Michigan and senior research scientist at the Institute for Social Research.

SHELLY LUNDBERG is professor of economics at the University of Washington.

SARA MCLANAHAN is professor of sociology and public affairs at Princeton University.

DANIEL R. MEYER is professor in the School of Social Work at the University of Wisconsin-Madison.

ROBERT A. MOFFITT is professor of economics at Johns Hopkins University.

KELLY MUSICK is assistant professor of sociology at the University of Southern California.

CONSTANTIJN (STAN) W.A. PANIS is senior economist at RAND.

KAREN PENCE is an economist with the Board of Governors of the Federal Reserve System in Washington, D.C.

Nancy E. Reichman is research staff member at the Office of Population Research at Princeton University.

Julien O. Teitler is assistant professor in the School of Social Work at Princeton University.

Dawn M. Upchurch is associate professor of public health at the University of California at Los Angeles.

Acknowledgments

The chapters in this volume are drawn from a conference held in April 1999 at the Institute for Research on Poverty (IRP) at the University of Wisconsin-Madison. The organizers—Judi Bartfeld, Larry Bumpass, Robert Haveman, Barbara Wolfe, and Lawrence Wu—had two goals in planning this conference. The first was to provide a forum in which social scientists from the disciplines of demography, economics, and sociology could jointly review the state of basic research on nonmarital fertility. The second was to provide objective information and analysis relevant to public and policy discussions of nonmarital fertility. The chapters in this volume thus touch on a number of topics, including trends in nonmarital fertility within the United States and Europe, the increasing importance of childbearing within cohabiting unions, issues of child support, the interrelationship of nonmarital childbearing and federal programs such as Aid to Families with Dependent Children and its successor, Temporary Assistance for Needy Families, and the consequences of nonmarital childbearing for the social and economic well-being of families and children.

Funding for the conference was provided by IRP and the Office of the Assistant Secretary for Planning and Evaluation (ASPE), which we gratefully acknowledge. Contributors to this volume benefited from comments by two reviewers engaged by the Russell Sage Foundation and from discussions during the conference led by Jan Hoem, George Clarke, Lee Lillard, Robert Plotnick, Michael Rendall, James Walker, and Robert Willis. Much of the organizational burden of running the conference was borne by Elizabeth Evanson, who carried out these duties with her usual good cheer and great skill. We wish also to acknowledge the valuable support given to this project by Suzanne Nichols, director of publications at the Russell Sage Foundation, and Eric Wanner, the foundation's president; Barbara Wolfe, director of IRP; members of IRP's National Advisory Committee, who made valuable suggestions concerning the content of the conference; Christine Bachrach, Demographic and Behavioral Sciences Branch, National Institute of Child Health and Human Development; and Patricia Ruggles and Donald Oellerich of ASPE.

Introduction

The last 30 years have been a social disaster largely because people have felt free to enter into—or leave—any relationship they wanted. The result has been abandoned women and children, births out of wedlock and fatherless children. Children need a mother and a father. Marriage must be preserved as an institution intended to bring a man and woman together. It is not hateful or exclusionary to say these things.

(Bauer 2000)

[That] family relationships occupy an important but ever shrinking space in our lives . . . is the continuation of a long-term process and is not confined to any one country. . . . There is no reason to think that these processes are exhausted or likely to reverse.

(Bumpass 1990)

Sexual behaviour has never anywhere been confined to procreative behaviour, procreative behaviour confined to marriage, and marriage confined to the official celebrations established by society.

(Laslett 1980)

Nonmarital fertility, with its consequences for women, children, and social institutions such as marriage and the family, has increasingly captured the attention of researchers, policymakers, and the public. Heated debate on the subject in the mid-1990s (Whitehead 1993) culminated in the 1996 Personal Responsibility and Work Opportunity Reconciliation Act (PRWORA), one goal of which was to achieve reductions in nonmarital childbearing. To this end, the federal government now awards $100 million annually to the five states with the largest reductions in the proportion of births outside of marriage.

There has been both good and bad news since passage of the PRWORA. The good news is that the percentage of births to unmar-

ried women stopped increasing after 1995 (see figure I.1). For social scientists, this represents a striking break from the previous
trends. The bad news is that the percentage of children born outside of marriage remains high even after the enactment of PRW-
ORA. One of every three children born in 1999 was to an unmarried mother; this percentage has been unchanged since 1995.

Because the percentage of births to unmarried women is simply
the ratio of unmarried births to all births, social scientists have long
understood that changes in this index can be driven by changes in
nonmarital childbearing, changes in marital childbearing, or changes
in both. Computing separate time-series for birth rates to married
and unmarried women (see figure I.1) reveals that much of the
increase in the percentage of births to *unmarried* women over the last
four decades has in fact been driven by declines in the rate of childbearing among *married* women. This means that even if the change
from a welfare system based on Aid to Families with Dependent
Children (AFDC) to one based on Temporary Assistance for Needy
Families (TANF) played a role in arresting the steady increase in the
proportion of children born out of wedlock, it appears not to have
turned back the clock on out-of-wedlock births. Nonmarital childbearing shows no sign of subsiding, here at the beginning of the new
century, in either absolute numbers or social impact.[1]

Continuing high rates of nonmarital childbearing lead commentators like Gary Bauer (2000) to be concerned about the health of social
institutions such as marriage and family, but historians (Laslett 1980)
also remind us that "bastardy" has been present from time imme-
morial. Moreover, as the demographer Larry Bumpass argues, the
trends underlying nonmarital fertility are rooted in long-term historical processes that transcend national boundaries. Addressing the
issues underlying this debate is not unlike determining how one
might judge whether nonmarital fertility is relatively high or low.
One way to try to answer this question is provided by comparing
levels of nonmarital childbearing in the United States, as in figure I.1.
Another is to compare levels of nonmarital fertility in the United
States with other industrialized countries.

Research by Kiernan (this volume) and Ventura and Bachrach
(2000) contains surprising information on the latter means of comparison (see figure I.2). The United States falls roughly midway
between the highest and lowest levels of nonmarital fertility in
twenty industrialized nations. Substantially higher proportions of
births to unmarried women are found in Scandinavia and the for-

Figure I.1 Percentage of Births to Unmarried Women and
Birth Rates for Married and Unmarried Women
Aged Fifteen to Forty-Four, United States,
1960 to 1999

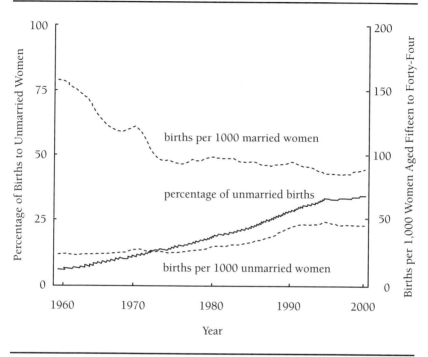

Source: Ventura and Bachrach (2000).

mer East Germany, where roughly one of every two births is outside
of marriage, and in France, the United Kingdom, and Finland,
where more than one of every three births is nonmarital. Levels in
Austria, Canada, and Ireland are slightly lower than in the United
States, and they are lower still in the Netherlands and Portugal. The
lowest levels are recorded in the former West Germany, Spain, Italy,
Switzerland, Greece, and Japan.

Nearly all of these countries, moreover, have witnessed sharp increases in nonmarital fertility: several countries have experienced a
doubling or more in the percentage of such births since 1980. It is
these findings that have led social scientists like Bumpass to argue
that recent trends in nonmarital fertility reflect other social forces—
the increasing participation of women in the labor force, continuing

Figure I.2 Percentage of Births Occurring to Unmarried Women in Selected Industrialized Nations, 1980 and 1998

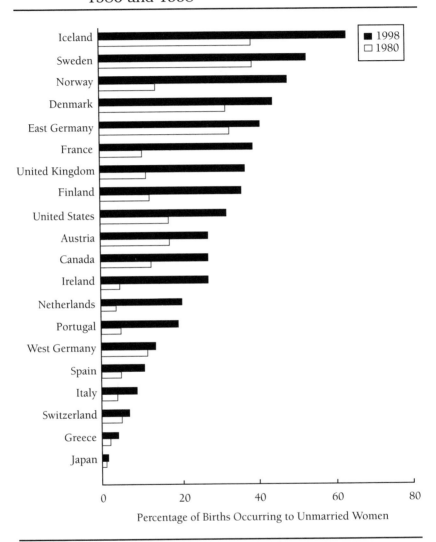

Percentage of Births Occurring to Unmarried Women

Source: Kiernan (this volume); Ventura and Bachrach (2000).
Note: Most recent data are from 1997 for Sweden, France, Finland, Canada, and West Germany, and from 1995 for East Germany, Spain, and Switzerland.

high levels of divorce, the almost universally high levels of sexual activity prior to marriage, and the increasingly widespread diffusion of cohabitation—and that these social forces, in turn, are transforming the institutions of marriage and the family in ways that transcend national boundaries. Or as the economist Shelley Lundberg puts it at the close of this volume, we must keep in mind that nonmarital childbearing is likely to represent a response by individuals to fundamental changes in the long-term contract represented by marriage.

An extremely important (and rapidly evolving) focus of research on nonmarital fertility is childbearing by cohabiting couples. Here, too, there are important differences between the United States and Europe, as the chapters in this volume reveal. The overwhelming proportion of European nonmarital births are to two unwed parents who are coresiding. In the United States, fewer than half of births outside of marriage are to cohabiting parents. As a result, U.S. children born to unmarried mothers are likely to spend more years, on average, than their European counterparts growing up without a father. This difference is of concern to social scientists and policymakers because, all else being equal, a family with an absent father has less access to his income, as well as to the emotional and social resources of a second parent. The greater prevalence of father absence in the United States may partly explain why child poverty is higher, and many child and adolescent outcomes are worse, in the United States than in Europe. Moreover, social provisions for children are generally less generous in the United States than in Europe, further exacerbating national differences in family and child well-being.

The striking differences in nonmarital fertility by race and ethnicity in the United States underlie further differences between this country and the European nations. For American whites, births within cohabiting unions have risen sharply, accounting for virtually all of the observed increase in white nonmarital fertility. This pattern closely resembles trends observed across Europe. By contrast, births within cohabiting unions account for a far smaller proportion of nonmarital births to black women—fewer than one out of five—and over time, births within cohabiting unions have constituted a declining fraction of nonmarital births to black women.

Viewed one way, births within cohabiting unions resemble births within marital unions—two biological parents are present, incomes and other resources are presumably shared, and household work and childrearing activities can be, at least in principle, divided between two adults. Viewed another way, however, births within cohabiting unions are closer to births to single, noncohabiting women in that cohabiting unions are far less stable than marital unions. As a result, children born within a cohabiting union are more likely to spend fewer years living with both biological parents than children born within a marital union. Moreover, what we observe—the presence or absence of a marital or cohabiting union—is but a crude proxy for what is far more difficult to observe: the commitment of the adults to one another and to the child, commitments which may vary over time.

What is clear is that children born outside of marriage spend more of their lives below or at the poverty line, in part because of the number of years they spend in families headed by a single mother. This raises a serious issue: social underinvestment in children in families headed by a single mother. When this occurs, liberals have traditionally argued that other social agents—typically state or federal agencies—should address the difference. However, a dilemma for policymakers is that the social and economic resources intended for children very often assist parents as well, as it is difficult to target policies in ways that benefit children but not parents. This has led conservatives to argue that programs such as AFDC may have fostered behaviors that are deemed socially undesirable—for example, the view that AFDC may have contributed to the rise in out-of-wedlock childbearing.

However troublesome these issues are, the questions they raise must be balanced against two facts: substantial proportions of this nation's children are raised in poverty, and children born to unmarried mothers are among those at the highest risk of poverty.

TRENDS AND INTERNATIONAL COMPARISONS

For researchers, one difficulty posed by nonmarital fertility is that it lies at the intersection of several processes by which families are formed: childbearing, marriage, and, increasingly, cohabiting unions. The contributors to this volume show how researchers have addressed the conceptual, theoretical, methodological, and empirical issues posed by nonmarital fertility. Nevertheless, these issues remain challenging.

For example, researchers are only now beginning to grapple with the additional analytic issues that arise when cohabitation is included in their behavioral and statistical models. In this volume, seven of the twelve chapters proceed without attention to births occurring within cohabiting unions (Kaye; Moffitt; Foster and Hoffman; Bartfeld and Meyer; Korenman, Kaestner, and Joyce; Haveman, Wolfe, and Pence; Upchurch, Lillard, and Panis). The remaining chapters (Wu, Bumpass, and Musick; Kiernan; Ermisch; McLanahan et al.; Lichter and Graefe) distinguish, at least some of the time, between births to married couples, births to cohabiting couples, and births outside either marital or cohabiting unions. Some of this inconsistency is attributable to data limitations: several major U.S. surveys lack information that would allow researchers to identify a nonmarital birth within a cohabiting union. Another reason concerns the evolving nature of nonmarital childbearing. Whether to bear a child within marriage, within a cohabitating union, or outside of either arrangement may well mean something quite different now than it did twenty years ago.

In chapter 1, Lawrence Wu, Larry Bumpass, and Kelly Musick pose several questions about nonmarital fertility in the United States: How has nonmarital childbearing changed in recent decades, and what are the components of this change? Do nonmarital first births differ from later births? How does nonmarital fertility differ by age of mother and race and ethnicity? To what extent is nonmarital fertility attributable to childbearing by cohabiting couples?

Our examination of trends in nonmarital childbearing during the last twenty-five years reveals startling differences by race. As noted previously, one of three U.S. births now occurs outside of marriage. This proportion in the early 1990s was one in four for white women, compared with seven in ten births for black women. Black-white differences are equally stark with respect to nonmarital first births and births to cohabiting couples. In the early 1990s, one in three first births to white women were nonmarital, while more than eight in ten first births to black women were nonmarital.

How does nonmarital fertility vary with the age of the mother? Despite a marked shift toward nonmarital childbearing at older ages, nonmarital fertility in the United States still tends to occur at young ages, with half of all nonmarital first births between 1990

and 1995 to teenage women. Age differences are even more apparent when marital and nonmarital first births are juxtaposed. For
marital first births to both black and white women, the mean age at
first birth rose by five years, from twenty-three to twenty-eight, between 1970 and 1995. For nonmarital first births during this
twenty-five-year period, the mean age at first birth rose from twenty
to twenty-one for white women and from nineteen to twenty-one
for black women. Thus, unmarried women in the mid-1990s were,
on average, seven years younger than their married counterparts
when they gave birth to their first child, with well over half of
nonmarital first births occurring during the teen years for both
black and white women. As a result, the *initiation* of nonmarital
childbearing in the United States appears strongly tied to patterns
of early family formation.

What impact does marital or union status have on nonmarital
second births? We find that most women proceed to a second birth
irrespective of their marital or union status at their first birth. Nevertheless, union status at first birth is highly associated with union
status at second birth: marital first births are overwhelmingly followed by marital second births, cohabiting first births by cohabiting
second births, and single first births by single second births. One
reason for this association is the sharp decline in marriage following a nonmarital first birth, particularly for black women. Perhaps
more interestingly, union instability appears considerably greater for
women who bear their first child within a cohabiting union. Cohabitating women are more than twice as likely to experience the
dissolution of their union following a first birth than their married
counterparts.

Kelleen Kaye's findings, reported in chapter 2, will be of particular interest to state policymakers given PRWORA's cash bonuses to
states with the largest reductions in the percentage of nonmarital
births. She finds that nonmarital births ranged in 1997 from 64 and
45 percent in the District of Columbia and Mississippi to 20 and 15
percent in Idaho and Utah. Nonmarital births are particularly concentrated among those with the least education and among women
in their teens or early twenties.

Minority populations are large in the District of Columbia and
Mississippi but small in Idaho and Utah. Because of this, Kaye asks
how state rankings would be altered if the racial and ethnic composition of each state were equalized to that of the nation as a whole.

This exercise yields some surprises: Indiana, Nevada, Pennsylvania, Rhode Island, and Wisconsin rank high in nonmarital childbearing after standardization, owing in part to high levels of nonmarital childbearing among minorities in these states. Kaye also finds that national trends in the percentage of births to unmarried women are mirrored at the state level, but that states exhibit a pattern of "regression to the mean." This means that many of the largest increases occurred in states with the lowest levels in 1980, and many of the smallest increases took place in states with the highest levels in 1980.

The next two chapters broaden the scope of the volume by looking at nonmarital fertility outside of the United States. In chapter 3, Kathleen Kiernan documents substantial variation in nonmarital childbearing across Europe. An important contribution of this piece is Kiernan's focus on childbearing among cohabiting couples. The main lesson is that it is impossible to understand recent changes in European nonmarital fertility without understanding the very substantial rise in childbearing within cohabiting unions across all European nations. Despite widely varying initial levels of nonmarital fertility, nearly all nations have moved away from the initiation of childbearing within marriage and toward its initiation within a cohabiting union. A key finding is that the proportion of women having a first child within a union—either marital or cohabiting—exhibits little change for successive cohorts of women. Kiernan's estimates also show that first births outside either a cohabiting or marital union are less common in Europe (with only two exceptions, Austria and Great Britain) than among white women in the United States.

As in the United States, cohabiting unions in Europe are more likely than marital unions to dissolve following the birth of a first child, but union dissolution rates are noticeably lower in Europe than in the United States. (As noted earlier, Great Britain is an exception to this rule.) Overall, the trend within Europe (like that for whites in the United States) is toward childbearing within de facto unions, rather than de jure unions. It seems likely that the greater stability of European cohabiting unions will lead, all else being equal, to more favorable child outcomes in Europe than in the United States.

As noted in Kiernan's findings, nonmarital fertility in Great Britain seems to run counter to its European neighbors, and in chapter

4, John Ermisch sheds considerable light on these differences. Ermisch's findings suggest that U.S. and British nonmarital fertility share some striking similarities in ways that set both apart from most of Europe. Indeed, the proportion of births occurring outside of marriage is even higher in Great Britain than in the United States. In both countries, nonmarital childbearing is especially prevalent during the teen years. Paralleling trends in Europe and in the United States, increases in the percentage of nonmarital births in Britain are due primarily to a rise in cohabiting first births. And relative to marital births, births within cohabiting unions or outside of any union occur disproportionately to women from poorer socioeconomic backgrounds.

Another similarity between Great Britain and the United States is the instability of cohabiting unions, relative to marital unions, following a birth. Ermisch calculates that 30 percent of children born within marital unions will experience the divorce of their parents prior to their sixteenth birthday; for children born within a cohabiting union, 64 percent will experience their parents' separation through the dissolution of their cohabiting or marital union. (These estimates are remarkably similarly to the life table estimates obtained by Wu, Bumpass, and Musick, reported in chapter 1.) Ermisch's estimates of the consequences of unstable unions and marriages for British children in terms of how many years they will live in a single-mother family are nearly identical to the estimates of Bumpass and Lu (2000) for U.S. children, again suggesting striking similarities in the experiences of British and U.S. children.

WELFARE, CHILD SUPPORT, AND PUBLIC POLICY

The next set of chapters focus on welfare, child support, and other public policy issues. Robert Moffitt breaks important new ground in chapter 5 by examining time-series data on the relationship between AFDC and nonmarital births. A large economic literature (for a review, see Moffitt 1998) has examined this relationship in cross-section, and the consensus among social scientists is that AFDC benefits exerted a statistically significant but small effect on nonmarital births. A persistent puzzle, however, is how to square these cross-sectional findings with trends in nonmarital births and AFDC generosity—nonmarital births increased dramatically in recent decades, while the inflation-adjusted real value of AFDC benefits fell markedly over the same period.

Moffitt's results suggest that there is in fact no real inconsistency between the time-series and cross-sectional evidence. One possibility is that falling AFDC benefits acted over time to reduce nonmarital births but other factors pushed nonmarital births in the opposite direction. Following a long tradition in labor economics, Moffitt posits that changing labor market opportunities for women (as proxied by female wage rates) influenced women's childbearing decisions, but he also augments these analyses by examining the effects of male wages and the relative wages of males and females. It is interesting to note that male wages, while implicit in economic models of the family (Becker 1973), have played a central role in some influential sociological accounts of nonmarital childbearing (Wilson 1987).

Moffitt's empirical analyses rely on a series of stylized time-series models employing random year effects, with data drawn from a time-series of male and female wage rates, combined with national time-series data on AFDC, food stamps, and Medicaid benefits between 1968 and 1996. The results are consistent with both the arguments that emphasize the role of AFDC and those that focus on male and female labor market opportunities. Moffitt's results suggest that the rise in female headship over the last thirty years has *not* been due primarily to changes in the generosity of welfare benefits. As a result, other factors, such as declines in marriage or changes in labor market conditions, are more likely to explain the dramatic rise of female headship in the United States.

In chapter 6, E. Michael Foster and Saul Hoffman examine the linkage between AFDC and nonmarital childbearing along more traditional lines. The important innovation in their analysis is to ask whether this relationship varies with the age of the mother. This question confronts a serious substantive difficulty: during the teen years, adolescents undergo remarkable changes, not just physically but also cognitively and socially. This is a point emphasized by psychologists in the areas of child and adolescent development. It is also (or should be) of consequence to economists, sociologists, and demographers. It is a particularly relevant factor to Foster and Hoffman because, as they note, one might expect older women (or those at risk of a nonmarital second birth) to act more deliberately and "rationally" than teenage women or women who have not yet given birth. Thus, one might expect older women, or women at higher birth orders, to be more sensitive to variation across states (and perhaps across time) in welfare generosity in ways expressed in behaviors related to marriage and fertility. As Foster and Hoffman note, this sort of age variation cannot be motivated from economic models in which women are thought to maximize utility over their lifetime, although it can be motivated from models in which women are viewed as relatively myopic, using current benefits as a proxy for probable short-run benefits.

A second point of departure for Foster and Hoffman is an influential paper by Mark Rosenzweig (1999), who finds a greater association between AFDC and nonmarital childbearing than has been found in other studies. Like Rosenzweig (1999), Foster and Hoffman employ state fixed-effects models (as they do in a companion paper, Hoffman and Foster 2000). Their consideration of nonmarital fertility through age thirty moves beyond both papers, however, by distinguishing between nonmarital first and second births and by allowing the association between AFDC and nonmarital fertility to vary with age. Their results give some support to the idea that the effect of AFDC varies with the age of the mother, in that welfare discourages younger women from marrying and encourages women in their twenties to bear children outside of marriage, particularly at higher birth orders. Still, their estimates for the effects of AFDC on marriage and nonmarital fertility prove quite sensitive to the inclusion or exclusion of state fixed-effects. As Foster and Hoffman note, the resulting findings are difficult to interpret. The argument for including state fixed-effects is that they capture unobserved state-level factors that may affect both a state's level of welfare generosity and, in turn, the nonmarital fertility of women residing there. Failure to correct for such unobservables can bias estimates controlling for state fixed-effects. But fixed-effects estimates reduce precision and can amplify biases created by measurement error. As a result, the absence of a statistically significant effect need not imply the true absence of an effect.

In chapter 7, Sara McLanahan, Irwin Garfinkel, Nancy Reichman, and Julien Teitler report on early findings from the Fragile Families Project, an important data collection effort in twenty cities consisting of interviews with young mothers and fathers in hospital settings at the time of birth. They present analyses based on data for 1,764 mothers in seven cities—Austin, Baltimore, Detroit, Newark,

Oakland, Philadelphia, and Richmond. They find that although only a small proportion are married at the time of birth, the vast majority of mothers and fathers report themselves as romantically involved. This is an intriguing finding and one that differs considerably from both depictions of men as engaged in a contest to win status by fathering many children out of wedlock (Anderson 1990; Willis 1999) and accounts in which women perceive fathers as unreliable breadwinners (Edin and Lein 1997).

If parents are unmarried but romantically involved, are they cohabiting? McLanahan and her co-authors answer this question by providing not one but several sets of estimates of cohabitation. One gives substantially larger proportions of births within cohabiting unions than national estimates, while another agrees substantially with national estimates. What could account for these discrepancies? All else being equal, the tendency of social scientists to trust reports based on shorter rather than longer durations of recall would favor the estimates from Fragile Families rather than those from national estimates, which rely on retrospective reports. The time periods also differ: the most recent national estimates come from the early 1990s, and Fragile Families estimates cover the late 1990s. Thus, increases in cohabitation among minorities—or concealment of cohabiting unions by AFDC recipients—could account for these differences.

It is also possible that, by interviewing respondents at the time of birth, Fragile Families catches parents at a time of unusual optimism, perhaps biasing responses toward more socially acceptable answers. Indeed, the alternative estimates set forth in this chapter suggest that this optimism may play a significant role. For example, about 60 percent of white and Hispanic mothers and 40 percent of black mothers report that they cohabited with the father of their child at the time of birth. However, these percentages drop to around 50 percent for whites and Hispanics and to 28 percent for blacks when this item is combined with questions about whether the baby will live with both parents and whether the father is listed on the household roster. These latter percentages are very close to national estimates of the percentage of nonmarital births to cohabiting couples.

Whatever the precise estimate for cohabitation, these results are important because they show that substantial numbers of fathers are present at birth and that many appear ready and willing to be involved in raising their children. Nevertheless, McLanahan and her colleagues caution that father involvement is likely to decline over time among those couples who do not marry or who break off their relationship. Certainly, some couples will eventually marry, although it must be borne in mind that marriage is likely to differentially select on the least fragile of these families. Still, this picture is strikingly similar to that given by Frank Furstenberg (1995) in summarizing the findings from his Baltimore study: "The intentions of fathers far outstrip their ability to make good on their goal of becoming involved caretakers. Whether by design, desire, or default many fathers retreat—some almost immediately but most after their initial efforts end in frustration or their motivation lags." Although unmarried parents may express hopes and desires similar to those of married parents, their unions are subject to a variety of circumstances—disruption and poverty among them—that make their families unusually fragile.

In chapter 8, Judi Bartfeld and Daniel Meyer report on a little-examined phenomenon—the role of child support in providing income to families in which a child is born outside of marriage. Issues related to child support have grown in importance since the passage of the Family Support Act of 1988, which led to increased efforts to establish paternity and stricter enforcement of child support awards. Bartfeld and Meyer restrict their analysis to never-married women with children present in the household at the time of survey and use nine years of repeated cross-sectional data to construct synthetic cohorts of women and children.

Their findings suggest that relatively few households in this sample receive child support. Nevertheless, among those who do receive some child support, it amounts to a substantial fraction of household income. Interestingly, the probability of child support receipt rises (and reliance on public assistance declines) with the age of the oldest child in the household. At least two explanations for this association are possible: as children become older, the earnings of fathers may also increase; and as an unmarried woman gives birth to children by different men, the likelihood that she will receive child support from at least one of them may increase. Although Bartfeld and Meyer do not find evidence of this latter effect, analyses of Wisconsin households by Maria Cancian and her colleagues (2000) suggest that both explanations have merit. In any event, the kinship relations of families formed by nonmarital childbearing do seem to be more complicated than relations in more traditional families, and these complexities may have implications for policies directed at families with nonmarital births.

CONSEQUENCES FOR CHILDREN AND ADULTS

Despite widespread expectations that nonmarital childbearing carries adverse consequences for the children born into these families, there is surprisingly little empirical research on the subject. The next two chapters in this volume attempt to fill this gap. In chapter 9, Sanders Korenman, Robert Kaestner, and Theodore Joyce examine outcomes during infancy and early childhood, and outcomes during adolescence and early adulthood are the subject of chapter 10 by Robert Haveman, Barbara Wolfe, and Karen Pence.

Both sets of authors are sensitive to the fact that women who give birth outside of marriage tend to be more disadvantaged than their married counterparts. Indeed, a central difficulty in interpreting the association between nonmarital fertility and child outcomes is determining whether an observed association is causal or an artifact generated by unobserved factors that may predate the birth of the child. Korenman, Kaestner, and Joyce address this issue by employing fixed-effects models that use sibling and cousin comparisons, which control for unobserved factors common to siblings or cousins, and by employing models that assume that unintended births represent an exogenous fertility shock relative to intended births. By contrast, Haveman, Wolfe, and Pence employ a random-effects probit model, which allows outcomes for children from the same family to be correlated.

Korenman and his colleagues find that nonmarital births are far more likely to be reported as unintended than are marital births, but that this difference accounts for very little of the differential in parenting behaviors, infant health, or child development observed for marital and nonmarital births. Controlling for unobserved factors common to siblings or cousins further reduces this difference, sometimes substantially. Their results speak less clearly, however, on the effects of an out-of-wedlock birth on child development. In models that ignore unobserved factors common to siblings or cousins, they find sizable and significant disadvantages for children born outside of marriage, but the estimates of these effects lose

statistical significance in models with family fixed-effects. The difficulty is that the effect of being born to a never-married woman
remains sizable; hence, it is unclear whether the large but statistically insignificant estimates in their fixed-effects models are due to
the absence of a true effect or to the lack of statistical power. They
obtain similar results from models that assume that unintended
births represent an exogenous fertility shock. As a result, Korenman
and his colleagues conclude that the "evidence for an effect of being
born to a never-married woman on child development is mixed."

In chapter 10, Haveman and his colleagues examine whether being born to an unmarried mother raises a woman's propensity to
bear a child out of wedlock herself or lowers the likelihood of com-
pleting high school. Like Foster and Hoffman, they ask if consequences may vary with the age of the respondent's mother, and if
disadvantage may be particularly severe for children of the youngest
mothers. Their findings suggest that the factors influencing education completion are distinct from those influencing childbearing
outside of marriage. Children born outside of marriage are less
likely to complete high school than children born within marriage,
regardless of their mother's age. Thus, mother's marital status is a
more potent predictor than her age in accounting for whether her
children will complete high school. By contrast, children born to
young mothers are much more likely to have a teen nonmarital
birth than children born to older mothers, an association that holds
for children born both within and outside of marriage. Thus,
mother's age, as opposed to her marital status at birth, is the more
potent predictor of whether her daughter will give birth to a child
as an unmarried teen. These findings point to the intergenerational
transmission of *early* family formation, but not to the intergenerational transmission of *nonmarital* childbearing. The latter finding
may appear surprising, but my colleagues and I (Wu and Martinson
1993; Wu 1996) reached an identical conclusion in analyses of two
data sources different from that used by Haveman and his colleagues.

The next two chapters look at the consequences of a nonmarital
birth for adults. Both chapter 11 by Daniel Lichter and Deborah
Graefe and chapter 12 by Dawn Upchurch, Lee Lillard, and Constantijn Panis ask the same question: Are unmarried women who
give birth less likely to marry after the birth than their unmarried
counterparts who have not given birth outside of marriage? Lichter

and Graefe also ask whether a nonmarital birth affects a woman's subsequent likelihood of entering a cohabiting union, while Upchurch, Lillard, and Panis ask whether a nonmarital birth affects the stability of marital unions for those women who marry after the birth.

As in previous chapters, a central difficulty lies in establishing whether an observed association is causal. Both sets of authors are sensitive to this problem, but they adopt quite different approaches to it. Lichter and Graefe supplement estimates from standard regression models with two additional sets of estimates that compare pregnancies of unwed women that are brought to term with those that are aborted or resulted in miscarriages, and that compare unwed mothers whose children reside in their household with unwed mothers whose children do not live with them. Upchurch, Lillard, and Panis use a simultaneous equation hazard model, which allows unobserved factors to be correlated across equations for marriage, marital dissolution, fertility, and education. These models, they argue, help control for the endogeneities between these joint processes and for the resulting differential selection into marital and fertility statuses.

Despite quite different data and methodological approaches, the two chapters obtain remarkably similar results. Upchurch and her colleagues find considerable evidence of endogeneities between the processes underlying marriage and fertility. Their results imply that nonmarital childbearing depresses marital prospects in both direct and indirect ways. That there are indirect effects suggests that women are differentially selected into motherhood while unmarried and that this plays a substantial role in their subsequent marital prospects. Lichter and Graefe, similarly, report evidence that a nonmarital birth lowers a woman's subsequent prospect of entering a marital union, although they find no significant effect on her subsequent prospects of entering a cohabiting union. Taken together, these results shed useful light on the important issue of the union and marital formation patterns of women who have had a child outside of marriage. Marriage and cohabitation are ways in which women may respond to the prospect of raising a child as a single parent. Indeed, these alternatives are likely to be even more germane to women under a TANF policy regime, in which time limits on benefits may influence their marriage and fertility decisions.

The last two chapters are by Shelley Lundberg and Andrew Cherlin and represent the disciplines of economics and sociology, respectively. The conference organizers approached these two distinguished social scientists to serve as rapporteurs for the conference papers, and we are exceedingly fortunate to have their responses. Lundberg and Cherlin reflect more generally on the questions raised in this volume and on a variety of empirical issues about which we know less than we should. They describe the broader social context in which nonmarital childbearing might be situated, and glean the policy lessons (and dilemmas) implied by the empirical findings assembled in this volume.

NOTE

1. There is, as yet, no consensus within the research community on whether PRWORA has in fact played a major role in arresting the steady increase in nonmarital childbearing. It is important to note that much of what appeared in PRWORA had roots in earlier welfare experiments undertaken in individual states. With this in mind, some researchers have found (Horvath-Rose and Peters 2000) that at least some of the variation across states and time in nonmarital childbearing can be linked to the timing of waivers issued by the federal government to states. There are, however, substantial grounds for caution. Horvath-Rose and Peters find that time limits on welfare benefits and work requirements by states had surprisingly little effect on nonmarital childbearing and that even the effect of family caps and AFDC-UP waivers were small relative to trends during this period. Similarly, Klerman and Haider (2000) find that even such seemingly obvious consequences of PRWORA, such as the quite precipitous drop in welfare rolls, may not be causally related to PRWORA provisions such as time limits on welfare benefits.

REFERENCES

Anderson, Elijah. 1990. *Streetwise: Race, Class, and Change in an Urban Community.* Chicago: University of Chicago Press.

Bauer, Gary. 2000. "Fuzzy Morality." Op-ed piece, *New York Times*, October 8, 2000.

Becker, Gary S. 1973. "A Theory of Marriage." In *Economics of the Family: Marriage, Children, and Human Capital,* edited by Theodore W. Schultz. Chicago: University of Chicago Press.

Bumpass, Larry L. 1990. "What's Happening to the Family: Interaction

Between Demographic and Institutional Change." *Demography* 27(4): 483–98.

Bumpass, Larry L., and Hsien-Hen Lu. 2000. "Trends in Cohabitation and Implications for Children's Family Contexts." *Population Studies* 54(1): 29–41.

Cancian, Maria, Robert Haveman, Daniel R. Meyer, and Barbara Wolfe. 2000. "Before and After TANF: The Economic Well-Being of Women Leaving Welfare." Special Report No. 77, Institute for Research on Poverty, University of Wisconsin–Madison.

Edin, Kathryn, and Laura Lein. 1997. *Making Ends Meet.* New York: Russell Sage Foundation.

Furstenberg, Frank F., Jr. 1995. "Dealing with Dads: The Changing Roles of Fathers." In *Escape From Poverty: What Makes A Difference for Children?,* edited by P. Lindsay Chase-Lansdale and Jeanne Brooks-Gunn. New York: Cambridge University Press.

Hoffman, Saul D., and E. Michael Foster. 2000. "AFDC Benefits and Non-Marital Births to Young Women." *Journal of Human Resources* 35(2): 376–91.

Horvath-Rose, Ann, and H. Elizabeth Peters. 2000. "Welfare Waivers and Non-Marital Childbearing." Working paper 128, Joint Center for Poverty Research, Northwestern University and University of Chicago.

Klerman, Jacob, and Steven Haider. 2000. "A Stock-Flow Analysis of the Welfare Caseload: Insights from California Economic Conditions." Paper presented at the 2000 Annual Meetings of the Population Association of America, Los Angeles, Calif.

Laslett, Peter. 1980. "Preface." In *Bastardy and its Comparative History,* edited by Peter Laslett, Karla Oosterveen, and Richard M. Smith. Cambridge, Mass.: Harvard University Press.

Lillard, Lee A., Michael J. Brien, and Linda J. Waite. 1995. "Premarital Cohabitation and Subsequent Marital Dissolution: A Matter of Self-Selection?" *Demography* 32(3): 437–57.

Moffitt, Robert A. 1998. "The Effect of Welfare on Marriage and Fertility." In *Welfare, The Family, and Reproductive Behavior: Research Perspectives,* edited by Robert A. Moffitt. Washington, D.C.: National Academy Press.

Rosenzweig, Mark R. 1999. "Welfare, Marital Prospects, and Nonmarital Childbearing." *Journal of Political Economy* 106(6, pt. 2): S3–S32

Ventura, Stephanie J., and Christine A. Bachrach. 2000. "Nonmarital Childbearing in the United States, 1940–99." *National Vital Statistics Reports,* 48(16). Washington, D.C.: National Center for Health Statistics.

Whitehead, Barbara Dafoe. 1993. "Dan Quayle Was Right." *Atlantic Monthly* (April): 47–84.

Willis, Robert J. 1999. "A Theory of Out-of-Wedlock Childbearing." *Journal of Political Economy* 106(6, pt. 2): S33–S64.

Wilson, William Julius. 1987. *The Truly Disadvantaged: The Inner City, the Underclass, and Public Policy.* Chicago: University of Chicago Press.

Wu, Lawrence L. 1996. "Effects of Family Instability, Income, and Income Instability on the Risk of a Premarital Birth." *American Sociological Review* 61(3): 386–406.

Wu, Lawrence L., and Brian C. Martinson. 1993. "Family Structure and the Risk of a Premarital Birth." *American Sociological Review* 58(2): 210–32.

PART I

Trends and International Comparisons

CHAPTER 1

Historical and Life Course Trajectories of Nonmarital Childbearing

Lawrence L. Wu, Larry L. Bumpass, and Kelly Musick

Cohabitation and nonmarital fertility are profoundly transforming the family experiences of both children and parents (Smith, Morgan, and Koropeckyj-Cox 1996; Bumpass and Raley 1995; Bumpass, Raley, and Sweet 1995). Approximately half of all children spend some time in a single-parent family while growing up, yet roughly two-fifths of such families are begun by an *unmarried* birth (Bumpass and Raley 1995; Bumpass and Sweet 1989). A substantial minority of single-parent families are thus begun by the childbearing of single women or cohabiting couples. Social scientists and policymakers alike have been slow to grapple with the possibility that many of the difficulties faced by both children and parents may flow not only from parental divorce—a traditional focus of social scientific research—but from the ongoing social changes associated with cohabitation, nonmarital childbearing, *and* divorce (see, for example, McLanahan and Sandefur 1994).

If family life is evolving, so too is the nature of nonmarital childbearing. Among white women, nonmarital birth rates doubled at all ages between the mid-1970s and the mid-1990s (Ventura et al. 1995). Moreover, while nonmarital first births have been and continue to be prevalent among teenage women, nonmarital births increasingly consist of higher-order births to non-teen women (Foster and Hoffman 1996). As of the early 1990s, second- and higher-order nonmarital births accounted for 48 percent of births to unmarried white women and fully 60 percent of births to unmarried black women (Ventura 1995). Nonmarital fertility has also increased substantially among women over age nineteen. In 1970 one-half of all nonmarital births were to teenage women, but by the early 1990s nonmarital births to women age twenty and older accounted for more than two-thirds of all nonmarital births (Ventura et al. 1995).

Although the link between cohabitation and nonmarital fertility is less well understood, it is increasingly clear that changes in nonmarital fertility have been affected significantly by ongoing trends in cohabitation (Bumpass, Raley, and Sweet 1995; Bumpass and Lu 2000). In the early 1990s about 40 percent of nonmarital births officially classified as creating single-mother families were in fact births to cohabiting couples (Bumpass and Lu 2000). Cohabitation was prevalent among AFDC populations; Moffitt, Reville, and Winkler (1998) report cohabitation rates as high as 18 to 25 percent for AFDC recipients in some age groups, prior to the welfare reforms of 1996. Moreover, for whites, trends in nonmarital fertility appear to have been driven almost entirely by increases in births within cohabiting unions during the 1970s and 1980s, while trends for blacks are reduced substantially when accounting for cohabiting births (Bumpass and Raley 1995).

These observations point to significant shifts in the nature of nonmarital fertility—from first births to higher-order births, from childbearing during the teen years to childbearing at later ages, and from births that occur outside of informal unions to births that are increasingly linked to the formation (and dissolution) of cohabiting unions. To unravel these issues, we take a descriptive first step by tracing women's pathways through marital, union, and nonunion childbearing in recent decades. One difficulty is that trajectories within these populations typically show enormous variability in family experience (Martinson and Wu 1992; Rindfuss 1991). Documenting such variation is essential, we believe, to understanding family change, but the resulting complexity of family experience can be daunting both descriptively and analytically. To manage this complexity, we describe selected components of the processes underlying nonmarital fertility, starting at the broadest level of description and then successively refining the detail of our focus.

We begin by examining change over time in the broad contours of nonmarital childbearing over the last twenty-five years. We find that increases in nonmarital fertility during the last twenty-five years have been driven largely by dramatic increases in nonmarital *first* births. Widely cited figures from vital statistics indicate that the proportion of births occurring outside of marriage has risen sharply: as of the mid-1990s, one in three births is nonmarital (Ventura 1995). We find that the proportion of first births occurring outside of marriage has increased even more dramatically. We estimate that more than four of five first births to black women and fully one of three to white women occurred outside of marriage in the mid-1990s; hence, the fraction of nonmarital *first* births for white women equals—and for black women substantially exceeds—the one-in-three proportion of *all* births occurring outside of marriage. These trends are mirrored in stark black-white differences in the union status of unmarried first births: of births to recent cohorts of first-time unmarried white women, over 40 percent occurred in a cohabiting union, while for black women the corresponding figure is 12 percent.

These levels of *first* births to unmarried women signal dramatic changes in the life course of women as growing numbers of women choose to initiate motherhood outside of formal marriage. Although recent research (for example, Geronimus and Korenman 1993; Hoffman, Foster, and Furstenberg 1993a, 1993b; Haveman, Wolfe, and Pence, this volume; Korenman, Kaestner, and Joyce, this volume) shows that the consequences of a teen birth are less dire than those put forth by Campbell (1968), we also now know that there is considerable diversity in outcomes for teen mothers (Furstenberg, Brooks-Gunn, and Morgan 1987). Still, poverty remains high in single-mother families, especially for those single mothers who gave birth while unmarried. Thus, continuing increases in nonmarital fertility provide considerable grounds for concern about the socioeconomic well-being of recent cohorts of U.S. children.

It is important to emphasize that not all behaviors related to nonmarital childbearing have accelerated over the last twenty-five years. Indeed, our results suggest relative stability along several behavioral dimensions. We find little change in the proportion proceeding from a first to second nonmarital birth for white women during recent decades, although we do observe a modest increase in this progression for black women. For both black and white women, our results suggest only a small increase in the average age at first birth for women who bear their first child outside of marriage, while the proportion of nonmarital first births to teen mothers has declined modestly. These latter findings nevertheless raise serious concerns. During this period there have been substantial increases in the mean age at first birth for women who initiate childbearing within marriage, in contrast to only small increases in age at first birth for unmarried women, large proportions of whom still give birth during their teen years. Because teen childbearing remains highly correlated with socioeconomic disadvantage to off-spring, trends indicating *widening* disparities in age at first birth may serve to further exacerbate the already substantial differentials in the social and economic circumstances of families in which childbearing is initiated within versus outside of marriage.

We conclude by examining the trajectories of women through marital and cohabiting unions and tracing how these union experiences relate to married and unmarried childbearing. To do so, we must describe initial marital, union, and fertility statuses and then follow women forward in time as these statuses change. To make this task manageable, we restrict our attention to a cohort of women with first births in the early 1980s.

We find that more than seven in ten women progress to a second birth within ten years of a first birth. Differences by union status at first birth in the progression to a second birth are modest and decline with duration since first birth. What is remarkable is that second births to unmarried women are nearly as prevalent as second births to married women. We also find that union status at first birth is highly associated with union status at second birth: marital first births are almost always followed by marital second births, cohabiting first births are most likely to be followed by cohabiting second births, and single first births are most likely to be followed by single second births. Nevertheless, these results indicate greater similarity than difference in women's fertility trajectories among those who have initiated childbearing, whether within or outside of marriage or within or outside of a cohabiting union.

By contrast, women's union trajectories exhibit substantial variability, especially for women who are single or cohabiting at first birth. What is notable is that we observe variability in union and marital trajectories both across individuals and within an individual's life span. Couples who bear children within a cohabiting union are substantially more likely to dissolve their union subsequently than are couples who bear children within a marital union. Thus, while children born within cohabiting unions resemble those born within marital unions in that both biological parents are present at the birth of the child, these children are also much more likely to experience the disruption of their parents' union than are children born within marital unions. This finding is notable because accumulating evidence suggests that turbulent family environments may carry adverse consequences for children (see, for example, An, Haveman, and Wolfe 1993; Capaldi, Crosby, and Stoolmiller 1996; Capaldi and Patterson 1991; Cherlin et al. 1991; Wu 1996; Wu and Martinson 1993; Wu and Thomson forthcoming).

In interpreting these latter results, it is important to keep in mind both the rapid pace of change across first-birth cohorts and the fact that following a 1980 to 1984 first-birth cohort forward to 1995 spans a considerable length of time with respect to changes in cohabitation and unmarried childbearing. Of course, these changes reflect the reality experienced by recent cohorts: women in this period initiated childbearing under one regime and then proceeded through a period characterized by dramatic and rapid changes in childbearing, union formation, and union dissolution. Thus, conclusions and interpretations of our findings must be tempered by the realization that the object of our inquiry—the union and fertility trajectories of women—is itself a moving target.

DATA AND METHODS

We analyze data from two sources: the June supplements to the 1990 and 1995 Current Population Surveys (CPS), and the 1995 National Survey of Family Growth (NSFG).

JUNE CURRENT POPULATION SURVEY

The CPS is the monthly survey conducted by the Bureau of the Census to document changes in labor force status. Supplements to the CPS on specific topics ranging from school enrollment to family and marital status are issued periodically. The June CPS has collected marital and fertility data on a roughly five-year cycle that provide detailed event histories for up to three marriages and for up to five births. In analyzing trends over time, we have pooled data from the 1990 and 1995 June CPS. Pooling the data in this way provides us with large samples and hence relatively stable estimates of period trends. A significant drawback of these data, however, is that they lack retrospective information on respondents' entries and exits from cohabiting unions. As a result, the CPS lets us distinguish only between married and unmarried births; hence, our analyses of cohabitation rely on data from the 1995 National Survey of Family Growth (NSFG).

NATIONAL SURVEY OF FAMILY GROWTH—CYCLE 5

The NSFG is a periodic survey conducted by the National Center for Health Statistics with the primary goal of providing estimates of the factors affecting the U.S. birth rate and the reproductive health of women in the United States. The sample universe consists of women age fifteen to forty-four. Marital and fertility histories have long been a part of the content of this survey, but cycle 5 provides complete cohabitation histories for the first time, as well as detailed education, employment, and living arrangement histories. Interviews averaging 105 minutes were conducted with 10,847 respondents over the first ten months of 1995 (Potter et al. 1998).

METHODS

In both data sources, we construct estimates by comparing dates in marriage or union histories with dates in fertility histories. Because of variation in the duration between separation and divorce and in the proportion of disrupted marriages that ever divorce, we include as nonmarital those births that occur either between separation and divorce or after separation for women who separate but never divorce (Sweet and Bumpass 1990; Castro-Martin and Bumpass 1989). Our definition differs from that used in the birth registration system; hence, when comparing trends obtained from vital statistics with trends estimated from survey data, we revert to the birth registration definition, using the timing of divorce, not separation, to distinguish between marital and nonmarital births.

We begin our analyses of trends in nonmarital fertility during the 1970s through the early 1990s with an examination of period estimates, followed by estimates obtained from competing-risk life table methods. In these analyses, we rely primarily on pooled data from the June 1990 and 1995 CPS, which provide large samples over a long historical span. We then turn to a more detailed examination of the experiences of women whose first birth occurred during the period 1980 to 1984. In these analyses, we rely heavily on data from the 1995 NSFG but present some CPS analyses for comparative purposes. By focusing on a cohort of first births occurring between 1980 and 1984, we have at least ten years in which to observe the joint union and fertility trajectories of women following a first birth.[1] We examine the union status of women five and ten years after the first birth and, for those women who go on to have a second child, the union status of the second birth. We then describe women's pathways through their union and fertility statuses in the ten years following their first birth. To simplify this discussion, we focus attention on the major trajectories that capture over 90 percent of all pathways from a first birth. The remaining pathways constitute a diverse set and are not easily summarized.

RESULTS

TRENDS OVER TIME

To establish the context for this discussion, we begin with figure 1.1, which presents well-known trends in the nonmarital fertility ratio since 1970. For a given calendar year, the nonmarital fertility ratio gives the number of births occurring outside of marriage expressed as a percentage of all births. The CPS estimates are derived from the comparison of women's retrospective reports of marital and fertility histories, whereas the vital statistics series is based on the registration of births.

Figure 1.1 Black-White Trends in Births to Unmarried Women, 1970 to 1998

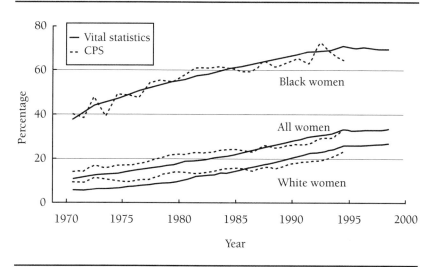

Source: Vital statistics on natality; June 1990 and 1995 Current Population Surveys.

The middle set of curves reports estimates for the entire U.S. population. Here we see the widely cited and dramatic rise in the percentage of births occurring outside of marriage—one in three by the late 1990s. The upper and lower sets of curves show corresponding increases in nonmarital childbearing among black and white women, with about one in four births to white women occurring outside of marriage and nearly seven of ten births to black women occurring outside of marriage in 1998. It is worth noting that the nonmarital fertility ratio for both whites and blacks rose steadily throughout the 1970s and 1980s until 1995, then flattened out after 1996. The post-1996 period coincides with recent welfare reforms but was also preceded by declines in teenage pregnancy and increases in teenage contraceptive use (Kaye, this volume; Ventura et al. 2000).

Despite very different estimation procedures, there is good agreement overall between the trends from CPS and vital statistics. Both sets of estimates reflect a marked increase in the proportion of births to unmarried women, and both indicate a roughly linear increase over this period. For blacks, the CPS and vital statistics trends agree closely, while for whites, CPS estimates indicate a slightly less rapid increase, with estimates falling above the vital statistics series in the 1970s and early 1980s and below this series in the most recent period. Although vital statistics reports on unmarried childbearing have generally been regarded as the "gold standard" against which other data sources can and should be calibrated, we think it is important to acknowledge that both vital statistics and CPS data may be affected by the stigma attached to unmarried childbearing in ways that may both vary over time and operate differentially by race and ethnicity.

Although these two series produce qualitatively similar patterns, conclusions about the magnitude of trends, as well as decompositions of these trends (see, for example, Smith, Morgan, and Koropeckyj-Cox 1996), may be especially sensitive to slight differences in estimated levels of nonmarital childbearing during the 1970s, particularly for white women. Moreover, it is important to note the conceptual ambiguity posed by births that occur between marital separation and divorce: some will have been conceived prior to separation, and some will have been conceived months or even years after marital separation. Nevertheless, these conceptual issues, as well as the slight differences in the precise magnitude of these

Figure 1.2 Black-White Trends in Marital, Cohabiting, and Single Births to Women Under Age Thirty

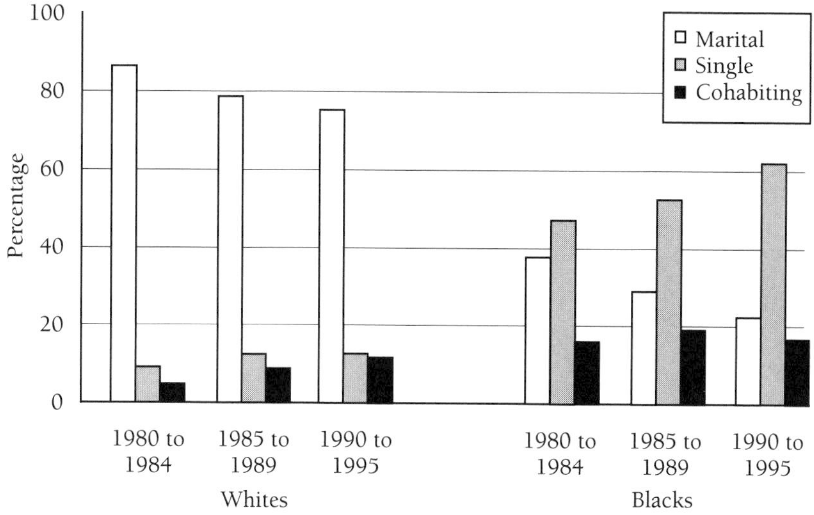

Source: 1995 National Survey of Family Growth.

trends, should not obscure the fact that both sets of estimates in figure 1.1 show substantial increases in the proportion of children born outside of marriage between the 1970s and early 1990s, and that both vital statistics and the CPS provide close—and remarkably high—estimates for current levels of unmarried childbearing.[2]

Figure 1.2 presents trends in the distribution of births occurring within marital unions, cohabiting unions, and outside of any union for white and black women in the National Survey of Family Growth. The unshaded bars give the percentage of births occurring within marriage, the shaded bars the percentage occurring outside of either marital or cohabiting unions, and the dark bars the percentage occurring within cohabiting unions, with percentages for adjacent bars summing to 100. Because the NSFG sample consists of women age fifteen to forty-four in 1995, we avoid issues of age truncation by restricting the sample in figure 1.2 (and in subsequent analyses using the NSFG) to women under age thirty at the time of birth. This age restriction results in a series extending only from 1980 to 1995.

Although the great majority of births to white women throughout this period occurred within marital unions, births within marital unions have nevertheless declined, while those occurring within cohabiting unions or outside of any union have increased. Of births to white women between 1980 and 1984, 86 percent occurred within marital unions, 5 percent within cohabiting unions, and 9 percent outside of either a marital or cohabiting union. Marital births to white women declined steadily over this period, falling in the period 1990 to 1995 to 76 percent of all births to white women. Births within cohabiting unions and outside of any union rose, with 12 percent of births to white women from 1990 to 1995 occurring within a cohabiting union and 13 percent outside of either a marital or cohabiting union.

Trends differ considerably for black women, for whom births outside of either a marital or cohabiting union predominate, rising from 47 to 62 percent of all black births between the 1980s and early 1990s. During this period, marital births fell sharply, from 37 to 22 percent, while births within cohabiting unions fluctuated between 16 and 19 percent.

Figure 1.2 also suggests a growing divergence in the family situations of black and white children. As of the early 1990s, three in four births to white women occurred within a marital union; of the remaining one in four white births, approximately equal numbers occurred in a cohabiting union or outside of any union. By contrast, only 22 percent of births to black women in the early 1990s occurred within marital unions; of the remaining 78 percent, four in five were to single mothers, and only one in five occurred within a cohabiting union. Put another way, the great majority of white infants are born into households in which both biological parents are present—91 percent of whites born between 1980 and 1984 and 87 percent of those born between 1990 and 1995 had both biological parents residing in the same household—while for blacks, 53 percent of infants born between 1980 and 1984 and only 38 percent of those born between 1990 and 1995 were in families in which both biological parents were co-residing.

Figures 1.1 and 1.2 track period change in the relative numbers of births within and outside of marital or cohabiting unions, but neither speaks to the evolving demographic composition of such births. We address this issue in figure 1.3, which presents period trends in the age and parity distribution of nonmarital births. Overall there are only minor fluctuations in either the age or parity distribution of births to unmarried white women, but the trends in both the age and parity composition of births to unmarried black women are marked.

The first panel of figure 1.3 presents period trends in the percentage of births by age to unmarried white and black women. For whites, the percentage of nonmarital births occurring to teen women declined modestly from 38 percent between 1970 and 1974 to 33 percent between 1990 and 1995. At the other end of the age spectrum, births to unmarried white women in their thirties rose from 12 percent between 1970 and 1974 to 15 percent between 1990 and 1995. Changes in the age composition of nonmarital births are more marked for black women, for whom the proportion of nonmarital births to teen mothers declined markedly, from 50 percent between 1970 and 1974 to 32 percent between 1990 and 1995. Correspondingly, more nonmarital births to black women now occur after the teen years, with the percentage of such births to women age twenty-five to twenty-nine increasing more than twofold, from 9 to 19 percent, and the percentage to women age thirty and over increasing by over half, from 8 to 13 percent, between the 1970 to 1974 period and the 1990 to 1995 period.

Although these data document a steady upward shift in the age composition of births, from teen childbearing to childbearing over a broader range of ages, nonmarital childbearing remains concentrated among younger women. This holds for both whites and blacks: in two out of three nonmarital births between 1990 and 1995, the mother was under twenty-five, and nearly half of these were teenagers.

Figure 1.3 also presents period trends in the parity distribution of births to unmarried white and black women. For unmarried white women, 43 percent of births between 1970 and 1974 were second- or higher-order, a figure that rose to 47 percent in the 1990 to 1995 period; for third- or higher-order births, percentages rose only slightly, from 19 to 21 percent during this period. For unmarried black women, births between 1970 and 1995 have become increasingly weighted toward higher-order births. Second- or higher-order nonmarital births accounted for 44 percent of all births to unmarried black women between 1970 and 1974, rising to 59 percent in the 1990 to 1995 period; third- or higher-order nonmarital births accounted for 19 percent of nonmarital black births in the 1970 to 1974 period and for 31 percent in the 1990 to 1995 period.

Figure 1.3 Black-White Trends in the Age and Cumulative Parity Distribution of Nonmarital Births

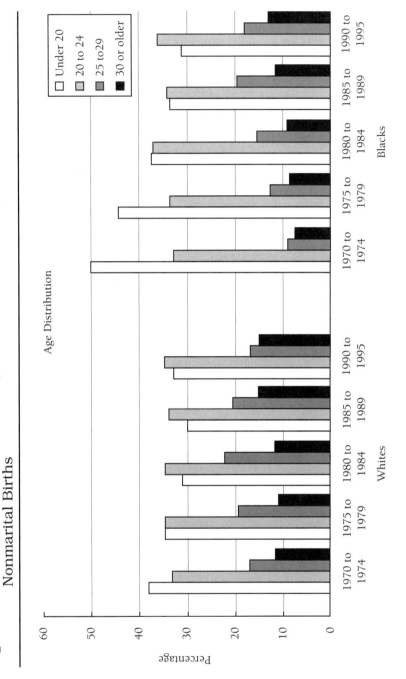

Age Distribution

Whites

Blacks

Legend:
- Under 20
- 20 to 24
- 25 to 29
- 30 or older

Parity Distribution

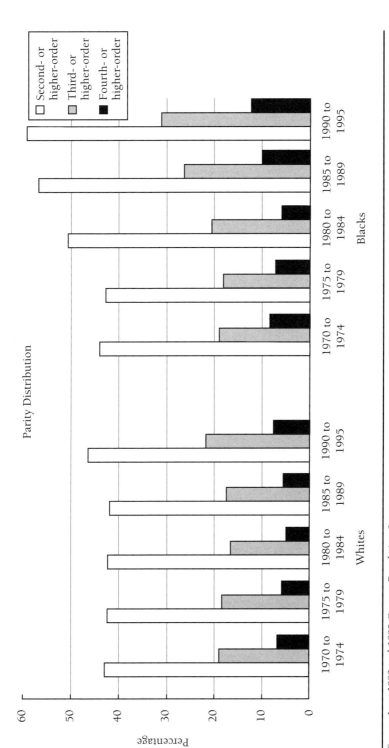

Source: June 1990 and 1995 Current Population Survey.

Thus, of births to unmarried black women in the early 1990s, fully three out of five were second- or higher-order births, and nearly one in three was a third- or higher-order birth.

What might account for increases over time in the absolute numbers, proportion, and distribution by parity of births outside of marriage? Figure 1.4 provides clues as to the role of nonmarital and cohabiting *first* births. The figure first presents black-white trends in the proportion of first births to married and unmarried women using data from the June 1990 and 1995 CPS. Although the proportion of first births occurring outside of marriage increased substantially for both white and black women, there are stark differences in level by race. For whites, 85 percent of first births between 1970 and 1974 occurred within a marital union; in the early 1990s, 66 percent of first births were marital. By contrast, 59 percent of black first births in the early 1970s, and fully 81 percent in the early 1990s, occurred outside of a marital union. Thus, black-white trends in the marital status of first births virtually mirror each other: the percentage of first births occurring *outside* of marriage to black women in the 1990s nearly equals the percentage of first births occurring *within* marriage to white women in the 1970s.

Figure 1.4 also uses data from the 1995 NSFG to provide black-white trends in the proportion of first births occurring in a marital union, in a cohabiting union, or in neither a marital nor a cohabiting union. Among white women, there was a marked rise in the proportion of cohabiting first births, from 5 percent of first births in the 1980 to 1984 period to 12 percent in 1990 to 1995. The proportion of first births to white women that occurred in neither a marital nor a cohabiting union also rose substantially, from 13 to 16 percent over this period. Thus, first births to cohabiting white women increased much more quickly than first births to single white women in the period between 1980 and 1995, with a 128 percent increase in the proportion of cohabiting first births during this period, compared to a 29 percent increase in the proportion of single first births.

Trends in the union status of first births differ modestly for black women, with dramatic declines in the proportion of marital first births, an overall increase in single first births, and a relatively constant proportion of cohabiting first births. First births to cohabiting black women constituted between 10 and 13 percent of all black first births, while first births in neither a marital nor cohabiting union rose from 57 to 72 percent between 1980 and 1995. For black women in the early 1990s, fewer than two of ten first births were to married women, roughly one out of ten were to cohabiting women, and more than seven of ten were to single women; for whites, about seven of ten first births were to married women, roughly one out of ten were to cohabiting women, and fewer than two of ten were to single women. Thus, in the early 1990s, 43 percent of first births to unmarried white women occurred in families in which two biological parents were co-residing; for blacks, the corresponding figure is 12 percent.

Figure 1.4 suggests a substantial decline over time in marital first births and a substantial increase in first births occurring in cohabiting unions or outside of any union. However, the period between 1970 and 1995 also coincided with changes in other dimensions of family life, including delays in age at marriage and age at initiation of childbearing. Figure 1.5 presents trends, by marital status, in mean age at first birth and the percentage of births to teen mothers for white and black women. Results show that mean age at entry into motherhood has increased for women with both marital and nonmarital first births, but that the pace of change varied markedly by marital status. The upper two curves plot the mean age at first birth for white and black women with a marital first birth.[3] For both white and black women, the mean age at first birth increased substantially, from roughly twenty-three years in 1970 to around twenty-eight years in 1995, with the rise consistent with trends in delayed age at marriage. Although the black curve tends to lie slightly below the white curve, there is considerable similarity between the two curves. Note, however, that marital fertility among first-time black mothers is concentrated within an increasingly small and potentially selected population.

Among women with a nonmarital first birth, black-white differences in mean age at first birth appear to have narrowed, although this statement must be qualified by the considerable sampling variability in these curves. For white women with a nonmarital first birth, mean age at first birth has fluctuated between twenty and twenty-two years, declining somewhat in the early 1990s. For black women with a nonmarital first birth, the mean age at first birth has risen steadily, from nineteen in 1970 to twenty-one in 1994.

Figure 1.5 also presents parallel trends in the percentage of first births occurring to teen women—those age nineteen or younger.

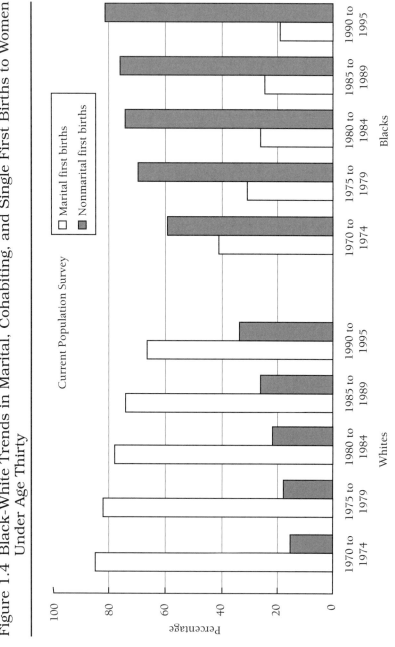

Figure 1.4 Black-White Trends in Marital, Cohabiting, and Single First Births to Women Under Age Thirty

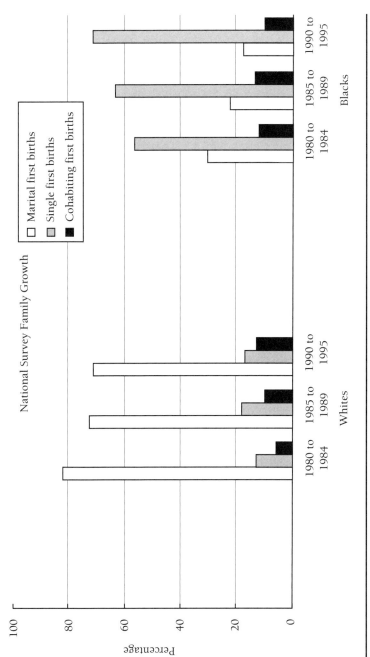

National Survey Family Growth

Source: June 1990 and 1995 Current Population Survey; 1995 National Survey of Family Growth.

Figure 1.5 Black-White Trends in Mean Age at First Birth and in First Births to Teenage Mothers, by Marital Status at First Birth

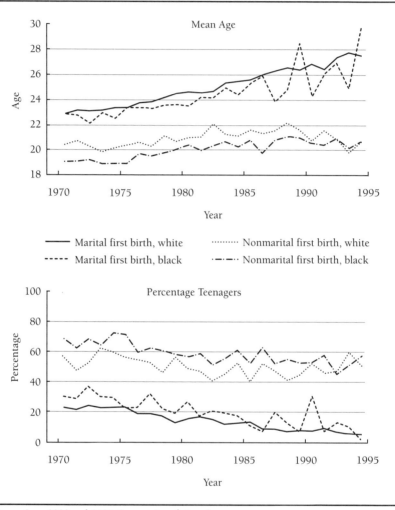

Source: June 1990 and 1995 Current Population Survey.

Despite considerable sampling variability, the proportion of non-marital first births to black teen mothers declined modestly, from about 70 percent in 1970 to just below 60 percent in 1995. For first births to unmarried white teen mothers, levels fluctuated between 40 and 60 percent, averaging around 50 percent between 1970 and

1995. By contrast, first births among married teen women declined noticeably for both white and black women, from around 35 percent in the early 1970s to around 11 percent in the early 1990s for blacks, and from around 20 percent in the 1970s to less than 10 percent in the early 1990s for whites.

Overall the trends in the mean age at first birth and percentage of teen births in figure 1.5 suggest a modest convergence by race, on the one hand, and a more marked divergence between married and unmarried births, on the other hand. We find that black/white differentials in both the mean age at first birth and the proportion of teen births have narrowed somewhat over time, although these patterns exhibit substantial sampling variability. Previous studies have documented similarities among black and white women with marital first births; however, our results also point to a possible modest narrowing in mean age at first birth and the proportion of teen births among those with nonmarital first births. These findings on the narrowing of differences between blacks and whites also echo Rindfuss and Parnell's (1989) observation regarding the increasing importance of marital status and the relative declining significance of race, *conditional* on selection into marriage.

Figure 1.5 also reveals a growing divergence in mean age at first birth and the proportion of teen births for women who were married, and those who were not, when they first became mothers. This divergence is notable for at least two reasons. First, studies have found a consistent association between *early* childbearing and socioeconomic disadvantage. (See, for example, Hoffman et al. 1993a, 1993b; but see also Geronimus and Korenman 1993, and Korenman et al., this volume, for cautions about the causal nature of this association.) Second, *delayed* childbearing is typically held to carry greater parental investment in offspring, both as a consequence of the higher earnings and life cycle accumulation that delayed childbearing affords to parents and as a consequence of the typical attributes of parents who delay childbearing (see, for example, Becker 1991; Oppenheimer 1994). Thus, the diverging trends in figure 1.5 point to possible demographic and life cycle components that may further exacerbate inequalities in the socioeconomic circumstances of children born within and outside of marital unions.

Although the period estimates in figures 1.1 through 1.5 provide a glimpse of trends in U.S. marital and nonmarital childbearing, they say little about the *trajectories* of childbearing and marriage experienced by successive cohorts of women. Figure 1.6 provides an initial step toward this goal by reporting competing-risk life table estimates of the cumulative probability of experiencing the transition from a first to a second birth, cross-classified by marital status at birth. These life table estimates can be interpreted as giving the expected proportion making each transition, conditional on not making a transition to another state during the period of exposure to risk.

As in previous figures, we trace change over time by conditioning on first births occurring in the periods 1970 to 1974, 1975 to 1979, 1980 to 1984, and 1985 to 1989. Although the June 1995 CPS could, in principle, yield ten years of exposure for first births occurring in the 1985 to 1989 period, for some transitions (and in particular, the transition from a marital first birth to a nonmarital second birth), the number of second-birth events is small for first births in that period. To make estimates comparable across first-birth cohorts, we present cumulative proportions of women experiencing a second birth within eight and a half years of a first birth.

The results in the upper left-hand section of figure 1.6 provide life table estimates for the transition from a marital first birth to a marital second birth. Over this period, white women have uniformly higher probabilities than black women of following this trajectory. There is a slight upward trend for white women, with probabilities increasing about three percentage points for white women, but no apparent trend for black women.

The upper right-hand section of figure 1.6 gives life table estimates for the transition from a nonmarital first birth to a nonmarital second birth. Estimates fluctuate between 35 and 38 percent for white women, and rise from 55 to 65 percent for black women between the 1970 to 1974 period and the 1985 to 1989 period. Thus, black women are substantially more likely than white women to progress from a nonmarital first birth to a nonmarital second birth, with the black-white differential increasing over this period.

How large are these trends? A natural comparison is with trends in the percentage of first births occurring outside of marriage in figure 1.4. For whites in figure 1.4, these percentages rose from 15 to 26 percent between the 1970 to 1974 period and the 1985 to 1989 period; for blacks, the increase was from 59 to 75 percent. These trends correspond to relative increases of 69 and 28 percent for first births to unmarried white and black women, respectively. By contrast, the trends in figure 1.6 for the transition from a non-marital first birth to a nonmarital second birth correspond to a relative decrease of 4 percent for whites and a relative increase of 17 percent for blacks. Trends in the initiation of nonmarital childbearing (69 and 28 percent increase for whites and blacks, respectively) thus substantially outweigh trends in the progression from a nonmarital first birth to a nonmarital second birth (a 4 percent decrease and a 17 percent increase for whites and blacks, respectively).

The bottom part of figure 1.6 presents estimates for two other transitions—from a nonmarital first birth to a marital second birth, and from a marital first birth to a nonmarital second birth. As expected, whites are substantially more likely than blacks to have a marital second birth given a nonmarital first birth, with black/white differences fluctuating between 18 and 23 percent over the period. There is only a modest decline in the probability of this transition between the 1970s and 1980s for both white and black women (49 versus 44 percent for white women, and 30 versus 26 percent for black women for the 1970 to 1974 and 1985 to 1989 periods, respectively). Estimated probabilities for the final transition—from a marital first birth to a nonmarital second birth—are much lower than for other transitions and are subject to considerable sampling variability.

To this point, our analyses have examined births conditional on marital status, yet doing so arguably conditions away too much, given that this period witnessed substantial delays in women's entry into marriage (Cherlin 1992). Indeed, a number of researchers see the role of declining marital prospects as central to understanding nonmarital childbearing (An, Haveman, and Wolfe 1993; Bennett, Bloom, and Miller 1995; Duncan and Hoffman 1990; Lichter and Graefe, this volume; South and Lloyd 1992; Upchurch, Lillard, and Panis, this volume; Wilson 1987). It is also important to recognize that an increasing mean age at first marriage implies increasing numbers of nonmarital births even in the absence of changing reproductive behaviors by virtue of the longer durations of exposure to the risk of childbearing outside of marriage (Bumpass and McLanahan 1989).

Figure 1.7 replicates results reported by Bumpass and Lu (2000) on trends in marriage subsequent to a first unmarried birth. Overall the results suggest little trend in the likelihood of marriage follow-

Figure 1.6 Competing-Risk Estimates of Black-White Trends in the Cumulative Probability of a Second Birth Within Eight and a Half Years of a First Birth, by Marital Status of First and Second Birth.

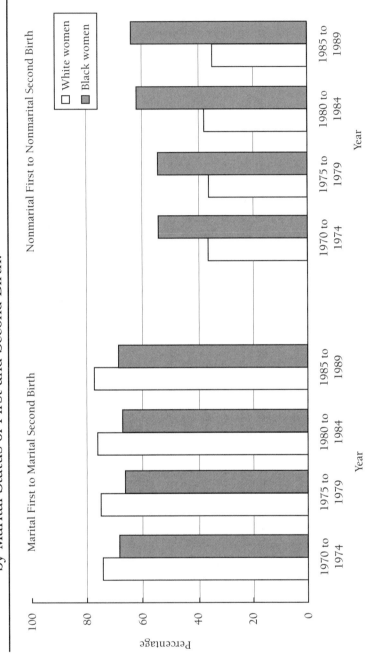

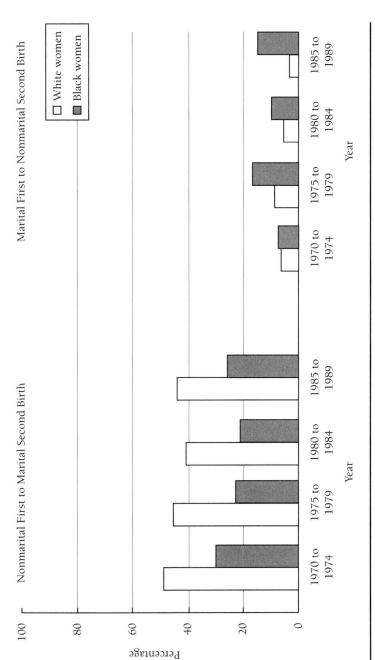

Nonmarital First to Marital Second Birth

Marital First to Nonmarital Second Birth

Year

Year

Percentage

White women
Black women

Source: June 1990 and 1995 Current Population Survey.

Figure 1.7 Black-White Trends in the Cumulative
          Probability of Marriage Within Eight and a
          Half Years of a Nonmarital First Birth

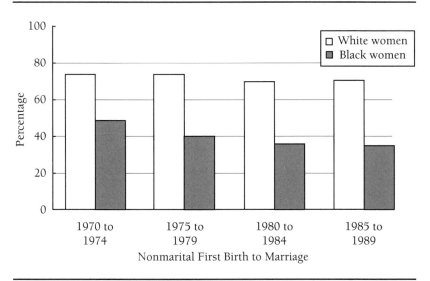

Source: June 1990 and 1995 Current Population Survey.

ing a nonmarital first birth for white women, but they do show a significant decline for black women. For white women, life table estimates of the cumulative probability of marriage within eight and a half years of a nonmarital first birth decline only slightly, from 73 to 70 percent between the 1970 to 1974 period and the 1985 to 1989 period. By contrast, we observe a notable decline in marriage probabilities for black women, from 49 to 34 percent, between the early 1970s and late 1980s.

These results also provide insight into trends in previous figures. For example, we noted the relative lack of change in the parity distribution of nonmarital births to white women in figure 1.3, despite a clear upward trend in figure 1.1 in the proportion of births occurring to unmarried white women. Although a full decomposition of the trends in figures 1.1 and 1.3 would necessarily require accounting for other demographic processes (see, for example, Smith, Morgan, and Koropeckyj-Cox 1996), these results are nevertheless consistent with the large increases in the proportion of first births to unmarried white women observed in figure 1.4, the small changes in the probability of marriage given a nonmarital first birth observed in figure 1.7, and the relatively unchanging progression from a first to second nonmarital birth for white women observed in figure 1.6. Similarly, recall that black women were characterized by both an upward trend in the nonmarital fertility ratio and a shift toward higher-order nonmarital births in figures 1.1 and 1.3. These findings are likewise consistent with the dramatic increase in the proportion of first births to unmarried black women observed in figure 1.4, the substantial decline in marriage for unmarried black mothers observed in figure 1.7, and the modest increases in the progression from a first to second nonmarital birth observed in figure 1.6.

These observations suggest that, for white women, upward trends in the nonmarital fertility ratio appear driven primarily by increases over the last twenty-five years in the proportion of *first* births outside of marriage, while the absence of any substantial trend in the progression from a nonmarital first birth to a nonmarital second birth accounts for the relative stability in the parity composition of nonmarital births among white women. For black women, increases in the nonmarital fertility ratio appear to result primarily from the dramatic rise in nonmarital first births *and* substantial declines in marriage, and only secondarily from more modest increases in progression from a first nonmarital birth to a second nonmarital birth. Similarly, the shift in the parity distribution of black nonmarital births toward higher-order parities appears due to a modest increase in the progression from a nonmarital first to a nonmarital second birth, coupled with increases in the duration of exposure to the risk of higher-order nonmarital births resulting from declining marital prospects.

UNION STATUSES AFTER FIVE AND TEN YEARS

We now turn attention away from historical change and toward a more intensive examination of union and fertility trajectories. Our analytic strategy is to follow a single cohort of women—those with first births occurring in the period 1980 to 1984—over a ten-year period, using data from the 1995 NSFG.[4] By permitting us to differentiate between births to married, cohabiting, and single women, these data let us focus particular attention on the role of cohabitation in shaping women's trajectories of nonmarital childbearing.

Figure 1.8 Second Births at Five and Ten Years After First Birth, for First Births Occurring Between 1980 and 1984 to Women Under Age Thirty

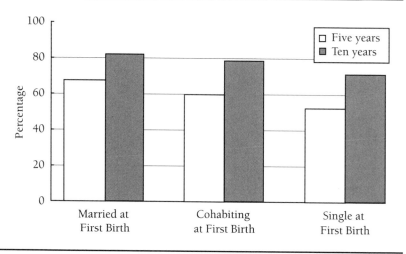

Source: 1995 National Survey of Family Growth.

An advantage of this analytic strategy is that it traces trajectories through union and fertility statuses as experienced by a cohort of women exposed to a uniform, albeit changing, set of period influences. A drawback is that it necessarily limits the number of NSFG women analyzed, with the available sample sizes too small to compare the experiences of white and black women. And as noted earlier, we restrict our NSFG analyses to first births to women under age thirty to avoid issues of truncation induced by the age structure of the 1995 NSFG sampling frame.

Figure 1.8 presents estimates for the percentage of women with a second birth at durations of five and ten years after first birth by union status at first birth. Note that these cross-classifications of initial statuses with statuses five and ten years later ignore intervening changes in union status. For example, women married at first birth may experience a second birth within a cohabiting union, and women cohabiting at first birth may have a second birth within a different cohabiting union.

Does subsequent fertility differ by union status at first birth? The answers in figure 1.8 reveal notable similarities across women of different union status at first birth. Women married at first birth are the most likely—and women single at first birth the least likely—to have a second birth; nevertheless, differences by union status at first birth are modest and decline with duration since first birth. Within five years of a first birth, 68 percent of those who were married, 59 percent of those who were cohabiting, and 52 percent of those who were single at first birth proceed to a second birth. At ten years' duration, similarities are even more apparent, with second births to 82, 78, and 71 percent of women whose union status at first birth was married, cohabiting, and single, respectively. Thus, for women in this cohort of first births, very high proportions proceed to a second birth, with only modest variation by union status at first birth.

Is union status at second birth associated with union status at first birth? The results in figure 1.9 are striking. Among those who progress to a second birth within five or ten years of a first birth, union status at first birth is highly associated with union status at second birth, with marital first births followed by marital second births, cohabiting first births most likely to lead to cohabiting second births, and single first births usually preceding single second births. Of second births occurring within five or ten years to women married at first birth, more than 96 percent occur within marriage. Moreover, of these marital second births, nearly all occurred within the same marriage (results not presented). Patterns among unmarried births are similar at both five and ten years after first birth. Five years after first birth, fully 60 percent of second births to women cohabiting at first birth are within cohabiting unions, with another 39 percent of these second births occurring in marital unions. Finally, a plurality of second births to women who were single at first birth occur to women single at second birth—48 percent at five years' duration, with 32 percent of second births occurring within marital unions, and 20 percent of second births occurring within cohabiting unions.

Figure 1.9 also suggests divergence in the populations at risk of a *non-union* birth. Union first births—those occurring in either a cohabiting or marital union—are followed only very rarely by non-union second births, that is, second births outside of either a cohabiting or marital union. Non-union second births are extremely infrequent for those with marital first births—constituting under 3 percent of second births to these women at both five and ten years' duration—but non-union second births are nearly as rare among

Figure 1.9   Union Status of Women at Second Birth Five
and Ten Years After First Birth, for First
Births Occurring Between 1980 and 1984 to
Women Under Age Thirty

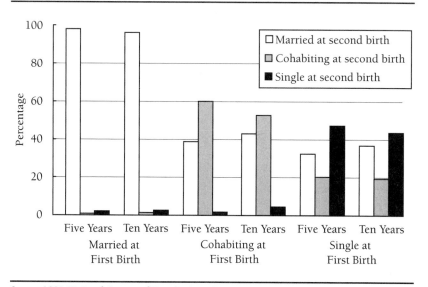

Legend:
- ☐ Married at second birth
- ▥ Cohabiting at second birth
- ■ Single at second birth

X-axis groups:
- Five Years / Ten Years — Married at First Birth
- Five Years / Ten Years — Cohabiting at First Birth
- Five Years / Ten Years — Single at First Birth

Y-axis: Percentage (0 to 100)

Source: 1995 National Survey of Family Growth.

women with cohabiting first births: only 3 and 5 percent at five and ten years' duration. On a cautionary note: in analyses not reported, we find that the proportion of non-union second births to women cohabiting at first birth rises substantially for later NSFG cohorts of first births. Hence, this bifurcation has continued to evolve over time from a pattern involving *non-union* births to one involving *nonmarital* births. The evolving nature of this bifurcation is yet another aspect of an issue raised at the outset of this chapter—namely, that in following a cohort of first births forward in time, we are selecting on women who initiated childbearing under one regime and whose subsequent fertility and union history took place during a period of extremely rapid change with respect to childbearing, union formation, and union dissolution.

One motivation behind the construction of figure 1.9 is the idea that the situations of children born to parents who are cohabiting or married might be similar by virtue of the fact that both biological parents are present at birth. Figure 1.9 provides some indirect evidence supporting this hypothesis—showing, for example, that cohabiting first births tend to be followed by cohabiting second births. Moreover, in results not reported, we find that just under 70 percent of these cohabiting second births occurred within the same cohabiting relationship. Still, what figure 1.9 does not reveal is the extent to which these union statuses are stable or transitory.

Figure 1.10 provides a first look at this question by cross-classifying women's union statuses at first birth and at five and ten years after first birth. These results show that women who were married at first birth are overwhelmingly married five and ten years later (85 and 82 percent, respectively), although it should be noted that 12 percent of those observed to be married ten years after first birth have divorced and remarried (results not shown). Of the 18 percent of women who were married at first birth but who subsequently separated, most are single (11 and 14 percent at five and ten years after a first birth), with relatively few cohabiting (3 and 4 percent). Although this last finding may appear inconsistent with what we know about cohabitation following a marital disruption (Bumpass, Sweet, and Cherlin 1989; Martinson and Wu 1998), it must be remembered that this group of women is selected from those who ever experienced a marital disruption by virtue of a first birth followed by a marital separation, all within a five- or ten-year period.

Union statuses following first birth are considerably more diverse for women not married at first birth. At five years' duration, union status at first birth is highly associated with subsequent union status for those not married at first birth. Women cohabiting at first birth are almost as likely to be cohabiting five years later as to be married (36 versus 41 percent), and considerably less likely to be single (23 percent), while women who were single at first birth are most likely to be single five years later (51 percent, versus 33 and 17 percent married and cohabiting, respectively). At ten years' duration, the association between union status at first birth and subsequent union status persists for women who were married or single at first birth; however, women cohabiting at first birth are most likely to be married (51 percent) but least likely to be cohabiting (19 percent), with the single state falling in between (30 percent). Hence, though there is substantial movement into marriage among mothers who were either cohabiting or single at their first birth, these flows into marriage are relatively modest during the five years following a first birth. As a result, many of those cohabiting at first

Figure 1.10   Union Status Five and Ten Years After First
Birth, for First Births Occurring Between
1980 and 1984 to Women Under Age Thirty

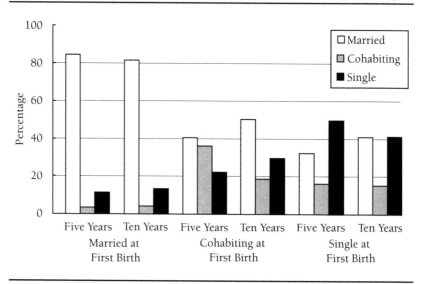

Source: 1995 National Survey of Family Growth.

birth are cohabiting five years later, and of those single at first birth, substantial proportions are single five years later.

Figure 1.11 presents a more direct look at the stability of cohabiting and marital unions by comparing life table estimates of the cumulative probability of experiencing a union dissolution within ten years after a first birth for women cohabiting or married at first birth. There are several possible outcomes of interest for a woman cohabiting at first birth: she may have remained in the same cohabiting union ten years after first birth; she may have married her cohabiting partner and remained in this marital union ten years after first birth; she may have married her cohabiting partner but then divorced; or she may have separated from her cohabiting partner without marrying. We censor women in the first two cases (at ten years' duration) and define the last two as union dissolutions, the event of substantive interest.

Figure 1.11 reveals striking differentials in union dissolution by status at first birth, with cohabiting unions more than twice as likely as marital unions to dissolve following a first birth. Life table

Figure 1.11   Cumulative Probability of Union Dissolution
Following a First Birth, by Union Status at
First Birth for First Births Occurring
Between 1980 and 1984, for Married and
Cohabiting Women Under Age Thirty

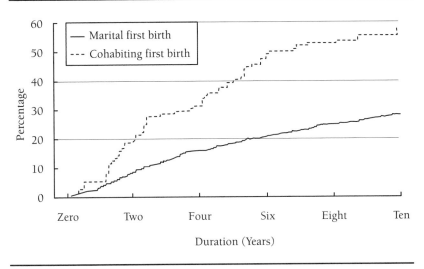

Source: 1995 National Survey of Family Growth.

estimates suggest that 31 percent of those cohabiting at first birth
and 16 percent of those married at first birth have experienced a
union dissolution within four years after a first birth; within eight
years after a first birth, the corresponding percentages are 54 and
25 percent.

TRAJECTORIES OVER TEN YEARS

Figures 1.12 and 1.13 present simple descriptions of the major trajectories culminating in a second birth (or no second birth) over
ten years. The first column gives the percentage of all trajectories
captured by each pathway; the numbers at the bottom of the column give the total for pathways represented in the figure. The second column restates these same trajectories conditional on status at
first birth, with the totals representing the percentage of pathways
from each initial status. We would emphasize the highly descriptive
nature of figures 1.12 and 1.13—in particular, the simple percent-

ages reported do not account for a woman's duration of exposure while in any particular status, nor do they accurately reflect the likelihood that she will eventually occupy a particular status.

We begin with results from the CPS. As can be seen in the totals reported in the first column of figure 1.12, virtually all pathways followed within ten years of the first birth can be represented by nine distinct trajectories through fertility and marital statuses. The most common path is from a marital first birth through an intact marriage to a marital second birth. Although we might expect this trajectory to be even more dominant, in fact it represents only half of the trajectories between a first and second birth. The next most common path is from an unmarried first birth to an unmarried second birth, representing 15 percent of observed trajectories. Paths to no second birth, whether begun by a marital or nonmarital first birth, account for another 21 percent of observed trajectories. Among those with nonmarital first births, a nonmarital second birth was two-thirds as likely (15 versus 9 percent) as a marital second birth.

The second column provides an alternative view of the same process by giving percentages separately by marital status at first birth. It is no surprise that 77 percent of the transitions for women married at first birth consisted of second births within intact marriages. Nonetheless, 30 percent of women with a marital first and second birth subsequently disrupted within ten years of the first birth (results not reported), while only 4 percent of women with a marital first birth had a nonmarital second birth. Another 17 percent of women with a marital first birth did not have a second birth within ten years—whether within an intact marriage or following a marital disruption.

About one-quarter of women with nonmarital first births proceeded to a marital second birth, although nearly one-third of these marriages ended within ten years (results not reported). About 30 percent of these unmarried first-time mothers did not have a second birth—either after marriage or while remaining single. But the most prevalent trajectory among these women was to a second nonmarital birth (43 percent). Hence, these simple tabulations again reveal a picture of quite distinctive trajectories of childbearing that depend heavily on mother's marital status at first birth: marital first births are overwhelmingly followed by marital second births, and nonmarital first births are disproportionately followed by nonmarital second births.

Figure 1.12 Major Marriage and Fertility Trajectories, by
Marital Status at First Birth, for First Births
Occurring Between 1980 and 1984 to
Women Under Age Thirty

	Percentage Distribution Unconditional on Marital Status at First Birth	Percentage Distribution Conditional on Marital Status at First Birth
Marital second birth	50%	77%
No second birth	6	10
Remarried second birth	2	3
Unmarried second birth	2	4
No second birth	5	7
Total	—	101
Marital second birth	9	26
No second birth	5	15
Nonmarital second birth	15	43
No second birth	5	14
Total	99	98

Marital first birth → Intact, Split
Nonmarital first birth → Marry

Source: June 1995 Current Population Survey.
Note: Some percentages sum to more than 100 percent because of rounding.

Figure 1.13 extends these analyses using data from the 1995
NSFG to distinguish between union statuses—married, cohabiting,
or single. We report sixteen pathways that account for 97 percent of
all trajectories observed. The resulting complexity of trajectories
defies easy summary, but several findings of note are suggested by
the second column of figure 1.13.

Figure 1.13 Major Union and Fertility Trajectories, by
Union Status at First Birth, for First Births
Occurring Between 1980 and 1984 to
Women Under Age Thirty

	Percentage Distribution Unconditional on Union Status at First Birth	Percentage Distribution Conditional on Union Status at First Birth
Marital first birth		
Intact — Marital second birth	55%	77%
Intact — No second birth	7	9
Split — Remarried second birth	2	3
Split — Unmarried second birth	2	3
Split — No second birth	6	9
Total	—	101
Cohabiting first birth		
Intact — Cohabiting second birth	3	36
Marry — Marital second birth	2	29
Marry — No second birth	0.3	4
Split — Marital second birth	0.4	5
Split — Cohabiting second birth	0.4	5
Split — No second birth	1	16
Total	—	95
Single first birth		
Marry — Marital second birth	5	26
Marry — No second birth	2	12
Cohabit — Cohabiting second birth	3	14
Nonmarital second birth	6	28
No second birth	2	12
Total	97	92

Source: 1995 National Survey of Family Growth.
Note: Some percentages sum to more than 100 percent because of rounding.

For women with a marital first birth, CPS and NSFG estimates of the percentage of women who follow various trajectories agree closely and differ by no more than two percentage points in figures 1.12 and 1.13. Among mothers who were cohabiting at their first birth, the three most common pathways account for 81 percent of observed trajectories, with the remaining three trajectories covering another 14 percent. We emphasize again that union dissolution after a second birth is common among this pool of women. It is nonetheless striking that the two most common trajectories to a second birth occur among women within the same intact union— 36 percent within the same cohabiting union and 29 percent to women who have married their cohabiting partner. These two trajectories constitute just under two-thirds of all trajectories observed for women cohabiting at first birth. Second births within marital or cohabiting unions account for another 10 percent of trajectories; these trajectories are characterized by the breakup of the cohabiting union at first birth, followed by a subsequent cohabiting or marital union, followed by a second birth.

Five major pathways describe 92 percent of the trajectories among single first-time mothers. Two of these result in no second birth: 12 percent through marriage, and another 12 percent outside of either a marital or cohabiting union during the ten years of observation. About one-quarter of single first-time mothers subsequently married and had a marital second birth, with another 28 percent remaining single and continuing to a second unmarried birth. Cohabiting births account for 14 percent of these trajectories, compared to the 41 percent noted earlier for women who cohabited at first birth. Only 40 percent of women who were single at first birth proceeded to a second birth within a cohabiting or marital union; by contrast, almost three-fourths of those cohabiting at first birth proceeded to a second birth in either a cohabiting or marital union. These findings thus emphasize once again that experience subsequent to a first birth depends heavily on the union status of the first birth.

DISCUSSION

Unmarried childbearing has increased to the point where, as of the mid-1990s, one-third of all births in the United States are to unmarried mothers. Although significant in itself, this stark statistic masks considerable complexity. It is frequently assumed that unmarried births create mother-only families; in fact, fully two-fifths of such births now occur in families with two unmarried parents. Similarly, policymakers and researchers often proceed as if unmarried births are predominantly first births, whereas one-half of such births are second- or higher-order births, and fully one-quarter are third- or higher-order.

In addition to increases in the level of nonmarital childbearing, there has been a shift over time toward higher-order nonmarital births. According to our estimates, this shift has occurred primarily among black women, with little change in the parity distribution of nonmarital births to white women. At the same time, the prevalence of higher-order nonmarital births to white women is also much higher than is generally appreciated. Of births to unmarried white women, we estimate that 43 percent were second- or higher-order, and that 19 percent were third- or higher-order, as of the early 1970s; these percentages rose modestly to 47 and 21 percent, respectively, in the early 1990s. By contrast, of births to unmarried black women, 44 percent were second- or higher-order, and 19 percent were third- or higher-order in the early 1970s, with these percentages rising substantially to 59 and 31 percent in the early 1990s.

These trends in both the numbers and parity distribution of nonmarital births have coincided with a much more dramatic increase in *first* births to unmarried women. We estimate that the percentage of first births occurring outside of marriage rose from 15 to 33 percent between the early 1970s and early 1990s for white women and from 59 to 81 percent for black women. Thus, in recent years, four out of five first births to black women and fully one out of three to white women occurred outside of marriage. Changes in the likelihood of progressing from a first to second nonmarital birth appear much less central to overall trends in nonmarital childbearing. Life table estimates reveal little trend in these parity progressions for white women and a modest increase for black women. Thus, our findings suggest the somewhat paradoxical conclusion that the shift in the distribution toward higher-parity nonmarital births is in fact primarily a consequence of the rising number of women who initiate childbearing outside of marriage and only secondarily a consequence of changes in subsequent reproductive behavior within this pool of unmarried mothers. Widening black-white differentials in higher-order nonmarital births are also a result of declining rates of marriage for black women following a nonmarital first birth.

These findings also suggest, somewhat paradoxically, that we re-direct attention back to the circumstances characterizing first births to unmarried mothers. In this regard, the processes leading to a first birth outside of marriage continue to be concentrated in the teen years and early twenties, while first births within marriage have become increasingly prevalent among women in their mid- to late twenties. And despite the very large numbers of nonmarital first births to black women, we find little difference over the last twenty-five years between black and white unmarried mothers in the age at which they initiate childbearing. To us, these trends suggest yet another way in which the gulf between the married and unmarried has widened, while the divide between racial groups has narrowed *conditional* on marriage.

Of course, the other crucial element to understanding the circumstances characterizing first births to unmarried mothers is marriage itself; thus, when we say that the gulf between the married and unmarried has widened while the divide between racial groups has narrowed conditional on marriage, this statement may condition away too much of real substance. The view that declining marriage is essential to understanding nonmarital fertility, articulated forcefully by Wilson (1987), gains even greater relevance when juxtaposed with studies suggesting that poverty—and particularly persistent child poverty—has been especially concentrated in households headed by never-married women (Duncan and Rodgers 1991; Hoffman and Foster 1997). Nevertheless, our results make us skeptical about the policy potential of simplistic calls to recon-stitute marriage and fatherhood within these populations (see, for example, Blankenhorn 1995; Popenoe 1996). The decision not to marry is, after all, the "revealed preference" of the pregnant woman and her potential spouse, and the information known to the woman about the marriageability of the father most surely exceeds that available to the researcher or policymaker (Lundberg, this volume). Furthermore, because the *initiation* of nonmarital childbearing re-mains stubbornly concentrated among teenage women, we suspect that other factors—not the least of which concerns the unplanned nature of many such pregnancies—are critical to understanding the social context in which unmarried pregnancies are conceived and brought to term.

As we have emphasized repeatedly, any attempt to understand evolving differences in the reproductive behaviors of the married and unmarried must also grapple with the remarkable increase in cohabitation. Births within cohabiting unions now constitute a significant fraction of first births that occur outside of marriage. Cohabiting first births have quadrupled for white women, from below 4 to 16 percent from the 1970s to the early 1990s, with two out of five nonmarital first births to white women now occurring in families with two unmarried parents. Cohabiting first births have also been a fixture among black women, but the proportion of such births has held steady at around 10 to 13 percent, while the prevalence of births to single black women has risen substantially over time. Consequently, first births to cohabiting black women have constituted an increasingly smaller fraction of the pool of first births to blacks that occur outside of formal marriage.

To what extent does a woman's union status at first birth shape her subsequent trajectory of childbearing? Our results are consistent with the view that two-child norms remain strong in the United States, with only modest differences emerging between married, cohabiting, and single mothers. Thus, the progression to a second birth remains prevalent among those who have initiated a first birth, with similarities across union status at first birth far outweighing differences. Nevertheless, a woman's union status at second birth is highly contingent on her union status at first birth, with marital first births overwhelmingly followed by marital second births, cohabiting first births leading to cohabiting second births, and single first births leading to single second births.

We are interested in distinguishing between births to married, cohabiting, or single women primarily because we are thus able to identify births in which two biological parents—married or unmarried—are co-residing at the birth of a child. In this respect, marital and cohabiting unions might be thought to provide children with roughly similar circumstances at birth relative to births to single women. But a complication is that the family situations of children at birth correlate only imperfectly with their family situations in later life (Martinson and Wu 1992); in particular, the lives of substantial numbers of children will be disrupted by the dissolution of their parents' marital or cohabiting unions (Bumpass and Raley 1995; Bumpass and Sweet 1989).

Are the families of children born within cohabiting unions less stable than the families of children born within marital unions? Our answer is yes, with striking differentials by union status at first birth. Of women whose first child was born between 1980 and 1984, more than half of those cohabiting at first birth experienced a union dissolution within eight years, compared to one in four dissolutions for those married at first birth. This finding mirrors recent empirical studies documenting the greater instability of marriages preceded by cohabitation (Bennett, Blanc, and Bloom 1988; Teachman and Polonko 1990; but see Lillard, Brien, and Waite 1995). Our analyses do not tell us, however, whether this greater instability is a consequence of the decision by parents to cohabit, of the decision to bear a child prior to marrying, or of characteristics of the parents (for example, lower earnings potentials) that may predate the birth of the child and that may in turn contribute to union instability. Answers to these and other questions are critically important to social scientists and policymakers interested in understanding parental behaviors in these domains. Still, when viewed from the perspective of *children,* these results are troubling if, as some evidence suggests, family instability is associated with negative consequences for children later in life (see, for example, Cherlin et al. 1991; Wu 1996; Wu and Martinson 1993).

Our analyses have been self-consciously descriptive and, as noted earlier, do not speak to issues of causality. Yet authors as diverse as Becker (1991) and Rindfuss and Parnell (1989) view marriage and fertility as inextricably intertwined. Indeed, we would add other components—the planned or unplanned nature of pregnancies, the processes influencing the formation and dissolution of cohabiting unions, and the turbulence or lack thereof in women's families of origin *and* of choice—to the mix of endogeneities that recent research has begun to document (Lillard, Brien, and Waite 1995; Brien, Lillard, and Waite 1999; Korenman, Kaestner, and Joyce, this volume; Upchurch, Lillard, and Panis, this volume). Given the complexity of these issues, it is dangerous to venture predictions, particularly during a period of rapid social change. Nevertheless, the overall story that emerges from our findings provides, to our eyes, evidence of an evolving divergence between those who bear children within marriage and those who do not.

APPENDIX

Figure 1.A1 provides a more direct comparison of the estimates from the June 1990 and 1995 CPS and 1995 NSFG presented in

Figure 1.A1 Comparison of Trends in the Proportion of First Births Occurring Within and Outside of Marriage

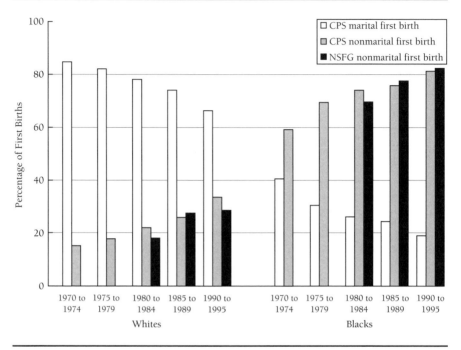

Source: June 1990 and 1995 Current Population Survey; 1995 National Survey of Family Growth.

figures 1.4 and 1.5. The white and gray bars repeat the estimates presented in figure 1.4; the black bars present the estimates from the 1995 NSFG corresponding to a definition of nonmarital child-bearing obtained by summing the proportions of first births occurring in a cohabiting union or outside of a marital or cohabiting union. We do not report NSFG estimates for the period 1970 to 1979 because the sampling universe of the 1995 NSFG consists of women age fifteen to forty-four in 1995; hence, since NSFG respondents were born between 1951 and 1980, only a small fraction were at risk of a first birth from 1970 to 1979. Moreover, first births to NSFG respondents between 1970 and 1979 would not be representative of all first births in this period by virtue of the upper age limit of forty-four in the 1995 NSFG.

For the period 1980 to 1995, figure 1.A1 shows close agreement

Table 1.A1 Percentage Married Ten Years After First
Birth and at Second Birth, by Marital Status
at First Birth, for First Births Occurring
Between 1980 and 1984, for Women Under
Age Thirty

	Percentage Married Ten Years After First Birth		Percentage Married at Second Birth	
	CPS	NSFG	CPS	NSFG
Married at first birth	82.8	82.1	96.8	96.3
Not married at first birth	47.6	44.4	36.8	38.7

Source: June 1995 Current Population Survey; 1995 National Survey of Family Growth.

between the estimates from the 1995 NSFG and from the June 1990 and 1995 CPS and 1995 NSFG for the proportion of first births occurring outside of marriage. For white women, NSFG estimates are slightly lower than CPS estimates for 1980 to 1984 and for 1990 to 1995, but higher in the period 1985 to 1989. By contrast, for black women, NSFG estimates are slightly higher than CPS estimates, except for the 1980 to 1984 period. CPS estimates provide somewhat smoother patterns for trends over time owing to the larger sample sizes provided by pooling data over the June 1990 and 1995 CPS. Trends from the 1995 NSFG mirror those in the CPS closely, however, despite the smaller NSFG sample sizes.

Table 1.A1 presents some selected comparisons of estimates from both the June 1995 CPS and the 1995 NSFG for women with a first birth by age thirty that occurred between 1980 and 1984. The left-hand side of table 1.A1 shows that about 82 percent of those who were married at first birth were married ten years later, and that less than half of those who were unmarried at the first interview were unmarried ten years later. The right-hand side of table 1.A1 gives a corresponding set of results for marital status at second birth within ten years of a first birth. Estimates from the CPS and NSFG again agree closely. In both surveys, about 96 percent of women with second births who were married at first birth had marital second births; of those not married at first birth, somewhat less than 40 percent had marital second births. Overall, results from these two data sources agree closely, with estimates from the CPS and NSFG deviating by at most three percentage points in the upper panel and by less than two percentage points in the lower panel.

Earlier versions of this chapter were presented at the 1999 annual meetings of the Population Association of America and at the 1999 Conference on Nonmarital Fertility, Institute for Research on Poverty, University of Wisconsin–Madison. We thank Steven P. Martin, S. Philip Morgan, Michael Rendall, and Halliman Winsborough for helpful discussions and comments. Research funding from the National Institute of Child Health and Human Development (HD 29550 and HD 22433) and research facilities provided under HD 05876 to the Center for Demography and Ecology are gratefully acknowledged.

NOTES

1. Examining more recent first-birth cohorts would result in greater truncation of women's union and fertility trajectories. Although these issues can be addressed easily with life table techniques, the use of these procedures is complicated by the sheer diversity of trajectories through union and fertility statuses of women following a first birth and by the rapidity of period change across recent first-birth cohorts. These considerations and the descriptive nature of our analyses have led us to adopt the analytic strategy described here.

2. Recall that in figure 1.1 only we use the date of divorce, not the date of marital separation, to classify births as marital or nonmarital. CPS estimates are derived from a woman's retrospective recall of the timing of marital events and births as obtained in 1990 or 1995, whereas estimates from vital statistics are collected from women at the time of birth. Although retrospective data on dates of births and marriage are typically reported with high accuracy (Pendleton, McCarthy, and Cherlin 1989; Wu, Martin, and Long, forthcoming), retrospectively reported dates of *divorce* are arguably less accurate, with data quality declining with duration since divorce. Raley and Bumpass (1999) find no evidence, however, for such deterioration in data quality. Similar issues of data quality can be raised about vital statistics, which employ varying procedures to estimate marital status across states and over time (see, for example, Ventura et al. 1995). In this context, one interpretation of the slight differences in figure 1.1 is that the declining stigma associated with nonmarital births affected trends obtained from vital statistics more than those from the CPS. Note that this possi-

bility, which supposes changes in stigma over time and the likelihood of differences in stigma's effects between whites and blacks, is consistent with the finding that the differentials noted in figure 1.1 are limited to whites only.

3. The greater fluctuation for estimates for black women after 1985 reflects the relatively small numbers of black women with marital first births in this period.

4. In analyses not reported, we compared, to the extent possible, NSFG and CPS estimates for figures 1.8 through 1.13. Throughout, we find remarkable agreement between these two sources, with estimates typically within two to five percentage points—the expected sampling error—of one another. See also figure 1.A1.

REFERENCES

An, Chong-Bum, Robert Haveman, and Barbara Wolfe. 1993. "Teen Out-of-Wedlock Births and Welfare Receipt: The Role of Childhood Events and Economic Circumstances." *Review of Economics and Statistics* 75(2): 195–208.

Becker, Gary S. 1991. *A Treatise on the Family.* Enlarged edition. Cambridge, Mass.: Harvard University Press.

Bennett, Neil G., Ann Klimas Blanc, and David E. Bloom. 1988. "Commitment and the Modern Union: Assessing the Link Between Premarital Cohabitation and Subsequent Marital Stability." *American Sociological Review* 53(1): 1277–38.

Bennett, Neil G., David E. Bloom, and Cynthia K. Miller. 1995. "The Influence of Nonmarital Childbearing on the Formation of First Marriages." *Demography* 32(1): 47–62.

Blankenhorn, David. 1995. *Fatherless America: Confronting Our Most Urgent Social Problem.* New York: Basic Books.

Brien, Michael J., Lee A. Lillard, and Linda J. Waite. 1999. "Interrelated Family-Building Behaviors: Cohabitation, Marriage, and Nonmarital Conception." *Demography* 36(4): 535–52.

Bumpass, Larry L., and Hsien-Hen Lu. 2000. "Trends in Cohabitation and Implications for Children's Family Contexts in the United States." *Population Studies* 54(1): 29–41.

Bumpass, Larry L., and Sara S. McLanahan. 1989. "Unmarried Motherhood: Recent Trends, Composition, and Black-White Differences." *Demography* 26(2): 279–86.

Bumpass, Larry L., and R. Kelly Raley. 1995. "Redefining Single-Parent Families: Cohabitation and Changing Family Realities." *Demography* 32(1): 97–109.

Bumpass, Larry L., Kelly Raley, and James A. Sweet. 1995. "The Changing

Character of Stepfamilies: Implications of Cohabitation and Nonmarital Childbearing." *Demography* 32(3): 425–36.

Bumpass, Larry L., and James A. Sweet. 1989. "Children's Experience in Single-Parent Families: Implications of Cohabitation and Marital Transitions." *Family Planning Perspectives* 21(6): 256–61.

Bumpass, Larry L., James A. Sweet, and Andrew Cherlin. 1989. "The Role of Cohabitation in Declining Rates of Marriage." *Journal of Marriage and the Family* 53(4): 913–27.

Campbell, Arthur A. 1968. "The Role of Family Planning in the Reduction of Poverty." *Journal of Marriage and the Family* 30(2): 236–45.

Capaldi, Deborah M., Lynn Crosby, and Mike Stoolmiller. 1996. "Predicting the Timing of First Sexual Intercourse for At-Risk Adolescent Males." *Child Development* 67(2): 344–59.

Capaldi, Deborah M., and G. R. Patterson. 1991. "Relation of Parental Transitions to Boys' Adjustment Problems: I. A Linear Hypothesis. II. Mothers at Risk for Transitions and Unskilled Parenting." *Developmental Psychology* 27(3): 489–504.

Castro-Martin, Teresa, and Larry L. Bumpass. 1989. "Recent Trends in Marital Disruption." *Demography* 26(1): 37–51.

Cherlin, Andrew J. 1992. *Marriage, Divorce, Remarriage.* Revised and enlarged edition. Cambridge, Mass.: Harvard University Press.

Cherlin, Andrew J., Frank F. Furstenberg Jr., P. Lindsay Chase-Lansdale, Kathleen E. Kiernan, Philip K. Robins, Donna Ruane Morrison, and Julien O. Teitler. 1991. "Longitudinal Studies of Effects of Divorce on Children in Great Britain and the United States." *Science* 252(5011): 1386–89.

Duncan, Greg J., and Saul D. Hoffman. 1990. "Welfare Benefits, Economic Opportunities, and Out-of-Wedlock Births Among Black Teenage Girls." *Demography* 27(4): 519–36.

Duncan, Greg J., and Willard Rodgers. 1991. "Has Children's Poverty Become More Persistent?" *American Sociological Review* 56(4): 538–50.

Foster, E. Michael, and Saul D. Hoffman. 1996. "Nonmarital Childbearing in the 1980s: Assessing the Importance of Women Twenty-five and Older." *Family Planning Perspectives* 28(3): 117–19.

Furstenberg, Frank F., Jr., Jeanne Brooks-Gunn, and S. Philip Morgan. 1987. *Adolescent Mothers in Later Life.* Cambridge: Cambridge University Press.

Geronimus, Arline, and Sanders Korenman. 1993. "The Socioeconomic Costs of Teenage Childbearing: Evidence and Interpretation." *Demography* 30(2): 281–96.

Hoffman, Saul D., and E. Michael Foster. 1997. "Economic Correlates of Nonmarital Childbearing Among Adult Women." *Family Planning Perspectives* 29(3): 137–40.

Hoffman, Saul D., E. Michael Foster, and Frank F. Furstenberg Jr. 1993a. "Reevaluating the Costs of Teenage Childbearing." *Demography* 30(1): 1–13.

———. 1993b. "Reevaluating the Costs of Teenage Childbearing: Response to Geronimus and Korenman." *Demography* 30(2): 291–96.

Lillard, Lee A., Michael J. Brien, and Linda J. Waite. 1995. "Premarital Cohabitation and Subsequent Marital Dissolution: A Matter of Self-Selection?" *Demography* 32(3): 437–57.

Martinson, Brian C., and Lawrence L. Wu. 1992. "Parent Histories: Patterns of Change in Early Life." *Journal of Family Issues* 13(3): 351–77.

———. 1998. "The Competing Risks of Remarriage and Nonmarital Cohabitation Among White Women in the United States." NSFH working paper 79. Madison: Center for Demography and Ecology, University of Wisconsin.

McLanahan, Sara S., and Gary Sandefur. 1994. *Growing Up with a Single Parent.* Cambridge, Mass.: Harvard University Press.

Moffitt, Robert A., Robert Reville, and Anne E. Winkler. 1998. "Beyond Single Mothers: Cohabitation, Marriage, and the U.S. Welfare System." *Demography* 35(3): 259–78.

Oppenheimer, Valerie Kincade. 1994. "Women's Rising Employment and the Future of the Family in Industrial Societies." *Population and Development Review* 20(2): 293–342.

Pendleton, Audrey J., James McCarthy, and Andrew Cherlin. 1989. "The Quality of Marriage and Divorce Data from Surveys." U.S. National Center for Health Statistics, PHS 90–1241, *Challenges for Public Health Statistics in the 1990s: Proceedings of the 1989 Public Health Conference on Records and Statistics.* Washington: U.S. Government Printing Office.

Popenoe, David. 1996. *Life Without Father.* New York: Free Press.

Potter, Frank J., Vincent G. Iannacchione, William D. Mosher, Robert E. Mason, and Jill D. Kavee. 1998. "Sample Design, Sampling Weights, Imputation, and Variance Estimation in the 1995 National Survey of Family Growth." *Vital and Health Statistics*, series 2, no. 124. Hyattsville, Md.: National Center for Health Statistics.

Raley, R. Kelly, and Larry L. Bumpass. 1999. "Estimating Levels of Marital Disruption: Differential Data Quality by Source and Trends by Race, Age at Marriage, and Education." Working Paper 99-27, Center for Demography and Ecology, University of Wisconsin–Madison.

Rindfuss, Ronald R. 1991. "The Young Adult Years: Diversity, Structural Change, and Fertility." *Demography* 28(4): 493–512.

Rindfuss, Ronald R., and Allan M. Parnell. 1989. "The Varying Connection Between Marital Status and Childbearing in the United States." *Population and Development Review* 15(3): 447–70.

Smith, Herbert L., S. Philip Morgan, and Tanya Koropeckyj-Cox. 1996. "A

Decomposition of Trends in the Nonmarital Fertility Ratios of Blacks and Whites in the United States, 1960 to 1992." *Demography* 33(2): 141–52.

South, Scott J., and Kim M. Lloyd. 1992. "Marriage Markets and Nonmarital Fertility in the United States." *Demography* 29(2): 247–64.

Sweet, James A., and Larry L. Bumpass. 1990. "Disruption of Marital and Cohabitation Relationships: A Social-Demographic Perspective." In *Close Relationship Loss: Theoretical Approaches,* edited by Terri Orbuch. New York: Springer-Verlag.

Teachman, Jay D., and Karen A. Polonko. 1990. "Cohabitation and Marital Stability in the United States." *Social Forces* 69(1): 207–20.

Ventura, Stephanie J. 1995. "Births to Unmarried Mothers: United States, 1980–1992." *Vital and Health Statistics,* series 21, no. 53. Hyattsville, Md.: National Center for Health Statistics.

Ventura, Stephanie J., Christine A. Bachrach, Laura Hill, Kelleen Kaye, Pamela Holcomb, and Elisa Koff. 1995. "The Demography of Nonmarital Childbearing." In *Report to Congress on Out-of-Wedlock Childbearing,* U.S. Department of Health and Human Services. *Vital and Health Statistics,* series 21, no. 56. Hyattsville, Md.: National Center for Health Statistics.

Ventura, Stephanie J., William D. Mosher, Sally C. Curtin, Joyce C. Abma, and Stanley Henshaw. 2000. "Trends in Pregnancies and Pregnancy Rates by Outcome: Estimates for the United States, 1976–1996." *Vital and Health Statistics,* series 21, no. 56. Hyattsville, Md: National Center for Health Statistics.

Wilson, William Julius. 1987. *The Truly Disadvantaged: The Inner City, the Underclass, and Public Policy.* Chicago: University of Chicago Press.

Wu, Lawrence L. 1996. "Effects of Family Instability, Income, and Income Instability on the Risk of a Premarital Birth." *American Sociological Review* 61(3): 386–406.

Wu, Lawrence L., Stephen P. Martin, and Daniel A. Long. Forthcoming. "Comparing Data Quality of Fertility and First Sexual Intercourse Histories." *Journal of Human Resources.*

Wu, Lawrence L., and Brian C. Martinson. 1993. "Family Structure and the Risk of a Premarital Birth." *American Sociological Review* 58(2): 210–32.

Wu, Lawrence L., and Elizabeth Thomson. Forthcoming. "Race Differences in Family Experience and Early Sexual Initiation: Dynamic Models of Family Structure and Family Change." *Journal of Marriage and the Family.*

CHAPTER 2

Differences in Nonmarital Childbearing Across States

Kelleen Kaye

The rising share of births that occur outside of marriage has received a great deal of attention from policymakers, researchers, and the media. This attention stems from a variety of concerns, including those stemming from findings that children born outside of marriage are more likely to be in poverty, more likely to be on public assistance, and more likely to become pregnant as teens (U.S. House of Representatives 1996). The health status of unmarried women and their babies is also generally less favorable. The National Center for Health Statistics (NCHS) states that "unmarried mothers are less apt to receive adequate prenatal care, more likely to smoke during pregnancy and less likely to gain weight during pregnancy" (Ventura 1995).

Much of the research on trends in nonmarital births has centered on differences in fertility among various demographic subgroups (defined by age, race, and other characteristics), and this research has drawn policy attention to various populations over time. In understanding the impact of various subpopulations on nonmarital births, it is useful to examine these relationships at the state level. The role of demographic subgroups varies widely across states, and for reasons greater than basic differences in the racial and ethnic makeup of the population, as will be shown later in the chapter. Understanding the demographics of nonmarital childbearing at the state level has also become more important to policymakers since the welfare reform debate of the 1990s and the passage of the Personal Responsibility and Work Opportunity Reconciliation Act of 1996 (PRWORA).

PRWORA replaced Aid to Families with Dependent Children (AFDC) with Temporary Assistance for Needy Families (TANF), a change that shifted much of the focus of welfare-related issues to the state level. The stated purposes of this legislation include "prevent[ing] and reduc[ing] the incidence of out-of-wedlock pregnancies." One provision of PRWORA, the Bonus to Reward Decrease in Illegitimacy Ratio, focuses particular attention on state-level changes in nonmarital births. This provision seeks to encourage state-level policy and program development around these issues through an award of $100 million annually to approximately five states that achieve the largest decrease in the proportion of births that occur outside of marriage.[1] Additional evidence is needed before we can examine the impact of the bonus on policy development. However, the bonus has served to focus increased attention on the issue of nonmarital childbearing in many states.[2]

In an effort to help inform policy and research around nonmarital childbearing, this chapter looks at the contributions of various subpopulations to trends in nonmarital births and the differences in these contributions across states, highlighting examples of demographic characteristics that could have implications for state-level policymakers. This work expands on a variety of nonmarital birth statistics presented by researchers at the National Center for Health Statistics and elsewhere by providing additional state-level detail and using decomposition analysis to estimate the amount of increase in nonmarital childbearing attributable to each demographic group.

BACKGROUND

The percentage of births that occur outside of marriage increased from roughly 18 percent in 1980 to about 32 percent in 1994, remaining relatively unchanged between 1994 and 1997.[3] During this time the birth rate among unmarried white women roughly doubled, while the rate declined slightly among black women. The most significant declines among black women have occurred in the last seven years. After rising sharply between 1980 and 1991, unmarried birth rates among black adults and teens have fallen since 1991 by over 20 percent (based on findings presented in Ventura, Martin, et al. 1999; and Ventura, Mathews, et al. 1999). Thus, the gap between unmarried birth rates for white and black women has narrowed substantially, although the rate for black women remains more than twice that for white women (73.4 births per 1,000 unmarried women compared to 44.0 births). NCHS reports that the gap in nonmarital birth outcomes persists even after controlling for differences in education, the best measure of socioeconomic status in the vital statistics data (Ventura 1995).

The nonmarital birth ratio is affected by changes in unmarried birth rates, as well as in married birth rates and marriage rates. Smith, Morgan, and Koropeckyj-Cox (1996) find that, among both white and black women, decreases in marriage rates and increases in nonmarital birth rates pushed the nonmarital birth ratio upward between 1983 and 1992, although marriage rates were a more important factor for black women and nonmarital birth rates were a more important factor for white women. This upward trend in the ratio was partially offset by increases in married birth rates and changes in the age distribution, both of which pushed the ratio downward slightly. In addition to these factors, NCHS reports that sharp increases in sexual activity during the 1980s were only partially mitigated by increases in contraception. During this same period, abortion rates declined. Among women who become pregnant outside of marriage, the proportion of those who marry prior to the birth has also been falling, particularly among black women (see Ventura 1995; Bachu 1991).

Perhaps one of the most important factors affecting the intersection of marriage and fertility is the increasing prevalence of cohabitation. Findings cited in Wu, Bumpass, and Musick (this volume) indicate that during the 1970s and 1980s births within cohabiting unions accounted for a substantial share of the upward trend in nonmarital first births among black women, and nearly the entire upward trend among white women.[4]

Nonmarital birth outcomes are also affected by many other factors, including differences in social norms, economies and labor markets, family planning, public assistance, and other social policies. Kathleen Kiernan (this volume) compares the increase in nonmarital births across nine European countries with varying policy regimes and demographic and cultural characteristics. She finds differing perspectives on nonmarital childbearing across Europe: marriage is a more predominant setting for childbearing in southern and middle European countries compared to Nordic countries, among which Sweden is the only country to have more first births within cohabiting unions than within married unions.

Variations in economies, policies, demographics, and social norms also affect nonmarital birth outcomes across states in the

United States, although less work has been done to examine these differences. NCHS reports indicate that the proportion of births outside of marriage in 1997 varied from 0.166 in Utah to 0.633 in the District of Columbia. While some states experienced declines of less than 13 percent between 1991 and 1997, others experienced declines of 20 percent or more (see Ventura, Martin, et al. 1999; and Ventura, Mathews, et al. 1999).[5]

The findings presented here expand on existing work, providing additional state-level detail and estimating the proportion of increases in the nonmarital birth ratio attributable to various demographic groups across states. The chapter first discusses briefly the nonmarital birth ratio and composition of nonmarital births at the national level in 1997, then examines how these factors vary across states. The chapter then examines the increase in the nonmarital birth ratio from 1980 to 1997, the population groups that contributed to this increase, and variations in the contributions across states. The population groups are defined by age, race, Hispanic origin, birth order, and mother's education at the time of birth.

METHODOLOGY

MEASURES OF NONMARITAL BIRTHS

There are several commonly used measures of nonmarital births: the number of nonmarital births; the birth rate among unmarried women; and the ratio of nonmarital births to total births. Although these statistics are related, they each provide different information.

Number The number of nonmarital births is a basic count of births occurring outside of marriage. To the extent that policymakers are concerned about the economic or other implications of nonmarital births, the number describes the size of the population involved. The number of nonmarital births is also informative because it is easily broken down to describe the proportion attributable to various subgroups of the population. The demographic makeup of nonmarital births tends to reflect that of the general population. For example, large states generally have more nonmarital births than small states. In states where Hispanics account for a large portion of the population, they tend to account for a larger portion of nonmarital births. However, the fact that the demographic makeup of nonmarital births does not mirror the underlying population completely highlights differences in birth and marriage behavior across populations.

Although the number of nonmarital births is informative, changes in this measure are difficult to interpret. For example, the number of nonmarital births has been rising, but the number does not indicate how much of this change is simply due to general increases in the population of childbearing age. Also, if more nonmarital births are to Hispanic women than to black women in a particular area, this higher proportion could indicate either that Hispanics make up a larger share of the population of unmarried women or that unmarried Hispanic women are more likely to give birth.

Rate The likelihood that an unmarried woman will give birth is an important measure because it controls for these differences in the population. It provides a clearer picture of how nonmarital childbearing has changed over time and how it may differ among various populations. The likelihood that unmarried women will give birth is called the nonmarital birth rate, and it is expressed as the number of nonmarital births per 1,000 unmarried women of a particular demographic group.

Ratio The ratio of nonmarital births to total births is also a useful measure. It describes nonmarital births relative to total births and thus controls for changes in overall fertility. If childbearing among unmarried women is rising much faster than among women overall, this increase might be of greater concern to policymakers than if the two are rising in a similar fashion.

The nonmarital birth ratio, or the proportion of births that occur outside of marriage can be stated as follows:

$$\frac{\text{Nonmarital Births}}{\text{Total Births}} = \frac{\text{Nonmarital Births}}{\text{Nonmarital Births} + \text{Marital Births}} =$$

$$\frac{\text{Unmarried Women} \times \text{Nonmarital Birth Rate}}{\text{Unmarried Women} \times \text{Nonmarital Birth Rate} + \text{Married Women} \times \text{Marital Birth Rate}}$$

This equation shows that the nonmarital birth ratio is affected not only by the birth rate of single women but also by the rate at which women marry and the birth rate among married women. The equation also shows that the number of nonmarital births, the nonmarital birth rate, and the nonmarital birth ratio are all related.[6] Although the nonmarital birth ratio can be informative for this reason, research on trends in the ratio can be hard to interpret because it confounds the factors of marriage rates and single and married birth rates. Numerous studies have used decomposition analysis to disentangle these factors for different demographic groups at the national level; however, such analysis cannot be replicated at the state level owing to data limitations. For many states, inter-censal data do not provide reliable population estimates by marital status for demographic groups; thus birth rates for these groups cannot be calculated.

ANALYTIC METHODS

For these reasons, the decomposition analysis presented here cannot disentangle the effects of marriage rates and single and nonmarital birth rates at the state level. However, it does answer a fundamental question by identifying the demographic groups that account for the increase in the nonmarital birth ratio and how their contributions vary across states. By describing the nonmarital birth ratio in terms of the number of marital and nonmarital births, and then breaking these births down further by age, race, Hispanic origin, education, and birth order, it is possible to estimate how much of the increase in the nonmarital birth ratio is attributable to each population group at the state level. Given that nonmarital birth rates are not available at the state level between census years, decomposing changes in the nonmarital birth ratio in this way is an alternative method available for examining variation in nonmarital fertility trends and composition across states.

Changes in the nonmarital birth ratio are decomposed into the effects of two factors: the number of marital births and the number of nonmarital births.[7] The changes attributable to marital and nonmarital births are then apportioned to changes in the subgroups that make up these births. For example, if 70 percent of the change in the nonmarital birth ratio is attributable to changes in nonmarital births and white teens make up 20 percent of the change in nonmarital births, then the increase in the nonmarital birth ratio attributable to nonmarital births among white teens would be approximately 0.70 × 0.20, or 14 percent. The total effect of a particular demographic group on the nonmarital birth ratio would depend on both its nonmarital and marital birth outcomes.

These results capture two potential effects. A particular demographic group can contribute to changes in the overall nonmarital birth ratio either because the nonmarital birth ratio within that group changed or because births to that group became a larger or smaller share of overall births. This effect can be seen when the nonmarital birth ratio is written in the following way. For simplification, the decomposition is written in terms of two populations, adults and teens, but the equation could be further expanded to include other demographic groups defined by race, Hispanic origin, education, or birth order.

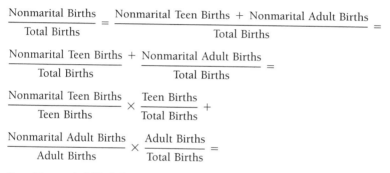

$$\frac{\text{Nonmarital Births}}{\text{Total Births}} = \frac{\text{Nonmarital Teen Births} + \text{Nonmarital Adult Births}}{\text{Total Births}} =$$

$$\frac{\text{Nonmarital Teen Births}}{\text{Total Births}} + \frac{\text{Nonmarital Adult Births}}{\text{Total Births}} =$$

$$\frac{\text{Nonmarital Teen Births}}{\text{Teen Births}} \times \frac{\text{Teen Births}}{\text{Total Births}} +$$

$$\frac{\text{Nonmarital Adult Births}}{\text{Adult Births}} \times \frac{\text{Adult Births}}{\text{Total Births}} =$$

Teen Nonmarital Birth Ratio × Teen Birth Share + Adult Nonmarital Birth Ratio × Adult Birth Share

The share of births to each demographic group—in this case teens and adults—is in turn a function of that group's share of the population as well as the birth rate per 1,000 women in that demographic group divided by the birth rate for the total population. Thus, the nonmarital birth ratio can be further rewritten as follows:

Nonmarital Birth Ratio = Teen Nonmarital Birth Ratio × (Teen Birth Rate/Total Birth Rate) × Teen Population Share
+ Adult Nonmarital Birth Ratio × (Adult Birth Rate/Total Birth Rate) × Adult Population Share

This equation shows that the demographic composition of the underlying population affects the nonmarital birth ratio, and it is used to estimate how the ratio varies across states or over time if the makeup of the population is held constant.

DATA SOURCES

The data for this analysis come from two sources. Vital statistics data provide information on births for 1980 and 1997. Population estimates from the U.S. Bureau of the Census are used to calculate the distribution of the female population by age, race, and Hispanic origin for 1980 and 1997.

VITAL STATISTICS DATA

This project is primarily based on vital statistics data for marital and nonmarital births by state for 1980 and 1997 from the National Center for Health Statistics. These data are submitted by states to NCHS each year through the Vital Statistics Cooperative Program. The data contain information about the race and Hispanic origin of the mother, birth order, marital status, mother's education, and mother's age at time of birth.[8] Vital statistics are based on almost universal reporting of births and are a reliable source of birth data at the state level.[9]

Nonetheless, there are important differences in the reporting of marital status across states and over time. In 1980, forty-four states and the District of Columbia used a direct question to determine marital status. The remaining states (California, Connecticut, Michigan, Nevada, New York, and Texas) used an inferential procedure based on a comparison of the child's and parents' surnames and the presence of information about the father. However, by 1997 California, Nevada, and Texas had added a direct question on marital status, and the inferential procedures used in Michigan and New York had been significantly improved.[10] Thus, by 1997 the reporting of nonmarital births was fairly consistent across states.

The improvements in data collection implemented in these states probably affect comparisons of 1997 to 1980 much less than if 1997 were being compared to a more recent historical period such as the early 1990s. This is because sources of error in the previous inferential procedures, such as differing surnames among married couples and hyphenated surnames (particularly among the Hispanic population), were less prevalent in 1980 compared to today. Nonetheless, these differences should be taken into account when considering the results presented here.[11]

Population Data

Calculations that control for differences in the underlying female population by age, race, and Hispanic origin rely on published population counts from the U.S. Bureau of the Census for 1980 and 1997. State-level birth rates by race and Hispanic origin for 1997 were generated by the Statistical Export and Tabulation System. This interface, published by NCHS, not only contains detailed natality data but also tabulates birth rates for various populations.

RESULTS

This section briefly discusses nonmarital childbearing at the national level, then describes in more detail how nonmarital childbearing varies across states. Findings are presented first for 1997, and then with respect to changes between 1980 and 1997.

1997 Nonmarital Births, National

Ratio of Nonmarital Births   Although the nonmarital birth ratio was 0.324 in 1997, it is well known that the proportion is much higher for some populations than others. Figure 2.1 shows the nonmarital birth ratio for each race/ethnic group overall, as well as by age, education, and birth order within each race/ethnic group.

As would be expected, within each of the three race/ethnic groups, some subgroups tend to be at higher risk than others, such as teens and women with lower education, but there are interesting differences between the race/ethnic groups as well. Among black women, the likelihood that a birth will occur outside of marriage is relatively high for all population groups examined, even adults and more highly educated women, and the difference between high-risk and low-risk groups is narrower, indicating that nonmarital childbearing in this subgroup is more than a matter of age or socioeconomics. Also, the proportion of births outside of marriage is generally higher among Hispanic women compared to white women,

Figure 2.1 Nonmarital Birth Ratio, for Various Subpopulations, 1997

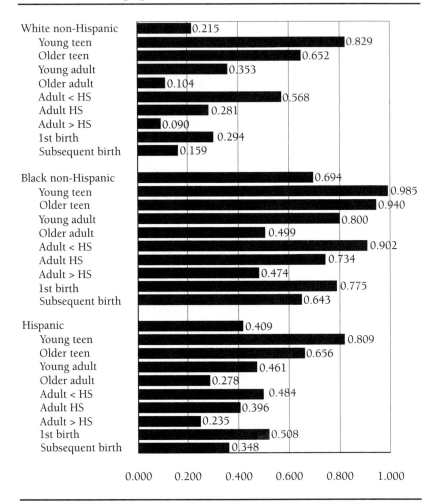

Source: Author's compilation based on data from 1997 Natality Data Set.
Young teen = less than eighteen
Older teen = eighteen to nineteen
Young adult = twenty to twenty-four
Older adult = over twenty-four
Adult < HS = less than twelve years of education
Adult HS = high school graduate
Adult > HS = more than twelve years of education
1st birth = has given birth once
Subsequent birth = has given birth more than once

but the ratio is higher for white women when comparing relatively high-risk groups such as teens and adults with less education.

Although these results show which populations are most likely to experience births outside of marriage, they do not show which populations account for the majority of nonmarital births. The likelihood that a birth will occur outside of marriage is high among teens, for instance, but teens account for less than one-third of all nonmarital births because they account for a small portion of the population and their overall birth rate is lower than the aggregate birth rate.

Composition of Nonmarital Births   Table 2.1 shows the proportion of nonmarital births attributable to each demographic group. Forty percent of nonmarital births occurred among non-Hispanic white women, 32 percent among non-Hispanic black women, and 23 percent among Hispanic women. Young adults accounted for the largest share, followed by older adults and then teens. The age distribution was fairly similar among white non-Hispanic, black non-Hispanic, and Hispanic mothers. Fully 50 percent of nonmarital births were to teens or were subsequent births to young adults, many of whom probably had their first birth as a teen. This proportion was somewhat greater among black women compared to Hispanic and white women. Among younger and older adults, between one-quarter and one-third had less than twelve years of education. The educational attainment was fairly similar among white and black non-Hispanic unmarried mothers but tended to be much lower among Hispanic unmarried mothers.[12]

1997 NONMARITAL BIRTHS, VARIATION ACROSS STATES

Ratio of Nonmarital Births   Thirty-three states had nonmarital birth ratios that were close to the national average of 0.324, lying within plus or minus 0.05 points. However, there are several noticeable outliers. Four states have ratios over 0.430, and another four states have ratios at 0.250 or below.

Figure 2.2 highlights those states with the highest and lowest nonmarital birth ratios. Because the likelihood that a birth will occur outside of marriage is higher for black women and Hispanic women, overall nonmarital birth ratios tend to be higher in states

Table 2.1 Distribution of Nonmarital Births, by Various Subpopulations, 1997

	All Nonmarital Births	White Non-Hispanic	Black Non-Hispanic	Other Non-Hispanic	Hispanic
Race-ethnicity					
White non-Hispanic	40%	—	—	—	—
Black non-Hispanic	32	—	—	—	—
Other non-Hispanic	4	—	—	—	—
Hispanic	23	—	—	—	—
Age					
Young teen	13	12	14	12	14
Older teen	18	19	17	14	16
Less than high school	8	8	7	6	10
High school	8	9	8	7	5
More than high school	1	1	1	1	1
First birth	13	16	11	11	11
Subsequent birth	5	4	6	4	5
Young adult	35	35	35	33	34
Less than high school	11	9	9	9	18
High school	16	17	17	16	12
More than high school	8	9	9	9	5
First birth	16	19	13	16	15
Subsequent birth	19	16	22	17	19
Older adult	34	33	34	41	36
Less than high school	9	6	6	10	19
High school	14	15	15	16	11
More than high school	11	13	12	14	6
First birth	9	11	7	12	8
Subsequent birth	25	23	27	29	28

Source: Author's tabulations based on data from 1997 Natality Data Set.
Note: Education proportions are calculated with respect to the 98.5 percent of births for which education was reported. Birth order proportions are calculated with respect to the 99.5 percent of births for which birth order was reported.

Figure 2.2 States with Highest Nonmarital Birth Ratios

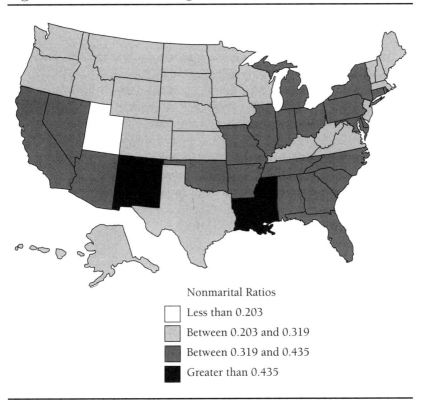

Nonmarital Ratios

☐ Less than 0.203

▨ Between 0.203 and 0.319

▨ Between 0.319 and 0.435

■ Greater than 0.435

Source: Author's tabulations based on data from 1997 Natality Data Set.

where these groups account for a larger share of the population. However, nonmarital birth ratios also vary across states because birth and marital outcomes within each race/ethnic group are likely to be affected by state-level differences in economies, social policies, and other factors.

The District of Columbia ranks highest in the country with a nonmarital birth ratio of .636—attributable in part to the fact that a large share of the female population in the District is black. The District's high overall nonmarital birth ratio is also attributable to the fact that the District's nonmarital birth ratio among black women is the second highest in the country. Mississippi and Louisiana are similar in this respect. Their overall nonmarital birth ratios rank second and third highest, at 0.439 and 0.454, respectively. The share of their population that is black is higher than the national average, and among black women their nonmarital birth ratios rank relatively high (ninth and fourteenth, respectively). New Mexico, with the fourth-highest overall nonmarital birth ratio at 0.435, has a higher-than-average share of Hispanic women and, among Hispanic women, a nonmarital birth ratio that ranks eighth highest in the nation. Thus, in these states, clearly the racial and ethnic composition of the population, as well as the birth and marital patterns within each race-ethnic group, account for the high nonmarital birth ratios.

These states would not be such extreme outliers if the racial and ethnic composition of their population mirrored the national average.[13] In this case, the District of Columbia and Mississippi would be among the one-third of states with the lowest nonmarital birth ratios, Louisiana would be in the middle third, and New Mexico would remain in the highest third. These rankings follow from the fact that nonmarital birth ratios for non-Hispanic white women are among the lowest in the country for the District and Mississippi, close to the national average in Louisiana, and significantly higher than the national average in New Mexico.

Several states would have a much higher nonmarital birth ratio if differences in population were controlled for by setting the race-ethnic composition equal to the national average. States whose ratio would rank among the top ten include Indiana, Nevada, Pennsylvania, Rhode Island, and Wisconsin. For example, although Wisconsin ranks thirty-seventh in actual nonmarital birth ratios, it would rank sixth if the composition of its population mirrored the national average. Among black women in Wisconsin, the nonmarital birth ratio is the highest in the country.

Naturally, the variability in the nonmarital birth ratios across states is significantly smaller once the racial and ethnic composition of the population is held constant: the standard deviation drops from .07 points for the actual ratio to .05 points for the adjusted ratio. However, clearly much of the variability remains.

Composition of Nonmarital Births   Not surprisingly, there is variability across states in the composition of nonmarital births as well. The following results provide a few examples of how the composition of nonmarital births varies across states and highlights the implications for policymakers.

Figure 2.3 Percentage of Nonmarital Births to Women
           with Less than Ten Years of Education

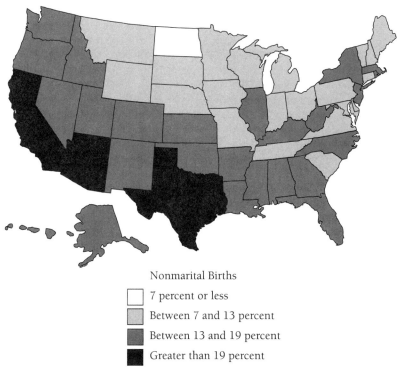

Nonmarital Births

☐ 7 percent or less

▨ Between 7 and 13 percent

▨ Between 13 and 19 percent

■ Greater than 19 percent

Source: Author's tabulations based on data from 1997 Natality Data Set.

Figure 2.3 shows the proportion of nonmarital births to women
with low educational attainment. Although it is widely known that
many women who have a child outside of marriage lack a high
school diploma, the fact is that a significant percentage of these
women have not gone even beyond the ninth grade. The proportion
of nonmarital births to women with less than ten years of schooling
ranges from just under 7 to 26 percent across states, with a standard deviation of .04. Those states with the highest proportions are
highlighted in black. These women left school before the tenth
grade or gave birth before the tenth grade. In either case, this finding supports other evidence of the need for school-based intervention programs to begin early. Additionally, roughly half of these

Figure 2.4 Percentage of Nonmarital Births to Women Under Age Twenty-Five with Prior Birth

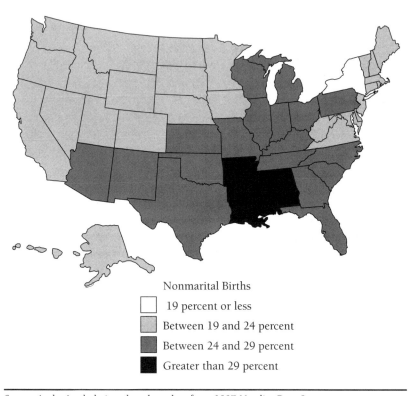

Nonmarital Births

☐ 19 percent or less

▢ Between 19 and 24 percent

▨ Between 24 and 29 percent

▪ Greater than 29 percent

Source: Author's tabulations based on data from 1997 Natality Data Set.

women with very low education were foreign-born, and it is likely that many were not even participating in the U.S. educational system, making it particularly difficult for policymakers to target interventions. Thus, it is not surprising that several of the states highlighted in figure 2.3 are in areas of high immigration, including Texas, California, and Arizona.[14]

Figure 2.4 shows the percentage of nonmarital births that are subsequent births to teens or to young adults, many of whom probably had their first birth as a teen. This proportion ranges across states from just under 19 to 33 percent, with a standard deviation of .03. This finding indicates that interventions targeted at teens who

Figure 2.5 Percentage of Nonmarital Births to Women Over Age Twenty-Five

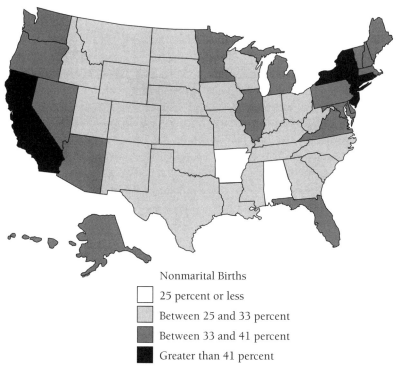

Nonmarital Births

☐ 25 percent or less

▨ Between 25 and 33 percent

▨ Between 33 and 41 percent

■ Greater than 41 percent

Source: Author's tabulations based on data from 1997 Natality Data Set.

have already had a first birth may be even more important in some states than in others, particularly Mississippi, Louisiana, Alabama, and Arkansas.

Policies focused on teens overall could play a larger role in addressing nonmarital childbearing in some states than in others. Nationally, 31 percent of nonmarital births are to teens, ranging from 22 to 39 percent across states. Furthermore, all teen births plus subsequent births among young adults account for as much as 60 percent of nonmarital births in some southern states. Some have argued, based on national data, that policies focused on teens do not address the majority of potential nonmarital births, but the teen years are an important point of intervention, particularly in some states.

Other states are dealing with the fact that a great share of nonmarital births occur among older adult women. Figure 2.5 shows the percentage of nonmarital births to women over twenty-five, ranging across states from just under 25 to 47 percent, with a standard deviation of .06. Because older women having nonmarital births are different from younger women (for example, they tend to be more educated, they are more likely to have had a prior birth, and their union formation is probably different), the outcomes associated with nonmarital childbearing for this group and the implications for research and policy need to be better understood. The share of nonmarital births to women age twenty-five and over is highest in New York, the District of Columbia, Connecticut, New Jersey, and California.[15]

Policy attention often focuses not only on those demographic groups that make up the majority of current nonmarital births but also on those groups that account for the increase. Examining the demographic composition of recent increases in nonmarital childbearing can sometimes suggest future trends and directions for policy and research.

NATIONAL INCREASE IN NONMARITAL BIRTH RATIO, 1980 TO 1997

As noted earlier, there are several measures of trends in nonmarital childbearing, each with its own strengths and weaknesses. One advantage of the nonmarital birth ratio is that it can be used to examine changes in nonmarital births within the context of overall changes in fertility. Another advantage is that the ratio can be decomposed at the state level in ways that do not rely on population counts for unmarried women. Between 1980 and 1997 the ratio increased from 0.184 to 0.324, or 0.140 points. The findings presented in table 2.2, which describes how much of this increase is attributable to each population group, are based on the decomposition analysis described earlier.

Findings by Age, Race, and Birth Order   Births among white women accounted for nearly all of the increase in the nonmarital birth ratio

Table 2.2 Contribution of Various Subpopulations to the Increase in the Nonmarital Birth Ratio, by Race, 1980 to 1997

	White	Black	Other	Total
Young teen	8%	−1%	0%	8%
First birth	7	−1	0	7
Subsequent birth	1	−0	0	1
Older teen	16	1	1	18
First birth	12	1	0	13
Subsequent birth	4	1	0	5
Young adult	45	7	1	53
First birth	23	2	1	26
Subsequent birth	22	5	1	27
Older adult	14	10	−1	22
First birth	1	2	−1	1
Subsequent birth	12	8	−1	20
Total	82	17	1	100

Source: Author's tabulations based on 1980 and 1997 vital statistics data provided by the National Center for Health Statistics.

during this period, or 82 percent, with more than half of this contribution in turn attributable to births among young adults.[16] Births among black women accounted for 17 percent of the increase, with the greatest share attributable to births among older adults and virtually none attributable to births among teens. Among young adults, the increase was roughly split between first births and subsequent births, although first births were a larger factor for white women and subsequent births were a larger factor for black women. Among older adults, nearly all of the increase is attributable to subsequent births.

These findings suggest that the role played by different demographic groups may be shifting over time. For example, among black women, subsequent births account for roughly half of current nonmarital births, but for over three-quarters of the increase in the nonmarital birth ratio attributable to black women.

The Role of Births to Hispanic Women   These findings are presented by race but do not distinguish according to Hispanic origin, and most Hispanic women are classified as white. The amount of the increase in the nonmarital birth ratio attributable to births among

Hispanic women can only be approximated because in 1980 only twenty-two states reported Hispanic origin for the mother. Nonetheless, the approximation described here is likely to be reliable, given that these twenty-two states included 87 percent of the Hispanic population at the time. If we assume that this 87 percent was representative of the Hispanic population as a whole in 1980, we can estimate total married and nonmarital births in 1980 and include these figures in the decomposition analysis.[17]

According to these estimates, nearly 40 percent of the increase in the nonmarital birth ratio attributable to births among white women would be due to births among Hispanic women.[18]

The Role of Changes in the Population   The significant effect of the Hispanic population on changing fertility patterns raises a related issue: Does the increase in the nonmarital birth ratio simply reflect changes in the composition of the population, or were there important changes in marital and birth outcomes during this time? In fact, the proportion of births that occur outside of marriage increased substantially within each race-ethnic group between 1980 and 1997. Based on the approximations of 1980 Hispanic marital and nonmarital births described earlier, the nonmarital birth ratio for white non-Hispanic women and Hispanic women roughly doubled during this time. The ratio for black women, already very high at .561, increased by roughly one-quarter. Had the composition of the population with respect to race and Hispanic origin remained unchanged at 1980 proportions, the overall nonmarital birth ratios still would have increased from 0.184 to 0.297 between 1980 and 1997.

INCREASE IN NONMARITAL BIRTH RATIO, VARIATION ACROSS STATES

Variation in the Increase   Although the national nonmarital birth ratio increased by over 75 percent between 1980 and 1997, this increase varied widely across states. Figure 2.6 shows the level of the nonmarital birth ratio in 1980 for each state, as well as the level reached by 1997. Some of the largest increases occurred in states with the lowest ratios in 1980, including New Mexico, Nevada, Wyoming, and Arizona. It is not surprising that the smallest increase occurred in the District of Columbia, where the ratio was

Figure 2.6 Nonmarital Birth Ratio, by State, 1980 and 1997

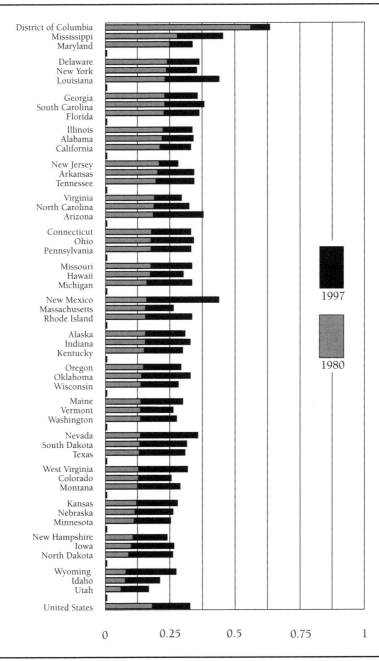

Source: Author's compilation based on 1980 and 1997 vital statistics data provided by the National Center for Health Statistics.

already so high in 1980 that it was probably approaching a threshold.

These findings raise the question of whether the nonmarital birth ratios across states are converging to a threshold. The evidence presented here does not indicate that such a threshold has yet been reached. If this were the case, we would expect the cross-state variation in nonmarital birth ratios to decrease over time. Although the variance is somewhat lower in 1997 compared to 1980, the difference is not statistically significant, and if the outliers of the District and Utah are excluded, the variance has actually increased during this time.

There does seem to be some evidence that the geographic patterns of nonmarital births have shifted over time. States with the highest ratios in 1980 included many of the states in the Southeast, as well as states along the East Coast such as Delaware, New York, Maryland, and New Jersey. Their relative ranking among states has fallen over time, however, while the ranking among many of the Southwest, Central, and Great Lakes states has increased.

The relative contributions of each demographic group to the increase in the nonmarital birth ratio at the national level, shown in table 2.2, are quite different in some respects from the picture that forms at the state level. It is not practical to summarize the sources of increase across all states, but the remainder of this section presents a few interesting examples that highlight the variation in compositional changes across states.

Increase Attributable to Young Adults   Although nationally just over 50 percent of the increase in the ratio is attributable to births among young adults, across states this contribution ranges from a low of 30 percent in the District of Columbia to 82 percent in Massachusetts, with a standard deviation of .08. In the District of Columbia, fully 79 percent of the increase is attributable to births among older adults, and births among teens actually pushed the ratio downward, making a negative contribution of 8 percent to the total change. Both the positive contribution among adults and the negative contribution among teens occurred primarily among black women.

In Massachusetts, where births among young adults accounted for 79 percent of the increase, births among older adults actually put downward pressure on the ratio, making a negative contribution of 3 percent of the total change. Births among teens accounted for 22 percent of the increase. The positive contribution among both young adults and teens occurred primarily among white women.

Increase Attributable to Teens   While births among teens pushed the nonmarital birth ratio lower in the District, as noted earlier, the increase in the ratio attributable to teens ranged as high as 42 percent (in Texas) and had a standard deviation across states of .09. In Texas births among young adults accounted for another 60 percent of the increase, and births among older adults pushed the ratio downward slightly, making a negative contribution of 3 percent of the total change. Births among Hispanic women accounted for roughly one-third of the increase overall, with over one-half of this increase attributable to teens.[19]

Increase Attributable to Other Groups   The contribution of other groups to the increase in the ratio varied across states as well. For example, while first births accounted for 47 percent of the increase in the nonmarital ratio nationally, their contribution ranged from a low of 36 percent in Maryland to 61 percent in New Hampshire, with a standard deviation of .06 points. Subsequent births to teens or young adults accounted for 33 percent of the increase nationally and ranged from a low of 21 percent in New Jersey to a high of 44 percent in Georgia, with a standard deviation of .05. The percentage of the increase attributable to adult women with less than twelve years of schooling varied from 6 percent in North Dakota to 30 percent in Massachusetts, with a standard deviation of .07.[20] As would be expected, the increase in the ratio attributable to births among young teens was fairly low across all states, as was the increase attributable to black teens.

CONCLUSION

This chapter has examined the trends in and demographic composition of nonmarital birth outcomes across states. Although the ratio of nonmarital to total births has increased steadily across all states between 1980 and 1997, the paths followed in many states vary widely in terms of the size of the increase and the role of various demographic subgroups. It was not feasible to present findings for each demographic group across all states, but the chapter highlights a few outcomes of interest. For example, the increase in the nonmarital birth ratio attributable to births among young adults, births among teens, births among less-educated women, and first births versus second births differed greatly in many states compared to the national average. The composition of current nonmarital births in many states also differs substantially from the national average. Much of this variation remains even after controlling for differences in the racial and ethnic makeup of the underlying population, reflecting the role of other state-level factors. These probably include state-level differences in economies and labor markets, as well as social norms and policies. Just as Kiernan (this volume) concludes that there are "not just one but several European perspectives on nonmarital childbearing," there are also several perspectives on nonmarital childbearing across the United States.

The views expressed here are those of the author and should not be attributed to her employer, the Department of Health and Human Services. The author gratefully acknowledges helpful comments from Pat Ruggles, Don Oellerich, and Julie Isaacs. Christine Bachrach, Vicki Freedman, Susan Hauan, Matt Stagner, and Larry Wu also provided helpful comments on an earlier draft. The author benefited greatly from comments, expertise, and data provided by Stephanie Ventura.

NOTES

1. More specifically, a state must be among the top five states with the largest reduction in their ratio of nonmarital to total births during the most recent two years for which data are available compared to the prior two years. A qualifying state must also show that its abortion rate during the most recent year for which data are available is lower than the abortion rate for 1995.
2. Examples of recent press coverage include Meyers (1998), Owen (1998), Tampa Tribune (1997), and American Political Network Abortion Report (1997).

3. NCHS reports that there was a slight increase in 1998, with 33 percent of births occurring outside of marriage (see Ventura, Martin, et al. 2000).

4. For additional information about trends and antecedents related to nonmartial childbearing, see Ventura, Bachrach, et al. 1995.

5. Birth rates at the state level are not calculated separately for unmarried teens, but the majority of teen births occur outside of marriage. (See Ventura, Martin, et al. 1999 ; and Ventura, Mathews, et al. 1999.)

6. The nonmarital birth ratio is also sometimes expressed as a percentage. For example, a ratio of 0.324 would indicate that 32.4 percent of births occur outside of marriage.

7. This part of the analysis is based on the technique described by Das Gupta (1993) and later used by Smith and his colleagues (1996) to decompose changes in the nonmarital birth ratio.

8. Hispanic origin was reported by twenty-two states in 1980, but not by all states until 1993. Education was reported for all states in 1997, but not by California, Texas, and Washington in 1980. These variables are included in the analysis to the extent that the data are available.

9. It should be noted that some researchers have expressed concern over differences in national nonmarital fertility trends as measured by vital statistics data compared to Current Population Survey data, particularly through 1985 (see Wu, Bumpass, and Musick, this volume).

10. More specifically, Michigan began considering paternity acknowledgments in determining marital status by 1994, and New York City made its inferential process more consistent with that of the rest of the state in 1997.

11. More specifically, NCHS reports that the 1997 changes in California had little effect on total numbers of nonmarital births compared to the previous year, but did affect the age distribution of nonmarital births. Nevada showed a similar pattern. Reporting changes in New York City affected the overall numbers of nonmarital births reported compared to the previous year, as well as the age distribution. Reporting changes in Michigan and Texas are primarily aimed at correcting the underreporting that occurred during the late 1980s and early 1990s and so are likely to have only a small impact on the analysis presented here (for more detail, see NCHS, various years; and Ventura, Martin, et al. 1999).

12. This finding probably results from a combination of factors. NCHS reports that the educational attainment of Hispanic women in general tends to be much lower. Its findings also show that birth rates

among less-educated Hispanic women are much greater than among more highly educated Hispanic women, and that this gap is much larger for Hispanic women compared to white and black non-Hispanic women (see Mathews and Ventura 1997).

13. These findings illustrate an example in which the state-level proportions of the population that are white non-Hispanic, black non-Hispanic, Asian or Pacific Islander, American Indian, and Hispanic are held constant to the national population. Standardizing to a different population would result in different rankings.

14. When this analysis is limited to native-born women, Texas and Arizona still have a relatively high proportion of nonmarital births to women with very low education, ranking first and third in the nation. California, on the other hand, ranks quite low in such an analysis.

15. The inferential procedure used to determine marital status in New York may somewhat inflate the proportion of nonmarital births to older women. The extent to which Connecticut or New Jersey residents have their births in New York could affect results in those states as well, although less than 1 percent of births to residents of these states occurred in New York.

16. These findings refer to all white women, including most Hispanic women, because not all states' vital records identified Hispanic origin in 1980. An approximation that accounts for births among Hispanic women separately is detailed later in the chapter.

17. This is a reasonable assumption, given that in 1997, a year for which Hispanic origin was reported for all states, the Hispanic birth rate and nonmarital birth ratio for these twenty-two states was similar to that for the Hispanic population in the nation as a whole.

18. The important effect of Hispanic births on changes in fertility is also described in Mathews et al. (1998). This report indicates that from 1989 to 1995, among Hispanic women, both total birth rates and nonmarital birth rates increased much faster than among the overall population. This report also suggests that one contributing factor is the high level of cohabitation among Hispanic women.

19. Texas is one of the states that reported Hispanic origin in both 1980 and 1997. As noted earlier, the changes in reporting of marital status that were made during this time should be taken into account when considering these results.

20. Results based on education are not shown nationally because years of schooling was not reported in California, Texas, and Washington in 1980. These results represent outcomes for the remaining states.

REFERENCES

Bachu, Amara. 1991. "Fertility of American Women: June 1990." Current Population Reports. Series P-20, No. 454. Washington: U.S. Government Printing Office.

Das Gupta, Prithwis. 1993. *Standardization and Decomposition of Rates: A User's Manual.* Current Population Reports. Special Study Series P-23, No. 186. Washington: U.S Government Printing Office.

Mathews T. J., and Stephanie J. Ventura. 1997. "Births and Fertility Rates by Educational Attainment: United States, 1994." *Monthly Vital Statistics Report* 45(10). Hyattsville, Md.: National Center for Health Statistics.

Mathews, T. J., Stephanie J. Ventura, Sally C. Curtin, and J. A. Martin. 1998. "Births of Hispanic Origin, 1980–1995." *Monthly Vital Statistics Report* 46(6). Hyattsville, Md.: National Center for Health Statistics.

Meyers, Marcia. 1998. "State Targets Illegitimacy in Welfare Reform Project; $100 Million Bonus to MD Is Possible." *Baltimore Sun*, April 7.

National Center for Health Statistics. Various years. *Technical Appendix from Vital Statistics of the United States: Natality.* Hyattsville, Md.: National Center for Health Statistics.

Owen, Penny. 1998. "Agency May Offer States Bonus for Reducing Illegitimate Births." *Daily Oklahoman,* June 1.

"Shaming Pregnant Teens Won't End Illegitimate Births." 1997. *Tampa Tribune,* March 30.

Smith, Herbert, Philip Morgan, and Tanya Koropeckyj-Cox. 1996. "A Decomposition of Trends in the Nonmarital Fertility Ratios of Blacks and Whites in the United States, 1960–1992." *Demography* 33(2): 141–52.

"Unwed Births; States Competing for Cash; VA Claims Victory." 1997. *American Political Network Abortion Report* (April 1).

U.S. House of Representatives. 1996. *Personal Responsibility and Work Opportunity Reconciliation Act of 1996: Conference Report to Accompany H.R.3747.* Washington: U.S. Government Printing Office.

Ventura, Stephanie J. 1995. "Births to Unmarried Mothers: United States, 1980–1992." *Vital and Health Statistics,* 21(53). Hyattsville, Md.: National Center for Health Statistics (June).

Ventura, Stephanie J., Christine A. Bachrach, Laura Hill, Kelleen Kaye, Pamela Holcomb, and Elisa Koff. 1995. "The Demography of Out of Wedlock Childbearing." In *Report to Congress on Out-of-Wedlock Childbearing,* U.S. Department of Health and Human Services. *Vital and Health Statistics,* series 21, no. 56. Hyattsville, Md.: National Center for Health Statistics.

Ventura, Stephanie J., Joyce A. Martin, Sally C. Curtin, and T. J. Mathews.

1999. "Births: Final Data for 1997." *National Vital Statistics Reports* 47(18, April). Hyattsville, Md.: National Center for Health Statistics.

Ventura, Stephanie J., Joyce A. Martin, Sally C. Curtin, T. J. Mathews, and Melissa M. Park. 2000. "Births: Final Data for 1998." *National Vital Statistics Reports* 48(3). Hyattsville, Md.: National Center for Health Statistics.

Ventura, Stephanie J., T. J. Mathews, and Sally C. Curtin. 1999. "Declines in Teenage Birth Rates, 1991–98: Update of State and National Trends." *National Vital Statistics Reports* 47(26). Hyattsville, Md.: National Center for Health Statistics.

CHAPTER 3

European Perspectives on Nonmarital Childbearing

Kathleen Kiernan

Across Europe more and more children are being born outside first marriage, the conventional locus for the transition to parenthood. This chapter examines this development for Western European nations using mainly data from the United Nations Economic Commission for Europe (ECE) European Fertility and Family Surveys (FFS).

I commence with an overview, based on vital registration data, of the level of nonmarital childbearing across Western European nations and changes in this level over the last two decades. The in-depth analysis is confined to nine countries that encompass nations with somewhat different cultural and demographic regimes. For these nations, I examine the partnership context of first births in terms of whether the transition to motherhood was made prior to entry into any union; within a first cohabiting union; within a first marriage; or after a first partnership had ended. In addition to examining the extent of these types of behavior across nations, I also ascertain whether within nations such behaviors varied with respect to age at first birth, educational level, religious observance, and family background. Having set the scene, I focus on women who had a nonmarital birth. I track women who had a child prior to any partnership and estimate the extent to which they subsequently entered a partnership and also how long they spent as single mothers; I also examine whether these behaviors varied according to background characteristics. For the set of women who had their non-marital birth within a cohabiting union, I estimate the extent to which they legalized their union and whether this tendency varied according to background factors. I complete the analysis with an assessment of the relative risk of dissolution according to whether the transition to motherhood was made within a cohabiting or a marital union. Finally, I briefly review some of the policy responses to these developments.

THE RISE IN NONMARITAL CHILDBEARING

In recent decades, across most European states as in the United States (Kaye, this volume), there have been noteworthy increases in the proportions of births occurring outside of legal marriage, but there continues to be marked variation in the extent of nonmarital childbearing across nations. As we see in figure 3.1, at one extreme are the Nordic countries, where well over 40 percent of births in 1997 were outside marriage, and at the other extreme are the southern European countries of Italy and Greece, where, along with Switzerland, under 10 percent of births occurred outside marriage. Between these two extremes, two broad groupings can be discerned. A set of countries with ratios between 10 and 20 percent, including the geographically close Benelux countries and the former West Germany, and a set with 25 percent or more that encompasses Ireland (which has experienced one of the most notable changes—up from 8 percent in 1985 to 27 percent in 1997), the United Kingdom, France (with remarkably similar trends), Austria, and Finland. In 1975 only six of the nineteen countries represented here had nonmarital birth ratios of more than 10 percent; in 1985 the number of countries had increased to ten, and by 1997 it numbered sixteen. In 1975 Sweden and Iceland were dramatic outliers. This is much less the case today. We recognize that these comparisons of trends over time and space using the nonmarital birth ratio are unlikely to be as robust as comparisons based on nonmarital birth rates, which take into account the population at risk. Unfortunately, data on nonmarital birth rates are not as readily available as the ratio data, which are easier to calculate and simpler to understand.

One of the important engines behind the rise in nonmarital childbearing is the rise in cohabitation that has occurred, particularly since the beginning of the 1980s, in many European countries. However, there is a good deal of diversity across European states in the incidence of cohabitation. Cohabitation is strikingly most common in the Nordic countries and France, relatively rare in southern European countries and Ireland, and somewhere in between these two extremes in the remainder of the western Euro-

Figure 3.1 Nonmarital Births per One Hundred Births, 1997

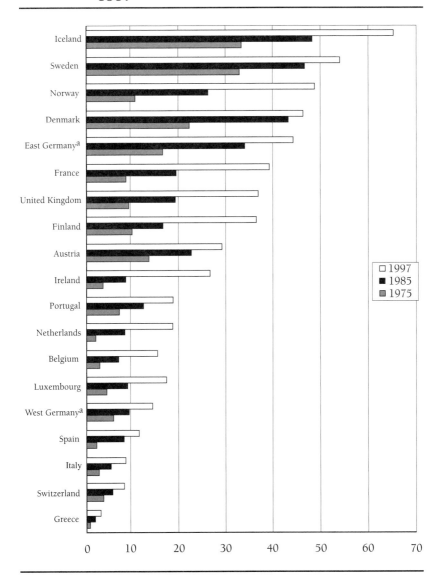

Source: Author's compilation based on data from *Recent Demographic Developments in Europe*. Council of Europe 1999: Strasbourg, France.
[a] Data are still published separately for the two regions of Germany.

pean countries. (For a detailed analysis of recent trends in cohabitation in western Europe, see Kiernan 1999.) Across Europe levels of cohabitation and childbearing outside marriage tend to be in accord: countries with high levels of cohabitation have higher rates of nonmarital childbearing, and vice versa. However, there are exceptions. Britain and Ireland have higher levels of childbearing outside marriage than one would expect from cohabitation estimates alone, and the Netherlands and West Germany have lower rates of nonmarital childbearing than might be anticipated from their levels of cohabitation.

In the remainder of the chapter, I use data from the ECE European Fertility and Family Surveys—and in the case of Britain (which did not participate in the FFS) the British Household Panel Survey (BHPS)—to investigate the transition to nonmarital childbearing in nine West European countries: two Nordic countries, Sweden and Norway; two southern European countries, Italy and Spain; three middle European countries, Switzerland, West Germany,[1] and Austria; and two northwestern European countries, France and Great Britain. This selection broadly encompasses the four levels of nonmarital childbearing highlighted in figure 3.1, and it also includes the four largest countries in terms of population in western Europe: Germany, Britain, France, and Italy.

EUROPEAN FERTILITY AND FAMILY SURVEYS

The European Fertility and Family Surveys were carried out primarily in the first half of the 1990s under the auspices of the United Nations Economic Commission for Europe. More than twenty countries have participated in this enterprise, and here I make use of data from a range of western European countries. The dates of interviews in these countries, along with the age range of the respondents and sample sizes, are shown in table 3.1. With the exception of Norway, the surveys all took place in the first half of the 1990s. All FFS data come from standard recode files supplied by the individual countries to the Population Activities Unit at the UN Economic Commission for Europe.

The timing and elapsed time for some of the surveys need to be borne in mind when making comparisons. The FFS data sets include a core of questions common to all countries and others that

Table 3.1 UN ECE Fertility and Family Surveys and the
British Household Panel Survey: Interview and
Sample Characteristics

Country	Year	Age Range	Total Sample	Number of Women
Fertility and Family Surveys				
Norway	1988 to 1989	Twenty to forty-three[a]	5,758	4,510
Sweden	1992 to 1993	Twenty-three to forty-three[b]	5,741	3,811
Austria	1996	Twenty to fifty-four	6,429	3,863
Switzerland	1994 to 1995	Twenty to forty-nine	6,076	3,460
West Germany	1992	Twenty to thirty-nine[c]	5,096	3,058
France	1994	Twenty to forty-nine	5,050	2,747
Italy	1995 to 1996	Twenty to forty-nine	6,082	4,311
Spain	1994 to 1995	Eighteen to forty-nine	6,037	3,406
British Household Panel Survey				
Great Britain	1992	Sixteen to ninety-seven[d]	9,459	2,537

Source:
[a] Data collected only on women born in 1945, 1950, 1955, 1960, 1965, and 1968 and men born in 1945 and 1960.
[b] Data collected only on women born in 1949, 1954, 1959, 1964, and 1969 and on men born in 1949, 1959, and 1964.
[c] Comparisons with West Germany must be interpeted in light of the significantly smaller age range of its sample.
[d] Analysis restricted to 2,537 women aged twenty to forty-five years.

were asked in some countries but not others. All these countries included men and women in their samples, and with the exception of Norway and Sweden, information was collected on men and women in the same age range. Data collectors in these two countries took a different strategy. Instead of collecting information on all ages within a given range, they focused on a series of birth cohorts: each country interviewed only women and men born in certain years. Details on the questionnaire can be found in the *Ques-*

tionnaire and Codebook: Fertility and Family Surveys (UN 1992), and technical matters relating to the individual countries can be found in the available *Standard Country Reports* (UN ECE 1996).

The Fertility and Family Surveys included a full partnership and birth history. The partnership history incorporated dates of marriages and any other co-residential heterosexual intimate relationships. The question pertaining to nonmarital partnerships was: "Have you ever lived in the same household with someone with whom you had an intimate relationship but did not marry?" The British Household Panel Survey collected a retrospective partnership and fertility history in wave 2, carried out in 1992 (Buck et al. 1994). John Ermisch (this volume) uses the same data set for a detailed examination of childbearing outside marriage in Britain. The BHPS includes men and women age sixteen and over, and for our comparative analyses, the sample was restricted to women age twenty to forty-five in 1992—a total of 2,537. The BHPS definition of a partnership differed from that of the FFS in that a time constraint was placed on the partnership. The question was: "Have you ever lived as a couple for three months or more?" An examination of the FFS data showed that only a negligible proportion of partnerships were reported as lasting less than three months (around five in one thousand cases).

The variation in the age range of the samples in the different countries presented some difficulties. Germany had the most age-restricted sample, which included only persons age twenty to thirty-nine. Limiting my analysis to this age range would have precluded the two oldest cohorts in the Swedish and Norwegian samples, and all the other countries included women age twenty to forty-five. To maximize the amount of information included in the analysis for the widest range of countries, I included women in the twenty-to-forty-five age range while recognizing that doing so has implications for interpretation of the German data.

PARTNERSHIP CONTEXT OF FIRST BIRTH

The analysis starts with an examination of the partnership context of first births. Table 3.2 shows the proportions of women in the various countries who made the transition to motherhood before they had participated in any co-residential partnership; within their first partnership, which was a cohabitation; within their first marriage; or after the dissolution of their first partnership (either a co-habitation or a marriage). To provide a perspective on the variation in the popularity of motherhood, the final column gives the proportion of the total number of women in the different countries who had had a first birth.

To help us ascertain whether within a given country there has been any temporal change in behavior, table 3.3 shows the proportion of women age twenty-five to twenty-nine who had a child in different contexts and the analogous proportion found among women currently age thirty-five to thirty-nine, but only including the births they had ten years or more prior to the survey date. The more direct comparison that can thus be made between two different cohorts at a similar stage in the life course is more rigorous than a cross-sectional comparison between those currently age twenty-five to twenty-nine and age thirty-five to thirty-nine. In the absence of life-history data, the latter is often the only comparison that can be made.

In Spain and Italy, and to a lesser extent Switzerland, it is clear that first marriage is the preeminent context for first births, and that there has been little change in the extent of marital births in the latter two countries. In the remainder of the countries, the picture is less clear-cut.

It is clearly the case for almost all these European countries that it is normative to become a mother in one's first partnership. With the exception of Sweden, 10 percent or less in the most recent cohort of women (those age twenty-five to twenty-nine years) who were mothers had their first child after their first partnership had ended, but as we see in table 3.3, there is evidence of an upward trend in this type of behavior in many of the countries.

Having a child prior to a partnership is a minor practice in many countries, including countries with high levels of nonmarital childbearing and countries with low levels (table 3.2). For example, the overall proportion of women who had a child prior to any union was only 7 percent in Sweden and 6 percent in France. The extent of out-of-partnership births is somewhat higher in Norway, and notably higher in Austria, although the latter is a special case in that it has a long history of marriage following a first birth (Prinz 1995). One also sees from table 3.3 that in most countries the proportion of births prior to a first partnership has hardly changed over recent cohorts, and that in most countries that proportion has, if anything,

Table 3.2 Partnership Context at First Birth, by Age at First Birth

Country	Before Any Partnership	In First Cohabiting Union	In First Marriage	After First Partnership Ended	Total Percentage with First Birth
Norway[a]					
Twenty-five to twenty-nine	12%	28%	53%	8%	68%
Thirty-five to thirty-nine	13	7	75	4	91
Twenty to forty-five	12	18	65	5	62
Sweden[b]					
Twenty-five to twenty-nine	6	53	23	19	66
Thirty-five to thirty-nine	6	53	30	12	92
Twenty to forty-five	7	51	29	13	74
Austria					
Twenty-five to twenty-nine	21	29	47	3	70
Thirty-five to thirty-nine	20	20	53	7	91
Twenty to forty-five	20	22	53	5	73
Switzerland					
Twenty-five to twenty-nine	4	8	78	10	45
Thirty-five to thirty-nine	5	8	76	11	83
Twenty to forty-five	5	7	77	11	66

West Germany[c]

Twenty-five to twenty-nine	11	17	64	8	38
Thirty-five to thirty-nine	11	8	73	8	75
Twenty to thirty-nine	10	13	70	7	45
France					
Twenty-five to twenty-nine	9	22	62	7	56
Thirty-five to thirty-nine	5	11	80	4	91
Twenty to forty-five	6	14	74	6	71
Great Britain					
Twenty-five to twenty-nine	15	17	59	8	54
Thirty-five to thirty-nine	4	4	82	9	80
Twenty to forty-five	9	9	75	8	65
Italy					
Twenty-five to twenty-nine	4	5	90	1	36
Thirty-five to thirty-nine	5	3	90	1	83
Twenty to forty-five	5	3	90	1	61
Spain					
Twenty-five to twenty-nine	8	6	85	—	47
Thirty-five to thirty-nine	4	3	92	1	92
Twenty to forty-five	5	3	90	1	65

Source: Author's calculations based on data from FFS and BHPS.
[a] Data collected from 1950 and 1960 cohorts are equivalent to data for ages thirty-five to thirty-nine and twenty-five to twenty-nine.
[b] Data collected from 1954 and 1964 cohorts are equivalent to data for ages thirty-five to thirty-nine and twenty-five to twenty-nine.
[c] Note the smaller age range of the West German sample.

Table 3.3 Comparison of Partnership Context at First
Birth Among Women Age Twenty-Five to
Twenty-Nine, with Partnership Context at First
Birth Ten Years or More Prior Among Women
Age Thirty-Five to Thirty-Nine

Country	Before Any Partnership	In First Cohabiting Union	In First Marriage	After First Partnership Ended
Norway[a]				
Twenty-five to twenty-nine	12%	28%	53%	8%
Thirty-five to thirty-nine	14	6	77	2
Sweden[b]				
Twenty-five to twenty-nine	6	53	23	19
Thirty-five to thirty-nine	6	59	29	6
Austria				
Twenty-five to twenty-nine	21	29	47	3
Thirty-five to thirty-nine	24	18	54	3
Switzerland				
Twenty-five to twenty-nine	4	8	78	10
Thirty-five to thirty-nine	8	9	79	4
West Germany				
Twenty-five to twenty-nine	11	17	64	8
Thirty-five to thirty-nine	14	8	75	3
France				
Twenty-five to twenty-nine	9	22	62	7
Thirty-five to thirty-nine	10	16	72	3
Great Britain				
Twenty-five to twenty-nine	15	17	59	8
Thirty-five to thirty-nine	6	4	86	3
Italy				
Twenty-five to twenty-nine	4	5	90	1
Thirty-five to thirty-nine	6	2	92	—
Spain				
Twenty-five to twenty-nine	8	6	85	—
Thirty-five to thirty-nine	5	2	92	—

Source: Author's calculations based on data from FFS and BHPS.
[a] Data collected from 1950 and 1960 cohorts are equivalent to data for thirty-five to thirty-nine and twenty-five to twenty-nine.
[b] Data collected from 1954 and 1964 cohorts are equivalent to data for thirty-five to thirty-nine and twenty-five to twenty-nine.

generally decreased. The major exception to this trend is Great Britain, where the proportion of births prior to a first partnership has more than doubled, from 6 to 15 percent.

In most countries the proportion of women having their first child in a first partnership, whether a cohabitation or a marriage, has changed little over the two cohorts shown in table 3.3. The exceptions are Sweden, where there has been a movement toward having a first child after a first partnership has ended—up from 6 to 19 percent of first births—and Britain, where there has been a striking increase in the proportion of women having a child before they form a partnership. In most countries the trend has been away from having a child within marriage to having a child within a cohabiting union, but the proportion of women having a child outside a partnership per se has exhibited little change.

CHARACTERISTICS ACCORDING TO TYPE OF FIRST PARTNERSHIP

I now turn to an examination of the effect of age at first birth and a range of background characteristics on births that occur in different partnership contexts. What follows is a straightforward description of variation according to background characteristics for women across the whole range of reproductive ages included in the samples, since my purpose is to examine similarities and differences across countries in these domains.

AGE AT FIRST BIRTH

Table 3.4 shows the average age at first birth among women according to the partnership context of their first birth. This table makes clear the unsurprising finding that the women who had their first child after a first partnership had ended have the highest mean age at first birth—around twenty-seven years in most countries. At the other end of the spectrum, in most countries the women who had a child prior to forming any co-residential partnership have the youngest average age at childbearing—usually within the twenty-to-twenty-one age range, which is some two years younger on average than that observed for women who had their first child within their first partnership.

The story is less clear-cut when we compare the average ages at first birth of those who were in cohabiting and marital unions. Any comparison or interpretation is, of course, complicated by the fact that in countries where the propensity to have children in cohabiting rather than marital unions has recently increased, other things being equal, women who have children within a cohabiting union are likely to be selected for relative youthfulness. From table 3.4 we

Table 3.4 Average Age at First Birth Among Women Age Twenty to Forty-Five, by Partnership Context of First Birth

Country	Before Any Partnership	In First Cohabiting Union	In First Marriage	After First Partnership Ended	All Mothers	Number in Sample
Norway[a]	20.7	22.2	23.4	26.9	23.1	2,590
Sweden[b]	20.6	22.9	24.5	26.8	23.7	2,812
Austria	21.0	22.1	23.3	26.7	22.7	2,758
Switzerland	20.1	24.9	25.4	28.9	25.5	2,198
West Germany[c]	20.4	23.9	24.1	26.9	23.9	1,247
France	20.3	23.2	23.8	27.4	23.7	2,502
Great Britain	19.1	21.4	23.7	27.6	23.5	1,629
Italy	22.4	24.0	24.2	29.1	24.1	2,457
Spain	21.3	23.2	24.0	26.9	23.9	2,243

Source: Author's calculations based on data from FFS and BHPS.
[a] Data collected from 1950 and 1960 cohorts are equivalent to data for ages thirty-five to thirty-nine and twenty-five to twenty-nine.
[b] Data collected from 1954 and 1964 cohorts are equivalent to data for ages thirty-five to thirty-nine and twenty-five to twenty-nine.
[c] The age range in West Germany is twenty to thirty-nine.

see that in most countries cohabiting women have their first child on average at a younger age than those in marital unions. The extreme example is Great Britain, where there is a difference of 2.3 years between women in the two types of union in the average age at birth. We can observe the same tendency in Sweden, Norway, and Austria, where there is more than one year's difference in the average age at first birth for these two groups of women. As table 3.2 demonstrates, in Sweden there has been little change over recent cohorts in the extent to which women are having their first child in cohabiting versus marital unions, but in Britain and Norway there have been marked increases over time in the proportions having a child in a cohabiting union. In most of the other countries, cohabiting women tend to have their first child at a younger age than married women, as in Spain and Switzerland. In Italy, West Germany, and France, however, there are only small differences between these two groups of women.

BACKGROUND CHARACTERISTICS

The Fertility and Family Surveys included only a limited amount of background information on the respondents, but I was able to examine three pertinent dimensions, namely: variation according to educational level; religious observance; and experience of parental separation. Not all countries obtained information on all these dimensions.

EDUCATIONAL LEVEL

For all countries, information on educational level was categorized relatively crudely into three levels: women at level 1 had achieved a presecondary education; level 2 women had a secondary-level education (high school equivalent); level 3 broadly encompassed the college graduate or equivalent group. In table 3.5, I have divided the women into two educational groups: nongraduates, and college graduates or the equivalent. Note from the final column of table 3.5 that the proportion of graduate-or-equivalent women is highly variable across nations, from a low of 9 percent in Italy to a high of 41 percent in Norway.

In some countries, such as Austria, West Germany, and Italy, there is a weak relationship between educational level and the con-

Table 3.5 Partnership Context at First Birth Among Women Age Twenty to Forty-Five, by Educational Level

Country	Before Any Partnership		In First Cohabiting Union		In First Marriage		After First Partnership Ended	
	Non-Graduate	Graduate	Non-Graduate	Graduate	Non-Graduate	Graduate	Non-Graduate	Graduate	Graduates
Norway[a]	15%	8%	18%	17%	62%	69%	4%	6%	41%
Sweden[b]	8	5	56	40	24	38	12	16	35
Austria	20	20	21	22	54	53	5	4	18
Switzerland	5	3	6	10	79	70	10	16	12
West Germany[c]	10	13	13	14	71	63	7	10	12
France	8	2	16	7	72	83	3	8	18
Great Britain	10	3	10	6	74	78	6	13	23
Italy	5	7	3	4	91	87	1	2	9
Spain	5	3	3	4	90	89	1	3	12

Source: Author's calculations based on data from FFS and BHPS.
[a] Data collected from 1950 and 1960 cohorts are equivalent to data for ages thirty-five to thirty-nine and twenty-five to twenty-nine.
[b] Data collected from 1954 and 1964 cohorts are equivalent to data for ages thirty-five to thirty-nine and twenty-five to twenty-nine.
[c] The age range in West Germany is twenty to thirty-nine.

text of first birth. In the remainder of the countries, there are indications that nongraduates are more likely than their graduate contemporaries to have a child before forming any partnership, and in several countries nongraduates are more likely than graduates to have their first child in their first partnership. In Sweden, as in France and Great Britain, marital childbearing is more frequent among the graduate group. There may indeed be no generalizable patterns across nations with respect to educational level, but given the crudeness of the measure as well as the variation in educational participation rates across nations and cohorts, we cannot be sure that this is the case.

RELIGION

Turning to religion, in table 3.6, I divided the women into two groups: those who responded to the question on how often they attended a religious service by reporting that they practically never did, and all the rest. This question measures current religious observance rather than childhood observance or observance prior to motherhood, so we cannot say with any certainty whether the more secular women were more likely to have a child in a certain partnership context. Nor can we determine whether, for example, having had a child outside marriage affected their level of religious observance. In all the countries, it is clear that those who became mothers within marriage were more religious than their counterparts who had their first child in other contexts.

PARENTAL DIVORCE

The final background factor I examined was whether the women had experienced parental separation or divorce during childhood. There is evidence for Great Britain and the United States that children who experience parental divorce are more likely to cohabit and to have a child outside marriage (Kiernan 1992; McLanahan and Bumpass 1988; Thornton 1991). Many of the Fertility and Family Surveys included a question on whether the parents of the respondents had ever separated or divorced and the respondent's age when it occurred. Norway did not include this question, and the British Household Panel Survey did not distinguish in its retrospective questions between dissolution due to death and dissolution

Table 3.6 Partnership Context at First Birth Among Women Age Twenty to Forty-Five, by Church Attendance

Country	Before Any Partnership		In First Cohabiting Union		In First Marriage		After First Partnership Ended		Reporting None
	Some Church Attendance	No Church Attendance	Some Church Attendance	No Church Attendance	Some Church Attendance	No Church Attendance	Some Church Attendance	No Church Attendance	
Norway[a]	11%	12%	11%	21%	74%	60%	4%	6%	63%
Sweden[b]	6	7	42	56	40	23	12	14	62
Switzerland	4	6	4	9	85	69	7	15	35
West Germany[c]	8	13	11	16	76	60	5	11	38
Great Britain	7	10	6	12	80	69	8	8	43
Italy	4	9	3	6	92	82	1	3	9
Spain	4	5	2	4	92	88	1	2	47

Source: Author's calculations based on data from FFS and BHPS.

[a] Data collected from 1950 and 1960 cohorts are equivalent to data for ages thirty-five to thirty-nine and twenty-five to twenty-nine.

[b] Data collected from 1954 and 1964 cohorts are equivalent to data for ages thirty-five to thirty-nine and twenty-five to twenty-nine.

[c] The age range in West Germany is twenty to thirty-nine.

due to divorce. The proportion of women who had experienced parental separation or divorce during childhood varied across the countries. It was very low in Italy and Spain, at 2 to 3 percent, and notably higher in France and Sweden, at 10 to 13 percent; in the remainder of the countries, it was around 10 percent.

There are some notable similarities and differences to be observed in table 3.7. In all countries, women who did not experience a parental divorce were more likely than those who did to have their first child within their first marital partnership. Conversely, in all countries except Sweden—where having a child within a cohabiting union is the majority practice—those who experienced parental divorce during childhood were more likely to have a child within a cohabiting union than those women without such an experience. Women who experienced parental divorce were also significantly more likely than those without such an experience to have their first child after their first partnership ended.

There are some differences across nations with respect to the propensity to have a child prior to any union. In the southern European countries of Spain and Italy, where having a child outside a union is rare, differences according to experience of parental divorce are small. In Austria, where such behavior is more prevalent—and indeed, its history in this realm is unique—the experience in childhood of the dissolution of their parents' marriage also made little difference in the propensity of women to become mothers prior to forming any kind of co-residential partnership. In the remainder of the countries, women who experienced parental divorce during childhood were more likely to have a child prior to any partnership, as has been found to be the case in the United States and Great Britain.

WOMEN WHO HAD A CHILD OUTSIDE A PARTNERSHIP

Having provided a broad overview of the partnership context of first births across a range of European nations, I now examine partnership trajectories following the birth of the child, as Wu, Bumpass, and Musick do in this volume for the United States. I begin by focusing on the group of women who had their first child prior to living with any partner. Earlier in this chapter, we saw that they tended on average to be younger at first birth than women who

Table 3.7 Partnership Context at First Birth Among Women Age Twenty to Forty-Five, by Experience in Childhood of Parental Divorce

Country	Before Any Partnership		In First Cohabiting Union		In First Marriage		After First Partnership Ended		Total Experienced Parental Divorce
	Parental Divorce	No Parental Divorce	Parental Divorce	No Parental Divorce	Parental Divorce	No Parental Divorce	Parental Divorce	No Parental Divorce	
Sweden[a]	10%	6%	51%	51%	21%	30%	19%	13%	13%
Austria	18	20	27	20	41	56	13	4	11
Switzerland	8	4	13	6	63	80	15	10	10
West Germany[b]	13	9	20	12	54	72	13	6	10
France	12	4	22	13	59	78	6	5	10
Italy	2	5	10	3	77	91	12	1	2
Spain	8	5	10	3	73	91	6	1	3

Source: Author's calculations based on data from FFS.

Note: This question was not asked in Norway or Great Britain.

[a] Data collected from 1954 and 1964 cohorts are equivalent to data for ages thirty-five to thirty-nine and twenty-five to twenty-nine.

[b] The age range in West Germany is twenty to thirty-nine.

became mothers within their first partnership. Now I pose a number of questions about partnership formation after the birth of the child. To what extent do these mothers cohabit, marry, or continue to live without a partner, and among those who enter a partnership, how long after the birth do any of these events occur?

I provide some simple descriptive statistics on this issue, then proceed to examine the issue using life table techniques.

TYPE OF FIRST PARTNERSHIP

Table 3.8 gives simple descriptive statistics on the proportions of women who had not entered a partnership by the time of the survey; the proportions of those who had entered a cohabiting union, subdivided into those unions that had and had not subsequently been converted into marriage; and finally, the proportions of those who had married without cohabiting after the birth of their child. Unfortunately, we have no information on whether the mother married the putative father of the child. In most countries, the majority of women who had a child on their own, more than 70 percent, subsequently cohabited or married. Sweden had the lowest proportion of never-partnered mothers, at 12 percent. Most of the other countries were clustered in the 15 to 24 percent range, with France and West Germany as outliers at 29 percent.

Among those who entered a union, the majority practice was to cohabit rather than to marry directly. The exceptions to this were the two southern European countries of Spain and Italy, where two out of three mothers who had a child on their own went on to marry. Among those whose first partnership was a cohabitation, some went on to marry that partner. Consequently, the ultimate proportions of women who married after having a baby on their own were not insubstantial in several countries. In six out of the nine countries, the proportion was 50 percent and above, and in the three remaining countries the proportion was in the 38 to 45 percent range.

I also attempted to examine whether younger women who had a child prior to a partnership were more or less likely to enter a partnership than their recent predecessors. However, it was difficult to disentangle whether changes across cohorts were real or whether the passage of more time had provided a larger window of time within which partnerships might be formed.

Table 3.8 Type of First Partnership Following First Birth Among Women Age Twenty to Forty-Five Who Had Their First Child Prior to Any Partnership

Country	No Partnership	Cohabiting, No Marriage	Cohabited, Then Married	Married Directly	Number in Sample
Norway[a]	17%	26%	20%	37%	313
Sweden[b]	12	49	28	10	192
Austria	21	36	18	25	574
Switzerland	16	21	36	27	110
West Germany[c]	29	26	19	26	128
France	29	20	35	15	211
Great Britain	24	20	20	35	143
Italy	23	4	9	64	124
Spain	15	16	4	65	107

Source: Author's calculations based on data from FFS and BHPS.

[a] Data collected from 1950 and 1960 cohorts are equivalent to data for ages thirty-five to thirty-nine and twenty-five to twenty-nine.
[b] Data collected from 1954 and 1964 cohorts are equivalent to data for ages thirty-five to thirty-nine and twenty-five to twenty-nine.
[c] The age range in West Germany is twenty to thirty-nine.

DURATION BEFORE FORMATION OF FIRST PARTNERSHIP

For the women who had had a baby prior to any partnership, I used life table techniques to estimate the duration from the time the baby was born to the time of entry into a partnership, if this had occurred, or the date of interview if there had been no partnership.

The first column in table 3.9 shows the median duration to first partnership for women in the various countries. Note that the spread is quite wide: the shortest durations are seen in Norway and Britain, with median durations of around two and a half years, and the longest duration, around six years, is seen in West Germany. Table 3.9 also shows the proportions of women who had formed a partnership by the first, second, or fifth anniversary of the birth of their child. In most countries, the proportion who had left solo motherhood by the time their child was one year old was in the 20 to 30 percent range. By the time their child was five years old,

Table 3.9 Duration Until First Partnership Among Women Age Twenty to Forty-Five Who Had Their First Child Prior to Any Partnership: Life Table Estimates

Country	Median Duration to Partnership (Months)	Entered a Partnership Within Twelve Months	Entered a Partnership Within Two Years	Entered a Partnership Within Five Years
Norway[a]	28	30%	45%	69%
Sweden[b]	40	29	37	63
Austria	53	17	31	55
Switzerland	44	28	37	60
West Germany[c]	74	14	32	42
France	52	27	43	62
Great Britain	32	29	46	65
Italy	61	30	35	51
Spain	48	27	37	59

Source: Author's calculations based on data from FFS and BHPS.
[a] Data collected from 1950 and 1960 cohorts are equivalent to data for ages thirty-five to thirty-nine and twenty-five to twenty-nine.
[b] Data collected from 1954 and 1964 cohorts are equivalent to data for ages thirty-five to thirty-nine and twenty-five to twenty-nine.
[c] The age range in West Germany is twenty to thirty-nine.

Table 3.10 Relative Risks from a Cox Proportional Hazard Model on Partnership Formation After Having a Child Outside of a Union, for Women Age Twenty to Forty-Five

Variables	Norway	Sweden	Austria	Switzerland	West Germany	France	Great Britain	Italy	Spain
Parental divorce	NA	1.21	1.14	1.1	.97	1.59	NA	.29	.38**
No religion	.86	1.41*	NA	.94	.72	NA	1.03	.99	.78
Education: level 1	NA	1.02	.83	1.03	.83	1.81**	1.36	.29***	1.50
Education: level 2	1.13	.91	1.02	1.30	.45	1.59	0.93	.38**	.92
Twenty to twenty-four at first birth	.70***	.53***	.83*	1.37	.99	.55***	.81	.66	.63*
Twenty-five to twenty-nine at first birth	.55**	.41***	.72*	1.49	.26*	.19***	.18*	.35***	.98
Thirty or older at first birth	.35**	.45*	.56*	1.14	.39	.37**	—	.35***	.29*
Number in sample	308	192	561	96	113	200	133	108	107

Source: Author's calculations based on data from FFS and BHPS.
* = .10 level
** = .05 level
*** = .01 level

typically more than one in two of the mothers had cohabited or married.

FACTORS AFFECTING ENTRY INTO PARTNERSHIP

I was also interested in whether the propensity to enter a partnership varied according to age at first birth, educational level, church attendance, and experience of family disruption in childhood. I used proportional hazard models estimated by the Cox partial likelihood method for this analysis. The analysis included age at first birth subdivided into four categories: under age twenty, twenty to twenty-four, twenty-five to twenty-nine, and thirty or older; the reference category was the teenage group. The education variable had three categories representing low, medium, and high levels of education, and the reference group was the highest level. Religion and experience of parental divorce were dichotomous variables, and the reference categories were, respectively, attendance at church and no experience of parental divorce during childhood. A series of analyses were performed: the first included only age at first birth in the model; the second included the set of covariates relating to religion, education, and parental divorce; and a third included both age at first birth and the covariates. Results are given in terms of relative risk ratios—that is, the excess risk for a particular group compared with the reference group.

Table 3.10 provides a summary of the relative risks of forming a partnership after giving birth prior to any partnership, taking into account all the factors. My analyses showed that there was little variation within and across nations in the risk of forming a partnership according to attendance at church. The possible exception was Sweden, where there were indications that those who had never attended church were more likely to enter a partnership than their counterparts who attended church. With respect to educational level and experience of parental divorce, there was also little variation within and between nations: women with high levels of education and no experience of parental divorce were as likely to enter a partnership as those with lower levels of education and experience of parental divorce. Italy was the exception in that women with lower levels of education were less likely to form a partnership than the more highly educated women. However, there was some evidence for five out of the nine countries—Sweden, Norway, Austria,

France, and Italy—that those who had their children at a young age were more likely to form a partnership than those who had their first child at an older age. In Switzerland, Spain, West Germany, and Great Britain, however, there was a weaker association between age at first birth and propensity to enter a partnership after the birth.

WOMEN WHO HAD A CHILD WITHIN A COHABITING UNION

The set of nonmarital births includes not only those born outside a union but those born within a cohabiting union. Here I examine this latter group and inquire to what extent these unions convert into marriages. Or to put it in the parlance of the past: To what extent are children born outside a marital union legitimated by the subsequent marriage of their parents?

Table 3.11 provides life table estimates of the proportion of women who had legalized their union by one, three, and five years after the birth of their baby. It is apparent from table 3.11 that there is some variation across nations in the extent to which cohabiting unions are converted into marriages. Great Britain exhibits the lowest proportion at around one-third, and the highest set includes Switzerland, Austria, Italy, and Sweden, with around 70 percent or more having married. We can also examine the pace at which the cohabiting unions were converted into marriages. By the first anniversary of the birth of the child, between 18 and 39 percent of the women had married; in most countries, it was in the 18 to 21 percent range. The pace of conversion gathered speed in the first few years after the birth and then slowed down. For example, in many countries the proportion of women who married between the first and third birthdays of their baby almost doubled, but between the third and fifth birthdays, the pace of conversion to marriage slowed down.

Again using proportional hazard models, I examined whether the risk of converting a cohabitation to a marriage varied according to age at first birth, church attendance, educational level, and experience of parental divorce. The effects of these variables varied across nations (table 3.12). In Austria, women who had experienced a parental divorce and had had their first child within a cohabiting union were less likely to legalize that union than those who had not

Table 3.11 Marriage Rates and Life Table Estimates of
Duration to Marriage Among Women Aged
Twenty to Forty-Five Who Had Their First
Child in a Cohabiting Union

Country	Proportion Married	Married Within Twelve Months	Married Within Three Years	Married Within Five Years	Number in Sample
Norway[a]	57%	31%	60%	66%	457
Sweden[b]	69	20	44	56	1,425
Austria	73	21	55	69	606
Switzerland	78	39	68	75	151
West Germany[c]	56	27	49	55	162
France	47	25	33	45	565
Great Britain	36	18	30	39	150
Italy	70	34	55	70	86
Spain	45	21	37	46	67

Source: Author's calculations based on data from FFS and BHPS.
[a] Data collected from 1950 and 1960 cohorts are equivalent to data for ages thirty-five to thirty-nine and twenty-five to twenty-nine.
[b] Data collected from 1954 and 1964 cohorts are equivalent to data for ages thirty-five to thirty-nine and twenty-five to twenty-nine.
[c] The age range in West Germany is twenty to thirty-nine.

experienced parental divorce during childhood. Swedish and Norwegian women who did not attend church were less likely to convert their union into a marriage, and in France there was some evidence that those who had their children at a younger age were more likely to convert their union into marriage compared with those who became mothers at older ages. In Norway, West Germany, Switzerland, and Great Britain, there was little statistical difference in the risk of converting a cohabiting union into a marriage according to the background variables. In the remaining countries, the story was more mixed.

Why do women choose to marry rather than continue to cohabit? What is the trigger for marriage? These are questions to which we as yet have few answers. The FFS did not collect information on why people chose to marry rather than continue to cohabit after having a child. However, some relevant information was collected in a 1993 Eurobarometer Survey carried out in the then-twelve member states of the European Union. In this survey, respondents were asked about their level of agreement to a list of

Table 3.12 Relative Risks from a Cox Proportional Hazard Model on Marriage Formation After Having a Child Within a Cohabiting Union, for Women Age Twenty to Forty-Five

Variables	Norway	Sweden	Austria	Switzerland	West Germany	France	Great Britain	Italy	Spain
Parental divorce	NA	.92	.67***	.70	.91	.89	NA	.99	.92
No religion	.58****	.81***	NA	.96	1.45*	NA	.85	.72	.66
Education: level 1	NA	.73***	.82	1.08	1.28	.85	.73	1.57****	.87
Education: level 2	1.05	.86**	.87	1.05	1.02	1.00	1.34	1.34****	1.11
Twenty to twenty-four at first birth	1.01	1.28***	.99	1.03	.85	.56***	.89	.33**	3.25**
Twenty-five to twenty-nine at first birth	.77	1.15	1.00	1.54	.67	.34****	.31	.82	.75
Thirty or older at first birth	1.19	1.47**	.44**	.78	.46	.24**	.38	.52	.67
Number in sample	454	1,422	597	131	152	558	101	70	67

Source: Author's calculations based on data from FFS and BHPS.
* = .10 level
** = .05 level
*** = .01 level
**** = .001 level

eleven reasons for getting married (Malpas and Lambert 1993). The top response (62 percent) related to committing oneself to being faithful to one's partner. The next most important reason, with 51 percent in complete agreement, was "to guarantee the rights of the children," and in third place was proving "to the other person that you really love him/her" (41 percent). Thus, we might infer that commitment and the rights of children are important elements in the decision to marry. These are responses for all groups, but the ordering of the importance of the responses did not vary significantly according to gender, marital status, or past history of cohabitation. Similarly, in a recent British study (Haskey 1999), the two main reasons for marrying given by those who had cohabited with their future spouse had to do with strengthening the relationship and with children.

In the final section, I examine the policy position of children in out-of-wedlock families.

PARTNERSHIP DISSOLUTION

The final issue I explored was the extent to which children born into cohabiting unions, compared with those born to married parents, were more or less likely to experience the separation of their parents, and did parental marriage after the birth make any difference? I used life table analysis to estimate the survival probabilities of partnerships, with the clock starting at the birth of the child, not the onset of the union. I estimated life tables for women who had a marital birth and among those who had a nonmarital birth; marriage was included as a time-varying covariate. Table 3.13 shows the proportion of unions surviving three and five years after the birth of the first child for all marital unions and cohabiting unions and for the two subsets of cohabiting unions: those that had converted into marriages by the time of the survey and those that had not.

In all the countries included in our analysis, children born within marriage were less likely to see their parents separate than those born in a cohabiting union. Within the set of cohabiting unions, those that had not been converted into marriages were the most fragile: at least one in five of these unions had dissolved by the time the child was five years old. Among children born within marriage or cohabiting unions that subsequently converted to mar-

Table 3.13 Life Table Estimates for Unions Surviving
Three and Five Years After First Birth Among
Women Age Twenty to Forty-Five, by Type of
First Partnership

Country	Partnership Percentage Surviving Thirty-Six Months	Partnership Percentage Surviving Sixty Months	Number in Risk Set
Norway[a]			
Married	97%	94%	1,677
Cohabitation	87	82	456
Cohabited-married	98	95	131
Cohabited only	79	71	325
Sweden[b]			
Married	96	93	817
Cohabitation	90	84	1,424
Cohabited-married	97	94	493
Cohabited only	84	75	931
Austria			
Married	97	94	2,161
Cohabitation	92	86	670
Cohabited-married	98	96	246
Cohabited only	86	71	424
Switzerland			
Married	97	95	2,191
Cohabitation	82	73	166
Cohabited-married	95	86	65
Cohabited only	64	53	101
West Germany[c]			
Married	95	91	873
Cohabitation	92	85	161
Cohabited-married	97	91	45
Cohabited only	89	80	116
France			
Married	97	95	1,522
Cohabitation	85	78	258
Cohabited-married	94	90	96
Cohabited only	82	70	168
Great Britain			
Married	96	92	1,242
Cohabitation	71	57	149
Cohabited-married	90	75	43
Cohabited only	61	48	106

Table 3.13 *Continued*

Country	Partnership Percentage Surviving Thirty-Six Months	Partnership Percentage Surviving Sixty Months	Number in Risk Set
Italy			
Married	99	98	2,677
Cohabitation	95	91	90
Cohabited-married	—	—	31
Cohabited only	93	82	59
Spain			
Married	99	98	1,540
Cohabitation	79	67	74
Cohabited-married	—	—	16
Cohabited only	71	51	58

Source: Author's calculations based on data from FFS and BHPS.
[a] Data collected from 1950 and 1960 cohorts are equivalent to data for ages thirty-five to thirty-nine and twenty-five to twenty-nine.
[b] Data collected from 1954 and 1964 cohorts are equivalent to data for ages thirty-five to thirty-nine and twenty-five to twenty-nine.
[c] The age range in West Germany is twenty to thirty-nine.

riages, there was little difference in their chances of witnessing the breakup of their parents' marriage by their fifth birthday in Sweden, Norway, Austria, and West Germany; less than one in ten of these children had experienced parental separation. However, in Switzerland, and more noticeably in Great Britain, children born into marital unions were more likely to see their parents remain together until their fifth birthday than those children born into a cohabiting union that converted into a marriage. In Italy and Spain, the number of dissolutions occurring to converted unions were too small for reliable estimates to be made.

POLICY BACKGROUND

In this final section, I take a brief look at the policy background to these developments. In European nations, the legal relationship between parents and their children has rarely been determined by parenthood alone but has depended on whether the child's parents were legally married to each other. The legal position of children born outside marriage has historically tended to reflect social attitudes to nonmarital childbearing; those attitudes have varied over time and space and from one social or cultural group to another. Over the course of the twentieth century, there have been shifts toward improving the legal position of children born outside marriage, but the speed and extent of such changes have been quite variable across nations. For example, as early as 1917 the Swedish government banned the use of the term "illegitimate" in all official documents, whereas it was not until some seventy years later, in 1987, that such legislation was enacted in England and Wales. Progress has tended to be slower in terms of, for example, children's rights to inherit from their father. In Sweden it was not until 1969 that children born within and outside marriage had the same rights, whereas Norway was a forerunner in tackling this issue, granting rights of inheritance to all children in 1916 (Eekelaar and Katz 1980).

In all the nations included in this analysis, married couples have automatic parental rights and responsibilities as soon as the child is born, and unmarried mothers, whether they are cohabiting or not, automatically have the same rights and responsibilities as married mothers. The position of cohabiting fathers, however, is less clear-cut. In all the countries, when paternity has been established, unmarried fathers have a financial duty to maintain their children, and in most countries, they can establish parental responsibility by making some form of formal declaration (European Observatory on National Family Policies 1996), but they have no automatic rights over their children. However, there is some variation with respect to guardianship and custody (Millar and Warman 1996). Guardianship (analogous terms include "care" and "parental responsibility") refers to the right to make decisions regarding the rearing of the child, while custody (residence or control) refers to the right to make everyday decisions concerning the child and the provision of day-to-day care. In Sweden, France, Norway, and Great Britain, after the parental relationship has been formalized, both parents can share parental obligations and rights equally, as married couples do. In Austria and Spain, both parents can share parental rights and responsibilities, but only with the agreement and ratification of the courts, and in Germany and Italy, at the discretion of the courts, the father can gain some rights to guardianship but not necessarily to custody. Given that cohabitation does not automatically confer the rights of married fatherhood, it is as though a couple never lived together at all if they separate. Generally speaking, across European nations the issues associated with children born outside marriage and their position vis-à-vis their parents have been discussed and codified in recent years, and the public policy debate has moved from a focus on the obligations and responsibilities arising from marriage to the obligations and responsibilities of parenthood (Millar and Warman 1996).

CONCLUSION

Across the European countries studied here, there are marked commonalities and differences in the extent, context, and outcomes of nonmarital childbearing. The norm is undoubtedly to become a mother within a first partnership, but in many countries the trend has been for more and more women to make the transition to motherhood within a de facto rather than a de jure union. The increases in nonmarital childbearing in the majority of European countries are attributable to women having babies within a cohabiting union rather than on their own, and with the notable exception of Great Britain, there is little evidence of a movement to solo motherhood. Even single mothers do not eschew entering unions: a substantial majority subsequently form partnerships, either marital or cohabiting. Nevertheless, across most European nations children are less likely to see their parents split up if they are born to married parents than to cohabiting parents.

There remain marked differences in Europe in the level of nonmarital childbearing and the saliency of marriage as the context for having children. Marriage is still a preeminent setting for having a child in the southern European countries and the middle European countries of Switzerland and West Germany, but this is much less the case in the Nordic countries. Indeed, Sweden is the only country with more first births within cohabiting unions than marital unions. In sum, we can say that there is not just one but several European perspectives on nonmarital childbearing behavior.

The Economic and Social Research Council (ESRC) of the United Kingdom provided the funding for this project. The ESRC Data Archive supplied the British Household Panel Survey. The Fertility and Family Surveys were supplied by the Population Activities Unit at the United Nations Economic Commission for Europe in Geneva. Thanks are also due to the Advisory Group of the FFS program of comparative research and Statistics Sweden for permission granted under identification number 06 to use the FFS data in this study. A version of this paper appeared previously in *Population Trends* 98 (Winter 1999). London: Office for National Statistics.

NOTE

1. East Germany was not included within the "Western Europe" set given its different history for much of the post-war period.

REFERENCES

Buck, Nick, et al. 1994. *Changing Households: The British Household Panel Survey 1990–1992*. Essex, Eng.: ESRC Research Center on Micro-Social Change.

Eekelaar, John, and Sanford Katz. 1980. *Marriage and Cohabitation in Contemporary Societies*. Toronto, Can.: Butterworth.

European Observatory on National Family Policies. 1996. *A Synthesis of National Family Policies, 1995*. Brussels: European Commission.

Haskey, John 1999. "Cohabitational and Marital Histories of Adults in Great Britain." *Population Trends* 96: 13–24.

Kiernan, Kathleen. 1992. "The Impact of Family Disruption in Childhood on Transitions Made in Young Adult Life." *Population Studies* 46(2): 213–34.

———. 1999. "Cohabitation in Western Europe." *Population Trends* 96s: 25–32.

Malpas, Nicole, and Pierre-Yves Lambert. 1993. *Europeans and the Family.* Brussels: Commission of the European Communities.

McLanahan, Sara, and Larry Bumpass. 1988. "Intergenerational Consequences of Family Disruption." *American Journal of Sociology* 94(1): 130–52.

Millar, Jane, and Andrea Warman. 1996. *Family Obligations in Europe.* London: Family Policy Studies Center.

Prinz, Christopher. 1995. *Cohabiting, Married Single.* Aldershot, Eng.: Avebury.

Thornton, Arland. 1991. "Influence of Marital History of Parents on the Marital and Cohabitational Experiences of Children." *American Journal of Sociology* 96(4): 868–94.

United Nations. 1992. *Questionnaire and Codebook: Fertility and Family Surveys in Countries of the ECE Region.* New York: United Nations.

United Nations, Economic Commission for Europe. 1996–99. *Fertility and Family Surveys in Countries of the ECE Region.* Economic Studies 10h. Geneva: ECE.

CHAPTER 4

Cohabitation and Childbearing Outside Marriage in Britain

John Ermisch

There has been a dramatic rise in the percentage of births in England and Wales that occur outside marriage, from 9 percent in 1975 to 37 percent in 1997, with the upward trend becoming steeper after 1980 (see figure 4.1; Babb and Bethune 1995). Many other Western countries have also seen large increases in this percentage from 1975 to 1995, but England and Wales rank among those with the largest increases (Kiernan, this volume, figure 3.1). In particular, Britain's rate of increase in nonmarital births exceeds that in the United States (see Kaye, this volume).

Out-of-wedlock births may occur in a live-in partnership or outside of one. This chapter shows that three-fifths of births outside marriage are currently occurring in a cohabiting union, and it argues that the advent of widespread cohabitation without legal marriage is primarily responsible for the increase in out-of-wedlock childbearing in Britain. An important reason for public interest in the partnership context of births is the implication of that context for the number of years a child will spend with one parent. The chapter uncovers substantial differences in the average number of years a child lives with one parent over his or her childhood according to whether he or she was born outside a live-in partnership, in a cohabiting union, or in a marriage. Analysis of the British Household Panel Survey (BHPS) for 1991 to 1997 indicates that births outside marriage, whether outside a live-in partnership or in a cohabiting union, occur disproportionately to women with poorer economic opportunities and from poorer social backgrounds.

The first section examines changes over time in the outcomes of conceptions outside marriage; the second investigates the role of cohabiting unions in these changes; and the third considers the implications of the statistical analyses for identifying the causes of the changes in childbearing outside marriage. The fourth section

Figure 4.1 Births Outside of Marriage in Great Britain,
1964 to 1996

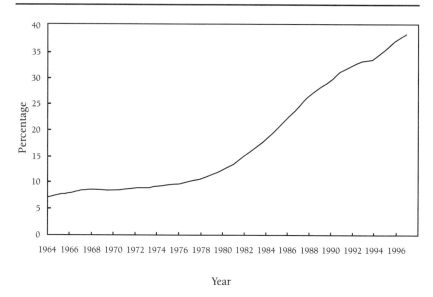

Source: Author's compilation.

estimates the average number of years that children born into different partnership contexts spend with one parent. The next two
sections examine the socioeconomic characteristics of women who
become mothers outside marriage, distinguishing between those
who give birth outside a live-in partnership and those who become
mothers in a cohabiting union. The seventh section draws together
the main conclusions.

THE CHANGING OUTCOMES OF
CONCEPTIONS OUTSIDE MARRIAGE

Marriage decisions may be strongly linked to *current* childbearing
decisions. Marriage may intervene between conception and birth,
either because it was planned that way or in response to the pregnancy. Figures 4.2 and 4.3 show, for two important age groups, the
percentages of conceptions in each year that (1) were aborted, (2)
led to births within marriage, (3) led to births outside marriage in
which both parents were present at the registration of the birth

Figure 4.2 Outcomes of Conceptions Outside of Marriage,
Women Under Twenty

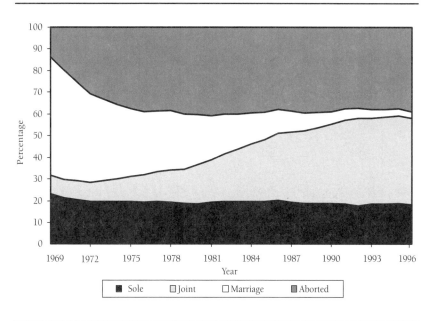

Source: Author's compilation.

(providing their names and addresses on the registration form), or (4) led to births outside marriage in which the birth was registered by the mother alone.[1] The data cover the period since 1969, which was the first full year of operation of the 1967 Abortion Act. In each five-year age group up to age thirty-four, a growing proportion of conceptions were terminated by abortion until the mid-1970s, after which time a relatively constant or declining proportion of conceptions were aborted.[2]

Two interesting features of the patterns illustrated in figures 4.2 and 4.3 are also evident for women age twenty-five to thirty-four. One is the decline in the proportion of conceptions that produced a birth within marriage, and the other is the rise in the proportion leading to births registered jointly by both parents, particularly for women under twenty-five. The decline in premarital conceptions leading to marital births (many of which may have been "shotgun marriages" in response to a pregnancy) was particularly sharp for women under twenty, from 55 percent of conceptions in 1969 to

Figure 4.3 Outcomes of Conceptions Outside of Marriage, Women Age Twenty to Twenty-Four

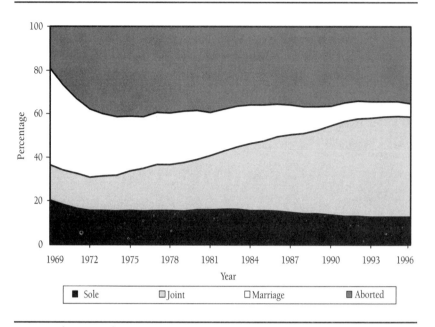

Source: Author's compilation.

3 percent in 1996. The corresponding percentages for women age twenty to twenty-four were 45 percent (1969) and 6 percent (1996). There was a complementary rise between 1969 and 1996 in the percentage of conceptions leading to births outside marriage jointly registered by both parents: from 9 percent to 40 percent for women under twenty, and from 16 percent to 46 percent for women age twenty to twenty-four.

Removal of abortions from the base in these figures indicates the context of births conceived outside marriage. Although the majority of such births among women under twenty-five in marriages in 1969 (63 percent of those to women under twenty and 55 percent of those to women age twenty to twenty-four), it was very rare to have a birth conceived before marriage but born within a marriage by 1996. (For these two age groups, only 5 percent and 9 percent, respectively, had such births within marriage.)

For each of the five-year age groups from fifteen to thirty-four, a large majority of births conceived outside marriage are now also born outside marriage *and jointly registered by both parents*. The percentages for the four age groups in 1996 are, from youngest to oldest, 66 percent, 71 percent, 73 percent, and 73 percent. The proportion of births conceived outside marriage and registered by the mother alone has either declined (for ages twenty to thirty-four) or remained about the same (for women under twenty). What meaning can be attached to the fact that these out-of-wedlock births are jointly registered by both parents?

COHABITATION AND CHILDBEARING OUTSIDE MARRIAGE

For a subset of jointly registered births, the meaning is clearer. About three-fourths of all jointly registered births outside marriage in 1997 were to parents living at the same address. These can be plausibly interpreted as births to a couple in a cohabiting union. Thus, it appears that about three-fifths of all recent out-of-wedlock births occur in cohabiting unions.[3] Elsewhere (Ermisch 1997) I have estimated that a similar proportion of extramarital *first* births are born in cohabiting unions, on the basis of life table estimates using partnership and childbearing histories from the British Household Panel Survey (see appendix). Although this is a higher proportion than in the United States (see Wu, Bumpass, and Musick, this volume), it is not high in comparison with a number of European countries (see Kiernan, this volume, table 3.2).[4] Some of the implications of births in cohabiting unions compared with marital births and out-of-partnership births are discussed later in the chapter.

The percentage of jointly registered births for which parents live at the same address varies markedly with the age of the mother. In 1996, 59 percent of jointly registered extramarital births to women under twenty were to parents at the same address, rising to 73 percent for births to women age twenty to twenty-four, and to 79 percent and 80 percent for births to women age twenty-five to twenty-nine and age thirty to thirty-four, respectively.[5] When these percentages are combined with the proportions of births conceived outside marriage that were jointly registered, we obtain the estimates of the percentages of such births within either marriage or a cohabiting union shown in table 4.1.

More than three-fifths of births conceived outside marriage are

Table 4.1 Family Context of Births Conceived Outside
Marriage, 1996

	Births Inside a Marriage	Births Inside a Cohabiting Union[a]	Births Inside Either Type of Co-Residential Union
Fifteen to nineteen	4.9%	38.6%	43.5%
Twenty to twenty-four	9.4	51.8	61.2
Twenty-five to twenty-nine	11.4	57.6	69.0
Thirty to thirty-four	12.1	58.3	70.4
Fifteen to forty-four	9.7	52.8	62.5

Source: Birth Statistics (various years, tables 12.5, 3.9, and 3.10).
[a] Product of the percentage of births conceived outside of marriage that are jointly registered and the proportion of jointly registered births outside of marriage for which the parents are living at the same address.

currently born into a union in which the parents live together, with this proportion rising with the age of the mother (see table 4.1). Most of these (over 80 percent) are in cohabiting unions. Estimates from the British Household Panel Survey indicate that about 30 percent of births within first cohabiting unions were conceived outside of the union.[6] Thus, for some, the cohabiting union may have been a response to the pregnancy, as marriage had been in the past. The rise with the age of the mother in the percentage of births conceived outside marriage but born inside marriage suggests that many such births were conceived in a cohabiting union, and that marriage was either a response to the pregnancy or pregnancy and marriage were planned jointly. The BHPS life history data indicate that, among women born since 1950 having first births within marriage, 28 percent of first births conceived before marriage (5 percent of all marital first births) were conceived in a cohabiting union with the husband preceding the legal marriage.[7]

The contribution of the increase in childbearing within cohabiting unions to the increase in births outside marriage is suggested by the fact that the growth in these has primarily been among women in their twenties (and to a lesser extent among women age thirty to thirty-four). In contrast to U.S. whites (see Kaye, this volume, figure 2.1), only about one-tenth of the increase in the nonmarital birth ratio is accounted for by births to teenagers. We can, however, be more specific about the contribution of the increase in childbearing within cohabiting unions to the increase in the proportion of births outside marriage.

Cohabitation without legal marriage has become the dominant mode of first partnership: about 70 percent of women's first partnerships are now cohabiting unions, compared with 30 percent among women born in the 1950s who formed partnerships in the 1970s and early 1980s (Ermisch and Francesconi 2000). An associated development is the delay of marriage in women's lives; for instance, 68 percent of women born in 1964 had married by their thirtieth birthday, compared with 88 percent of women born in 1951 (*Marriage and Divorce Statistics* 1994, table 3.12). The postponement of marriage has caused the enormous increases since 1975 in the percentage of women in their twenties and early thirties who are not married, as documented in table 4.2.

A simple decomposition of the change in the ratio of births outside marriage to births inside marriage indicates that the increase in the prevalence of childbearing outside marriage is primarily attributable to this increase in the proportion of women who are not married.[8] Table 4.3 shows the results of this decomposition for four five-year age groups for two time intervals. We see that, for each of the five-year age groups, about 80 percent or more of the increase between 1975 and 1996 in the proportion of births born outside marriage is accounted for by the increase in the proportion of women of these ages who are not married. In other words, less than one-fifth of the increase can be attributed to the increase in the fertility rate of unmarried women relative to the fertility rate of married women. This strongly suggests that it has been the steep

Table 4.2 Unmarried Women, 1964 to 1996

Age Group	1964	1975	1985	1996
Fifteen to nineteen	93.3%	92.0%	97.1%	99.2%
Twenty to twenty-four	42.2	43.2	66.0	85.3
Twenty-five to twenty-nine	15.6	17.3	32.5	55.1
Thirty to thirty-four	11.4	12.1	21.0	37.4

Source: Birth Statistics (various years, appendix table 2).

Table 4.3 Births Outside Marriage and Change in Marriage Rates

Age Group	Births Outside of Marriage (1964)	Births Outside of Marriage (1975)	Births Outside of Marriage (1996)	Increase Due to Change in Proportion Not Married (1964 to 1996)[a]	Increase Due to Change in Proportion Not Married (1975 to 1996)[a]
Fifteen to nineteen	22.7%	32.3%	87.9%	68.1%	86.9%
Twenty to twenty-four	7.4	8.8	56.6	74.3	78.2
Twenty-five to twenty-nine	4.5	4.4	29.5	86.4	79.7
Thirty to thirty-four	4.7	5.3	21.7	89.1	91.8

Source: Author's calculations from birth registration information reported in *Birth Statistics* (various years, tables 3.1 and appendix table 2).

[a] For the i-th age group, let R_i = (births outside of marriage)$_i$ / (births within a marriage)$_i$; P_i = (unmarried population)$_i$ / (married population)$_i$; and f_i = (fertility rate of unmarried women)$_i$ / (fertility rate of married women)$_i$. Then, by definition, $R_i \equiv P_i f_i$, and $\Delta \ln(R_i) \equiv \Delta \ln(P_i) + \Delta \ln(f_i)$, where $\Delta \ln(x_i)$ is the change in the natural logarithm of variable x between two years. The $\Delta \ln(P_i)$ component indicates the contribution of the change in the proportion of the female population who are not married to the change in the logarithm of R_i.

increase in the proportion of women who cohabit in their first partnership that lies behind the increase in childbearing outside marriage.

There has also been a large increase, however, in the proportion of cohabiting unions that produce children. Life table estimates from the BHPS life history data indicate that the percentage of women who started first cohabiting unions and became mothers while cohabiting was 18 percent for women born between 1963 and 1976, an increase from 9 percent for those born between 1950 and 1962 (Ermisch 1997).[9]

More direct identification of the relative roles of increasing cohabitation, increasing childbearing within cohabiting unions, and births outside a live-in partnership in the increase in the proportion of births outside marriage is possible with the aid of estimates of partnership and fertility transition rates from the BHPS life history data. Consider two synthetic cohorts of women: one subjected to the transition rates of women born between 1950 and 1962, from their sixteenth birthday onward, and another subjected to the transition rates of women born between 1963 and 1976 (with first partnership rates at age twenty-eight and over, based on women born between 1950 and 1962; for details, see appendix). In the 1950 to 1962 cohort, 10 percent of first births (by age thirty-three) were outside marriage, one-third of these in a cohabiting union. The out-of-wedlock first-birth ratio increases to 29.2 percent for the cohort of women born after 1962, three-fifths of these in a cohabiting union.[10] If the rates of first entry into a cohabiting union and marriage had remained the same as for the 1950 to 1962 cohort, the out-of-wedlock first-birth ratio would have increased only to 15.6 percent; thus, 71 percent of the 19.2-percentage-point increase in the out-of-wedlock first-birth ratio between the two cohorts can be accounted for by the large increase in the propensity of women to cohabit in their first partnership. If we also hold the first-birth rate within cohabiting unions to its value for the 1950 to 1962 cohort, the out-of-wedlock first-birth ratio would have increased only to 12.6 percent. It follows that 86 percent of the increase in the out-of-wedlock first-birth ratio can be accounted for by the combined increase in the tendency to cohabit in first partnerships and in the first-birth rate within cohabiting unions.[11]

CAUSES OF INCREASE IN CHILDBEARING OUTSIDE MARRIAGE

Recent analysis of out-of-wedlock childbearing in the United States (Akerlof, Yellen, and Katz 1996) puts forward the hypothesis that the decline in "shotgun marriage" (that is, marriage in response to a premarital pregnancy) and the concomitant rise in childbearing outside marriage is the consequence of the legalization of abortion and the advent of female contraception. They argue that, in the absence of abortion and contraception, women asked for and obtained an implicit promise of marriage in the event of pregnancy; men gave the promise because that was the only way they could engage in sexual activity outside marriage. When abortion and contraceptives became readily available, men could easily obtain sexual satisfaction without making such promises and were therefore reluctant to commit to marriage in the event of a pregnancy. Women who, in the absence of female contraception and abortion, would not have engaged in premarital sexual activity without such a promise felt pressured to do so without any assurances from the man once these became available. Women who became pregnant in these circumstances but did not wish to have an abortion would have had their child outside marriage, while formerly the child would have been born within marriage. Does this argument have wide applicability when a large proportion of births outside marriage are in cohabiting unions?

Some doubt about the argument of these authors in the British case arises immediately from inspection of figure 4.1. Although the contraceptive pill was introduced in the early 1960s and abortion became legal in 1969, there was only a small increase in the percentage of births outside marriage between 1964 and 1979.[12] Why would it take so long for the impact of female contraception and legal abortion to be felt? When changes in the percentage of out-of-wedlock births are examined separately by age group, the trend between 1964 and the late 1970s is flat for women age twenty to twenty-four, twenty-five to twenty-nine, and thirty to thirty-four, after which it goes steeply upward. The trend in this percentage was also upward, however, from 1970 to 1980 for teenage mothers.

An important piece of evidence put forward by Akerlof and his colleagues (1996) to support their arguments is the major contribution made by the decline in what they call the "shotgun marriage" rate (the proportion of births conceived outside marriage but born inside marriage) to the increase in the proportion of births outside marriage. I have undertaken a similar decomposition for each of the five-year age groups in table 4.3. Although 88 percent of the increase in the proportion of births outside marriage to British women under twenty between 1969 and 1996 can be accounted for by the decrease in the shotgun marriage rate, its fall accounts for only 59 percent, 27 percent, and 15 percent, respectively, of the 1969 to 1996 increase in the out-of-wedlock birth proportion among women age twenty to twenty-four, twenty-five to twenty-nine, and thirty to thirty-four.[13] This pattern reflects the smaller role played by shotgun marriage in the resolution of premarital conceptions for older mothers.

The advent of widespread cohabitation has an important role to play in the decline in the institution of shotgun marriage. Not only do more conceptions occur within cohabiting unions, but, as noted earlier, 30 percent of births within first cohabiting unions were conceived outside the union; thus, some of these may be "shotgun cohabiting unions." Although legal abortion and female contraception were undoubtedly necessary conditions for cohabitation to flourish, the large role of childbearing within cohabiting unions in Britain makes the story much more complex than allowed for by the argument of Akerlof and his colleagues (1996). Their argument about the impact of the decline in the "promise to marry if pregnant" may have a larger role to play in explaining the increase in the proportion of out-of-wedlock childbearing among teenagers, although even among them nearly two-fifths of conceptions outside marriage are now born into cohabiting unions.

The analysis of the previous section indicates that any explanation of the rise in childbearing outside marriage in Britain must explain in particular why cohabitation has increased so dramatically and, to a lesser extent, why more women in cohabiting unions have children.[14] The rise in the popularity of cohabitation as the form of one's first partnership appears to have little to do with the arguments put forward by Akerlof and his colleagues (1996) concerning the decline in the "promise to marry if pregnant"—other than the fact that widespread cohabitation was probably not conceivable without effective contraception and the availability of abortion.

PARTNERSHIP CONTEXT OF BIRTH AND
LIFE WITH ONE PARENT

We have seen that a majority of births conceived outside marriage in Britain occur within either a cohabiting union or a marriage. Nevertheless, there remain a majority of births conceived outside marriage by women under twenty and a large minority by women in their twenties that occur in neither a cohabiting union nor a marriage (see table 4.1). About 100,000 children per year are now born outside a live-in partnership.

An important reason for society's interest in the partnership context of births is its implications for the number of years a child will spend with two parents (or a parent and a stepparent). In popular discussion, it is often implicitly assumed that children born outside a live-in partnership continue to live with one parent for a long time. But many of their mothers begin a live-in partnership relatively quickly. Estimates from the BHPS life history data (for women born since 1950) indicate that 36 percent of women having a birth before their first live-in partnership began a marriage or cohabiting union within one year of the child's birth, and the median gap between the birth and entry into a partnership was twenty-two months. To assess the expected number of years that these children will spend with one parent, however, it is necessary to consider also the length of subsequent partnerships. For instance, 65 percent of these mothers cohabited in their first partnership after having the child, and about 50 percent of these cohabiting unions dissolved, giving rise to another spell of lone parenthood.

Similarly, we must take into account that the mothers of children born into cohabiting unions and marriages may see their union dissolve in the future. Although cohabiting unions into which children are born tend to last longer than childless ones, only about one in ten last ten years or longer after the birth of the first child.[15] About one-half dissolve, and 40 percent are turned into marriage.[16] Thus, more childbearing within cohabiting unions is not indicative of a major substitution of cohabiting unions for marriage as a long-term arrangement for the raising of children. Using union dissolution rates estimated from the BHPS, 70 percent of children born within a marriage will live their entire childhood (to their sixteenth birthday) with both natural parents, but only 36 percent of children born into a cohabiting union will live with both parents throughout their childhood.

A simple simulation of the potential sequences of partnership formation and dissolution, based on transition rates estimated from the BHPS, indicates that (first) children born outside a live-in partnership will spend, on average, 6.6 years with one parent, while children born into a cohabiting union average 4.3 years with one parent, compared with 1.7 years for children born within marriages.[17] These simulations make a point similar to that made by Wu, Bumpass, and Musick (this volume), namely, that the mother's and child's experience subsequent to a first birth is strongly associated with the union status at the first birth.

The socioeconomic composition of women who have their first child outside marriage is also of interest. The next two sections examine the characteristics of women who become mothers outside marriage, either outside a live-in partnership altogether or in a cohabiting union.

WHO BECOMES A MOTHER OUTSIDE A LIVE-IN PARTNERSHIP?

The probability of a first birth outside a live-in partnership can be viewed as the product of three probabilities: the probability of a childless woman becoming pregnant while not in a live-in partnership; the probability of having the baby conditional on being pregnant (that is, not having an abortion); and the probability of having the baby outside a partnership conditional on having the child. The first probability depends on whether a woman is sexually active and whether she uses contraceptives. Sexual activity tends to increase with age, but so might the efficiency of contraceptive practice. These factors are also likely to depend on family background (for example, see Lundberg and Plotnick 1995). Socioeconomic factors other than these are likely to have their most important influence on the latter two probabilities—that is, a woman's decision on how to resolve a pregnancy outside a live-in partnership, and whether to move in with the father if she has the baby. An important element in these decisions is her assessment of the other opportunities open to her. For instance, women with better labor market or education opportunities face higher costs of having a baby and are thus more likely to terminate the pregnancy (see, for example, Olsen and Farkas 1990).

Earlier analysis of the entry into motherhood of British women outside a partnership found that women from poorer social backgrounds were more likely to become mothers outside a live-in partnership (Ermisch 1997), but because it used the life history data from the BHPS, the covariates that could be examined were very limited. The present analysis uses the first seven waves of the BHPS panel data (1991 to 1997), which provide 2,575 woman-year observations on 845 never-married, childless women age sixteen to twenty-five not in a live-in partnership who were at risk of a first birth in the forthcoming year. Their annual out-of-partnership first-birth rate is 1.9 percent. This is a lower bound, however, because another 0.6 percent both had a child and entered a live-in partnership between annual waves of the BHPS, and it is not possible to determine which happened first.[18] About one-half of these births were to teenagers. Three-fourths of women having an out-of-partnership birth remained without a partner one year later, and most of those who moved in with a partner were not married. Table 4.4 shows associations between the out-of-partnership birth rate among never-married, childless women and various socioeconomic variables, including family background.

BIVARIATE ASSOCIATIONS

Unemployed young women (in the previous year) were six times more likely to have a first birth outside a partnership as those in employment, while full-time students (in the previous year) had the lowest birth rate.[19] Young women who had obtained qualifications below advanced (beyond American high school) level (as of the previous year) had a higher risk of giving birth outside a partnership than those with higher qualifications. These associations are consistent with the argument that such women face lower opportunity costs from having a child, as well as with the findings of Olsen and Farkas (1990), which indicate that better employment opportunities discourage childbearing outside partnerships.

Table 4.4 distinguishes those women who lived with their parents from those who did not. In four-fifths of the cases, housing tenure refers to parents' tenure. The main tenure difference in out-of-partnership first-birth rates is between young women who lived

Table 4.4 Out-of-Partnership Births to Never-Married, Childless Women Age Sixteen to Twenty-Five: Socioeconomic Variables

Variables	Births (Percentage)	Number in Sample
Main economic activity$_{t-1}$[a]		
In job	1.68	1,191
Unemployed	10.11	188
Full-time student	0.55	1,093
Other[b]	2.47	81
Highest educational qualification$_{t-1}$[c]		
Degree or higher	0.00	146
Teaching or other, or higher	1.85	270
A-level or nursing	0.28	717
O-level or GCSE, or other	2.10	1,237
No qualification	16.67	66
Still at school	0.00	35
Housing tenure[d]		
Owner-occupier, not with parents	0.00	130
Owner-occupier, with parents	0.83	1,567
LA or HA tenant, not with parents	2.63	38
LA or HA tenant, with parents	7.71	350
Other tenant, not with parents	0.86	350
Other tenant, with parents	1.20	83
Father's occupation when woman was fourteen[e]		
Professional	0.00	128
Managerial	1.58	380
Skilled, nonmanual	0.68	147
Skilled, manual	0.98	508
Semi-skilled, manual	2.45	163
Unskilled, manual	8.33	12
Armed forces	0.00	19
Missing	1.55	1,218
Mother's occupation when woman was fourteen[f]		
Professional	0.00	15
Managerial	1.33	301
Skilled, nonmanual	1.46	412
Skilled, manual	0.00	61
Semi-skilled, manual	0.00	185
Unskilled, manual	5.26	95
Not employed	2.76	471
Missing	1.93	1,035
Lived with both parents in previous year$_{t-1}$[g]		
Yes	1.21	1,488
No	2.76	1,087

(Table continues on p. 124.)

Table 4.4 *Continued*

Variables	Births (Percentage)	Number in Sample
Lived with both parents throughout childhood$_{t-1}$[h]		
Yes	1.25	1,846
No	4.84	434
Had nonlabor, nonbenefit income in previous year$_{t-1}$[i]		
Yes	0.77	1,420
No	3.37	1,069

Source: Author's compilation.
[a] Pearson Chi-square = 81.52 (p = 0.000).
[b] Mainly long-term sick or disabled and government training scheme.
[c] Pearson Chi-square = 96.89 (p = 0.000).
[d] Pearson Chi-square = 82.64 (p = 0.000).
[e] Pearson Chi-square = 12.38 (p = 0.089).
[f] Pearson Chi-square = 13.90 (p = 0.053).
[g] Pearson Chi-square = 8.25 (p = 0.004).
[h] Pearson Chi-square = 23.97 (p = 0.000).
[i] Pearson Chi-square = 21.00 (p = 0.000).

with their parents in social housing, who had an annual birth rate of 7.7 percent, and the rest (0.9 percent). Having parents who live in social housing is associated with coming from poorer families. In line with this reasoning, table 4.4 indicates that births outside a partnership were much more likely for women who had fathers working in semi-skilled or unskilled manual occupations (when the woman was fourteen).[20] Such women were also much more likely to have lived with their parents in social housing in the previous year. Table 4.4 also shows that, other than women whose mothers were in unskilled manual jobs, those whose mothers were in employment when they were fourteen were less likely to have an out-of-partnership birth than those whose mothers did not have jobs.[21]

Another aspect of family background is whether both parents were present throughout childhood. Table 4.4 indicates that young women who lived with both parents in the previous year were less than half as likely to have a birth outside a partnership as those who did not live with both parents. In the sixth wave of the BHPS (1996), all respondents were asked whether they lived with both natural parents up to the age of sixteen. The table shows that young women who did not live with both parents throughout their childhood were nearly four times more likely to have an out-of-partnership birth than those who did.[22] Indeed, such women were also much more likely to be unemployed, to be living with their parents in social housing, and to have low educational qualifications, and they were less likely to be a student (in the previous year in each case).

Having access to nonlabor, nonbenefit income in the previous year is associated with a much lower birth rate.[23] Young women who had an out-of-partnership birth also tended to have slightly lower pay (if they worked in the previous year), to have been unemployed more weeks in the previous year, and to have lower nonlabor, nonbenefit income than those who remained childless. There is little difference in average age between the two groups.

Multivariate Analysis

It is useful to look at these covariates with the out-of-partnership birth rate in a multivariate context, because many of the variables are clearly correlated with one another. The model estimated is a discrete-time, competing-risks transition rate model, the three risks being a birth outside a live-in partnership, entry into a cohabiting union, and a marriage. Under the conventional independence assumptions, the log-likelihood function factors into a sum of terms, each of which is a function of the parameters of a single transition rate only. As a consequence, we can estimate each of the competing-risk transition rates by treating the alternative outcomes as censoring at that point (see Narendranathan and Stewart 1993, 68). Furthermore, the resulting likelihood function is identical to that of a binary logit model for each type of transition (see Allison 1982, 74–75).

The transition rate to motherhood outside a partnership (conditional on being never married, childless, and not partnered at $t - 1$), p_{jt} is assumed to take the form:

$$\ln[p_{jt}/(1 - p_{jt})] = \beta X_{jt-1} \tag{1}$$

where X_{jt-1} is a vector of explanatory variables measured at $t - 1$ (or earlier), including woman's age, and β is a vector of parameters to be estimated.

The data used to estimate the model are annual observations on never-married, childless women who were neither cohabiting nor married and who were not full-time students in the previous year.[24] Some of these observations come from spells in progress at the beginning of the panel (1991). The contribution to the likelihood function of such observations must therefore condition on surviving in the never-married, childless, and not-partnered state up to the time of the start of the panel. Jenkins (1995) shows that, because of the "canceling of terms" in the conditional survivor probability, their likelihood contribution depends only on transition rates and data for years since the beginning of the panel, provided the total elapsed-spell duration is an element of X_{jt-1} in (4.1).[25] In this application, spell duration is the age of the woman for most of the women.[26] The potential elements of X_{jt-1} are those variables considered in table 4.4.

Note, however, that if there is unmeasured woman-specific heterogeneity (for example, fecundity or sexual activity), this convenient canceling in the likelihood does not occur, and in general, the distribution of the unobservable that shifts the transition rate differs between the women whose spell was in progress in 1991 and women who started their spell between 1991 and 1997. The model in (4.1) assumes that there is no residual heterogeneity.

Family background is captured by two variables: whether the woman came from an intact family (that is, lived with both parents throughout childhood), and whether she lived with her parent(s) in social housing in the previous year.[27] The parameter estimates in the first column of table 4.5 indicate that, after controlling for these background factors and educational attainment (as of the previous year), being unemployed in the previous year tripled the odds of a birth.[28] Higher educational attainments reduced the odds of a birth outside a partnership. Although consistent with the findings of Olsen and Farkas (1990), the measured impacts of unemployment and education in table 4.5 may be biased estimates, because the unobserved traits of women that increase the chances of a birth may also affect their risk of unemployment and their educational attainments. In the case of education, women who put low weight on the future consequences of a birth outside a live-in partnership may also invest less in education. The model in the second column of table 4.5 omits the potentially endogenous education variables, producing an even larger impact of unemployment.

Elsewhere (Ermisch 1999) I have attempted to address the endogeneity of a woman's unemployment by exploiting variation in the

Table 4.5 Parameter Estimates of Discrete-Time
Transition Rate Model of Entry into
Motherhood Outside a Partnership, for
Never-Married Women, Age Sixteen to
Twenty-Five, Who Were Not Full-Time Students
in Previous Year

	(1) Coefficient	(2) Coefficient	(3) Coefficient	(4) Coefficient
Age of woman$_t$	0.040 [0.50]	−0.023 [0.32]	0.168 [1.25]	0.101 [0.83]
Did not live with both parents up to age sixteen	0.914 [2.58]	1.089 [3.22]	1.139 [2.33]	1.283 [2.85]
Lived with parent(s) in social housing$_{t-1}$	1.694 [4.74]	1.853 [5.37]	1.241 [2.51]	1.472 [3.28]
Unemployed$_{t-1}$	1.218 [3.12]	1.389 [3.87]	—	—
Qualification below A-level$_{t-1}$	0.933 [1.88]	—	0.711 [1.21]	—
No qualification$_{t-1}$	1.937 [2.90]	—	2.269 [2.22]	—
Usual monthly pay$_{t-1}$	—	—	−0.00177 [1.97]	−0.00200 [2.15]
Amount of non-labor, nonbenefit income$_{t-1}$	−0.072 [1.65]	−0.093 [1.73]	−0.042 [1.91]	−0.0517 [1.95]
Constant	−6.110 [3.20]	−4.189 [2.77]	−7.746 [2.70]	−5.750 [2.49]
Number in sample	1229	1234	1029	1033
Model chi-square	68.73	61.3	34.49	31.65
(df)	(7df)	(5 df)	(7 df)	(5 df)

Source: Author's compilation.
Note: Ratio of coefficient to robust standard error in brackets.

characteristics of local labor markets (three hundred "travel-to-work areas") over time and space to instrument the number of weeks a young woman was unemployed in the previous year. It proceeds on the arguable assumption that any movement across labor markets is exogenous. This analysis does not reject the exogeneity of the number of weeks unemployed in the previous year, but this may be because the instruments are not strong enough.[29]

Another way to address the endogeneity of unemployment is to use the fact that the BHPS contains observations on sisters. If the unobservables affecting both unemployment and the risk of an out-of-partnership birth are common family factors, then we can eliminate them with a sibling-difference estimator. In the earlier sample, 213 sister pairs (living with their mother) could be identified, and they produced 7 out-of-partnership births. Assuming a simple linear probability model for the birth rate and controlling for age, the sister-difference estimate of the impact of being unemployed in the previous year on the out-of-partnership birth rate is 0.041, with a standard error of 0.037. Although not precisely estimated with this small sample, this is a large effect when viewed relative to the average out-of-partnership birth rate of 0.019. The estimate in the second column of table 4.5 implies a marginal impact of unemployment on the birth rate of 0.026. Thus, the difference estimator suggests that treating unemployment status as exogenous biases its impact downward.

The last two columns of table 4.5 confine the sample to those in a job in the previous year, for whom we can measure typical monthly pay. In each specification, higher monthly pay reduced the odds of an out-of-partnership birth, as expected by the opportunity cost hypothesis. Although the exogeneity of monthly pay may be questionable for similar reasons to those advanced for education and unemployment status, a Hausman-Wu test does not reject exogeneity of monthly pay (see Ermisch 1999).[30]

The associations of education, unemployment, and pay with out-of-partnership births in table 4.5 suggest that young women with limited economic and education opportunities were more likely to become mothers outside a partnership, a result consistent with the conclusion by Duncan and Hoffman (1990, 532), from their analysis of Afro-American teenagers, that "women with the least to lose are most likely to have children [outside marriage] during their teen years." It is also consistent with the findings of Olsen and Farkas (1990).

In all specifications, higher nonlabor, nonbenefit income (in the previous year) reduced the odds of a birth. The vast majority of women who had a birth outside a live-in partnership received substantial means-tested welfare benefits after becoming a mother (averaging £313 [$460] per month in our sample). The British benefit system taxes away other income at a 100 percent rate. Thus, higher nonlabor, nonbenefit income in the childless state is usually associated with a smaller difference in nonlabor income between having and not having a child outside a partnership, thereby favoring the childless state.

It appears that the variables indicating whether a young woman was from a non-intact family and whether she was living with parents in social housing capture a great deal of family background information. Looking across the columns of table 4.5, living with parents in social housing increased the odds of a birth by 3.5 (column 3) to 6.4 times (column 2),[31] and coming from a non-intact family increased the odds of a birth by 2.5 (column 1) to 3.6 times (column 4).[32] These results strongly suggest that young women from poorer backgrounds were more likely to have their first child outside a live-in partnership. Lundberg and Plotnick's (1995) findings suggest that family background affects all three probabilities mentioned at the outset of this section, with poorer background tending to raise the probability of becoming pregnant and to reduce the probability of abortion and the probability of moving in with the father (marriage, in their analysis).

FIRST BIRTHS WITHIN COHABITING UNIONS

As demonstrated earlier, a majority of births outside marriage are in cohabiting unions. In the 1991 to 1997 BHPS data, 4.7 percent of never-married, childless women who started the year in a cohabiting union gave birth in the union during the following year (and were cohabiting at the end of the year).[33] The median age of these births was about twenty-four. Table 4.6 shows how the annual birth rate in cohabiting unions varies with some characteristics of never-married, childless women and their partners. Associations with a range of variables similar to those in table 4.4 were considered, but those in table 4.6 were the only ones that approached statistical significance.

The bivariate associations indicate that a first birth within a cohabiting union is much more likely when the male partner is *not* employed, and that young women whose fathers were in semi-skilled or unskilled manual jobs (when the young women were

Table 4.6 First Births in Cohabiting Unions: Selected Socioeconomic Variables

Variables	Births (Percentage)	Number in Sample
Partner in paid employment at t − 1[a]		
Yes	3.9	623
No	11.0	82
Father's occupation when woman was fourteen[b]		
Professional	4.4	69
Managerial	1.8	168
Skilled, nonmanual	2.1	47
Skilled, manual	2.3	219
Semi-skilled, manual	10.3	58
Unskilled, manual	9.5	21
Armed forces	33.3	3
Missing	9.8	122

Source: Author's compilation.
[a] Pearson Chi-square = 8.24 (p = 0.004).
[b] Pearson Chi-square = 24.81 (p = 0.001).

fourteen) were much more likely to become mothers in a cohabiting union. Analogous to out-of-partnership first births, a discrete-time competing-risk transition rate model is estimated. An earlier analysis by Böheim and Ermisch (1998) found that union duration and age at the start of the cohabiting union does not have a significant effect on the birth rate; we assume a Markov model with age of the woman and the variables in table 4.6 as regressors.

The parameter estimates in table 4.7 indicate that young women whose fathers were in semi-skilled or unskilled manual jobs were five times more likely to become mothers in a cohabiting union as women with fathers in other occupations. The odds of having a child were about three times higher when the woman's partner was out of employment, suggesting that cohabiting couples who are not doing well economically are more likely to have a baby.[34]

CONCLUSIONS

This chapter has used birth registration data and the British Household Panel Survey to study the dramatic increase in childbearing outside marriage in Great Britain over the past twenty years. It finds that the increase in the proportion of births outside marriage can be

Table 4.7 Parameter Estimates of Discrete-Time
Transition Rate Model for First Births in
Cohabiting Unions, Never-Married Women

Variable	(1) Coefficient	(2) Coefficient
Age of woman$_t$	−0.032 [0.67]	−0.067 [1.30]
Partner in job$_{t-1}$	−1.068 [2.36]	−1.086 [2.62]
Father in professional or managerial job when woman was fourteen	0.082 [0.14]	—
Father in semi- or unskilled manual job when woman was fourteen	1.652 [2.94]	—
Father's occupation at age fourteen missing	1.376 [2.55]	—
Constant	−1.984 [1.39]	−0.371 [0.27]
Chi-square	25.15 (5 df) N = 705	8.54 (2 df) N = 705

Source: Author's compilation.
Note: Ratio of coefficient to robust standard error in brackets.

primarily accounted for by the increase in the tendency for women to cohabit in first partnerships, and secondarily by the increase in the birth rate within cohabiting unions. This increase in childbearing within cohabiting unions accounts for most of the increase in the out-of-wedlock birth ratio. There are substantial differences in the average number of years that a child lives with one parent over his or her childhood according to whether he or she is born outside a live-in partnership, in a cohabiting union, or in a marriage. Births outside marriage, whether outside a live-in partnership or in a cohabiting union, occur disproportionately to women with poorer economic opportunities and from poorer social backgrounds. In particular, being unemployed dramatically increases a woman's risk of having a birth outside a live-in partnership during the following year, and cohabiting couples in which the man is not employed are much more likely to become parents in the coming year. Further research needs to address the potential endogeneity of these employment variables in order to distinguish causal impacts from heterogeneity.

APPENDIX: THE BRITISH HOUSEHOLD PANEL SURVEY

In the autumn of 1991, the BHPS interviewed a representative sample of 5,500 households, containing about 10,000 persons. The same individuals are reinterviewed each successive year, and if they split off from their original households to form new households, all adult members of these households are also interviewed. Similarly, children in original households are interviewed when they reach sixteen. Thus, the sample remains broadly representative of the population of Britain as it changes through the 1990s. The core questionnaire elicits information about income, labor market behavior, housing conditions, household composition, education, and health at each yearly interview.

The second wave of the BHPS collected, during the last quarter of 1992, complete fertility histories and also histories of all spells of marriage and cohabitation from a representative sample of 9,459 adults age sixteen and over throughout Great Britain. These included both cohabiting unions that preceded legal marriage and those that were not associated with any marriage. Information on cohabitation was elicited by the following question: "As you know, some couples live together without actually getting married. Have you ever lived with someone as a *couple* for three months or more?" If the answer was yes, questioners then asked how many such partnerships the respondent had formed, and the months and years at which they started and stopped living with their partners. In conjunction with information from the panel waves, these data provide the best available British data for studying the dynamics of cohabiting unions and childbearing within such unions. Lelièvre (1993) explains the drawbacks of the next best available data source, the General Household Survey, for such analyses.

In the simulations comparing the 1950 to 1962 and the 1963 to 1976 synthetic cohorts, the two cohorts differ by the following set of transition rates: first-entry rates into marriage; cohabitation and a pre-partnership birth; birth, marriage, and dissolution rates among childless women within cohabiting unions; first-birth rates within marriage; and marriage and cohabitation rates after a pre-partnership birth. Both cohorts are assumed to have the same marriage and union dissolution rates after the birth of a child within a cohabiting union, but this does not affect the computations, that are of primary interest here. The first-entry rates into partnerships and a pre-partnership birth vary with age (as illustrated in Ermisch 1997, figure 6.1), but all subsequent transition rates are assumed to be constant with duration in each state (that is, a competing-risk Markov process is assumed for each of these processes).

I am grateful to the Economic and Social Research Council for financial support for this research, and to Marco Francesconi and anonymous reviewers for comments on earlier drafts.

NOTES

1. In the official statistics, *conceptions* are defined as pregnancies resulting in live births, stillbirths, or *legal* terminations under the 1967 Abortion Act; miscarriages and spontaneous and illegal abortions are excluded. Since abortions are available from the National Health Service at no financial cost to the woman, it appears likely that the statistics include virtually all induced abortions.

2. The four five-year age groups considered (that is, women under thirty-five) account for most of conceptions outside marriage, although their share has declined slightly: from 96 percent of conceptions outside marriage in 1969 to 92 percent in 1996. The data come from *Birth Statistics* (various years, table 12.5).

3. This may be a lower bound on the proportion of births outside marriage born to cohabiting couples because, as Lelièvre (1993, 112) notes, "a proportion of births registered jointly but with different addresses for the father and mother or registered by the mother only may also have occurred in *de facto* couples who start cohabiting after the birth."

4. A number of other non-Scandinavian countries have similarly large proportions. For instance, in France in the early 1980s three-fourths of births outside marriage were in a co-residential union (Leridon 1990). The proportion is also increasing in the United States. Bumpass and Lu (1998) find that 53 percent of extramarital births to American white women from 1990 to 1994 were to cohabiting parents, up from 33 percent of such births from 1980 to 1984.

5. There has been little change in these percentages since 1983 (when these data became available) for births to women age twenty and

over, and a gradual upward trend for births to women under twenty (from 56 percent in 1983 to 59 percent in 1996).

6. That is, the birth occurred less than nine months after the start of the cohabiting union; the estimate is based on women born since 1950. Estimates from the BHPS panel (1991 to 1995) and life history data are very similar, indicating from 25 to 31 percent of cohabiting union births were conceived outside the union.

7. Another 13 percent of first marital births were conceived before marriage, but not in a cohabiting union.

8. For the i-th age group, let R_i = (births outside marriage)$_i$/(births inside marriage)$_i$; P_i = (unmarried population)$_i$/(married population)$_i$, and f_i = (fertility rate of unmarried women)$_i$/(fertility rate of married women)$_i$. Then, by definition, $R_i \equiv P_i f_i$, and $\Delta\ln(R_i) \equiv \Delta\ln(P_i) + \Delta\ln(f_i)$, where $\Delta\ln(x_i)$ is the change in the natural logarithm of variable x between two years. The $\Delta\ln(P_i)$ component indicates the contribution of the change in the proportion of the female population who are not married to the change in the logarithm of R_i. Note that the proportion of all births in the i-th age group occurring outside marriage is $R_i/(1 + R_i)$. There are alternative forms of decomposition, such as in Cooper (1991). When the decomposition she used is applied to changes in the proportion of births outside marriage among women age fifteen to thirty-four between 1975 and 1996, the conclusion is similar; more specifically, the out-of-wedlock birth percentage among these women increased from 9.1 percent to 37.6 percent, but if the proportion married in each five-year age group remained the same as in 1975, the increase would only have been from 9.1 percent to 12.4 percent. Thus, 87 percent of the increase can be accounted for by the decline in the proportions married in each age group.

9. This increase appears to have also happened in France, where about one-fifth of first cohabiting unions started between 1977 and 1979 produced a child outside marriage (Leridon 1990).

10. The percentage of first births outside marriage is larger than the percentage of all extramarital births because a disproportionate number of births outside marriage are first births (see Cooper 1991, table 6). On the basis of Cooper's estimates (from the General Household Survey [GHS]) of the proportions of births that are first births inside and outside marriage, I estimate that from 1970 to 1982, about 14 percent of first births were outside marriage, and that from 1983 to 1992 about 30 percent of first births were outside marriage. Thus, the simulated proportions are of the right order of magnitude.

11. Using data from the 1989 GHS, Lelièvre (1993, 117) concludes that "seventy nine per cent of the increase across the two younger birth

cohorts [born between 1945 and 1954 and between 1955 and 1964] in the proportions having a birth [by age twenty-five] while single is due to births occurring during spells of cohabitation." This conclusion is in line with the argument here.

12. The use of the pill gradually became more widespread, especially with the provision, under the National Health Service, of free family planning services by clinics since 1974 and by general practitioners since 1975.

13. That is, if the proportion of births conceived outside marriage but born within a marriage had remained the same in 1996 as it had been in 1969, the increase in the proportion of births outside marriage to women age under twenty (twenty to twenty-four) would have been only 12 percent (41 percent) as high. The decomposition formula is $bom_{96} - bom_{69} \equiv (sr_{69} - sr_{96})bcom_{96} + (1 - sr_{69})(bcom_{96} - bcom_{69})$, where bom_t is the proportion of births outside marriage in year t; $bcom_t$ is the proportion of births conceived outside marriage in year t; and sr_t is the shotgun marriage rate in year t $[sr_t = (1 - bom_t)/bcom_t]$. The first term on the right-hand side of the equation is the contribution of the change in the shotgun marriage rate to the change in the proportion of births outside marriage.

14. Wu, Bumpass, and Musick (this volume) come to a similar conclusion for the United States. Analysis by Bumpass and Lu (1998) finds that almost all of the increase in childbearing outside marriage between the period 1980 to 1984 and the period 1990 to 1994 occurred among cohabiting women. During that same period, they find, the proportion of first unions that began as cohabitation increased from 46 to 59 percent, accounting for much of the decline in first marriage at ages below twenty-five.

15. Ermisch and Francesconi (2000) show that cohabiting unions into which children are born are much *less* likely to be converted into marriage and more likely to dissolve eventually than childless unions. This finding is consistent with Lelièvre's (1993, 120) results in her figure 7.7, from the 1989 GHS.

16. These estimates are based on year-to-year transitions from 1991 to 1995 from the panel data of the BHPS; estimates in Ermisch (1997) using the life history data from the BHPS produce nearly identical percentages.

17. Multi-state life table estimates for the United States by Bumpass and Lu (1998) are broadly similar to these, with expected years in a one-parent family of 7.7, 4.2, and 2.1, respectively. The simulation here employs duration-specific rates for entering a cohabiting union and marriage after a first birth outside a live-in partnership and constant

(Markov) transition rates for all subsequent partnership formation and dissolution rates.

18.   For two-thirds of these difficult-to-classify births, the mother is in a cohabiting union in the following year. There are, of course, competing risks to becoming a mother outside a partnership: 9.4 percent of these never-married, childless women enter a live-in partnership childless during the following year, and 75 percent of these cohabit rather than marry.

19.   Observations on two women who reported being on maternity leave or engaged in family care in the previous year are omitted from the analysis.

20.   This retrospective question was asked in the first wave of the panel (1991). Most of the missing observations on this variable are for those who entered the panel after the first wave, primarily because they reached the age of sixteen after the first wave. Babb and Bethune (1995) find that women whose fathers were in a manual occupation were more than twice as likely to have a birth outside marriage as women from a nonmanual background, but table 4.4 suggests that the manual/nonmanual comparison may hide important differences; see also table 4.6 for births in a cohabiting union.

21.   As was the case for information on father's occupation, most of the missing observations on this variable are for those who entered the panel after the first wave.

22.   The 295 fewer observations when using the latter variable reflect missing values, which mainly arise because panel members who were at risk for an out-of-partnership birth in earlier years of the panel were no longer in the panel at wave 6 (1996). "Temporary sample members" are excluded throughout the analyses.

23.   Nonlabor, nonbenefit income for these women is primarily private income transfers, education grants, and investment income.

24.   Full-time students were excluded because they produced only six births out of 1,093 woman-year observations.

25.   This convenient canceling result does not carry over to analogous continuous-time transition models (see Lancaster 1990, ch. 8).

26.   This is not the case for women who reenter the unpartnered, childless, never-married state after the dissolution of a cohabiting union, but analysis in Böheim and Ermisch (1998, table 2.2) indicates that such women contribute less than 10 percent of the woman-year observations. Furthermore, substituting age for age at start of spell and the log of duration improves the statistical fit of their model.

27.   Indicators of father's and mother's occupations when the woman was fourteen have been excluded from the set of background variables. This exclusion is supported by likelihood ratio tests.

28. Likelihood ratio tests indicate that it is acceptable to include women in "other activities" (see panel A of table 4.4) with those in employment, which is the reference group.

29. The identifying instrumental variables in this test are father's occupation when the woman was fourteen, the rate of inflow to unemployment, the rate of creation of new vacancies, and the unemployment rate in the local labor market. (All rates are expressed relative to the local area's labor force.) These variables are jointly significant in the weeks unemployed equation at the 0.01 level ($F_{6,\ 1174} = 11.32$).

30. The identifying instrumental variables in this test are as in the weeks-unemployed equation plus whether the woman's mother worked when the woman was fourteen. These are jointly significant in the pay equation, and the R^2 of the pay equation is 0.39.

31. One could also argue that co-residence with parents is a choice variable for young women, and so it also may be endogenous. Its exclusion does not, however, have a large effect on the other coefficients.

32. When observations in which the woman both has a child and enters a live-in partnership between annual waves of the BHPS are counted as out-of-partnership births, the impact of coming from a non-intact family in each specification is about half that in table 4.5, while the coefficients on the other variables are similar.

33. Thus, 4.7 percent represents a lower bound on the birth rate, because some of the cohabiting unions that were dissolved or converted into marriage during the year may have produced a child before the dissolution or conversion. If those who ended the year married with a child or never-married with a child were also deemed to have had the child during the cohabiting union, then the cohabiting union first-birth rate would be 7.2 percent. For nearly four-fifths of these ambiguous births, the couple was married at the end of the year. In addition, 27.9 percent either married their partner or dissolved their union childless during the year.

34. If those who ended the year married with a child or never-married with a child were also deemed to have had the child during the cohabiting union, the impacts of the partner's employment status and the father's socioeconomic group are much smaller.

REFERENCES

Akerlof, George A., Janet L. Yellen, and Michael L. Katz. 1996. "An Analysis of Out-of-Wedlock Childbearing in the United States." *Quarterly Journal of Economics* 111: 275–317.

Allison, Paul D. 1982. "Discrete-time Methods for the Analysis of Event Histories." *Sociological Methodology*, 61–98.

Babb, Penny, and Ann Bethune. 1995. "Trends in Births Outside Marriage." *Population Trends* 81: 17–22.

Birth Statistics. Various years. London: Her Majesty's Stationery Office.

Böheim, Rene, and John F. Ermisch. 1998. "Analysis of the Dynamics of Lone Parent Families." Working paper 98–8. Essex, Eng.: University of Essex, Economic and Social Research Council Research Center on Micro-social Change (August).

Bumpass, Larry, and Hsien-Hen Lu. 1998. "Trends in Cohabitation and Implications for Children's Family Contexts." Paper presented at the 1998 annual meetings of the Population Association of America, Chicago.

Cooper, Jaqui. 1991. "Births Outside Marriage: Recent Trends and Associated Demographic and Social Changes." *Population Trends* 63: 8–18.

Duncan, Greg J., and Saul D. Hoffman. 1990. "Welfare Benefits, Economic Opportunities, and Out-of-Wedlock Births Among Black Teenage Girls." *Demography* 27: 519–35.

Ermisch, John F. 1997. "Premarital Cohabitation, Childbearing, and the Creation of One-Parent Families." In *Economics of the Family*, edited by C. Jonung and I. Persson. New York: Routledge.

———. 1999. "Economic Opportunities and Births Outside Live-in Partnerships in Britain." Paper presented at the annual conference of the European Society for Population Economics, Turin (June). Available from the Institute of Social and Economic Research, University of Essex.

Ermisch, John F., and Marco Francesconi. 2000. "Educational Choice, Families and Young People's Earnings." *Journal of Human Resources* 35(winter): 143–76.

Jenkins, Stephen P. 1995. "Easy Estimation Methods for Discrete Time Duration Models." *Oxford Bulletin of Economics and Statistics* 57: 129–38.

Lancaster, Tony. 1990. *The Econometric Analysis of Transition Data.* Cambridge: Cambridge University Press.

Lelièvre, Eva. 1993. "Extramarital Births Occurring in Cohabiting Unions." In *New Perspectives on Fertility in Britain*, edited by M. Ní Bhrolcháin. London: Her Majesty's Stationery Office.

Leridon, Henri. 1990. "Extramarital Cohabitation and Fertility." *Population Studies* 44: 469–87.

Lundberg, Shelley, and Robert D. Plotnick. 1995. "Adolescent Premarital Childbearing: Do Economic Incentives Matter?" *Journal of Labor Economics* 13: 177–200.

Marriage and Divorce Statistics. 1994. Her Majesty's Stationery Office.

Narendranathan, Wiji, and Mark B. Stewart. 1993. "Modeling the Probability of Leaving Unemployment: Competing Risks Models with Flexible Baseline Hazards." *Applied Statistician* 42: 63–83.

Olsen, Randall J., and George Farkas. 1990. "The Effect of Economic Opportunity and Family Background on Adolescent Cohabitation and Childbearing Among Lone-income Blacks." *Journal of Labor Economics* 8: 341–62.

—

PART II

Welfare, Child Support, and Public Policy

CHAPTER 5

Welfare Benefits and Female Headship in U.S. Time Series

Robert A. Moffitt

Whether welfare benefits affect the marriage and fertility decisions of the low-income population has been the subject of much research. The substantial bias in the U.S. welfare system toward female-headed families, relative to either married couples or single, childless individuals, provides a clear financial incentive for behavior that makes eligibility for welfare benefits more likely or that avoids the loss of eligibility after it has been achieved, such as early nonmarital childbearing, postponement of marriage, divorce, and postponement of remarriage.

Elsewhere (Moffitt 1998) I have summarized the research literature through 1995. The existing literature typically uses individual data on women in different states with different welfare benefit levels and correlates those benefits with women's family structure, usually in a regression context controlling for other individual and state-level factors. A number of the studies also have data on individuals in different states over time and examine the correlation between changes in benefit levels and changes in family structure, again typically in a regression framework where state fixed effects are entered. More than sixty separate estimates of this type have been obtained in the literature, according to my 1998 review (see also Foster and Hoffman, this volume). Contrary to some other summaries of the evidence, my review found that the central tendency of this cross-sectional evidence is to reveal that there are indeed effects of welfare on some aspects of family structure, namely, marriage and nonmarital fertility. The validity of the central tendency is open to debate, however, in light of considerable unexplained dispersion in the estimates across studies; furthermore, there is disagreement about the magnitude of the effect across studies.

Nevertheless, despite the differences in results that remain, there is widespread agreement in the literature that the time-series evidence does not support an effect of welfare benefits on marriage and nonmarital fertility, for real benefits have been falling for more than twenty years—at least in the Aid to Families with Dependent Children (AFDC) program and now in the Temporary Assistance to Needy Families (TANF) program—while female headship has been increasing. Moreover, bringing other programs such as food stamps and Medicaid into the picture helps explain female headship increases in the late 1960s and early 1970s, when those programs were introduced and solidified, but does less well in explaining headship growth in the late 1970s and early 1980s, when such growth was still strong. Even the cross-sectional studies that have revealed the largest magnitude of welfare effects do not contravene these time-series correlations, for virtually all of the individual studies, including those with state fixed effects, enter year dummies into their regressions, thereby removing the time-series correlation from the data.

From one perspective, one could say that there is no puzzle at all and no contradiction between the cross-sectional and time-series evidence: there may have simply been some forces at work in time-series but not present in cross-section, forces that have pushed female headship up more than the falling welfare benefits have pushed it down. Consequently, it may still be the case that female headship might have risen even faster than it did if benefits had not fallen. But this tidy explanation is tautological and lacks credibility unless the other forces can be identified and empirically shown to have caused headship to rise.

In an attempt to identify those forces, this chapter focuses on labor market opportunity—as proxied by wage rates—as the potential other force pushing female headship rates up. Wages and other measures of labor market potential have played a central role in economic models of the family since the work of Becker (1973, 1981) and hence may seem to be an overstudied source of the rise in female headship. However, both the bulk of the theoretical work and most of the traditional empirical work on the subject give too exclusive a role to the female wage rate and too minor a role to the male wage rate. This chapter shows that the male wage is an essential part of the story and must be included for the effects of welfare benefits to be estimated correctly.

The role of male wages has not been completely ignored: the

work of Wilson (1987) and Wilson and Neckerman (1986) gives the role of males a central position in explanations of the family structure decisions of disadvantaged women, although much of this work is concerned with the labor force and unemployment rates of men rather than with male wages per se (for additional discussion of the role of men, see McLanahan et al., this volume). Several cross-sectional studies of welfare benefit effects that controlled for both male and female wages (Danziger et al. 1982; Hoffman and Duncan 1988; Lichter, LeClere, and McLaughlin 1991; Lichter, McLaughlin, and Ribar 1997; Schultz 1994) have generally found significant effects of both. However, neither the work of William Julius Wilson nor the cross-sectional studies are directed at the time-series issue, and hence the inconsistency between the cross-sectional and time-series evidence that motivates this chapter is left unresolved.

The results of the analysis indicate that the addition of female wages to a time-series headship equation reverses the sign on the AFDC benefit from negative to positive and, even in specifications where benefit effects are positive to begin with, makes them more positive. Adding the male wage to the equation makes the benefit coefficient even more positive. The results thus offer a possible explanation for the inconsistency between the cross-sectional and time-series correlations. Moreover, for both white and black women it is demonstrated here that the decline in the male wage for less-educated men has had more of an effect on female headship rates than any upward trend in female wages; thus, male wages play a critical role in time-series explanations of headship changes.

The next section briefly outlines an economic model of female headship that incorporates wage and benefit effects in the simplest possible way. The subsequent sections of the paper look at the time-series empirical evidence on wage and benefit effects and consider whether incorporating wages changes the sign of benefit effects.

THE ROLE OF WAGES AND BENEFITS IN THE SIMPLE STATIC ECONOMIC MODEL

Female headship is defined as a family structure in which a woman lives with her own children and without a partner. The simplest static model defines the marriage decision as based on utility differences between marriage to a particular potential mate and to a random draw from a set of mates with the same characteristics (Becker 1973). Conditional on the marriage decision, childbearing decisions are made from standard utility maximization by balancing the utility gains against the marginal costs.[2] Because female headship is both a marriage and a fertility decision, headship is said to occur when the woman chooses not to marry but to have children.[3] Assuming that women have individual utility functions containing, as arguments, leisure, the number of children, other consumption goods, and marriage itself, the following model captures the relevant considerations in minimal form:

$$K_{M=1} = f(W_m, W_f, P_K; X_m, X_f) \qquad (5.1)$$

$$K_{M=0} = g(W_f, P_K, B; X_f) \qquad (5.2)$$

$$M^* = V_{M=1}(W_m, W_f, K_{M=1}; X_m, X_f) - V_{M=0}(W_f, K_{M=0}, B; X_f) - C$$

$$M = 1 \text{ if } M^* \geq 0; M = 0 \text{ if } M^* < 0 \qquad (5.3)$$

where $M = 1$ if the woman is married and $M = 0$ if not; W_m is the male wage rate offered in the market, and W_f is that for the female wage; P_K is the money price of children; X_m represents the characteristics of potential male partners, and X_f female characteristics; and B is the welfare benefit. Equations (5.1) and (5.2) are demand-for-children equations conditional on marriage. In the married state, both wages have negative price effects and positive income effects, but if women spend more time in child-rearing than men, the female wage is more likely to have a net negative sign.[4] In the single state, specialization is more constricted and income is lower, leading to lesser childbearing than in the married state, but the sign on the female wage is still ambiguous. Welfare benefits, available only if not married, have a positive effect on childbearing not only because of their income effects but because they are tied to low levels of work effort.[5]

Equation (5.3) portrays the utility difference between being married and being single as M^*, which is the difference between the female quasi-indirect utility functions $V_{M=1}$ and $V_{M=0}$. In turn, these are conditioned on the pre-optimized number of children, K_M, but not on labor supply or other goods, minus a cost of marriage, C (search as well as divorce costs). The decision problem is portrayed as if it were a two-stage process in which a woman initially chooses the number of children she would have if she were married and the number she would have if she were not, then chooses whether to marry or not on the basis of these values of K and the other determinants of marriage. This is done for expositional purposes only, however; the model instead considers the decisions to be completely joint.

Wages in the marriage decision again have effects in different directions. An increase in the female wage raises income in both married and unmarried states and hence has no effect on the gain from marriage if utility is raised by the same amount in both, but raises that gain if marriage is a normal good. However, an increase in the male wage increases utility only in the married state, thereby increasing the gains from marriage unambiguously.[6] The effect of wages on marriage works through the choice of K as well, and it is here that the classic gains to marriage from specialization and division of labor (that is, increasing returns) occur in this model. Gains from specialization are greater the wider the gap between the two wage rates, which gives the wage ratio W_f/W_m a central role.[7] Assuming $W_m > W_f$, an increase in W_f/W_m reduces the gains to marriage and marriage rates fall. Finally, note that welfare benefits appear only in the unmarried state and thus have an unambiguously negative effect on gains to marriage.

Ignoring P_K, there are only three key determining variables in the model—the two wages and the welfare benefit (nontransfer, nonwage income is also ignored)—in addition to the exogenous characteristics X_m and X_f. Defining $F = 1$ as a woman's choice not to marry ($M = 0$) but to have children ($K_{M=0} > 0$), and $F = 0$ if she chooses to marry or not to have children—that is, a female headship indicator variable—we can work empirically with the reduced form expression

$$E(F \mid W_f, W_m, B, X_f, X_m) = G[\alpha + \beta(W_f/W_m) + \gamma(W_m + W_f) + \delta B + \theta X_f + \eta X_m] \qquad (5.4)$$

where G is a probability distribution function mapping the latent index inside the brackets into the unit interval. The two wage rates could be entered separately or in a variety of alternative functional forms but are entered here in ratio and additive form to assist in the interpretation of the effects of specialization, in the case of the ratio, and the income effects in the case of the wage sum. Thus, we expect $\beta > 0$ and $\gamma < 0$. The price-income distinction is not completely clean, for both variables capture different types of price and income effects to some extent; consequently, the expected signs are not completely unambiguous either.

However, we expect $\delta > 0$ unambiguously, and the question in the analysis is whether the omission of the two wage variables from the equation falsely leads to an estimated $\delta < 0$, as one observes as a raw correlation in the time-series data.

It is worth emphasizing that in this model when marriage does not occur, it is because there are no gains from marriage. Either utility is lowered by being married or the costs of marriage exceed the benefits. This view is at odds with traditional equilibrium models of the marriage market in which equal numbers of men and women always marry, because there are always gains to specialization, even at very low wages. The introduction of costs to marriage, and different utilities in the married and unmarried states, however, implies that the gains to specialization at low wages may be outweighed by negative factors. This model also does not need to rely on sex-ratio explanations to explain nonmarital fertility.

Clearly a model this simple misses many important factors. Other gains to marriage—such as those from public goods, alleviation of imperfect capital markets, and risk pooling (Weiss 1997)—are ignored. The general equilibrium nature of the marriage market is also ignored, and consequently so is the importance of imbalance of the two sexes; relatedly, the alternative to marriage is not necessarily being single but rather searching for another partner. Search considerations and matching considerations in the marriage market and other dynamics are also ignored in favor of the simplicity of the static model. Whether incorporation of these factors would materially change the expected wage and benefit signs in a female headship equation is unclear.

EMPIRICAL STRATEGY AND DATA

Given the focus of the analysis on explaining time-series trends in female headship, and also on determining whether the incorporation of wage effects resolves the inconsistency in the sign of welfare benefit effects in past cross-sectional and time-series studies, I follow an empirical strategy of focusing primarily on time-series variation in F, W_f, W_m, and B. Cross-sectional variables are incorporated to some extent by stratifying the analysis by educational level and age, but, conditional on education and age, only time-series, aggregate variation in the variables are utilized. Cross-sectional variation in B (for example, across geographic areas) is intentionally ignored in favor of a more purely time-series exercise.

I employed data from the March survey of the Current Population Survey (CPS) from 1968 to 1996. From each CPS I selected all men and women age eighteen to sixty-five with less than a high school education, and I stratified the sample in each year by birth cohort (grouped into five-year birth-year intervals). I also stratified the sample into two races, white and black, and did not examine other race groups. For each race and each birth cohort group in each year, I calculated a mean male wage rate, a mean female wage rate, and a female-headship rate.[8] The last is equal to the fraction of women in the group who have children but are not married. The wage rate is the average weekly wage (annual earnings divided by annual weeks of work) in real 1992 dollars over the previous calendar year, taken over workers in that year. (Tests for selection bias were also conducted.) Aggregate national real AFDC, food stamp, and Medicaid monthly benefits were available as well, and I computed a weighted sum of the three to arrive at an overall measure of welfare generosity.[9] Thus, we have a time series of data on female headship rates, male wages, female wages, and welfare benefits for the less-educated population over the years 1968 to 1996, stratified by birth cohort. Table 5A.1 shows the means of the variables.

We can estimate a linearized version of equation (5.4) on these group means:

$$F_{ct} = \alpha + \beta(W_f/W_m)_{ct} + \gamma(W_m + W_f)_{ct} + \delta B_t + \theta Age_{ct} \quad (5.5)$$

for birth cohort c in year t, where now all variables are means over individuals in a c-t group. The age of the group is the only variable controlled in the regression in addition to wages and benefits.

Equation (5.5) is extremely parsimonious and does not attempt to account for the many other changes in the social, economic, and policy environment that have occurred over the 1968 to 1996 period. Some of the other forces omitted have already been mentioned (such as sex ratios), but there have also been changes in contraceptive technology and the legal environment governing marriage, fertility, and abortion. Policy variables that are particularly important are changes in other aspects of the welfare system (welfare reform), the Earned Income Tax Credit (EITC), child support enforcement (see Bartfeld and Meyer, this volume), and the tax penalty to marriage. The aggregate time-series approach here could make very little progress in controlling for these factors because there are only twenty-nine annual observations in the data. The aim of the analysis here is therefore not to isolate the effect of welfare benefits in time series from the effects of these and other omitted factors, but rather the more modest goal of simply determining whether the addition of the two wage variables in equation (5.5) changes the sign or magnitude of the coefficient on B and hence whether the time-series evidence is consistent with a welfare effect at the simplest level.

We apply generalized least squares (GLS) to equation (5.5) to adjust for the effect of the grouping on sampling variance by using the number of observations in each cell; we assume the existence of a random year component in the error term when making this grouping adjustment. The random year effect is important because the key regressor of interest—the welfare benefit—varies only over time, not cross-sectionally, and hence implicitly has only 29 degrees of freedom (the number of years in the data), not the larger degrees of freedom suggested by the number of grouped observations (273 and 218 for the two race groups; see note 8). Ignoring the presence of a random year effect could result in seriously understated standard errors on the benefit coefficient. The appendix discusses the GLS procedure.

Figure 5.1 shows the mean female headship rate by race, taken over women age eighteen to sixty-five in each year of the CPS. As expected, the rate has risen monotonically over time. (Not shown graphically is the change in the composition of that trend, from divorce and separation in the early period to never-married single mothers in the later period.) Figure 5.2 shows the trends in welfare benefits—for AFDC alone (bottom line), for AFDC plus food stamps (middle line), and for AFDC plus food stamps plus Medicaid (top line). Benefits rose in the early period, particularly if food stamps and Medicaid are included, because these programs were being introduced and expanded over that period. Thus, the crude correlation between benefits and headship in this period is positive. But sometime after 1976, all benefit series reversed growth or slowed down. There is a significant difference if only AFDC bene-

Figure 5.1 Female Headship Rates, White and Black
Women Eighteen to Sixty-Five, 1968 to 1996

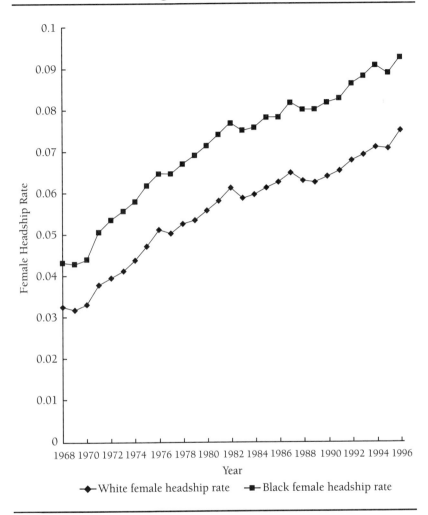

Source: Author's compilation.

fits are examined, for those fell monotonically after 1976, and benefits including both food stamps and Medicaid, which fell until 1982
but then rose again and subsequently fell again. The expansions of
Medicaid are primarily responsible for this difference. Even for this
more comprehensive measure of the benefit, however, there has

Figure 5.2 AFDC, Food Stamps, and Medicaid Benefits, 1968 to 1996

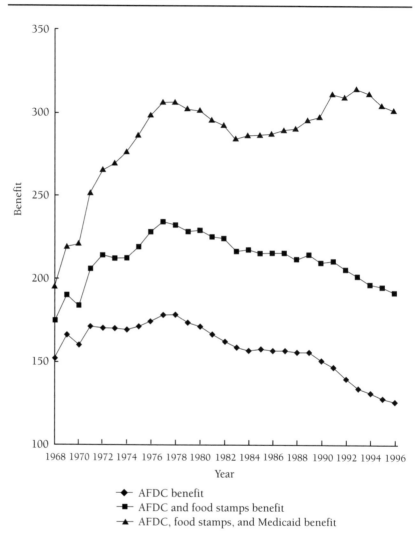

Source: U.S. Social Security Administration, 1998.

been a drastic overall slowdown in growth after 1976, and consequently the crude positive correlation between benefits and headship disappears.

Table 5.1 confirms these graphical trends with regression results. The table shows the coefficients on B_t from equation (5.5) omitting

Table 5.1 Regression Coefficients on Welfare Benefits
Without Wage Variables

	All Years	1976 and Up Only
AFDC Benefit	− 1.000*	− 0.702*
	(0.112)	(0.073)
AFDC + Food Stamp Benefit	0.342*	− 0.909*
	(0.130)	(0.096)
AFDC + Food Stamp + Medicaid Benefit	0.695*	0.235
	(0.050)	(0.156)

Source: Author's compilation.
Notes: Standard errors in parentheses; * designates significance at 10 percent level. All equations are estimated on the white population with less than twelve years of education and all include a fifth-order polynomial in age (the centered age of the birth cohort in each year). All coefficients are multiplied by 1000.

the wage variables, for different measures of the benefit and for different time periods. Both over all years and over the subperiod from 1976 forward, the AFDC benefit coefficient is negative. When food stamps are included, the coefficient is positive overall but negative in the period after 1976. When Medicaid benefits are included, the coefficients are positive in both time frames but weaker and insignificant after 1976.

ESTIMATION RESULTS

White Population   We first consider the white population, then the black population. The results for the white population are prefigured in simple graphical form in figure 5.3. The upper three lines of the figure show the life cycle profiles of female headship for three different birth cohorts (1930 to 1934, 1940 to 1944, and 1950 to 1954); we can see that headship rates have been rising over time, at least at young ages. The middle three lines in the figure show the life cycle profiles of female weekly wages for the same three cohorts and indicate, interestingly, extreme stability in that wage. Contrary to the conventional wisdom that female wages have been uniformly rising over time, real wages have not risen over this period for the less-educated population. The lack of growth reflects a general deterioration in the labor market for less-skilled workers over the last twenty years. Clearly, then, the female wage is unlikely to be by

Figure 5.3 Female Headship, Female Wage, and Female-Male Wage Ratio, by Birth Cohort, White Women, 1966 to 1998

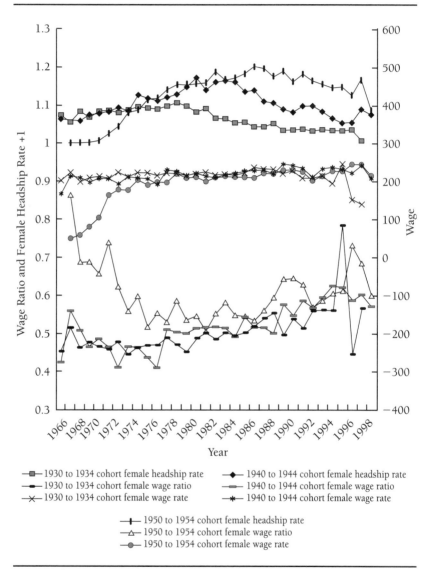

Source: Author's compilation.

itself a strong explanation for the growth in headship for this population.

The three lines in the lower portion of the figure show life cycle profiles of the female-to-male wage ratio, and here we see growth in the ratio over the three cohorts. Indirectly, these results imply, when combined with the lack of a female wage trend, a decline in the level of the real male wage for the less-educated population. This too has been well documented in the recent literature on the U.S. labor market and contrasts sharply with the wage trends for the more-educated male population; those trends have shown strong upward movement (for example, Levy and Murnane 1992; Katz and Autor 1999). For present purposes, the rise in the wage ratio implies a reduction in the gains to specialization and division of labor and hence a reduction in the gains to marriage, and this is consistent with the growth of female headship. It is important to note that changes over time in the male wage, not in the female wage, have influenced female headship according to these results.

Finally, although it is not shown in the figure, it follows from the two sets of wage plots that the sum of wages must have fallen (constant female wage, declining male wage), leading to income effects that should also lead to a decline in marriage and increase in female headship. Thus, both wage variables in equation (5.5) can be seen to have moved in a direction against marriage.

Table 5.2 shows the results of estimation of several specifications of equation (5.5).[10] Column 1 includes only the welfare benefit—the AFDC benefit alone, in this case—and no other variables except age (coefficients not shown). As expected, the AFDC benefit exhibits a significantly negative effect on female headship, inconsistent with cross-sectional evidence. However, when the female-male wage ratio is added to the equation, as in column 2, the sign on the AFDC benefit flips around to positive and is statistically significant, though only barely by conventional criteria. The coefficient on the wage ratio itself is positive and significant, as expected from the analysis in figure 5.3. Column 3 adds the wage sum to the equation and finds it to have a negative and significant sign, consistent with the simple economic model: even holding the ratio of male and female wages fixed, higher levels of wages result in more marriage. The coefficient on the welfare benefit almost doubles when the wage sum is added, a large increase in its magnitude; thus, when both "price" and "income" wage effects are controlled, welfare ben-

Table 5.2 Coefficients on Benefit and Wage Variables in
Headship Regressions: White Women Eighteen
to Sixty-Five, 1968 to 1996

	(1)	(2)	(3)	(4)	(5)
AFDC benefit	−1.000	0.274	0.381	—	—
	(0.112)	(0.137)	(0.142)		
AFDC plus food stamps benefit	—	—	—	0.720	—
				(0.086)	
AFDC plus food stamps plus Medicaid benefit	—	—	—	—	0.433
					(0.048)
W_f/W_m	—	0.389	0.344	0.283	0.167
		(0.032)	(0.036)	(0.028)	(0.031)
$W_m + W_f$	—	—	−0.128	−0.175	−0.142
			(0.048)	(0.042)	(0.041)

Source: Author's compilation.
Notes: N = 273. Standard errors in parentheses; all coefficients significant at the 10 percent level. All equations are estimated on the population with less than twelve years of education, and all include a fifth-order polynomial in age (the centered age of the birth cohort in each year). All coefficients are multiplied by 1,000 except that on the wage ratio.

efits become increasingly consistent with the cross-sectional evidence. Columns 4 and 5 add, in turn, food stamp benefits and Medicaid benefits to the welfare benefit-sum; these are more accurate representations of what the welfare system offers. Benefit effects are, on average, larger and more positive in this case than for the AFDC benefit alone.

These results constitute the basic findings of the analysis for white women and will be shown to hold up under a variety of sensitivity tests and alternative formulations. The analysis, as a whole, thus strongly supports an important effect of both female and male wages on marriage and female headship decisions.

Table 5.3 reinforces the importance of including both male and female wages by specifying them in a more conventional manner. In column 1, only the female wage is included, along with the three-benefit-sum. The wage coefficient is statistically insignificant, not surprisingly in light of figure 5.3. A misleading conclusion would be drawn from this result that female wages do not matter. Column 2 shows that this is not the case when the male wage is also entered, making the female wage coefficient positive and significant; the male wage coefficient is negative and significant.[11] The representation of wage effects in this way, rather than as wage ratio and

Table 5.3 Coefficients on Benefit and Wage in Female
Headship Regressions: White Women Eighteen
to Sixty-Five, 1968 to 1996

	(1)	(2)	(3)	(4)
Female wage	0.071	0.397	0.382	—
	(0.131)	(0.106)	(0.111)	
Male wage	—	−.409	−0.488	—
		(0.032)	(0.055)	
W_f/W_m	—	—	—	0.190
				(0.039)
$W_m + W_f$	—	—	—	−0.181
				(0.045)
AFDC plus food stamps plus	0.681	0.421	—	—
Medicaid benefit	(0.051)	(0.046)		
Year dummies	No	No	Yes	Yes

Source: Author's compilation.
Notes: N = 273. Standard errors in parentheses; all coefficients significant at the 10 percent level except that on female wage in column 1. All equations are estimated on the population with less than twelve years of education, and all include a fifth-order polynomial in age (the centered age of the birth cohort in each year). All coefficients are multiplied by 1,000 except that on the wage ratio.

wage sum, is fairly arbitrary and a matter of convenience, for they tell the same story: in column 2, an increase in the female wage and a decrease in the male wage (thus holding the sum constant) increases female headship, whereas an increase in both wages in the same amount decreases it, as implied by the fact that −.409 is greater in absolute value than .397. Finally, columns 3 and 4 replace the benefit sum with year dummies, in one case entering the two wages separately and in the other entering the wage ratio and wage sum; this specification is intended to test whether the specific form of welfare benefits or other period effects matters to the wage results. The answer is that it does not, for the wage coefficients maintain their previous pattern in this case as well.[12]

Another method of testing for the effect of the inclusion of wages on the estimated effect of benefits on female headship is to ask whether the model implies that female headship went up more than expected in the late 1970s and 1980s than would have been expected from the influence of wages alone. This is a necessary consequence of the results, for female headship did increase over the period and benefits fell, as shown in figures 5.1 and 5.2. To address this question directly, I estimate a model with only the two wage variables—the wage ratio and the wage sum—but without the benefit variable. (The age variables are also included.) If the interpretation given thus far is correct, the time series of headship rates predicted from this regression should overestimate the actual rate of female headship over the later years of the period.

Figure 5.4 shows the results graphically. The predicted female headship rates from the model show some fluctuation but exhibit an unmistakable upward trend that grows at a faster rate than actual headship, as can be seen from the top two lines in the figure. Although the level of headship is generally underpredicted, it is overpredicted for a few years in the late 1980s and early 1990s. The bottom line in the figure shows the pattern of residuals from the equation (that is, the difference in the top two lines).[13] The residuals show a corresponding monotonic downward trend (albeit with fluctuation) after around 1974. The residual plot is indeed of almost the exact same general shape as the plot of AFDC benefits and AFDC-plus-food-stamps benefits in figure 5.2. Thus, confirming the regression analysis, the inclusion of female and male wages in the model leaves an unexplained gap in actual and female headship that is consistent with the time-series patterns of welfare benefit changes.

Finally, we conduct three sensitivity tests to the model. The first two examine whether the estimates of benefit effects are stronger among subgroups that are more likely to be affected by welfare benefits and weaker among subgroups that are less likely to be affected by the welfare system. If the effects being estimated are completely spurious and a result of some more general trend, the benefit effects should not vary in the manner to be expected if they are truly reflecting welfare effects. Table 5.4 shows in its first column the estimates from column 5 in table 5.2 as baseline. The second column shows the effect of estimating the equation only on young women, who are the most likely to be welfare recipients and hence to respond; indeed, the welfare benefit coefficient grows larger for this group. The third column shows estimates on the sample of women with education greater than high school, who should be expected to respond less to changes in welfare benefits; indeed, the benefit coefficient drops sharply in this case.

The final column tests whether using a selectivity-bias-corrected wage, instead of the wage for workers only, affects the results. Fe-

Figure 5.4 Actual, Predicted, and Residual Female
Headship Rate from Models Without Benefits,
White Women, 1968 to 1996

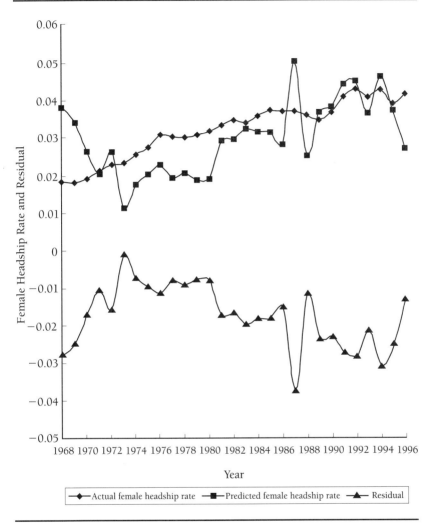

Source: Author's compilation.

male employment rates have risen over time, and this could be expected to artificially lower mean female wages, on the presumption
that most women entering the labor market have lower wages than
those previously working. Although it is not obvious how this
problem might affect benefit coefficients, it should be tested nev-

Table 5.4 Coefficients on Wage Ratio, Wage Sum, and Benefit Variables in Female Headship Regressions, White Women Eighteen to Sixty-Five, 1968 to 1996

	Basic Model	Estimates on Young Women Only[a]	Estimates on Women with Education Greater than High School	Selectivity-Bias Adjusted Wage[b]
W_f/W_m	0.167	0.164	0.063	0.273
	(0.031)	(0.048)	(0.011)	(0.167)
$W_m + W_f$	−0.142	−0.194	−0.030	−0.560
	(0.041)	(0.069)	(0.010)	(0.269)
AFDC + food stamps + Medicaid benefit	0.433	0.615	0.182	0.674
	(0.048)	(0.076)	(0.024)	(0.059)

Source: Author's compilation.
Notes: Standard errors in parentheses. All coefficients significant at the 10 percent level. All equations are estimated on the population with less than twelve years of education except column 3, and all include a fifth-order polynomial in age (the centered age of the birth cohort in each year). Wage sum and benefit coefficients multiplied by 1,000.
[a] Age less than or equal to forty.
[b] Unemployment rate identifies selection bias in wage equation; year polynomials identify wage coefficients.

ertheless. The results show that the benefit coefficients are larger than in the basic model (as are the wage coefficients) but the sign, significance, and order of magnitude are the same. Although these results are only suggestive, since they rely on identification assumptions that may be in error, they do provide at least one piece of evidence on the robustness of the benefit results to the problem of selectively missing wages.[14]

Black Population   The results for black women are discussed more briefly given that the framework and method have already been illustrated with the results for white women. Figure 5.5 shows the life course trends in headship, female wages, and the female-male wage ratio for the same three cohorts as in figure 5.3, but for black women. Headship has also risen among black women, with the effects concentrated at younger ages (under forty). Female wage rates have risen slightly for black women, but the magnitude of the growth has not been large and hence is unlikely to provide an explanation by itself for the trend in headship. The change in the female-male wage ratio is, contrary to that of white women, more mixed in its trend. There has been a rise in that ratio for the most recent cohort shown in the figure, at early ages, but the noise in the data makes this trend not completely clear-cut. Smoothing over the fluctuations, however, demonstrates that there has been an upward trend in this ratio for black women as for white women. Moreover, the decline in the black male wage implied by the combination of the female wage and female-male wage ratios in figure 5.5 is particularly strong in the early ages (thirty-five and under), which are also the ages when headship among the black population has risen the most (see top lines). The age-correspondence between these trends is somewhat closer than it was for the white population, for whom male wages have been dropping at ages somewhat later than the ages at which headship has risen (see figure 5.3).

The first column of table 5.5 shows the results of the basic model for black women. The wage ratio effect has a smaller magnitude than for white women but is still positive and significant. The effect of the wage sum is also negative and significant and of approximately same magnitude as for white women. However, the benefit coefficient is not only again positive and significant but is much larger than that for the white population, implying a large effect of

Figure 5.5   Female Headship, Female Wage, and Female-
Male Wage Ratio, by Birth Cohort, Black
Women, 1966 to 1998

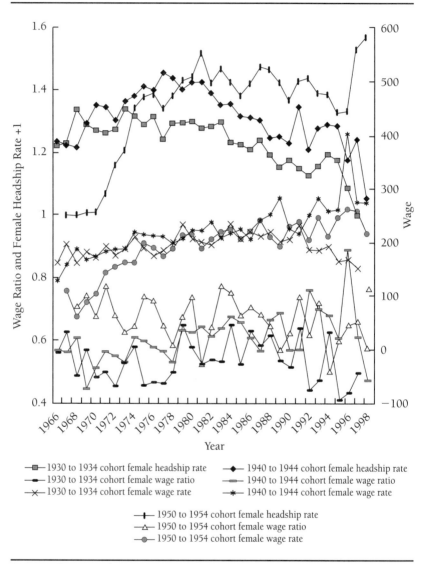

—■— 1930 to 1934 cohort female headship rate   —◆— 1940 to 1944 cohort female headship rate
—●— 1930 to 1934 cohort female wage ratio   —■— 1940 to 1944 cohort female wage ratio
—✕— 1930 to 1934 cohort female wage rate   —✱— 1940 to 1944 cohort female wage rate

—┼— 1950 to 1954 cohort female headship rate
—△— 1950 to 1954 cohort female wage ratio
—●— 1950 to 1954 cohort female wage rate

Source: Author's compilation.

Table 5.5 Coefficients on Wage Ratio, Wage Sum, and
Benefit Variables in Female Headship
Regressions Black Women Eighteen to
Sixty-Five, 1968 to 1996

	Basic Model	Estimates on Young Women Only[a]	Estimates on Women with Education Greater than High School
W_f/W_m	0.096	0.069	0.059
	(0.027)	(0.031)	(0.052)
$W_m + W_f$	−0.170	−0.253	−0.109
	(0.067)	(0.105)	(0.077)
AFDC + food	1.160	1.520	0.576
stamps + Medi-	(0.117)	(0.154)	(0.300)
caid benefit			

Source: Author's compilation.
Notes: N = 207. Standard errors in parentheses. All coefficients significant at the 10 percent level. All equations are estimated on the population with less than twelve years of education except column 3, and all include a fifth-order polynomial in age (the centered age of the birth cohort in each year). Wage sum and benefit coefficients multiplied by 1,000.
[a] Age less than or equal to forty.

welfare benefits. This finding is consistent with the higher welfare participation rates in welfare among the black population than among the white (Gottschalk and Moffitt 2001).

This stronger benefit effect can be seen in figure 5.6, where the predicted and actual headship rates from a model without benefits are shown for black women.[15] The residual plot at the bottom now shows a strong correspondence with the pattern of the AFDC-food-stamps-Medicaid plot shown in figure 5.2. The residual rose more strongly and later than for whites, all the way through the early 1980s, and did not fall as strongly or as rapidly thereafter as for whites. Although this residual plot is still not exactly in correspondence with the welfare benefit plot, it is more closely following it—at least for the most comprehensive benefit level—than for whites. This is what leads to the stronger estimated effect for black women.

The rest of the columns in table 5.5 show sensitivity testing for the black female results. When the analysis is restricted to younger women, the coefficient on the welfare benefit becomes even more positive than in the basic model. When the analysis is restricted

Figure 5.6 Actual, Predicted, and Residual Female
Headship Rate from Models Without Benefits,
Black Women, 1968 to 1992

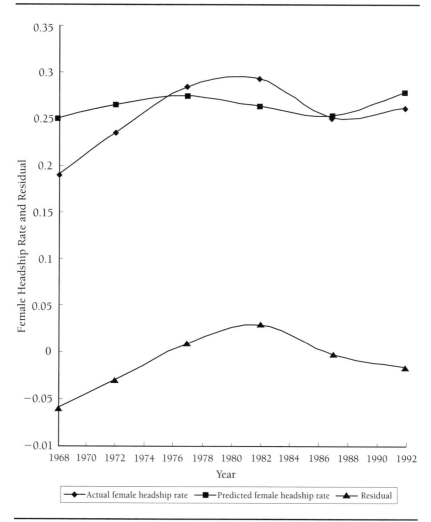

Source: Author's compilation.

only to more educated women, the benefit coefficient falls by 50 percent and becomes insignificant. Thus, the benefit effects are concentrated in the groups with the highest welfare participation rates, lending support against the hypothesis that the effects estimated are spurious and the result of general trends.

CONCLUSIONS

Time-series analysis has been relatively ignored in the literature on the effects of welfare benefits on female headship and nonmarital fertility. The relatively low number of degrees of freedom and the plethora of competing explanations from multiple changes in the market and society in time series make estimation with cross-sectional data naturally more attractive, and hence cross-sectional analysis should and will no doubt continue as the dominant mode of research. However, the time-series trend in female headship has dominated most public discussions of welfare effects, and it is therefore important to establish a possible explanation for that trend that is consistent with the cross-sectional evidence and allows both benefits and other factors to play a role.

This analysis has focused exclusively on the capability of male and female wage rates to provide, on their own and ignoring all other time-series factors, an explanation for the upward trend in female headship and for the inconsistency in unadjusted benefit-headship correlations between the two types of data. The results for both the white and black less-educated populations show that wages can provide such an explanation, in the sense that when both female and male wages are controlled in a time-series female headship regression, there is an unexplained residual that follows roughly the same time-series pattern as that of welfare benefits. There may be other time-series variables besides welfare benefits that follow this trend; however, the analysis is nevertheless consistent with benefits having played a role. Even without assigning benefits as the major factor in explaining the residual, the results strongly suggest that labor market factors, rather than governmental policy, may have been responsible for the secular rise in female headship in the United States over the last thirty years.

APPENDIX: GENERALIZED LEAST SQUARES PROCEDURE

The assumed model is:

$$y_{igt} = X_{igt}\beta + \varepsilon_{igt} \tag{5A.1}$$

$$\varepsilon_{igt} = \mu_t + \nu_{igt} \tag{5A.2}$$

for individual i in cohort group g in year t. We assume $E(\mu_t)$ = $E(v_{igt})$ = $E(\mu_t v_{igt})$ = 0 and $E(\mu^2_t)$ = σ^2_μ and $E(v^2_{igt})$ = σ^2_v. As noted in the text, one of the regressors (the welfare benefit) varies only over t.

We estimate the model in two stages. First we estimate the grouped regression

$$\bar{y}_{gt} = \bar{X}_{gt}\beta + \bar{\epsilon}_{gt} \tag{5A.3}$$

where the bars denote means taken over i within a g-t group, by OLS to produce the coefficient estimate b_{ols}. We use the microdata for each i to compute residuals

$$e_{igt} = y_{igt} - X_{igt}b_{ols} \tag{5A.4}$$

and we then estimate the variance components using the formula

$$\hat{\sigma}_v^2 = \frac{1}{M}\sum_g\sum_t\left\{\left[\frac{1}{n_{gt}-1}\sum_i(e_{igt}-\bar{e}_{gt})^2\right]\frac{n_{gt}}{n_{gt}-1}\right\}\left(\frac{N-M}{N-M-K}\right) \tag{5A.5}$$

$$\hat{\sigma}_\mu^2 = \left\{\frac{1}{M-1}\sum_g\sum_t(\bar{e}_{gt}-\bar{e})^2\right\}\left(\frac{M-1}{M-K-1}\right) - \frac{\hat{\sigma}_v^2}{\bar{n}} \tag{5A.6}$$

where M is the number of g-t groups, n_{gt} is the number of observations in group g-t, N is the grand sample size, K is the number of regressors, and $\bar{n}$ is the unweighted average of the n_{gt}. Equation (5A.5) estimates the variance of the within component as the unweighted average of the estimated within variances for each of the g-t groups, with a degrees-of-freedom adjustment. Equation (5A.6) estimates the variance of the between component in the traditional way by subtracting the variance of the mean of the within component from the between variance of the residuals. The average group sample size is used to scale down the within variance.

In the second stage, recognizing that the variance of the error term in equation (5A.3) is

$$\sigma_\mu^2 + [\sigma_v^2/n_{gt}] \tag{5A.7}$$

we reestimate equation (5A.3) with weighted least squares using the inverse of the square root of the estimates of this variance as

Table 5A.1 Means of the Variables in the Analysis

	White Women					Black Women				
	Mean	Standard Deviation	Minimum	Maximum		Mean	Standard Deviation	Minimum	Maximum	
Female headship (F)	0.096	0.058	0.001	0.217		0.253	0.123	0.008	0.506	
Female weekly wage (W_f)	201	35	71	253		183	41	78	307	
Male weekly wage (W_m)	375	91	88	504		317	77	86	425	
W_f/W_m	0.555	0.088	0.410	0.871		0.604	0.160	0.384	1.859	
$W_m + W_f$	577	123	161	732		500	108	165	706	
AFDC benefit	158	15	125	178		164	9	139	178	
AFDC plus food stamps benefit	211	14	175	234		214	15	175	234	
AFDC plus food stamps plus Medicaid benefit	284	29	195	314		278	30	195	311	

Source: Author's compilation.
Notes: N = 273 for white women, 207 for black women. Population includes all women with less than twelve years of schooling and in cohort-year cells with at least 100 observations. All dollar figures in 1992 constant dollars.

weights and using the estimates of the two error component variances obtained from the individual data to estimate the variance in equation (5A.7).

As Dickens (1990) has noted, if n_{gt} and σ^2_μ are sufficiently large, the variance of the error term in equation (5A.3) is essentially homoskedastic, and hence the GLS procedure does not produce standard errors very different from those of OLS. Our estimates of GLS and OLS standard errors turned out to be extremely close to one another, and this appears to be the reason (large cell sample sizes and relatively large random component variances).

The author would like to thank George Clarke, Jacob Klerman, and Larry Wu for comments, Xue Song and Zhong Zhao for research assistance, and the National Institute for Child Health and Human Development for financial support.

NOTES

1. Note that cohabitation is excluded as well as marriage in this definition. The census data used later in the chapter do not permit the separation of cohabitation and female headship, so the distinction is ignored here as well. In addition, nothing in the basic economic model distinguishes cohabitation from marriage, although I use the word *marriage* instead of *union* because the data used identify only marriage. Note as well that there is no distinction between female household headship and female family headship—that is, whether the woman lives in a household of her own or within a larger household, possibly headed by her parents.

2. It is impossible to do justice to the enormous literature on the economics of marriage and fertility by citation. For marriage, see the work of Becker (1973, 1981) and the review paper of Weiss (1997). For fertility, see the papers of Becker (1960) and Willis (1973) and the review paper by Hotz, Klerman, and Willis (1997).

3. Although the model is neutral on the issue, the empirical evidence suggests that the time-series increase in female headship is more a result of a decline in marriage than an increase in fertility, at least for the white population, and hence a shift of childbearing from married to unmarried women (Smith, Morgan, and Koropeckyj-Cox 1996).

4. When the "quality of children" (that is, expenditure per child) is

introduced, even the "income effects" may be negative (Becker and Lewis 1973; Willis 1973). See Becker (1965) for the basic household production model.

5. We ignore the possibility of welfare benefits for married couples.

6. Although awkward in many respects, this minimal model ignores the male utility gains from marriage. In a more realistic model, both males and females need utility gains to marry, and the chosen leisure, child, and consumption goods are the result of a collective decision mechanism involving both utility functions. However, the model here still allows male leisure and consumption to be in the female utility function. Consequently, even in this model complementarities between male and female leisure can give rise to gains from marriage; indeed, this was the source of gains originally identified by Becker (1973).

7. The two-stage portrayal of the decision process obscures this specialization effect to some extent, because the joint production of children, leisure, and other consumption is not portrayed in its fully joint form. As the model is written, the demand-for-children equation in (5.1) already incorporates the specialization decisions in the married state.

8. I also imposed the requirement that each race/cohort-year cell have a minimum of 100 observations, a restriction that is binding only for the black sample. There are 273 cells for the white population and 218 cells for the black population; these constitute the number of observations for the grouped regressions. Note as well that I used female *household* headship rather than female *family* headship; the latter was tested, with no difference in results. I ignored husband-wife differences in education and assumed that most marriages take place within the same, broad, less-than-high-school education group.

9. I used actual benefits rather than guarantee levels because the two are highly correlated. The three-benefit-sum equals the sum of the AFDC benefit and the food stamp benefit plus .368 of the Medicaid benefit; the .368 adjustment is for the in-kind nature of the Medicaid program. I also tested AFDC alone and AFDC-plus-food-stamp benefits alone.

10. Given the grouped nature of the data, the equation is estimated with least squares rather than with probit or logit.

11. The finding that female headship is a two-variable, not a one-variable, model is quite similar to the celebrated finding of Mincer (1962) that reconciling the cross-sectional and time-series relationship between labor force participation and wages of married women requires the introduction of the wage of the husband.

12. This may be the appropriate place to point out that there is still some cross-sectional variation in the data arising from the cohort variation (or, holding year fixed, age variation). In a pure time-series analysis, year dummies would absorb all variation and leave nothing for wages. In the year fixed-effects specification in columns 3 and 4, on the other hand, cross-cohort wage differences are correlated with cross-cohort headship differences.

13. The residuals in figure 5.4 do not have mean zero because population-size weights per cell were used in constructing the figure, but these weights were not used in the regression.

14. In a time-series analysis, where no cross-area variation is used, identification of selection effects is difficult. The selectivity effect in the wage equation is identified by the assumption that unemployment rate affects the probability of working but not wages directly, an assumption based on the research literature on the effects of the business cycle on the real wage; that literature shows that real wages are fairly cyclically insensitive. The wage coefficients in the headship equation are identified by the inclusion of polynomial year effects in the wage equation and not in the headship equation, thus implicitly allowing wage effects to pick up departures from the trends in the other variables in the equation (benefits and age).

15. Because of small sample sizes, the year-by-year plots show considerable fluctuation, which makes the figure difficult to view. The lines have therefore been smoothed for this group.

REFERENCES

Becker, Gary. 1960. "An Economic Analysis of Fertility." In *Demographic and Economic Change in Developed Countries*. Universities-National Bureau Conference Series, no. 11. Princeton, N.J.: Princeton University Press.

———. 1965. "A Theory of the Allocation of Time." *Economic Journal* 75(September): 493–517.

———. 1973. "A Theory of Marriage." In *The Economics of the Family*, edited by Theodore W. Schultz. Chicago: University of Chicago Press.

———. 1981. *A Treatise on the Family*. Cambridge, Mass.: Harvard University Press.

Becker, Gary, and H. Gregg Lewis. 1973. "Interaction Between Quantity and Quality of Children." In *The Economics of the Family*, edited by Theodore W. Schultz. Chicago: University of Chicago Press.

Danziger, Sheldon, George Jakubson, Saul Schwartz, and Eugene Smolensky. 1982. "Work and Welfare as Determinants of Female Poverty and Household Headship." *Quarterly Journal of Economics* 97(August): 519–34.

Dickens, William. 1990. "Error Components in Grouped Data: Is It Ever Worth Weighting?" *Review of Economics and Statistics* 72(May): 328–33.

Gottschalk, Peter, and Robert Moffitt. 2001. "Ethnic and Racial Differences in Welfare Receipt in the United States." In *America Becoming: Racial Trends and Their Consequences*, edited by N. Smelser, W. J. Wilson, and F. Mitchell. Washington, D.C.: National Academy Press.

Hoffman, Saul, and Gary Duncan. 1988. "A Comparison of Choice-Based Multinomial and Nested Logit Models: The Family Structure and Welfare Use Decisions of Divorced or Separated Women." *Journal of Human Resources* 23(Fall): 550–62.

Hotz, V. Joseph, Jacob Klerman, and Robert Willis. 1997. "The Economics of Fertility in Developed Countries: A Survey." In *Handbook of Population and Family Economics*, edited by Mark Rosenzweig and Oded Stark. Amsterdam and New York: Elsevier North-Holland.

Katz, Lawrence, and David Autor. 1999. "Changes in the Wage Structure and Earnings Inequality." In *Handbook of Labor Economics*, vol. 3A, edited by Orley Ashenfelter and David Card. Amsterdam and New York: Elsevier North-Holland.

Levy, Frank, and Richard Murnane. 1992. "U.S. Earnings Levels and Earnings Inequality: A Review of Recent Trends and Proposed Explanations." *Journal of Economic Literature* 30(September): 1333–81.

Lichter, Daniel, Felicia LeClere, and Diane McLaughlin. 1991. "Local Marriage Markets and the Marital Behavior of Black and White Women." *American Journal of Sociology* 96(January): 843–67.

Lichter, Daniel, Diane McLaughlin, and David Ribar. 1997. "Welfare and the Rise of Female Headed Families." *American Journal of Sociology* 103(July): 112–43.

Mincer, Jacob. 1962. "Labor Force Participation of Married Women: A Study of Labor Supply." In *Aspects of Labor Economics*, edited by Universities-National Bureau of Economic Research. Princeton, N.J.: Princeton University Press.

Moffitt, Robert. 1998. "The Effect of Welfare on Marriage and Fertility." In *Welfare, the Family, and Reproductive Behavior*, edited by Robert Moffitt. Washington, D.C.: National Academy Press.

Schultz, T. Paul. 1994. "Martial Status and Fertility in the United States." *Journal of Human Resources* 29(Spring): 637–69.

Smith, Herbert, S.Philip Morgan, and Tanya Koropeckyj-Cox. 1996. "A Decomposition of Trends in the Nonmarital Fertility Ratios of Blacks and Whites in the United States, 1960–1992." *Demography* 33 (May): 141–51.

U.S. Social Security Administration. 1998. *Social Security Bulletin: Annual Statistical Supplement*. Washington: Government Printing Office.

Weiss, Yoram. 1997. "The Formation and Dissolution of Families: Why Marry? Who Marries Whom? And What Happens upon Divorce?" In *Handbook of Population and Family Economics,* edited by Mark Rosenzweig and Oded Stark. Amsterdam and New York: Elsevier North-Holland.

Willis, Robert. 1973. "Economic Theory of Fertility Behavior." In *The Economics of the Family,* edited by Theodore W. Schultz. Chicago: University of Chicago Press.

Wilson, William J. 1987. *The Truly Disadvantaged.* Chicago: University of Chicago Press.

Wilson, William J., and Katherine Neckerman. 1986. "Poverty and Family Structure: The Widening Gap Between Evidence and Public Policy Issues." In *Fighting Poverty,* edited by Sheldon Danziger and Daniel Weinberg. Cambridge, Mass.: Harvard University Press.

CHAPTER 6

The Young and the Not Quite So Young: Age Variation in the Impact of AFDC Benefits on Nonmarital Childbearing

E. Michael Foster and Saul D. Hoffman

Discussions of nonmarital childbearing almost inevitably focus on teenagers. It is well known that, despite its recent decline, the teen birth rate in the United States is conspicuously high relative to other developed countries. Moreover, the problems of teen child-bearers are well documented (Maynard 1997), although the independent contribution of teen childbearing itself is in some doubt (Geronimus and Korenman 1992; Hoffman, Foster, and Furstenberg 1993; Hotz, McElroy, and Sanders 1997; Hoffman 1998).

Nonetheless, this heavy emphasis on teen childbearing is somewhat misplaced. Recent reports document the growing importance of women ages twenty and older among nonmarital child-bearers. Several statistics illustrate this trend. First, both women age twenty to twenty-four and those age twenty-five and older now account for a greater proportion of nonmarital births than teenagers do. In 1997, the most recent year for which fertility data are available, these two groups of non-teen women accounted for 35 percent and 34 percent of nonmarital births, respectively, while teens accounted for only 31 percent (Ventura et al. 1999). Second, older single women are more likely to have a nonmarital birth than teens. The nonmarital birth rate for women in their early twenties is nearly 70 percent higher than that of teens, while the rate for women in their late twenties is 33 percent higher. Even women age thirty to thirty-four have a nonmarital fertility rate that is nearly as high as that of teens (39.0 versus 42.2 births per 1,000 single women, respectively, in 1997). Third, during the 1980s and 1990s the nonmarital birth rate increased more rapidly for non-teens than for teens. Since 1980 the rate is up 53 percent for teens, 74 percent for twenty- to twenty-four-year-olds, 65 percent for twenty-five- to twenty-nine-year-olds, and 85 percent for thirty- to thirty-four-year-olds. Indeed, since its recent peak in 1994, the nonmarital birth rate for teens has fallen about 10 percent, while the rates for women in their twenties and thirties has fallen much less.

Furthermore, the economic status of older nonmarital child-bearers appears no better than that of their teenage counterparts (Hoffman and Foster 1997). For example, the poverty rates for teenage and older nonmarital child-bearers in the year after the birth are very similar (37 percent and 36 percent, respectively) and dwarf the figure for older married child-bearers (5 percent) (Foster, Jones, and Hoffman 1998).[1]

Nonetheless, teenagers have been the nearly exclusive focus of prior work on nonmarital childbearing, especially that research on the role of welfare in promoting these births. Recent research on older single child-bearers, however, suggests that the link between welfare and nonmarital childbearing at older ages deserves equal attention (Foster, Jones, and Hoffman 1998). That research indicates, for example, that in the year after a nonmarital birth, older single mothers are nearly 50 percent more likely to receive welfare (59 percent versus 41 percent) than their teenage counterparts. Furthermore, our own previous analyses (Hoffman and Foster 2000) indicate that the nonmarital fertility of women in their early twenties may be more sensitive to welfare generosity than is that of teenagers. In spite of this, whether the impact of welfare on fertility varies over the life course is largely unknown.

Why might welfare have a greater impact on the behavior of older women? One possibility is that older women act more deliberately. Their behavior may be more sensitive to welfare generosity because their fertility may be more intentional. Another explanation involves the mix of first and subsequent births. The likelihood of a second nonmarital birth may be more sensitive to welfare generosity, especially among women who are already receiving welfare. If so, welfare will appear to have a greater impact on the fertility of older women because a higher proportion of those births involve second and subsequent births. Finally, older women may be more likely to receive welfare after the birth because of a reduced ability to depend on family members for support. As a result, their behavior may be more sensitive to welfare generosity than is that of teens.

Age variation in the impact of welfare benefits on nonmarital fertility is the focus of this chapter. Using data from the 1979 cohort of the National Longitudinal Survey of Youth (NLSY), we examine the determinants of first and second nonmarital births with a special emphasis on age variation in the impact of welfare benefits. In order to explore timing issues more carefully, we organize our data in an event-history format. We estimate both standard models and also fixed-effects models that control for both year and state of residence.

The chapter has five sections. The first section reviews prior research on welfare and fertility. That review identifies what is known about the link between welfare benefits and nonmarital childbearing and discusses recent methodological advances that have shaped this work. The second section discusses our sample and the way in which we constructed our event-history data. The third reviews the methods we employ, while the fourth presents our findings. A discussion concludes the chapter.

PREVIOUS RESEARCH

The hypothesis that AFDC benefits affect decisions about marriage and fertility has a lengthy history. Empirical research on this issue spans more than a quarter-century and extends across a number of academic disciplines. The empirical literature that examines the effect of AFDC benefits on nonmarital fertility specifically is itself substantial, but most of that literature has focused on teen childbearing. Recent well-known papers include Duncan and Hoffman (1990), An, Haveman, and Wolfe (1993), and Lundberg and Plotnick (1995). Typically these studies find effects consistent with the underlying hypothesis—that is, a positive effect of AFDC benefits on the probability of a nonmarital or teen birth—but the quantitative impact is either relatively small or not statistically significant. For example, Moffitt's comprehensive 1998 survey includes nearly two dozen papers on the relationship between AFDC benefits and nonmarital childbearing, and the vast majority of these yield estimates that he classifies as "mixed" or "no effect." There is some tendency for effects to be larger for whites than for nonwhites, and more recent estimates tend to be larger than those in earlier studies. Because this literature is well known and reviewed elsewhere (Moffitt 1998), we do not discuss it here further.

A newer and still-developing literature has reexamined these issues using fixed-effects models that control for state and year (or cohort). In most previous research, the effect of welfare benefits on fertility behavior is identified from cross-sectional, point-in-time variation in AFDC benefits across states. This variation is substantial—on the order of five-to-one from high-benefit states to low-benefit states—and indispensable for reliable estimation. At the same time, researchers have been concerned that cross-state variation in AFDC benefits might be correlated with or even generated by other factors that influence fertility as well, such as unmeasured preferences or labor market conditions.[2] In that case, estimates of AFDC effects would be biased, capturing the combined influence of AFDC and the correlated omitted variables.[3]

Fixed-effects methods provide a potential solution to this problem. In practice, these models involve adding a dummy variable corresponding to each state to the analysis. The corresponding regression coefficients capture the impact of time-invariant, state-level factors on fertility. Estimation requires longitudinal data; otherwise, one cannot distinguish the impact of welfare benefits from the other, unmeasured state factors. The resulting estimated impact of welfare benefits on fertility is free of any bias caused by omitted state characteristics.[4]

Because they involve panel data, these analyses typically include year (or cohort) fixed effects to control for unobservable differences over time (or across birth cohorts). With this specification, the effect of AFDC benefits on fertility is identified by between-state variation in the change in AFDC benefits over time. In general, more recent cohorts of young women have faced less generous welfare alternatives, but this decline is not uniform over states.[5] In general, the between-state variation has narrowed over time as benefits in low-benefit southern states have not fallen as quickly as those in northeastern states (Moffitt 1998).

Two recent studies of AFDC effects on female headship have incorporated state fixed effects (Moffitt 1994; Hoynes 1997). Moffitt (1994) uses CPS data from 1968 to 1989 for a sample of women age twenty to forty-four with less than twelve years of education. Controlling only for observed state-level labor market conditions, Moffitt finds a modest but statistically significant positive effect of benefit levels on the probability that a white woman is a female head. The effect for black women is positive but not statistically significant. For both whites and blacks, the addition of state fixed effects produces an unexpected negative and statistically significant

AFDC effect. Analyzing data from the Panel Study of Income Dynamics (PSID), Hoynes (1997) finds that including state fixed effects eliminates the estimated positive AFDC effect on female headship for white women and halves the positive AFDC effect for black women; the resulting estimate, however, is still positive and statistically significant.[6] The results in Moffitt and in Hoynes are consistent with a positive relationship between AFDC benefits and state-level unobservables that encourage female headship. These findings suggest that estimates based on analyses that do not include state fixed effects may be biased upward.[7]

Two other recent papers have focused directly on early nonmarital fertility in a fixed-effects framework. Using panel data from the NLSY through 1985 and with controls for both state and birth cohort, Rosenzweig (1999) considers the effect of AFDC benefits on marital and nonmarital fertility through age twenty-two. AFDC benefits are measured by the guarantee for a family of two in a young woman's state of residence averaged across ages twelve to twenty. Other regressors include family income at age fourteen, whether there is an absent or unemployed father in the household at age fourteen, mother's education, race, and a girl's AFQT (Armed Forces Qualification Test) score.[8] Rosenzweig finds a large positive effect of welfare on the likelihood of a nonmarital birth. He reports that a one-standard-deviation decrease in AFDC benefits, equivalent to a 37 percent decline in mean benefits, would cause the probability of a nonmarital birth to fall from .104 to .073 (a decline of 30 percent) for the full sample, and from .170 to .096 (-43 percent) for a sample of women from low-income families.

In a replication of Rosenzweig's paper using data from the PSID,[9] we have provided evidence on both the impact of controlling for state fixed effects and the potential differential age effects of AFDC benefits on fertility (Hoffman and Foster 2000). Like Rosenzweig, we find a substantial impact of AFDC benefits on nonmarital fertility, but only when state fixed effects are included. This result is quite different from the earlier work of Moffitt and of Hoynes, who both found that controlling for state and cohort reduced the estimated impact of AFDC benefits.[10] In addition, to better understand why Rosenzweig's results differ from previous work, we have examined the sensitivity of parameter estimates to the age range over which the dependent variable is defined. We find that welfare generosity has no impact on nonmarital childbearing through age nineteen, even in models that include state fixed effects. For women in their early twenties, however, including state fixed effects produces large and statistically significant estimates of welfare effects.

A much smaller literature examines the link between welfare benefits and births among women with one or more children. Most of these studies use the incremental AFDC benefits following a birth, which vary across states, as the measure of welfare generosity. The findings are rather mixed. Acs (1996) and Fairlie and London (1997) find no relationship. Only Robins and Fronstin (1996), who include state fixed effects, find that the incremental benefits of having a second child increase the likelihood that a woman with one child will give birth.

In summary, the literature to date does not provide a clear and consistent picture of the effects of AFDC benefits on first and second nonmarital births, nor does it clarify whether these effects differ across the life course. The limited work with state fixed-effects models suggests that upward biases may be present in conventional models. Our work here extends that literature. We examine a wider age range, employ both conventional and fixed-effects models, and analyze both first and second nonmarital births.

MODEL AND METHODS

Our underlying approach is consistent with most previous empirical studies and relies on an economic rational choice model. That is, we assume (1) that young women make reasonably purposeful decisions about fertility and marriage, notwithstanding their occasional difficulty in negotiating these complicated issues; (2) that early nonmarital births are very likely to involve a subsequent spell of welfare receipt; and therefore (3) that the maximum utility following a nonmarital birth is an increasing function of the AFDC guarantee (the maximum benefits available to a family with no other financial resources). This yields a reduced-form empirical specification in which the probability of a nonmarital birth is a function of AFDC benefits as well as other determinants of the maximum utility available to a woman in marriage and other alternatives. In our empirical work, we do not assume that women are super-rational in the sense that they are solving a lifetime maximization problem. Rather, we treat them as relatively myopic utilitymaximizers, using current benefits as a proxy for likely short-run future benefits.

Our method here extends our previous work and that of Rosenzweig in three ways. First, those analyses classify women according to fertility only prior to age twenty-two. By extending the time frame through age thirty, we are able to consider the behavior of women through most of their childbearing years. Second, as noted earlier, in Rosenzweig's analyses women are classified according to whether they had *any* nonmarital births by age twenty-two. Women identified as nonmarital child-bearers include some who married (and potentially had a marital birth) before age twenty-two and then had a nonmarital birth after divorcing. As a result, this classification depends on an agglomeration of choices, including the timing of first birth, the timing of first marriage, the duration of first marriage, the timing of remarriage among divorced women, and fertility among divorced women who do not remarry. Any link between welfare and a woman's status at age twenty-two, therefore, is difficult to interpret. The impact of welfare may vary across these choices; furthermore, some women may not face some of these choices at all. We narrow the focus of our analyses to specific behaviors and limit the analysis of those behaviors to women who actually face those choices. In particular, we focus on the timing of first nonmarital births and on the timing of a second nonmarital birth among women who have had a nonmarital birth.

Third, we carefully examine the timing of these choices. Categorizing women according to their behavior through age twenty-two (or any arbitrary age) discards an enormous amount of information. It does not distinguish between single women giving birth at different ages, and as we have argued, this variation is of interest. Furthermore, the use of average AFDC benefits over an extended time period (that is, from age twelve to twenty) necessarily includes years that may be irrelevant to decisionmaking. For example, it is difficult to see how welfare generosity at age twelve would affect fertility behavior at age eighteen.

In order to examine the timing of choices and age variation in the impact of welfare, our analyses employ a discrete-time hazard framework. These analyses largely involve reorganizing the data, which we describe more fully later. Having done this, we simply analyze the data using a multinomial logit specification. (For a further discussion of discrete-time methods in the analysis of event histories, see Jenkins 1995, or Allison 1982; for an illustration, see Hoffman and Duncan 1995.) The outcomes we consider are whether a woman has a nonmarital first (or second) birth, whether she marries, and whether she does neither in a given time period.

All of our models include a set of individual and family background characteristics plus a measure of welfare generosity. In analyses of first births, we use payment levels for a family of two in a woman's current state of residence; for second births, we use the increase in benefits stemming from a second birth. In each case, we use a year-specific measure rather than an average over some extended time period. This formulation is consistent with a behavioral model in which women are myopic.

DATA

In this section, we describe the data we examine, identify the information on welfare generosity, and describe the person-year organization of our analysis files.

SAMPLE AND KEY VARIABLES

Our sample is drawn from the National Longitudinal Survey of Youth (NLSY), a national survey of over 6,000 women who were between ages fourteen and twenty-one in 1979. Our analyses are limited to the 4,274 women who participated in the 1996 interview.[11] Sample weights adjust for differences in initial selection probabilities and, to some extent, for subsequent differential sample attrition. For this reason, all calculations that follow are weighted.

Our analyses are based on information from the 1979 interview as well as fertility and marital information collected in the original interview and updated through 1996. We use this information to identify the woman's age at first birth and first marriage, and on that basis we ascertain her marital status at the time of the birth. We similarly determine whether a woman has had a second birth and her marital status at that time.

From the 1979 interview, we use individual information on age, race/ethnicity, and several measures of family background. Unfortunately, the data lack information on family income during childhood and early adolescence, a factor that is known from previous research to be an important predictor of early nonmarital fertility. Lacking that variable, we include a series of dummy variables identifying the two-digit occupation code for the respondent's mother/stepmother and her father/stepfather if that person worked at least part of the year in 1978.[12] We also include two measures of family structure—whether the respondent was living with both parents at age fourteen, and how many siblings the respondent had. Finally, we include information on mother's years of education coded into four categories: the mother was a high school dropout; the mother completed high school but had no further education; the mother obtained one to three years of postsecondary education; and the mother had four or more years of postsecondary education.

The data also include a measure of individual knowledge and skill, the Armed Services Vocational Aptitude Battery (ASVAB), which was administered in 1980. The ASVAB is a battery of ten tests; scores in four of these areas (arithmetic reasoning, word knowledge, paragraph comprehension, and numerical operations) are used to create a composite score, the Armed Forces Qualification Test (AFQT) score. We use the corresponding percentile score as a measure of ability (for more detail, see Center for Human Resource Research 1997).

WELFARE BENEFITS

Using data on state of residence in each year from 1979 to 1996, we merge data on state-level AFDC benefits. We calculate two measures of welfare generosity—the AFDC guarantee for a two-person family for first-birth analyses, and the amount by which benefits increase with a second birth for second-birth analyses. Benefits levels have been adjusted for inflation using the Consumer Price Index (CPI-U-X1). We use this index rather than the conventional CPI because it handles changes in the cost of housing more sensibly. All values of AFDC benefits have been converted into constant (1983–1984) dollars.

Note that, unlike some researchers, we have included neither food stamps nor Medicaid. We have not included food stamps because they are available to all poor families regardless of family structure; we have omitted Medicaid benefits because of difficulties in measuring their value. The literature is unclear on the effect of ignoring food stamps and Medicaid in estimating the impact of welfare. Hoynes (1997) finds a smaller impact when she omits food stamps than when they are included in the measure of welfare generosity. Fairlie and London (1997) find no difference.

CONSTRUCTION OF THE PERSON-YEAR FILE

In order to examine age variation in the impact of welfare on fertility and marriage, we organize our data into a format in which each person-year is a separate observation. This organization lends itself to hazard analyses and allows us to distinguish between women giving birth at different ages.

This format has several other advantages. First, it allows us to better account for residential mobility. In this framework, the state fixed effect can vary according to where the individual lived in each period, rather than where she lived in a single year, such as 1979, or at a particular age, such as age fourteen.[13] Second, organizing the data in person-years also avoids the awkwardness of basing the measure of welfare generosity on an extended age range (that is, age twelve to twenty) regardless of when a birth (or births) occurred. For women giving birth at early ages, an average measure of welfare generosity includes information on benefits after she gave birth. Unless women are rather forward-looking, these benefits are irrelevant. For women who have later births, available welfare benefits at earlier ages are also likely to be irrelevant. In an event-history framework, one can model fertility and marriage decisions as a function of welfare benefits that were relevant at the point when choices were made.

We generated two event-history files, each containing multiple observations for each woman. For the analysis of first births, the data file includes one observation for each year in which a woman is observed, beginning at 1979 and continuing through a first nonmarital birth, a first marriage (at which point she would no longer be at risk for a nonmarital birth), age thirty, or the end of the panel in 1996. We drop all person-years pertaining to age fourteen or older that occur prior to 1979. Because state of residence is unknown for those years, it is impossible to assign AFDC benefits accurately or to estimate a state fixed-effects model. We also exclude from the sample 717 person-years for individuals who lived in states where fewer than three nonmarital births or three marriages ever occurred. We do this because state fixed-effects logit estimation requires sufficient variation across alternatives for each state for which a fixed effect is estimated.[14] The resulting analysis file has 22,184 person-year observations.

To analyze the timing of second nonmarital births, we created a second person-year file. This file describes a woman's experiences from the time of a first nonmarital birth through marriage or a second nonmarital birth. This file includes a subset of individuals in the main file and includes only those women who had a first nonmarital birth. The file includes 3,361 person-year observations contributed by 849 women. Like the first file, it is limited to person-years occurring during or after 1979 and to states where three or more second nonmarital births and marriages occurred.

FINDINGS

Table 6.1 presents basic descriptive information about our first birth sample. All figures shown in the table were computed using the NLSY sample weights and are population estimates. The full sample includes 4,274 women, approximately equally divided between whites and nonwhites; about 70 percent of the nonwhites are black. As the table shows, 15 percent of the sample had a nonmarital birth by age thirty, but race differences are substantial (8 percent and 43 percent for whites and nonwhites, respectively).[15] Differences in the proportion ever married by age thirty are also substantial—the figure for whites (78 percent) is nearly double that for nonwhites (44 percent). The average AFDC guarantee is about $250 per month. Differences by race in parental education, occupational structure, family structure, and AFQT scores are substantial.

Figure 6.1 shows some further detail about the timing of nonmarital births. The figure shows the hazard rate of a nonmarital birth at age fourteen to thirty for white women and nonwhite women. For white women, the hazard rate is in the 1 to 1.5 percent range from age seventeen through twenty-one, then declines, rising above 1 percent only twice thereafter. For nonwhites, the hazard rate exceeds 5 percent continuously from age sixteen through age twenty-three, peaking at more than 8 percent at age twenty. Even at age thirty, it exceeds the highest hazard rate observed for white women.

Table 6.1 Descriptive Statistics: Sample for Analysis of First Births by Age Thirty

	White	Nonwhite	All
Outcome variable			
Marriage	78%	44%	71%
Nonmarital first birth	8	43	15
Neither	14	15	14
Family demographics			
African American	NA	69	14
Hispanic		31	6
Mother's education[a]			
Completed high school (only)	47	27	43
One to three years postsecondary education	11	7	10
Four years or more secondary education	11	4	9
Living with mother and father at age fourteen	79	55	74
Number of siblings	3.11	4.58	3.41
Mother's occupation[b]			
Professional	8%	6%	8%
Managers	3	1	3
Sales workers	5	1	4
Clerical and kindred	19	8	17
Craftsmen and kindred	1	1	1
Operatives	9	13	10
Nonfarm laborers	1	1	1
Farmers and farm laborers or managers	0	2	0
Service workers except private household	12	16	13
Private household	1	5	2
Does not know	3	3	3
Does not know mother and no stepmother	2	5	3
Father's occupation[c]			
Professional	12	3	11
Managers	15	5	13
Sales workers	6	1	5
Clerical and kindred	4	2	4
Craftsmen and kindred	21	15	20
Armed forces	1	1	1
Operatives	13	14	13
Nonfarm laborers	3	8	4
Farmers and farm managers	2	1	2
Farm laborers	0	3	1
Service workers except private household	5	7	5

Table 6.1 *Continued*

	White	Nonwhite	All
Does not know	4	8	5
Does not know father and no stepfather	8	22	11
Ability measure			
AFQT score	52.47	25.29	46.97
Missing data			
Missing AFQT score	4%	4%	4%
Missing mother's education	4	7	5
Welfare guarantee[d]			
Family of two	$219.85	$255.08	$248.46
Observations			
Persons	2,152	2,122	4,274
Person-years	12,666	10,620	23,286

Source: National Longitudinal Survey of Youth, 1979 cohort of young women.
Notes:
[a] Omitted category: high school dropout.
[b] Omitted category: mother did not work in preceding year.
[c] Omitted category: father did not work in preceding year.
[d] Welfare generosity is calculated as the appropriate welfare measure averaged across the person-years contributed by that individual to the analysis.

Figure 6.1 Nonmarital First-Birth Hazard Rate, by Age and Race

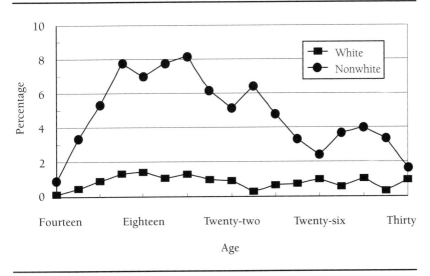

Source: Author's compilation.

FIRST BIRTHS

In table 6.2, we present our hazard estimates of the effect of AFDC benefits on the probability of a nonmarital first birth and of first marriage. We present estimates for three specifications for all observations, then separately by race-ethnicity. The specification for model A includes the full set of family background variables, but no fixed effects; for models B and C, we include year fixed effects and then both year and state fixed effects. In all three models, we constrain the effect of AFDC benefits to be equal at all ages; in table 6.3 below, we relax this assumption.

To simplify interpretation and exposition, we include only the AFDC coefficient estimates and report estimates of the marginal effect rather than the underlying beta coefficient.[16] In a multinomial logit framework, the coefficients have no natural interpretation as to magnitude or even sign; net effects depend on the full set of coefficient estimates. The estimates shown are the effect of a $100 increase in AFDC benefits on the annual hazard rate for the two alternatives. The marginal effects shown here are calculated at the mean values of all other independent variables.

In the first set of estimates in the first column, for all women and with no fixed effects, there is a small, positive, but statistically significant impact of AFDC benefits on the probability of a nonmarital birth and a larger negative impact on the probability of marriage. Controlling for year effects (column 2) has virtually no effect on the estimates, but in a pattern that we will see throughout this chapter, controlling for state fixed effects substantially changes the picture. In column 3, the nonmarital birth effect is halved to .0009, and its standard error doubles, leaving it well short of statistical significance. The marriage effect changes signs and more than doubles in absolute value.

Because these estimates are annual hazard rates, we need to transform them into a cumulative proportion to assess the impact of welfare in practical terms. Here the cumulative AFDC effect on a nonmarital birth is reasonably small, even for the largest estimate in column 1. The underlying average baseline hazard rate is 1.64 percent. With the constant annual impact of .19 percentage points per $100 increase in benefits, the proportion with a nonmarital birth would rise by about one percentage point (from 8 percent to 9 percent) at age twenty, 1.62 percentage points at age twenty-five,

Table 6.2 Estimated Marginal Impacts of AFDC
Generosity on the Hazards of a First
Nonmarital Birth and Marriage, for Women Age
Fourteen to Thirty

	Model A: Family Background Only	Model B: Year Fixed Effects Only	Model C: Year and State Fixed Effects
All (N = 22,184)			
Nonmarital birth			
Estimate	0.0019**	0.0018**	0.0009
Standard error	0.0004	0.0004	0.0010
Marriage			
Estimate	− 0.0043**	− 0.0039**	0.0084*
Standard error	0.0013	0.0014	0.0043
Nonwhites (N = 10,027)			
Nonmarital birth			
Estimate	0.0024	0.0020	− 0.0012
Standard error	0.0016	0.0017	0.0052
Marriage			
Estimate	− 0.0047**	− 0.0048**	− 0.0014
Standard error	0.0015	0.0016	0.0044
Whites (N = 6,852)			
Nonmarital birth			
Estimate	0.0024**	0.0020**	0.0009
Standard error	0.0006	0.0006	0.0016
Marriage			
Estimate	− 0.0041	− 0.0028	0.0084
Standard error	0.0027	0.0030	0.0090

Source: Authors' compilation.
Notes: Table entries represent the percentage point impact of a $100 increase in AFDC payments for a family of two. All models include the set of family background characteristics described in the text.
*$.10 > p > .05$.
**$p < .05$.

and 2.23 percentage points at age thirty, a trend that represents a 10 percent increase in the probability of a nonmarital birth by that age. Expressed as an elasticity, this is a moderate, though not trivial, impact. A $100 increase represents 40 percent of the average payment level in a given year. Thus, the estimated impacts yield a nonmarital birth elasticity of about .24. The fixed-effects estimates yield much smaller behavioral responses.

Our estimates for nonwhites (African Americans and Latinos)

and non-Hispanic whites are based on smaller samples because our estimation requires that any state included in the analyses include at least three individuals in each alternative. Because nonmarital births are relatively less common for white women, there is substantially more sample loss for whites than nonwhites (that is, more states are dropped in the analysis of whites). That accounts for the unusually high proportion of nonwhite women in the unweighted sample.[17]

Except for statistical significance, the general pattern of estimates for the two subgroups is quite similar. For both groups, we estimate a positive effect in model A for the probability of a nonmarital birth and a negative effect for marriage. The nonmarital first-birth estimate for nonwhites and the marriage estimate for whites fall just short of the 10 percent level of significance. The other two estimates are statistically significant. Again, we find that controlling for year effects has little impact, while further controlling for state fixed effects changes the estimates quite substantially. In both cases, there is no longer any evidence of an AFDC effect on a nonmarital birth. The marriage effect is near zero, and one-fourth its standard error for nonwhites and large but insignificant for whites.

The estimates in column 1, which are the largest, yield a cumulative increase in the proportion of white women with a nonmarital birth of 1.2 percentage points after five years and 2.2 percentage points after ten years. Since the underlying average baseline hazard yields a cumulative proportion with a nonmarital birth of only 4 percent at age twenty and 8 percent at age twenty-five, these changes are relatively large in proportional terms. For nonwhites, the proportional effects are smaller, causing a predicted increase from 23 percent to 24 percent at age twenty and from 41 percent to 42.5 percent at age twenty-five.

Table 6.3 relaxes the assumption of a constant AFDC effect by age. Our earlier PSID analyses (Hoffman and Foster 2000) provided indirect evidence that AFDC effects on nonmarital births were much higher for women in their early twenties than for teens. We test for such variation here by allowing the AFDC coefficient to vary across three age groups—age fifteen to eighteen, age nineteen to twenty-one, and age twenty-two and older. We again present estimates for all women and then separately by race. We report only the estimates from the state/year fixed-effects model. The table includes the marginal effects for each age group as well as the cor-

Table 6.3 Age Variation in Estimated Marginal Impacts of AFDC Generosity on the Hazards of Marriage and of a First Nonmarital Birth, for Women Age Fourteen to Thirty

	Fifteen to Eighteen	Age Subgroup Nineteen to Twenty-One	Twenty-Two and Older
All (N = 22,184)			
Nonmarital birth			
Estimate	0.0026	0.0028**	0.0014
Standard error	0.0017	0.0014	0.0011
p for H_0: no age variation			0.17
Marriage			
Estimate	−0.0406**	−0.0127*	−0.0021
Standard error	0.0087	0.0067	0.0046
p for H_0: no age variation			<0.01
Nonwhite (N = 10,027)			
Nonmarital birth			
Estimate	0.0006	0.0076	−0.0001
Standard error	0.0091	0.0077	0.0057
p for H_0: no age variation			0.08
Marriage			
Estimate	−0.0076	−0.0059	−0.0033
Standard error	0.0087	0.0071	0.0049
p for H_0: no age variation			0.67
Whites (N = 6,852)			
Nonmarital birth			
Estimate	0.0001	0.0011	0.0007
Standard error	0.0028	0.0023	0.0017
p for H_0: no age variation			0.81
Marriage			
Estimate	−0.0525**	−0.0185	−0.0033
Standard error	0.0171	0.0132	0.0094
p for H_0: no age variation			<0.01

Notes: Table entries represent the percentage point impact of a $100 increase in AFDC payments for a family of two. All models include the set of family background characteristics described in the text as well as state and year dummy variables.
H_0 = null hypothesis.
*.10 > p > .05.
**p < .05.

responding test statistic for the null hypothesis of no age differences.

In general, the estimated effects provide mixed support for a differential age effect. For the nonmarital birth effects, we cannot reject the hypothesis of no age variation at conventional levels (p = .17). It is striking that the estimated impact for women in their early twenties is significant while that for teens is not. This is due, however, to between-group differences in standard errors. The point estimates for the two groups are nearly identical. The estimated impact for women age twenty-two and older is roughly half that for the two younger groups. These findings imply that the impact of welfare drops with age.[18]

The estimated impact of welfare on the likelihood of a first marriage does appear to vary with age—the impact declines monotonically in absolute value. The effect for women age eighteen and younger is large and statistically significant; the effect for women age nineteen to twenty-one is smaller but also statistically significant. The effect on women age twenty-two and older is very small.

The separate estimates for nonwhites and whites are similar. In both cases, the estimates for a nonmarital birth rise and then fall with age, but none are statistically significant. Age variation for nonwhite women is marginally significant (p = .08), but not for whites. Marriage effects follow the same age pattern as for all women, declining steadily in importance. That variation is significant for white women (p < .01), but not for nonwhites (p = .67). The estimated impact is significant only for young white women.

SECOND BIRTHS

To gauge the impact of welfare on the likelihood that a woman will have a second nonmarital birth, we examine the experiences of those women in our main analyses who had an initial nonmarital birth before age thirty. In analyses presented in this subsection, we examine whether these women eventually marry, give birth out-of-wedlock again, or neither. Note that sample sizes are inadequate here to support separate analyses for whites and nonwhites. Table 6.4 describes the women included in this subsample. Nineteen percent of the women are observed as having a second birth at or before age thirty. Twenty percent marry.[19] As one would expect, compared to the women in the first-birth sample (see table 6.1), these women are far more likely to be nonwhite (58 percent versus 20 percent in the full sample) and to come from more disadvantaged backgrounds. Women in the full sample, for example, were 50 percent more likely to have lived with both parents at fourteen

Table 6.4 Descriptive Statistics: Sample for Analyses of Second Births

	All
Outcome variable	
Marriage	20%
Second nonmarital birth	19
Neither	61
Family demographics	
Black	51
Hispanic	7
Mother's education[a]	
Completed high school (only)	32
One to three years postsecondary education	5
Four years or more secondary education	2
Living with mother and father at age fourteen	50
Number of siblings	4.52
Mother's occupation[b]	
Professional	3
Managers	2
Sales workers	2
Clerical and kindred	8
Craftsmen and kindred	1
Operatives	12
Nonfarm laborers	0
Farmers and farm laborers/managers	1
Service workers except private household	19
Private household	4
Does not know	4
Does not know mother and no stepmother	5
Father's occupation[c]	
Professional	3
Managers	5
Sales workers	2
Clerical and kindred	2
Craftsmen and kindred	17
Operatives	17
Nonfarm laborers	8
Farmers and farm managers	0
Farm laborers	1
Service workers except private household	6
Does not know	8
Does not know father and no stepfather	23

(Table continues on p. 192.)

Table 6.4 *Continued*

	All
Ability measure	
AFQT score	26.33
Missing Data	
Missing AFQT score	4%
Missing mother's education	8%
Welfare Guarantee[d]	
Added benefits for second child	$65.87
Observations	
Persons	849
Person-years	3,551

Source: National Longitudinal Survey of Youth, 1979 cohort of young women.
Notes:
[a] Omitted category: high school dropout.
[b] Omitted category: mother did not work in preceding year.
[c] Omitted category: father did not work in preceding year.
[d] Welfare generosity is calculated as the appropriate welfare measure averaged across the person-years contributed by that individual to the analysis.

than were individuals included in the analyses of second births (74 percent versus 50 percent, respectively).

Figure 6.2 shows the hazard rates for our sample for the first ten years after a first birth. The rates are quite high, exceeding 10 percent in years two through four and year six. There is evidence of a declining hazard after six years.

In table 6.5, we examine the impact of AFDC benefits on a second nonmarital birth. Again, the data are in person-year format, beginning with the year following the birth and continuing through marriage, age thirty, or the end of the sample period. The model here is again a multinomial logit, and the model specification is the same as in the previous tables. In this case, the estimated marginal effect corresponds to a $25 increase in the incremental benefit associated with a second child. (This increase represents roughly one standard deviation for the incremental benefit.)

The estimated impact of welfare on both nonmarital births and marriage is statistically significant in both the ordinary regression (column 1) and year fixed-effects analyses (column 2). In analyses that include state fixed effects (column 3), both estimates are no longer statistically significant. In the case of the nonmarital birth effect, this loss of significance is almost entirely due to an increase in the standard error; adding the state fixed effects has virtually no

Figure 6.2 Second Nonmarital Birth Hazard Rate

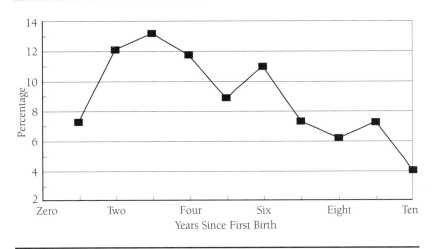

Years Since First Birth

Source: Authors' compilation.

Table 6.5 Marginal Impacts of AFDC Generosity on the Hazards of a Second Nonmarital Birth and of Marriage, for Women Age Fourteen to Thirty

	Model A: Family Background Only	Model B: Year Fixed Effects Only	Model C: Year and State Fixed Effects
Nonmarital Birth			
Estimate	0.0107**	0.0102**	0.0100
Standard error	0.0034	0.0035	0.0071
Marriage			
Estimate	− 0.0125**	− 0.0138**	− 0.0080
Standard error	0.0036	0.0038	0.0074

Source: Authors' compilation.
Notes: N = 3,551. Table entries represent the percentage point impact of a $25 increase in marginal payment for a second child. All models include the set of family background characteristics described in the text.
*.10 > p > .05.
**p < .05.

impact on the estimated marginal effect. The estimate in column 2 translates into an increase in cumulative (five-year) hazard from 34.0 percent to 37.6 percent. Using the marginal impact in column 3, the hazard increases to 37.1 percent. This implies an AFDC incremental benefits–second birth elasticity of about .23.

Adding the state fixed effects does reduce the estimated effect of welfare generosity on the likelihood that a woman who gave birth outside of marriage will marry. The corresponding marginal effect is not statistically significant.

CONCLUSION

In general, *once state fixed effects are included,* our estimates provide little indication of a welfare effect on decisions about marriage and fertility. Fixed-effects estimates (the third columns in tables 6.2 and 6.5) are either not statistically significant or of a counterintuitive sign. Although a confounding of welfare and state-specific trends in omitted variables (such as "conservatism" [Winkler 1994] or the relative wages of men and women [Moffitt, this volume]) or other statistical problems may have biased estimates downward in absolute value, the fixed-effects models offer little evidence that welfare encourages out-of-wedlock childbearing or discourages marriage.

We do find some modest confirmation that the effect of welfare varies by age. Welfare seems to discourage marriage at younger ages; for women in their early twenties, welfare appears to encourage nonmarital childbearing. This finding confirms our earlier results (Hoffman and Foster 2000) and is consistent with our earlier claim that Rosenzweig's results partially reflect the age range he used to define his dependent variable.

In separate analyses of whites and nonwhites, the welfare effects for different age subgroups are generally not significant. An exception is the marriage effect for white teens. In several cases, the race-specific coefficient estimates are rather large but not statistically significant. This imprecision reflects the fact that the variation in welfare benefits used to identify the model—between-state variation in the growth in benefits over time—is only a small portion (5 percent) of overall variation. As a result, the standard errors for the estimated welfare effects are large.

In general, including state fixed effects reduces AFDC effects on demographic behavior—a finding that is consistent with Moffitt

(1994) and Hoynes (1997). (Unlike Moffitt [1998], we find that adding state fixed effects reduces the welfare effect for both whites and nonwhites.) The fixed-effects results are in stark contrast to those from models that include only observed family and individual characteristics. Those models typically yield estimated welfare effects that are statistically significant and large in practical terms. *One's bottom line on whether welfare affects behavior, therefore, seems to depend on whether one believes analyses should include state fixed effects.*

Should state fixed effects be included? The case for including fixed effects is simple. They capture state-level determinants of welfare and fertility that otherwise are confounded with the impact of welfare. From this perspective, past analyses that omit fixed effects are clearly biased, and the fixed-effects estimates clearly preferred.

On the other hand, one might argue that fixed effects represent a case where the medicine is worse than the illness. Fixed-effects estimation may amplify any bias created by measurement error. After the time-invariant portion of the variance in welfare generosity is differenced-out, measurement error may explain a greater portion of the overall variance. This further attenuates the estimated impact of welfare generosity (see McKinnish 2000; Griliches and Hausman 1986). Furthermore, because of the required variation in the outcomes within states, analyses that include state fixed effects require large data sets. This requirement sharply limits the possibility of replicating new or unusual findings across multiple data sets.[20]

In addition, as discussed earlier, fixed-effects estimation carries a high price in terms of estimation precision. Adding the state fixed effects nearly triples the standard error of the marginal effect. (Compare columns 2 and 3 in table 6.2.) The importance of this loss of precision is particularly evident in the analysis of second nonmarital births (table 6.5). Although the point estimate in column 3 is virtually identical to that in column 2, the former is not statistically significant because its standard error is so large. As a result, one cannot reject the hypothesis of no welfare effect, but neither can one reject the hypothesis that the conventional estimate (column 2) and the fixed-effects estimate (column 3) are equivalent.[21] As a result, one might conclude that the omitted state-level factors do not bias the estimates in column 2. In that case, those estimates are preferred to those in column 3 on efficiency grounds, and our findings are reversed.

Statistical and practical problems therefore afflict fixed-effects estimation, but for analyses of welfare effects, there is a deeper conceptual problem. As discussed earlier, including year and state fixed effects in the model means that the effect of welfare is identified by cross-state variation in benefit time trends. Such blips in payment levels are transitory, and one might argue that individuals ignore such variation in making decisions (see Keane and Wolpin 1998; McKinnish 2000; or Moffitt 1998). In that case, fixed-effects estimation produces a different (and smaller) estimated welfare effect not only because it controls for state-level unobservables but also because it captures a different (and smaller) behavioral response. Whether this is the case depends on whether women are myopic and, if not, on how accurately they are able to forecast future benefit levels. If individuals are forward-looking, then fixed-effects estimates do not capture the impact of long-term changes in benefit levels that shape behavior. On the other hand, if individuals are myopic (or assume that all changes in benefit levels are permanent), then fixed-effects estimates do capture changes in welfare generosity that should affect behavior.

The issue of whether to include fixed effects therefore highlights a need for future research. That research needs to examine how women think about welfare and how they evaluate changes in welfare generosity. That information seems even more necessary in light of the complex changes made to welfare under the Personal Responsibility and Work Opportunity Reconciliation Act.

NOTES

1. Although income levels differ little, income sources do differ. Bartfeld and Meyer (this volume) find that among never-married mothers, women giving birth in their early twenties are more likely to receive child support.
2. Although their solution was ultimately unsuccessful, Ellwood and Bane (1985) is the earliest paper to consider this problem.
3. The most likely relationship is one in which states whose residents are more tolerant of nonmarital births provide more generous AFDC benefits. In that case, the estimated coefficient on the AFDC guarantee would be biased upward. The case of states like Mississippi and Alabama (low benefits, high nonmarital birth rate) suggests another possibility: perhaps states in which the majority disapproves of nonmarital births while a substantial proportion of the population has a

disposition toward them will offer low benefits to signal disapproval and attempt to reduce the number of births and state expenditures. This relationship would generate a negative bias in estimates of AFDC impact. Recent research has attempted to explain benefit levels in terms of state labor market conditions and voter preferences. Examples include Moffitt, Ribar, and Wilhelm (1998) and Ribar and Wilhelm (1999).

4.   As discussed later in the chapter, time-varying state characteristics or measurement error still may bias estimates of the effect of AFDC benefits.

5.   Average benefits have fallen about 30 percent in real terms since the early 1970s. There is substantial diversity, however, among states. Illinois, Pennsylvania, New Jersey, and Texas have experienced very large declines in real benefits—50 percent or more. On the other hand, Maine actually increased real benefits by 2 percent over this time period, and both California and Mississippi reduced them less than 10 percent. If the decline were uniform across states, both state and year (or cohort) fixed effects could not be estimated.

6.   Hoynes also estimates models that control for individual fixed effects, with and without state fixed effects. For black women, these models yield smaller and statistically insignificant estimates of AFDC effects.

7.   In a broader review of fixed-effects models and the link between welfare benefits and demographic outcomes, Moffitt finds some racial differences in the impact of including state fixed effects. In particular, he finds that state fixed-effects models produce smaller estimated welfare effects for whites but stronger effects for blacks.

8.   The NLSY includes information about state of residence only at birth, at age fourteen, and for all years beginning in 1979. Thus, state of residence is missing for many women at ages twelve to twenty, and in those years one cannot accurately assign potential AFDC benefits. To get around this problem, Rosenzweig determines welfare generosity at all ages using state of residence at age fourteen. He imputes family income based on parental occupation reported at age fourteen and income by occupation figures from the 1970 census.

9.   The PSID provides better measurement of state of residence and family income, but it uses smaller sample sizes and lacks a measure of cognitive ability like the AFQT.

10.   Rosenzweig does not present estimates from models that do not include fixed effects.

11.   The original NLSY sample included a subsample of disadvantaged whites and another of military personnel. These two subsamples

(combined n = 1,331) eventually were dropped from data collection and are not included in these analyses. We also exclude the 12 percent of the sample that attrited between 1979 and 1996.

12. We also distinguish individuals whose father/stepfather did not work from those for whom no information on the father/stepfather is available.

13. Allowing the state dummies to vary with residential mobility highlights the endogeneity of migration. This problem, however, exists whether the fixed effects are based on residence in 1979 or on respondent's actual residence in a given year. In reality, welfare generosity reflects decisions about migration regardless of which state fixed effects are used. Using dummy variables for where a woman actually lived in a given year seems preferable if only because it accurately describes her place of residence.

14. In states where there are no women in one category (for example, there are no nonmarital births), residence in those states predicts "success" or "failure" perfectly. Maximum-likelihood estimation does not converge; the estimation procedure attempts to make the corresponding coefficient estimate infinitely large (in absolute value). The presence of these observations has little impact on coefficient estimates, and including them (and the corresponding fixed effect) in the analyses may create computational instabilities (for estimation details, see Chamberlain 1980). To improve the stability of our estimates, we require three individuals in each choice for each state.

15. Because of censoring (that is, some women did not reach age thirty before 1996), these figures underestimate the true proportion of women who had a nonmarital birth by age thirty. The hazard estimates presented later in the chapter do allow for censoring.

16. The empirical model includes a minimum of fifty-two variables (including the many occupational dummy variables). Adding state and year fixed effects requires estimation of more than one hundred coefficients. The full results are available from the authors.

17. This feature of the analysis also explains why the observations for whites and nonwhites do not sum to the number of observations in the pooled analyses. In the pooled analysis, we are able to use states in which any woman had a nonmarital birth, regardless of her race.

18. An alternative explanation for this drop-off in the size of the welfare effect is unobserved heterogeneity—women whose fertility is most sensitive to welfare generosity may give birth earlier, leaving women who are less sensitive to welfare generosity in the pool of women at risk. We considered this possibility by introducing a gamma-distributed heterogeneity term into the model (see Meyer 1990). Doing so did not influence our findings.

19. These figures represent outcomes observed in the data. Because of censoring, these figures underestimate the proportion of women who will experience these events by age thirty. The hazard models employed below account for censoring.

20. The list of suitable data sets is short. Even the PSID may not be large enough. Our analyses of those data yielded different welfare effects when we included region fixed effects for states that otherwise would be excluded because of inadequate variation (Hoffman and Foster 2000). This finding may indicate that region dummies are not a good substitute for state dummies, or it may indicate that shifts in the composition of the states included in the analysis may influence parameter estimates. This implies that analyses of smaller data sets may produce different parameter estimates because they involve differing subsets of all states.

21. One can use a Hausman-like test to assess the statistical significance of the difference between the two coefficients. That difference is significant for neither the marriage nor the nonmarital birth estimate in table 6.5. For table 6.2, in only one instance (the marriage effect for the entire sample) is the difference between the two estimates statistically significant.

  This test has the form of the Hausman test—it is calculated as the difference in the estimates divided by the square root of the difference in their variances. However, it is not a true Hausman test, for two reasons. First, the test is based on marginal effects, not the underlying regression coefficients. Second, the estimates in column 2 are not random-effects estimates. This test, therefore, is not a formal test, but we believe it to be a reasonable illustration of how small the differences in coefficient estimates are in light of the imprecision of the fixed-effects estimates.

REFERENCES

Acs, Gregory. 1996. "The Impact of Welfare on Young Mothers' Subsequent Childbearing Decisions." *Journal of Human Resources* 31(4): 898–915.

Allison, Paul D. 1982. "Discrete-Time Methods for the Analysis of Event Histories." In *Sociological Methodology*, edited by S. Leinhardt. San Francisco: Jossey-Bass Publishers.

An, Chong-Bum, Robert Haveman, and Barbara Wolfe. 1993. "Teen Out-of-Wedlock Births and Welfare Receipt: The Role of Childhood Events and Economic Circumstances." *Review of Economics and Statistics* 75(2): 195–208.

Center for Human Resource Research. 1997. *NLSY79 Users' Guide: A Guide* to the 1979–1996 National Longitudinal Survey of Youth Data. Columbus: Ohio State University, Center for Human Resource Research.

Chamberlain, Gary. 1980. "Analysis of Covariance with Qualitative Data." Review of Economics and Statistics 47: 225–38.

Duncan, Greg J., and Saul D. Hoffman. 1990. "Welfare Benefits, Economic Opportunities, and Out-of-Wedlock Births Among Black Teenage Girls." Demography 27(4): 519–35.

Ellwood, David, and Mary Jo Bane. 1985. "The Impact of AFDC on Family Structure and Living Arrangements." In Research in Labor Economics, vol. 7, edited by Ronald Ehrenberg. Greenwich, Conn.: JAI Press.

Fairlie, Robert W., and Rebecca A. London. 1997. "The Effect of Incremental Benefit Levels on Births to AFDC Recipients." Journal of Policy Analysis and Management 16(4): 575–97.

Foster, E. Michael, and Saul D. Hoffman. 1996. "Nonmarital Childbearing in the 1980s: Assessing the Importance of Older Women." Family Planning Perspectives 28(3): 117–19.

Foster, E. Michael, Damon Jones, and Saul D. Hoffman. 1998. "Nonmarital Childbearing in the Post-Teenage Years: The Economic Status of the Women and Their Children." Journal of Marriage and the Family 60(1): 163–75.

Geronimus, Arline T., and Sanders Korenman. 1992. "The Socioeconomic Consequences of Teen Childbearing Reconsidered." Quarterly Journal of Economics 107: 1187–1214.

Griliches, Zvi, and Jerry A. Hausman. 1986. "Errors in Variables in Panel Data." Journal of Econometrics 31: 93–118.

Hoffman, Saul D. 1998. "Teen Childbearing Isn't So Bad After All . . . Or Is It?: A Review of the New Literature on the Consequences of Teen Childbearing." Family Planning Perspectives 30(5): 236–39.

Hoffman, Saul D., and Greg J. Duncan. 1995. "The Role of Incomes, Wages, and AFDC Benefits on Marital Disruption." Journal of Human Resources 30(1): 19–41.

Hoffman, Saul D., and E. Michael Foster. 1997. "Economic Correlates of Nonmarital Childbearing Among Adult Women." Family Planning Perspectives 29(3): 37–40.

———. 2000. "AFDC Benefits and Nonmarital Births to Young Women." Journal of Human Resources. 35(2): 376–391.

Hoffman, Saul D., E. Michael Foster, and Frank F. Furstenberg, Jr. 1993. "Reevaluating the Costs of Teenage Childbearing." Demography 30(1): 1–14.

Hotz, V. Joseph, Susan W. McElroy, and Seth G. Sanders. 1997. "The Impacts of Teenage Childbearing on the Mothers and the Consequences of Those Impacts for Government." In Kids Having Kids, edited by Rebecca A. Maynard. Washington, D.C.: Urban Institute Press.

Hoynes, Hillary W. 1997. "Does Welfare Play Any Role in Female Headship Decisions?" *Journal of Public Economics* 65: 89–117.

Jenkins, Stephen P. 1995. "Easy Estimation Methods for Discrete-Time Duration Models." *Oxford Bulletin of Economics and Statistics* 57(1): 129–38.

Keane, Michael P., and Kenneth I. Wolpin. 1998. "Estimating Welfare Effects Consistent with Forward-Looking Behavior." Unpublished paper.

Lundberg, Shelly, and Robert A. Plotnick. 1995. "Adolescent Premarital Childbearing: Do Economic Incentives Matter?" *Journal of Labor Economics* 13(2): 177–200.

Maynard, Rebecca A. 1997. "The Costs of Adolescent Childbearing." In *Kids Having Kids*, edited by Rebecca A. Maynard. Washington, D.C.: Urban Institute Press.

McKinnish, Terra. 2000. "Model Sensitivity in Panel Data Analysis: Some Caveats About the Interpretation of Fixed Effects and Differences Estimators." Working paper. Boulder: University of Colorado, Department of Economics.

Meyer, B.D. 1990. "Unemployment Insurance and Unemployment Spells." *Econometrica* 58(4): 757–82.

Moffitt, Robert A. 1994. "Welfare Effects on Female Headship with Area Effects." *Journal of Human Resources* 29(2): 621–36.

———. 1998. "The Effect of Welfare on Marriage and Fertility." In *Welfare, the Family, and Reproductive Behavior,* edited by Robert Moffitt. Washington, D.C.: National Academy Press.

Moffitt, Robert A., David C. Ribar, and Mark O. Wilhelm. 1998. "The Decline of Welfare Benefits in the United States: The Role of Wage Inequality." *Journal of Public Economics* 68: 421–52.

Ribar, David C., and Mark O. Wilhelm. 1999. "The Demand for Welfare Generosity." *Review of Economics and Statistics* 81(1): 96–108.

Robins, Philip K., and Paul Fronstin. 1996. "Welfare Benefits and Birth Decisions of Never-Married Women." *Population Research and Policy Review* 15(1): 21–43.

Rosenzweig, Mark R. 1999. "Welfare, Marital Prospects, and Nonmarital Childbearing." *Journal of Political Economy* 107(6): S3–32.

Ventura, Stephanie J., et al. 1999. "Births: Final Data for 1997." *National Vital Statistics Reports* 47(18). Hyattsville, Md.: National Center for Health Statistics.

Winkler, Anne E. 1994. "The Determinants of a Mother's Choice of Family Structure: Labor Market Conditions, AFDC Policy or Community Mores?" *Population Research and Policy Review* 13(3): 283–303.

CHAPTER 7

Unwed Parents or Fragile Families? Implications for Welfare and Child Support Policy

*Sara McLanahan, Irwin Garfinkel,
Nancy E. Reichman, and Julien O. Teitler*

Nearly one-third of all births in the United States today occur outside marriage, up from 6 percent in the early 1960s (Ventura et al. 1995). The proportions are even higher among poor and minority populations—40 percent among Hispanics and 70 percent among African Americans. Nonmarital childbearing also is increasing throughout the western European countries. Indeed, the rate of nonmarital births is higher in the Scandinavian countries (and France) than it is in the United States (Ventura et al. 1995). The United States is different from these other countries, however, in one important respect. Whereas in Europe the overwhelming majority of unwed parents are living together when their child is born, in the United States less than half of new unwed parents are cohabiting. Thus, children born outside of marriage in the United States are much more likely to be poor and much more likely to experience *father absence* than children born outside of marriage in other countries. Both poverty and father absence have been shown to have a negative effect on children's future life chances (McLanahan and Sandefur 1994; Duncan and Brooks-Gunn 1997).

In response to growing concern over the economic and social costs of nonmarital childbearing, policymakers have begun to pass laws that make it more difficult for unmarried fathers to abandon their children and for unmarried mothers to raise their children alone. In the 1980s, Congress passed a series of laws designed to increase paternity establishment and strengthen child support enforcement. The Personal Responsibility and Work Opportunity Reconciliation Act of 1996 (PRWORA) continues in this vein by providing incentives and requirements for states to increase paternity establishment, strengthen child support enforcement, and reduce nonmarital childbearing by requiring mothers to work while receiving welfare and by limiting the amount of time they can receive welfare. Taken together, the new laws make unmarried mothers more dependent on fathers and make it more difficult for unwed fathers to shirk their paternal responsibilities.

Underlying these new policies is the assumption that children would be better off if their parents lived together and their fathers were more involved in their lives. Although most people endorse these assumptions, their scientific basis is weak. We know very little about the capabilities of the men who father children outside of marriage, and we know even less about the nature of their relationships with the mothers of their children. If fathers are able (and willing) to assume more financial responsibility for their children, and if mothers and fathers are able to cooperate, children are likely to be better off under the new policy regime. Conversely, if fathers are unable to meet their obligations and if stronger child support enforcement increases parental conflict, children are likely to be worse off.

In this chapter, we use data from a new survey of unmarried parents, the Fragile Families and Child Wellbeing Study. In interviews with parents shortly after birth, the survey collects information from both mothers and fathers on a wide range of topics, including parents' relationship, attitudes toward marriage and parenthood, parents' human capital, and sources of income and social support. We use these data to address two questions: What is the nature of the relationship between unmarried parents? And what are the capabilities of unmarried parents, especially fathers?

Getting the facts straight about the nature of unmarried parents' relationships is critical for understanding the potential impact of the new child support and welfare laws and for designing effective programs and policies. Not only can policies be more effective if they are tailored to actual rather than presumed parental relationships, but they have the potential to influence the relationships themselves. If, for example, a mother and father are truly indifferent to one another, it makes sense to design programs that treat them as separate individuals. If, on the other hand, they are involved in a marriage-like relationship, it may be preferable to treat them as a family unit, capitalizing on a preexisting commitment.

Understanding unwed fathers' capabilities, resources, and psychosocial risk factors is also of critical importance. Two aspects of fathers' capabilities are particularly relevant: earnings and propensity to violence. Clearly, most mothers and children would be better off, economically speaking, if fathers provided more financial support. However, some advocates fear that forcing fathers to pay child support may have serious repercussions for mothers and children. Much of their concern is grounded in the belief that a substantial number of unmarried fathers have serious mental health problems, problems with drug and alcohol abuse, and/or problems with physical abuse and violence. Again, getting the facts straight about the prevalence of these problems is crucial for the design of effective policies and programs to better meet the needs of this population.

The next section of the chapter reviews existing literature. The third section discusses the survey design and variables. The fourth section presents the results of our analysis, and the fifth and final section discusses the policy implications of the findings.

To summarize briefly, we find that the vast majority of new unmarried parents are committed to one another and have *high hopes* of raising their child together. At the same time, parents' ability to support themselves and their new baby is seriously restricted by low education, lack of work experience, and low income. In order to strengthen fragile families and promote paternal involvement—both financial and emotional—policies must address these human capital needs as soon as possible after the birth of the child.

LITERATURE REVIEW

Recent figures suggest that the pattern of nonmarital childbearing in the United States is converging with that of the European countries, where the vast majority of unwed parents live together in marriage-like relationships. Whereas in the early 1980s about 25 percent of births outside of marriage in the United States were to cohabiting parents (Bumpass and Sweet 1989), by the early 1990s the percentage was 40 percent (Bumpass and Lu 2000). Non-Hispanic whites are the most likely to cohabit, followed by Hispanics and then blacks. The increase in cohabitation during the past decade was also greatest among non-Hispanic whites (33 percent to 50 percent). About half of the parents who are cohabiting when their child is born will eventually marry each other; most of the other half will end their relationship.

Relationships Within Fragile Families

There are several conflicting stories about the relationships between unmarried parents and between fathers and children. Anderson (1989) describes how young, inner-city men exploit young women in order to satisfy their sexual needs and gain status with their peers. Edin (1997), in contrast, suggests that mothers often refuse to marry (or live with) the fathers of their children, either because the men are unreliable breadwinners or because they have serious drug or alcohol problems.[1] Although these two pictures differ dramatically with respect to which parent is defining the relationship, both authors agree that marriage is not part of the future for most of these couples. Other researchers present a more cooperative picture, suggesting that many unwed couples start out with high hopes for maintaining a stable relationship only to find that they (or their partners) cannot meet their earlier expectations (Edin and Lein 1997; Furstenberg, Hughes, and Brooks-Gunn 1992). These arguments are similar to ones made by Liebow (1967) in his famous study of street-corner life: he suggested that men who are unable to provide economic support for their families disengage as a way of minimizing feelings of inadequacy.

Although formal child support agreements are less common among never-married fathers than among formerly married fathers, informal support, especially the purchase of goods and services for the child, appears to be very common (Edin and Lein 1997; Waller 1997; Marsiglio and Day 1997). Contact between nonresident fathers and their children is also quite high. Analyses of the NLSY data suggest that half of new unwed fathers see their children at least once a week (McLanahan et al. 1997). These authors speculate that the high levels of contact between fathers and children are probably due to the fact that the parents are still romantically involved. When the romantic relationship ends, father contact is likely to drop off sharply, as it does among divorced fathers.

Parents' Capabilities

Researchers and policymakers are especially interested in two aspects of fathers' capabilities: their earnings capacity and their propensity to violence. These two factors are fundamental to the success or failure of the new welfare and child support laws that envision a greater role for fathers in supporting their families.

The best evidence we have to date suggests that men who father children outside of marriage are younger, less likely to have a high school degree, and less likely to attend college than men who father children within marriage (Garfinkel, McLanahan, and Hanson 1998). Unwed fathers also work fewer hours per week and have much lower hourly wages ($10 to $13, in 1995 dollars) than married fathers ($21). Not surprisingly, the average income of never-married fathers is much lower than the average income of married fathers—$15,000 to $25,000 for unwed fathers as compared with $42,000 for married fathers. The difference is even more striking when we look at men in the lower tail of the income distribution. Garfinkel and his colleagues (1998) estimate that 40 percent of unwed fathers have annual incomes less than $7,000. Finally, unwed fathers report more disability, more depression, and more frequent drug and alcohol use than men who father children within marriage (Garfinkel et al. 1998).

Most estimates of unwed fathers' earnings (and other characteristics) are seriously limited by the fact that these men are underrepresented in national and local surveys. Cherlin, Griffith, and McCarthy (1983) were the first to note this problem. As many as 3.8 million nonresident fathers are not represented in the National Survey of Families and Households (NSFH), which is arguably the best data set in the United States for studying family relationships (Garfinkel et al. 1998).[2] About one-third of the "missing fathers" are not included in the sampling frame because they are in prison, in the military, or, most important, not counted by the census. The other two-thirds are in the survey but do not acknowledge their status. The "missing fathers problem" is especially serious for low-income fathers and for men who father children outside of marriage (see also Rendall et al. 1999; Sorensen 1995).

Clearly, most mothers and children would be more secure economically if nonresident fathers paid more child support. A concern, however, is that forcing fathers to pay child support may lead to unintended negative consequences that, in some instances, may outweigh the economic benefits. Much of this concern is based on the belief that many nonresident fathers have serious mental health problems, problems with drugs and alcohol abuse, and problems with physical abuse and violence. Four recent studies suggest that domestic violence among poor women and women on welfare is very high, with current prevalence ranging from 15 to 32 percent and lifetime prevalence ranging from 34 to 65 percent (Raphael and Tolman 1997). We must approach these figures cautiously, however, since the statistics are based on special populations (that is, welfare mothers) and do not distinguish between biological and social fathers. Moreover, estimates based on nationally representative data suggest that while unmarried fathers report more mental health problems and more problems with drugs and alcohol than married fathers, the overall prevalence of these problems is still very low (Garfinkel et al. 1998). According to the NSFH data, only 11 percent of unwed fathers report being depressed, and only 7 percent report having drug or alcohol problems.

DATA

The Fragile Families and Child Wellbeing Study follows a new cohort of (mostly unwed) parents and their children. The sample contains approximately 4,700 births (3,600 nonmarital, 1,100 marital) in 75 hospitals in 20 cities across the United States. The data are representative of nonmarital births in each of 20 cities and in U.S. cities with populations of 200,000 or more people. The survey collects information on pregnancy and birth outcomes, mother-father relationships, attitudes toward marriage and fatherhood, social support networks, employment and underground employment, income and sources of income, and demographic characteristics (for example, age, education, race, religion, and immigrant status). The initial interviews with the mothers and fathers are conducted in the hospital shortly after the birth of the child. Follow-up interviews with both parents are scheduled for when the child is twelve, thirty, and forty-eight months old. (For details about the research design, see Reichman et al. 2001.)

In this chapter, we use data from the baseline interviews with parents in seven cities: Oakland, Austin, Baltimore, Detroit, Newark, Philadelphia, and Richmond. These parents were interviewed between February 1998 and August 1999. Each city sample consists of a random sample of 250 nonmarital and 75 marital births. Response rates for mothers exceeded 90 percent. With the exception of Newark, response rates for married fathers and cohabiting fathers were 90 percent, and response rates for unmarried fathers were 75 percent.[3]

Table 7.1 reports the basic demographic characteristics of the unmarried mothers in our sample and compares them with the figures for unwed mothers in the United States as a whole. The seven-city Fragile Families sample has over twice the percentage of non-Hispanic blacks and a much smaller percentage of non-Hispanic whites than the population of unmarried mothers in the United States as a whole in 1998. This is not surprising since these seven cities have very high percentages of black residents. The percentages of Hispanics and women of other races, however, are similar in the two samples. The age distribution of the nonmarital births in the Fragile Families sample mirrors closely the distribution in the United States as a whole, despite the fact that our sample excludes very young teen mothers.[4] Interestingly, the percentage of respondents born in

Table 7.1 Selected Characteristics of Unmarried Mothers in the Fragile Families Seven-City Baseline Sample and the United States

	Fragile Families	United States
Race		
White non-Hispanic	8%	40%
Black non-Hispanic	69	32
Hispanic	19	24
Other	4	4
Age		
Under eighteen	5	12
Eighteen to nineteen	19	18
Twenty to twenty-four	38	35
Twenty-five to twenty-nine	22	19
Thirty to thirty-four	10	10
Thirty-five to thirty-nine	4	5
Forty or older	2	1
Other characteristics		
U.S.-born	87	83
First birth	36	48
At least high school graduate	59	56

Source: Figures for race, age, and nativity for the United States are for 1998 and come from U.S. Department of Health and Human Services, National Vital Statistics Report 48 (3, March 28, 2000). Figures for first births and education for the United States are from U.S. Department of Health and Human Services, Vital Statistics of the United States, 1993, vol. 1, Natality.

the United States is close to that of the U.S. population. Finally, the percentage of first births in the Fragile Families sample is somewhat lower than that in the United States (36 percent versus 48 percent), and the percentage of women with at least twelve years of education is a bit higher (59 percent versus 56 percent). These differences are probably due to the underrepresentation of very young teen mothers (under eighteen) in the Fragile Families sample.

Parental relationships and capabilities are the central foci of the Fragile Families survey. The questionnaires therefore include extensive information on both subjects. To measure *parents' relationship status,* we used information on whether parents were married or living together at birth, whether they were romantically involved with one another, whether the father's name was on the household roster, and whether the mother reported that the child would live with the father. At the one-year follow-up interview, mothers were asked again whether they were living with the father at the time of the child's birth. This information allows us to cross-check the information on cohabitation in several ways: by comparing mothers' direct reports about cohabitation with the names on their household rosters; by comparing the mothers' reports about cohabitation with their reports about who the child would live with; by comparing mothers' and fathers' reports of cohabitation for the subset of couples for whom we have information from both parents; and by comparing mothers' retrospective reports from the twelve-month interview with their baseline report. The latter comparison can be made in the two cities for which we now have follow-up data— Austin, Texas, and Oakland, California. As we discuss in detail later, these comparisons suggest that there may be some misreporting about cohabitation, but that any misreporting is not extensive enough to seriously distort our estimates of marital status or cohabitation.

In addition to the questions on cohabitation, mothers were asked to characterize their relationship with the father as "romantically involved on a steady basis," "involved in an on-again, off-again relationship," "just friends," "hardly talk to each other," or "never talk to each other." We combine this question with the information on cohabitation to construct a measure of relationship status.

We use the mother's reports of the father's contributions and behaviors during her pregnancy and his intentions for the future. Specifically, we look at whether the father gave her money or bought things for the baby, whether he visited the hospital, whether the baby will have the father's surname, and whether the father's name will be on the birth certificate. We also look at the mother's report of whether the father told her he would provide financial support during the coming year and whether she wants the father to be involved in raising the child.

The Fragile Families survey provides better information on the earnings and personal problems of unwed fathers than has been available from previous studies. First, the sample of fathers is more representative of unwed fathers in large cities than other surveys. The interviews with the fathers, together with the information we collect from the mothers about the fathers, give us information on 90 percent of the sampled population (nonmarital births). Second, the survey collects information on regular earnings and earnings from all other irregular jobs.[5]

We look at mothers' and fathers' human capital at baseline using mothers' reports of their educational attainment and employment status. For mothers, we also look at household income and whether they received welfare, food stamps, or public assistance in the past year. For fathers, we look at earnings using their own reports.

Psycho-social risk factors include substance abuse problems and violence. We use the mother's responses to three questions to determine whether she used drugs during pregnancy or has (or has ever had) a substance abuse problem: whether she used marijuana, crack cocaine, or heroin during pregnancy, whether drinking or using drugs ever interfered with her work or relationships, and whether she ever sought help or was treated for drug or alcohol problems. We use the mother's responses to the last two questions about the father to determine whether the father has (or had) a substance abuse problem.

If the mother indicates at any point during the interview, either as a response to a direct question or not, that the father ever abused, slapped, or hit her, we code the father as being violent.

RESULTS

We begin by looking at the relationships between unwed parents. As noted earlier, the ethnographic literature on parents' relationships presents conflicting pictures about the level of commitment between unmarried parents and the differences in commitment between mothers and fathers. Understanding the nature of these parents' relationships is important insofar as policymakers want to design programs that strengthen rather than weaken existing ties between mothers and fathers and between fathers and children. If most parents are neither cohabiting nor romantically involved, then child support enforcement is appropriate and we needn't be too concerned about programs that discourage marriage or cohabitation (for example, housing policy and welfare policy). Conversely, if parents are romantically involved and have plans to marry or live together, then child support is less salient and we need to make sure that our income-tested programs are not discouraging family formation.

The Nature of Parental Relationships

According to table 7.2, the vast majority of the parents in our sample (82 percent) are romantically involved at the time of their child's birth. Close to half (45 percent) are living together, and the other 37 percent are romantically involved but living apart. Nine percent of parents are not romantically involved but report being on friendly terms. Only 9 percent have little or no contact.

Among those in a romantic relationship, Hispanics and non-Hispanic whites are much more likely to be living together than are blacks and other races. Among those who are not romantically involved, white mothers are much more likely than other mothers to

Table 7.2 Relationship Status of Unmarried Parents in the Fragile Families Seven-City Sample, by Race-Ethnicity, from Mother Baseline Interviews

	White Non-Hispanic	Black Non-Hispanic	Hispanic	Other	Total
Living together	57%	39%	61%	40%	45%
Romantic or steady	20	44	23	38	37
Friends	7	9	7	12	9
Hardly or never talk	16	8	9	10	9
Number of mothers	147	1,238	336	58	1,779

Source: Authors' compilation.

Figure 7.1 Relationship Status of Unmarried Parents in the Fragile Families Seven-City Sample, by Race-Ethnicity, from Mother Baseline Interviews

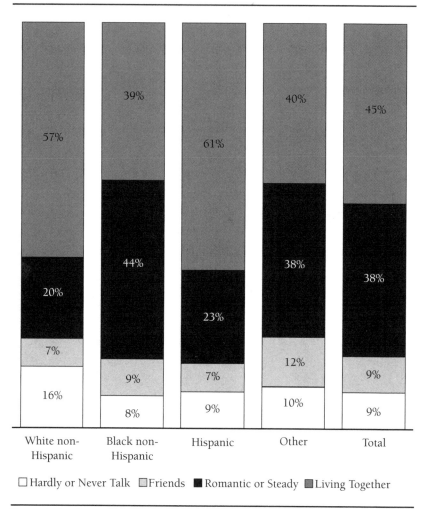

Source: Authors' compilation.

have minimal contact with the fathers. In short, white unwed parents appear to opt either for a marriage-like relationship (cohabitation) or no relationship at all (73 percent combined), whereas blacks tend to opt for something in between. These relationships for whites, blacks, and Hispanics are illustrated in figure 7.1.

Cohabitation Rates The Fragile Families cohabitation rate adjusted for the racial-ethnic distribution in the United States as a whole is 51.5 percent, or 12.5 percentage points higher than the figures for the early 1990s published by Bumpass and Lu (2000) using the National Survey of Family Growth (NSFG).[6] Comparing the two sets of figures broken down by mother's race, as shown in figure 7.2, we find that the discrepancy between our results and those of Bumpass and Lu (2000) is mostly due to difference among blacks (22 percent versus 40 percent). Though estimates of cohabitation are eight percentage points higher for both Hispanics and whites in the Fragile Families sample, they are not very different from what we might expect given the recent trend in cohabitation among whites and Hispanics (Bumpass and Lu 2000). The figures reported

Figure 7.2 Cohabitation Rates of Unmarried Parents in the Fragile Families Seven-City and NSFG Samples, by Race-Ethnicity

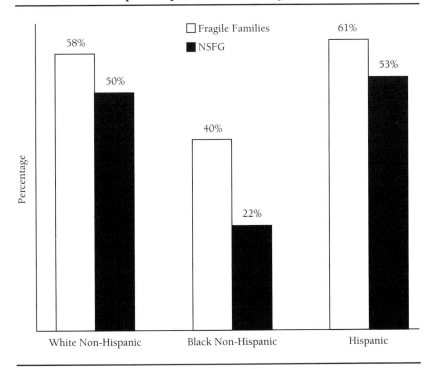

Source: Authors' compilation.

by Bumpass and Lu are based on births that occurred in the early 1990s, whereas our figures are based on births that occurred in 1998 and 1999.

We investigated a number of possible reasons for the discrepancy in cohabitation rates among blacks. In the appendix to this chapter, we present evidence that sampling differences are not responsible for the different estimates. A second hypothesis is that various ways of ascertaining cohabitation status can lead to significant differences in estimates. The Fragile Families data collected from different cohabitation status checkpoints lend some support to this hypothesis. In addition to the direct question on cohabitation ("Are you and [name of partner] living together?"), the Fragile Families Study collects information on the mother's household roster. It also asks her to list all the adults other than herself with whom the child will live. Mothers are less likely to list the father on the household roster or as one of the adults with whom the child will live than they are to report that they are cohabiting with the father. If we restrict the definition of cohabitation to include one of these other criteria, the estimates of cohabitation decrease substantially. The sixth row of table 7.3 shows the most conservative estimate, based on mothers' affirmative response to all three criteria: she cohabits with the father, lists the father on the household roster, *and* lists the father as one of the adults with whom the child will live. The more restrictive estimates are very close to the estimates reported by Bumpass and Lu (2000), who match relationship histories with children's birth dates. However, it is unclear which measure most *appropriately* captures cohabitation. The sensitivity of the estimates to the different measures suggests that cohabitation status is somewhat ambiguous. The figures in table 7.3 show that this is especially true for blacks, for whom the most restrictive measure reduces cohabitation estimates by about one-third. At the other extreme, estimates for Hispanics are much less sensitive to these restrictions. Additional evidence from in-depth interviews with a subset of parents in the Fragile Families study indicates that a substantial portion of non-cohabiting parents spend the night together several times a week, lending further support to the idea that cohabitation is an ambiguous concept.[7]

Finally, we hypothesized that the difference between the Fragile Families estimates and those based on the NSFG data are due to differences in when the questions were asked. The Bumpass and Lu

Table 7.3 Alternative Indicators of Cohabitation in the
Fragile Families Seven-City Sample, by Race-
Ethnicity, from Mother Baseline Interviews

	White Non-Hispanic	Black Non-Hispanic	Hispanic
Living together	57%	39%	61%
Baby will live with both parents	54	33	59
Father on household roster	50	35	57
Reporting living together and baby will live with both parents	52	30	57
Reporting living together and father on household roster	47	34	56
Reporting living together, baby will live with both parents, and father on household roster	46	27	53

Source: Authors' compilation.

(2000) estimates are based on retrospective data. Women in their sample were interviewed between zero and five years after the birth of their child. The Fragile Families estimates are based on information obtained shortly after the birth of the child. It is possible that cohabiting relationships that end soon after the birth of the child are not reported in retrospective surveys. We are able to partially reject this hypothesis by comparing reports obtained from the mothers' baseline questionnaires with reports obtained in the twelve-month interviews. The latter asks mothers, once again, whether they were living with the father when the child was born. We were able to carry out this test on the subset of mothers who had completed the twelve-month interviews—mothers in Oakland and Austin. Table 7.4 indicates there is only a trivial difference in reports at the two different time points. Note that our retrospective question covers only a single year. It is possible that questions covering a longer time frame would show a greater discrepancy with baseline reports.

Our exploration of the potential sources of differences between the NSFG and Fragile Families estimates of nonmarital cohabitation leads us to the following conclusion. The measures of cohabitation themselves may be responsible in part for the differences. Cohabitation estimates based on household rosters or expectations about

Table 7.4 Mothers' Reports of Cohabitation in the Fragile Families Seven-City Baseline Sample, by Race-Ethnicity (Two Cities)

	White Non-Hispanic	Black Non-Hispanic	Hispanic
Living together (baseline reports of mothers interviewed at twelve months)	60%	43%	62%
Living together at baseline (mother's report at twelve months)	62	43	62
Number of mothers	47	189	187

Source: Authors' compilation.

who the baby will live with produce substantially lower estimates than do responses to direct questions. However, given that the NSFG does not require as restricted a definition as our three combined criteria, this is unlikely to be the only explanation. One additional possibility is that cohabitation rates have increased substantially among blacks in the last decade, as they did among whites and to a lesser extent among Hispanics during the previous decade. Although it matters a great deal how we define cohabitation from a research perspective, what may matter most from a policy perspective is the finding that cohabitation is an ambiguous status and that certain cases are particularly fragile in this regard. There may be only trivial differences between racial groups in the proportion who are in romantic relationships at the time of the birth, but there are clear differences between racial and ethnic groups in terms of the stability and ambiguity of these relationships. Hispanics are the most likely to be unambiguously involved with each other. Blacks are as likely to be on romantic or friendly terms as other groups but are much less likely to be in marriage-like relationships. Whites fall somewhere in between.

Fathers' Behaviors and Intentions   Not only are most unmarried parents romantically involved at the time of the birth, but, as shown in table 7.5, most fathers also contributed financially during the pregnancy and intend to continue their involvement with the mother and child. About four out of five fathers contributed financially during the pregnancy, and three-quarters visited the mothers in the hospital (by the time the mother was interviewed). Future inten-

Table 7.5 Fathers' Behaviors and Intentions in Fragile
Families Seven-City Baseline Sample, by
Cohabitation Status

	Cohabiting	Not Cohabiting	Total
Father provided financial support during pregnancy (mother's report)	95%	69%	81%
Father visited mother in hospital (mother's report)	92	60	74
Baby will have father's surname (mother's report)	91	64	76
Father's name will be on birth certificate (mother's report)	97	79	87
Father intends to contribute (mother's report)	100	82	90
Mother wants father to be involved in raising child	100	87	93
Number of mothers	795	984	1,779

Source: Authors' compilation.

tions are even more positive: three out of four babies will have their
father's last name, slightly more have fathers who plan to contribute
financially, 87 percent of babies will have their father's name on the
birth certificate, and, perhaps most important, 93 percent of the
mothers want the fathers to be involved. Even among non-cohabi-
tors, 87 percent of the mothers want the fathers to be involved (see
table 7.5).

The myth that unwed fathers are not around at the time of the
birth could not be further from the truth. Though many of these
unmarried couples do not live together, they view themselves as
collaborative family units. This finding is true across all race-ethnic
groups. To the extent that small differences exist, involvement and
expectations for future involvement tend to be highest among
blacks (see table 7.6).

Finally, when asked about the future of their relationship, most
parents express optimism. About 80 percent of both cohabiting
mothers and fathers intend to marry their partner, and most of the
parents who are romantically involved but not living together plan
to live together or get married (about 75 percent of mothers and 90
percent of fathers who were interviewed) (results not shown in tables).[8]

Table 7.6 Fathers' Behaviors and Intentions in the Fragile Families Seven-City Baseline Sample, by Race-Ethnicity

	White Non-Hispanic	Black Non-Hispanic	Hispanic
Father provided financial support during pregnancy (mother's report)	73%	82%	80%
Father visited mother in hospital (mother's report)	76	73	79
Baby will have father's surname (mother's report)	73	74	87
Father's name will be on birth certificate (mother's report)	83	88	89
Father intends to contribute (mother's report)	85	91	90
Mother wants father to be involved in raising child	90	94	91

Source: Authors' compilation.

CAPABILITIES OF UNWED PARENTS

Clearly, parents' expectations about their relationship and the father's involvement are extremely high at the time of the birth. Whether these high expectations will be realized, however, depends at least in part on whether the parents have the resources they need to meet them. The Fragile Families Study collects data on parents' education, income, reliance on public assistance, and psycho-social risk factors, all of which are known to be good predictors of relationship stability.

Human Capital   Table 7.7 indicates that lack of education is a serious problem for these unmarried parents. Over 40 percent of the mothers and 35 percent of the fathers lack a high school degree. Three-quarters have no more than a high school degree. In today's world, where advanced training and education are increasingly important for employment and income stability, these numbers do not bode well for the future of these new parents. Hispanics are the worst off—61 and 57 percent, respectively, of mothers and fathers have not completed high school.

Table 7.7 Mothers' and Fathers' Human Capital in
Fragile Families Seven-City Baseline Sample,
by Race-Ethnicity

	White Non-Hispanic	Black Non-Hispanic	Hispanic	Total*
Mothers (from mother's report)				
Mothers with less than high school degree	33%	36%	61%	41%
Mothers with high school education only	35	40	26	36
Mothers who worked in past year	84	76	66	75
Mothers on welfare in past year	45	49	36	46
Mother's household income (mean)	$33,000	$22,000	$20,000	$22,000
Fathers				
Fathers with less than high school degree (mother's report)	29%	30%	57%	35%
Fathers with high school education (mother's report)	45	48	29	44
Fathers who worked in past year (mother's report)	83	79	84	80
Father's earnings (mean)	$23,000	$16,000	$15,000	$16,000

Source: Authors' compilation.
*Includes all women, even those who are not white, black, or Hispanic.

The financial resources of unwed parents are also limited. Although most mothers report that they worked the previous year, their average household income was $22,000, and close to half of the mothers received some support from public assistance, welfare, or food stamps (see table 7.7). The circumstances of fathers are no better. Among the fathers who were interviewed, the previous year's earnings averaged $16,000. Given the characteristics of the men who were *not* interviewed, the actual average income is likely to be even lower.

Table 7.8 Mothers' and Fathers' Risk Factors in Fragile Families Seven-City Baseline Sample, by Race-Ethnicity

	White Non-Hispanic	Black Non-Hispanic	Hispanic	Total
Mother has substance abuse problem (mother's report)	18%	14%	5%	12%
Father has substance abuse problem (mother's report)	15	5	7	6
Father is violent (mother's report)	4	5	7	5

Source: Authors' compilation.

Risk Factors   Approximately 12 percent of mothers and 6 percent of fathers have drug or alcohol problems, according to mothers' reports (see table 7.8). These figures are likely to be underestimates of the true rates.[9] There is substantial variation by race/ethnicity, with whites having the highest rates.

We discussed earlier the concern that child support enforcement and other policies designed to increase the involvement of fathers might put mothers at risk if the father is violent or has other psycho-social problems. These fears are justifiable in certain instances, but they do not accurately characterize the majority of unwed fathers. Overall, 5 percent of mothers reported being the object of some violent or abusive behavior on the part of the father. Again, the figures for violence and abuse are likely to be underestimates of true prevalence. It is important to be able to identify the fathers who are dangerous to mothers and children. It is also important to not let this small minority of fathers drive social policy toward all unwed fathers.

IMPLICATIONS FOR POLICY

The early findings from the Fragile Families Study reported in this chapter have important implications for social policy, particularly welfare and child support policy. Because these new parents are unmarried, they are automatically affected by child support policies. Because a large proportion of these couples have low earnings capacity, welfare policy is also likely to play a major role in their family formation decisions.   🐾

STRENGTHENING BONDS IN FRAGILE FAMILIES

That public policy should strive to reinforce the bonds between unwed fathers and mothers is not obvious. If a large proportion of either the mothers or fathers have no interest in, or are hostile to, co-parenting their child, attempts to strengthen these fragile family ties might be futile at best and harmful at worst. We know that parental conflict is harmful to children, and encouraging co-parenting among parents who do not get along is likely to increase parental conflict. One of the most important findings from the Fragile Families survey is the fact that the vast majority of unwed parents view themselves as families. At the time of the child's birth, 82 percent of unwed parents are still in a romantic relationship, about 80 percent believe their chances of marriage are good, and over 90 percent of the mothers want the father to be involved in raising the child. These findings suggest that, at a minimum, policies designed to strengthen fragile families are consistent with parents' objectives and therefore not foredoomed to failure.

Similarly, if many unwed fathers are violent toward the mothers or abuse drugs or alcohol, promoting father involvement might not be in the best interest of mothers and children. Many critics of welfare reform and stronger child support enforcement have argued that these policies are likely to increase domestic violence. Again, the information presented in this chapter suggests that only a small fraction of unwed fathers pose such a threat to mothers and children. Only 6 percent of mothers report that the father has a problem with drugs or alcohol, and only 5 percent report that he is physically abusive. Moreover, some mothers who report that the father is abusive or has a problem with drugs or alcohol are *currently in a romantic relationship with the father and want him involved in raising the child.* Thus, even in problem cases there are good reasons for treating unwed parents as a family unit and for trying to shape programs that help them deal with their problems (for example, training in conflict resolution or substance abuse treatment).

Given that strengthening fragile families appears to be a reasonable objective, we must ask whether our current policies are consistent with this objective. In many ways, current welfare and child support policies undermine rather than strengthen fragile family ties. To the extent that welfare policies or practices favor one-parent families over two-parent families, they discourage marriage and cohabitation and push fathers out of the picture. Under the old AFDC program, two-parent families in which the father worked more than one hundred hours per month were ineligible for assistance, and many states restricted the eligibility of two-parent families in other ways as well. More recently, state TANF programs appear to have reduced or eliminated most of these restrictions for two-parent families.

The absence of categorical restrictions, however, is not sufficient to make welfare policy neutral with respect to family formation. Because welfare is income-tested and tries to capture the economies of scale that result from living together, it creates an incentive for couples to live apart from one another (or feign living apart) when the father has earnings and the mother does not. Because ascertaining whether a couple lives together is costly, and because marriage creates the presumption of cohabitation, welfare encourages cohabitation over marriage. It also encourages non-coresidence over cohabitation.

One way to reduce the disincentives to marriage and cohabitation in welfare policy is to ensure that fathers who live apart from their children pay child support. Child support increases the costs of living separately. During the last twenty years, we have made substantial headway in increasing paternity establishment and child support payments among unwed fathers. (For a more complete discussion of this issue, see Garfinkel et al. 1998.) Further progress along these lines is desirable. But child support enforcement alone will not be sufficient. As discussed in more detail later, if child support obligations are grossly inconsistent with fathers' ability to pay, they may drive fathers away and discourage father involvement.

Another way to reduce the disincentives to marriage and cohabitation in welfare policy would be to count only a portion of fathers' earnings when determining eligibility and benefits for TANF. The problem with this solution is that it would increase welfare costs and caseloads. The time limits and work requirements of the new TANF program, however, limit these extra costs.

A third way to encourage marriage among fragile families is to expand policies outside of welfare. The Earned Income Tax Credit (EITC) is a good example of a policy that does just this. A father with earnings of $10,000 and a mother with one child and no earnings stand to gain over $3,000 from the EITC if they live together. On the other hand, the EITC, like the income tax of which it is a part, contains not only marriage bonuses but marriage penalties.

The incentives in the EITC and child support are more recent, and the former is much less well understood than the disincentives in the welfare system. Thus, part of the problem is knowledge. Welfare, paternity establishment and child support, and other programs need to do a better job of informing unwed parents about the relative benefits and costs of living together and getting married. It would also be helpful, though somewhat costly in terms of revenues lost, to eliminate the marriage penalties in the EITC and, more broadly, the federal income tax.

ADDRESSING FATHERS' LOW EARNINGS CAPACITY

The findings presented in this chapter show that a substantial proportion of unwed fathers have very low education and are not able to pay much child support. A major problem with the current child support system is that it frequently imposes child support obligations on low-income fathers that are unreasonably high. A large number of these unrealistic obligations arise because child support agencies or the courts base orders not on fathers' actual earnings but on presumptive minimum earnings (for example, the minimum wage for full-time, year-round work) or on how much the father earned in the past. Some fathers are required to pay back the mother's welfare or Medicaid costs. Finally, many fathers who become unemployed or incarcerated build up huge arrearages during these periods of unemployment. Such onerous child support obligations are rarely paid in full, but they do prompt fathers to avoid legitimate work for which their wages are easily attached, and they breed resentment on the part of fathers and mothers toward the system and perhaps each other. Given what we know about the low earnings capacity of many unwed fathers, these practices are not likely to be effective and are likely to have unintended negative consequences.

The most fundamental problem with the public child support system is that it does almost nothing to help fathers. At its inception, the federal office of child support enforcement viewed itself exclusively as a law enforcement agency. Federal and state offices of child support enforcement have come a long way since the early 1980s—including co-sponsoring experiments to help fathers obtain access to their children and experiments such as Parents' Fair Share to help fathers meet their child support obligations. But isolated experiments are not the same as institutional change. It is particularly important for low-income fathers that child support enforcement become a social welfare as well as a law enforcement agency. Only a small proportion of divorced fathers need help meeting their child support obligations. In contrast, a substantial proportion of unwed fathers need help. Whereas middle-class fathers typically establish visitation rights as part of their divorce agreements, low-income fathers rarely do so. This is because child support orders for low-income fathers are initiated by a state agency.

More generally, welfare and child support need to become father-friendly and family-friendly. If the parents reside together, they should be treated as a family by TANF, and services should be provided to fathers as well as mothers. The services for fathers, like those for mothers in TANF, should be geared primarily toward obtaining employment. In contrast to TANF, we would recommend that when either the mother or father demonstrates the potential to benefit from educational or other human investments, welfare support the upgrading of human capital.

Fathers who live with the mother and child should be required to establish paternity, but should not be required to pay child support. At the same time, most or all of the father's income should be counted in determining the mother's welfare eligibility and benefit level.

If the parents live apart, fathers should be required to pay child support, but the amount of the obligation should be proportional to their ability to pay. Paternity establishment and child support enforcement also should help fathers establish their rights to visitation. In short, both child support enforcement and welfare need to provide services to low-income fathers to help them make the best possible use of their limited human capital and, where appropriate, to encourage them to upgrade that capital.

The birth of a child is a very special moment for both parents. Thus, establishing the paternity of unwed fathers at the hospital gives the child support enforcement system a unique entrée into the lives of unwed mothers and fathers. Targeting services, such as education and job training, conflict resolution, and substance abuse treatment, at fathers soon after the birth of their new baby is also likely to have a greater payoff than offering them services years later, after their relationship with the mother has ended.

APPENDIX: DO SAMPLING DIFFERENCES ACCOUNT FOR HIGH BLACK COHABITATION RATES?

The Fragile Families and NSFG samples have slightly different age restrictions, and the Fragile Families sample is limited to large urban areas. The Fragile Families study does not restrict the upper age limit to thirty-nine years, as does the NSFG. On the other hand, it does have lower end age restrictions by not including mothers under eighteen in all hospitals. Since less than 2 percent of the Fragile Families unwed mothers are forty or older, it was only the differences in the proportion of teen mothers that we were concerned about. Nationally, 12 percent of unmarried births are to minors, compared to only 4 percent in the Fragile Families seven-city sample (see table 7.1). We reran our estimates using only the subset of eight hospitals where we included mothers of all ages, and the cohabitation figures did not change for any race or ethnic group.

The first seven cities in the Fragile Families study, on which our estimates of cohabitation are based, are not representative of unwed parents in all urban areas, and are even less representative of unwed parents in the United States. Although the Fragile Families cities are more distressed on average than the nation as a whole, there is considerable variation among them in this regard. When we look at cohabitation rates by city, only Detroit stands out as having significantly different (lower) cohabitation rates. Newark and Baltimore, which are as distressed as Detroit, have average or slightly higher cohabitation rates. The lack of a clear relationship between level of distress and cohabitation rates *within* the Fragile Families cities leads us to believe that the high level of distress of the seven Fragile Families cities overall does not explain the differential rates of cohabitation for blacks in the Fragile Families and NSFG samples.

Fewer than half of nonmarital black births in the United States are in places with less than 100,000 people (Ventura et al. 1995).

Thus, the cohabitation rate would have to be zero in these places in order for the lack of small cities and rural areas in the Fragile Families sample to explain the difference in cohabitation rates between the two samples.

We are grateful to Ofira Schwartz, Christina Norland, and Joseph Marchand for preparing the tables. The Fragile Families study is supported by grants from the A. L. Mailman Family Foundation, the Bendheim Thoman Center for Research on Child Wellbeing, the California HealthCare Foundation, the Charles Stewart Mott Foundation, Christian A. Johnson Endeavor Foundation, the Commonwealth Fund, the David and Lucile Packard Foundation, the Ford Foundation, the Foundation for Child Development, the Fund for New Jersey, the Healthcare Foundation of New Jersey, the Hogg Foundation, the John D. and Catherine T. MacArthur Foundation, the Kronkosky Charitable Foundation, Leon Lowenstein Foundation, the National Institute of Child Health and Human Development, National Science Foundation, the Public Policy Institute of California, the Robert Wood Johnson Foundation, the St. David's Hospital Foundation, St. Vincent Hospitals and Health Services in Indianapolis, the U.S. Department of Health and Human Services (ASPE and ACF), the William and Flora Hewlett Foundation, and the William T. Grant Foundation.

NOTES

1. Willis (1996) offers an economic explanation for the same behavior. He argues that unmarried women allow men to "free ride" (in terms of supporting their children) when there is a surplus of women and when women have an alternative source of support (for example, welfare).
2. Nonresident father status is also underreported in the NLSY, though the proportion of underreporting is somewhat lower.
3. In Newark, 58 percent of unwed fathers were interviewed.
4. Mothers who were less than eighteen years old were not interviewed in all hospitals because of parental consent restrictions imposed by some hospital institutional review boards.
5. Wherever possible, we use mothers' reports about fathers rather than fathers' own reports because the mothers' response rates are higher

than the fathers', and therefore they provide us with a less biased description of all fathers.

6. Since our seven-city sample overrepresents blacks and Hispanics, we adjusted the cohabitation rate by applying the racial/ethnic proportions in table 7.1 to the cohabitation rates for each group.

7. This information comes from research conducted by the MacArthur Network on the Family and the Economy.

8. The father reports are likely to be overestimated because they are based only on the unwed fathers who completed interviews.

9. The disparity between mothers' and fathers' rates is due to the more specific indicators (including drug use during pregnancy) for moms. Those numbers are more likely not to be underestimated as fathers' drug use.

REFERENCES

Anderson, Elijah. 1989. "Sex Codes and Family Life Among Poor Inner-City Youths." *Annals of the American Academy of Political and Social Science* 501: 59–78.

Bumpass, Larry, and Hsien-Hen Lu. 2000. "Trends in Cohabitation and Implications for Children's Family Contexts in the United States." *Population Studies* 54: 29–41.

Bumpass, Larry, and James Sweet. 1989. "National Estimates of Cohabitation: Cohort Levels and Union Stability." *Demography* 26: 615–25.

Cherlin, Andrew, Jeanne Griffith, and James McCarthy. 1983. "A Note on Maritally Disrupted Men's Reports of Child Support in June 1980 Current Population Survey." *Demography* 20(3): 385–89.

Duncan, Greg J., and Jeanne Brooks-Gunn. 1997. *Consequences of Growing up Poor.* New York: Russell Sage Foundation.

Edin, Katherine. 1997. "Why Don't Poor Fathers and Mothers Get Married?" Paper presented at the Urban Poverty Workshop, University of Chicago (March).

Edin, Katherine, and Laura Lein. 1997. *Making Ends Meet: How Single Mothers Survive Welfare and Low-Wage Work.* New York: Russell Sage Foundation.

Furstenberg, Frank F., Mary E. Hughes, and Jeanne Brooks-Gunn. 1992. "The Next Generation: The Children of Teenage Mothers Grow Up." In *Early Parenthood and the Coming of Age in the 1990s,* edited by Margaret K. Rosenheim and Mark F. Testa. New Brunswick, N.J.: Rutgers University Press.

Garfinkel, Irwin, Sara McLanahan, and Thomas Hanson. 1998. "A Patchwork Portrait of Nonresident Fathers." In *Fathers Under Fire: The Revolution in Child Support Enforcement.* New York: Russell Sage Foundation.

Liebow, Elliot. 1967. *Tally's Corner: A Study of Negro Streetcorner Men.* Boston: Little, Brown and Co.

Marsiglio, William, and Randal Day. 1997. "Social Fatherhood and Paternal Involvement: Conceptual Data and Policymaking Issues." Report prepared for the NICHD Conference on Fathering and Male Fertility: Improving Data and Research, Bethesda, Maryland, March 13–14.

McLanahan, Sara, and Gary Sandefur. 1994. *Growing Up with a Single Parent.* Cambridge, Mass.: Harvard University Press.

McLanahan, Sara, Irwin Garfinkel, Jeanne Brooks-Gunn, and Hongxin Zhao. 1997. "Fragile Families." Working paper #98–12, Princeton University, Center for Research on Child Wellbeing.

Raphael, Jody, and Richard M. Tolman. 1997. *Trapped by Poverty and Trapped by Abuse: New Evidence Documenting the Relationship Between Domestic Violence and Welfare: Executive Summary.* Chicago: Taylor Institute.

Reichman, Nancy E., Irwin Garfinkel, Sara McLanahan, and Julien O. Teitler. 2001. "Fragile Families: Sample and Design." *Children and Youth Services Review* 23(4): 303–26.

Rendall, Michael S., Lynda Clarke, H. Elizabeth Peters, Nalini Ranjit, and Georgia Verropoulou. 1999. "Incomplete Reporting of Male Fertility in the United States and Britain: A Research Note." *Demography* 36(1): 135–44.

Sorensen, Elaine. 1995. "Noncustodial Fathers: Can They Afford to Pay More Child Support?" Unpublished paper. Washington: Urban Institute.

Ventura, Stephanie J., Christine A. Bachrach, Laura Hill, Kelleen Kaye, Pamela Holcomb, and Elisa Koff. 1995. "The Demography of Out-of-Wedlock Childbearing." In *Report to Congress on Out-of-Wedlock Childbearing.* U.S. Department of Health and Human Services. *Vital and Health Statistics,* series 21, no. 56. Hyattsville, Md.: National Center for Health Statistics.

Waller, Maureen. 1997. "Redefining Fatherhood: Paternal Involvement, Masculinity, and Responsibility in the 'Other America.'" Ph.D. diss., Princeton University.

Willis, Robert. 1996. "Father Involvement: Theoretical Perspectives from Economics." Prepared for Conference on Fathers' Involvement, NICHD Family and Child Well-being Network, Bethesda, Md., October 10–11.

CHAPTER 8

The Changing Role of Child Support Among Never-Married Mothers

Judi Bartfeld and Daniel R. Meyer

The prevalence and economic hardship of single-parent families are major topics of concern. About half of all children are predicted to spend some time in a single-parent family (Bumpass and Raley 1995). This is particularly troubling because of the economic vulnerability of these families: over 40 percent of mother-only families fall below the official poverty line (Dalaker and Naifeh 1998). Economic hardship is especially pronounced among families headed by a never-married mother: for example, mean family income of never-married mothers is half that of previously married mothers, while the poverty rate among never-married mothers is twice that of previously married mothers—59 percent versus 31 percent.[1]

The economic plight of single-parent families, coupled with the heavy reliance of such families on public assistance, has led to an increased focus on private child support as a potential source of additional income. By private child support we refer to cash transfers made by nonresident parents to help support their children. The child support system has undergone substantial changes in the last twenty-five years. Legislation has targeted all stages of the process leading to child support collection, including efforts to promote paternity establishment, ensure that support orders are issued, increase the value of support ordered, and strengthen the enforcement system (Garfinkel, Meyer, and McLanahan 1998).

The welfare system has likewise been the subject of considerable attention. Beginning with the Family Support Act of 1988, the welfare system has increasingly emphasized job training and work requirements, and the 1990s saw a proliferation of waivers to run increasingly strict welfare programs in many states. These changes culminated in historic legislation replacing the Aid to Families with Dependent Children (AFDC) program with Temporary Assistance to Needy Families (TANF) in 1996. Among the more dramatic changes under TANF is the five-year lifetime limit on the receipt of benefits. The time-limited nature of benefits, combined with the restrictive nature of many state TANF programs, suggests that non-welfare income sources are becoming increasingly important to the long-term economic well-being of mother-only families. The current and potential role of child support as an ongoing income source to mother-only families is thus a critical topic, but it is not well understood.

The purpose of this chapter is to document the changing role of child support as an income source to never-married mothers during the 1990s. We focus on changes as children age and also on changes across years. To do this, we track the experience of successive cohorts of mothers as their children age, using synthetic cohorts of never-married mothers created from multiple panels of the Current Population Survey (CPS). Although our primary emphasis is on child support, we place our child support results in context by examining concurrent changes in other income sources. We focus our attention on 1989 to 1997, a period of profound change in the relative availability of public and private forms of support.

CHILD SUPPORT PATTERNS: BACKGROUND

Despite substantial changes in child support policy, aggregate child support outcomes did not change a great deal between 1978 and 1995 (Scoon-Rogers and Lester 1995; Scoon-Rogers 1999). Throughout this period, between 50 and 60 percent of resident mothers were owed support, about three-quarters of those mothers received some payment, and all outcomes were substantially better for divorced and separated mothers than for never-married mothers.

These aggregate outcomes mask improvements among some subgroups, however, particularly among never-married mothers. The paternity establishment rate for nonmarital births, measured as the number of paternities established in a year divided by the number of nonmarital births in the year, increased from 29 percent in 1987 to 46 percent in 1994 (U.S. House of Representatives 1998). Among all never-married mothers, the percentage with a child support order increased from about one-tenth in 1978 to more than one-third in 1995 (Scoon-Rogers 1999). The percentage of never-married mothers who actually receive child support has increased as well, from about 5 percent in the late 1970s to more than 15 percent in the late 1990s (Sorensen and Halpern 1999).

This evidence suggests that child support outcomes among never-married mothers have been improving over time, but we know very little about changes over time from the perspective of a particular cohort of mothers.[2] As a result, the extent to which time trends reflect improved outcomes among new versus existing mothers is not apparent. We know little about how child support outcomes change as children grow older, or about how such outcomes differ among mothers whose children were born at different times.

Theoretical models of child support transfers offer only limited insight into how child support might change as children grow older. Such models typically posit that child support transfers are affected by the nonresident parent's ability to pay, by the economic needs of the resident parent, by the strength of the ties between the nonresident parent and his or her ex-partner and children, and by the stringency of the child support system (e.g. Bartfeld and Meyer 1994; Beller and Graham 1993). These factors would have opposing influences on child support patterns. Because nonresident fathers' ability to pay typically increases over time, especially among fathers in nonmarital cases (Meyer 1995; Phillips and Garfinkel 1993), support could increase as children get older. The strengthening of the support system could likewise lead to an increase in support, since children in recent years have been growing up in tandem with a system that is becoming increasingly strict. On the other hand, ties between nonresident fathers and their children are thought to decline with time, potentially leading to lower child support. The Fragile Families study, discussed in chapter 7, provides valuable information about how father-child relations change over time and the implications for child support transfers.

Only limited efforts have been made to document changing patterns of child support over time using a case-based versus a calendar-based concept of time. Most of these efforts are limited to divorce cases and involve the use of cross-sectional data to compare support outcomes at varying intervals following separation or divorce. This research finds that the probability and amount of support is lower when more time has elapsed since the separation (Beller and Graham 1993; Seltzer 1991; Garfinkel and Robins 1994). An important limitation of this work is that the types of child support–eligible cases are changing (Beller and Graham

1993), as is the policy environment. Apparent differences between short-term and long-term child support outcomes could thus be confounded by cohort effects. That is, cross-sectional differences between child support outcomes in short-term and long-term cases could be reflecting differences over time in the characteristics of child support–eligible cases.

Recent research in Wisconsin uses longitudinal data to track aggregate and case-level child support outcomes over time, an approach that eliminates possible cohort effects by following a single cohort of single mothers (Meyer and Bartfeld 1998; Meyer and Hernandez 1999). Among nonmarital cases with paternity established between 1988 and 1992, aggregate compliance ratios declined only slightly over the first five years in which support was owed, from .48 to .46 (Meyer and Hernandez 1999). Results for an earlier cohort—1986 to 1988—showed a similar pattern, though compliance levels were higher (Meyer and Bartfeld 1998). There are no such cohort-based analyses of child support outcomes at the national level.

Research on child support receipts suggests that child support among never-married mothers continues to be relatively uncommon, but that among mothers who do receive support the amounts are not trivial. Although only 21 percent of never-married custodial mothers received child support in 1995, the average amount among those receiving support was $2,297, out of an average annual income of $13,889 (Scoon-Rogers 1999).

Child support trends over time are typically explored in isolation from trends in other income components. However, the previously noted gains in child support among never-married mothers suggest that the importance of child support as a component of mothers' income packages may be increasing. This could be compounded by recent declines in welfare participation among single mothers. The share of single mothers receiving welfare income, which hovered around 30 percent from the late 1970s to the late 1980s, fell from 29 percent to 23 percent between 1988 and 1996 (Meyer and Rosenbaum 1998). Furthermore, the failure of welfare benefits to keep pace with inflation over the past decades (U.S. House of Representatives 1998) suggests that welfare has become a less important part of the income package of many young mothers. Declining welfare receipts would increase the relative importance of other income sources, including child support. Reductions in welfare receipt would also have a direct impact on the amount of child support received by mothers: nonwelfare recipients receive all child support paid on their behalf, whereas welfare recipients receive only a portion, with the remainder retained by the state as partial reimbursement for welfare costs. If fewer mothers receive welfare, the amount of child support received will increase even if there is no increase in the amount paid.

On the other hand, there has been a substantial increase in the labor supply of single mothers, particularly over the past decade. Meyer and Rosenbaum (1998) report that the share of single mothers who worked in the past year increased from 73 percent to 82 percent between 1984 and 1996. This change occurred in conjunction with a decline in the availability of welfare benefits, as well as with strong growth in the performance of the economy. The gains from earnings could offset the decline in welfare receipt, and if larger than the gains from child support, could lead to a reduction in the relative importance of child support as a component of total income. As with the aggregate child support outcomes discussed earlier, we know little about the extent to which the changes in welfare participation and employment reflect changes across cohorts, or changes within particular cohorts as children age.

This chapter provides information on the changing role of child support as an income source for never-married mothers. We explore the income packages of several recent cohorts of never-married mothers, groups that face a substantially different policy regime from each other and from previous cohorts. By using a synthetic cohort approach, we disentangle changes in child support across cohorts from changes over time within a child's life. We place our child support results in a broader context by considering child support changes in tandem with changes in other income components. In doing so, we provide national evidence of the income patterns over time among recent cohorts of never-married mothers.

DATA AND METHODS

DATA AND SAMPLE

We draw our sample from the 1990 to 1998 March CPS, which provides us with detailed income data for the calendar years 1989 to 1997. The CPS approximates a representative national cross-section of the population.

Our primary sample includes never-married mothers whose oldest resident child was born between 1988 and 1995. We organize this sample into four successive cohorts of mothers—those who first became mothers in 1988 to 1989, in 1990 to 1991, in 1992 to 1993, and in 1994 to 1995. For each "synthetic cohort" we have income data for a period of two to eight years. For instance, for women who became mothers in 1989, we sample from March 1991 to March 1998, gathering income data for the calendar years 1990 to 1997, during which period the child born in 1989 was age zero to seven. Our total sample includes 6,003 mothers, with 197 to 377 mothers in each age-year cell (see Table 8A.1).[3]

The CPS is the best available data source for this analysis. Because it contains very recent data—through calendar year 1997—we can capture the effect of recent policy changes. Moreover, the overall sample is large enough to contain sufficient numbers of never-married mothers in each biennium to examine changes over time for multiple cohorts. Although it is not longitudinal, synthetic cohorts can be constructed that mimic key features of longitudinal data.

Although the data are in many ways well suited to this analysis, there are nevertheless some important limitations stemming from the lack of detailed information on either marital history or household relationships. We discuss these limitations later.

METHODS

Descriptive Data on Child Support Patterns   We begin by presenting descriptive data to illustrate the role of child support as an income source, focusing on changes as children age as well as changes across cohorts. Specifically, we illustrate the trajectory of child support outcomes as children age, looking separately at mothers of children born in successive two-year periods. We use weighted data and report child support amounts in constant 1997 dollars. We expect that later cohorts will have more favorable child support outcomes, reflecting the increasing emphasis on child support enforcement during the 1990s. The decreasing availability of public assistance in the latter half of the decade would also lead to higher child support receipts among those who otherwise would have had some support payments retained by the state to reimburse AFDC costs. As discussed earlier, the expected pattern of child support outcomes as children age is ambiguous.

Determinants of Child Support Receipt   We next use a multivariate approach to determine which factors are associated with receipt of child support among never-married mothers. A particular emphasis is on understanding the changing likelihood of receiving support as children age, controlling for demographic and time variables that also play a role. We estimate a probit model, with the dependent variable the receipt of any child support. Our primary independent variables of interest are a series of dummy variables for age of child (one through seven, with zero omitted) and a series of year dummy variables (1990 to 1997, with 1989 omitted). Note that the year refers to the calendar year that serves as the reference for income, which is the year prior to when the CPS data are collected. We include a variety of demographic variables that theory and prior research suggest may influence the likelihood of child support receipt: race (dummy variables for black, Hispanic, and other non-white); mother's age at birth (twenty to twenty-four, twenty-five to twenty-nine, and thirty or older, with teens omitted); and mother's education (high school graduate and college, with less than high school omitted). We further control for subsequent children, region, urban versus rural location, and current cohabitation status.[4] We use our model to generate predicted probabilities of receiving child support for a range of prototypical cases.

Child Support Relative to Other Income Sources   Our final analyses place child support in a broader context by exploring the changing importance of child support vis-à-vis other income sources. We present descriptive data on the changing likelihood of receiving public assistance and earnings and also present data on the relative contribution of child support and several other income sources to total income. We divide income into the following broad categories: child support, public assistance, other transfers, earnings, and all other income.

LIMITATIONS

The primary limitation of this data source is the lack of detailed information on either marital history or household relationships.

This affects the population to which we can generalize over time in two key ways.

First, we are unable to identify currently married or divorced mothers who originally became mothers owing to a nonmarital birth. Thus, we limit our attention to *never-married* mothers: those who had a nonmarital birth and remain unmarried x years later. Our target population therefore decreases over time. We can get some sense of the magnitude of this decline both from existing research on marriage rates following nonmarital childbearing and from changes in our weighted sample size as children age. Research indicates that the marriage rate following nonmarital childbearing is relatively low. Bumpass and Lu (1998) found that among never-married women who became mothers between 1985 and 1989, only 36 percent of whites and 13 percent of blacks had married five years later; these rates have decreased dramatically over the past several decades. We can also explore this in our sample by comparing the weighted sample sizes when children are less than one year old to sample sizes when children are older. In cohort 1, for which the greatest number of years are available, our weighted sample size decreases by 15 percent by the fifth year and by 23 percent by the seventh year. To the extent that the outcomes of interest are correlated with the likelihood of marriage, our results could be misleading. We are not aware of empirical evidence that child support outcomes are associated with differential marriage rates, however, and theoretical arguments about the direction of the relationship between child support and marriage are ambiguous.

A second concern is that we are unable to identify which mothers are cohabiting with the father of their child. Conceptually, we would prefer to exclude all such mothers from our sample, because we think of them as more similar to married mothers than unmarried mothers. In particular, we would not expect most such mothers to receive child support income. Although policy is somewhat ambiguous on this issue, we expect that cohabiting fathers would be more likely to contribute directly to their children's economic needs on a day-to-day basis than to contribute through the formal child support system.

Many cohabiting parents are appropriately excluded from our sample. When the father is designated as the household head, the child is linked in the data to the father rather than the mother. These cases are of necessity excluded from our analysis because we cannot identify the unmarried mother as such. Because we would prefer to exclude such mothers, this is not problematic. On the other hand, if the parents are cohabiting and the mother is designated as the household head, the child is linked to the mother in the record. In these cases, we are unable to determine whether the mother is cohabiting with the child's father or a new partner, and the mothers are included in our sample.[5]

An additional limitation with the CPS is underreporting of income. Research suggests that never-married mothers tend to underreport their income, particularly "unofficial" income from child support, earnings, or other informal sources (see, for example, Edin and Lein 1997). Although we do expect that the incomes are biased downward, we do not expect this to occur differentially either across cohorts or across ages, the primary focus of our analyses.

RESULTS

CHILD SUPPORT AMONG NEVER-MARRIED MOTHERS

We begin with descriptive information on child support receipt among never-married mothers, focusing on changes as children age and changes across successive cohorts. Figure 8.1 shows the mean amount of child support received (in constant 1997 dollars) by mothers whose oldest child is age zero to seven, for cohorts 1 through 4. Three findings are apparent: mean child support receipts are quite low at all ages for all cohorts; within each cohort mean child support receipts generally increase as children age; and for children of a given age mean child support receipts are generally higher in later cohorts. Thus, mean child support receipts in cohort 1 increase from $149 when children are age zero to $430 by the time children reach age seven, though the increase is not smooth in the later years. At age one—the oldest for which data from all cohorts are available—mean child support receipts are $152 for cohort 1, $322 for cohort 2, $330 for cohort 3, and $382 for cohort 4.

Focusing on means masks substantial variation across mothers. Only a relatively small minority of mothers receive support, though for those who do, the amounts are not trivial. Figure 8.2 shows the percentage of mothers receiving support. Again, we see that the likelihood of receiving support increases as children age and also increases across cohorts. Among cohort 1, the share of mothers re-

Figure 8.1 Mean Child Support Received by Never-Married Mothers, by Cohort

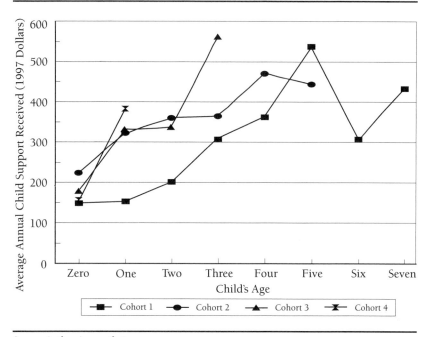

Source: Authors' compilation.
Note: Cohorts 1 through 4 represent never-married mothers who first became mothers in 1988 to 1989, in 1990 to 1991, in 1992 to 1993, and in 1994 to 1995, respectively.

ceiving support increases from 9 percent when children are age zero to 21 percent by age three, remaining roughly flat thereafter. Mothers in all four cohorts are equally likely to receive child support when their child is age zero (ranging from 9 to 11 percent), but as children age mothers in each successive cohort have higher receipt rates.[6] On the other hand, among those receiving something, there is no apparent pattern—either by age of child or by cohort—in the mean amount of support received (table 8.1).

Our reliance on a changing sample complicates the interpretation of these figures. With descriptive analyses, we are unable to differentiate between changes in the likelihood that a woman will receive child support as her child ages and changes in the characteristics of our target population (never-married mothers). It is possible that the women who leave our target population—those who marry—

Figure 8.2 Percentage of Never-Married Mothers
Receiving Child Support, by Cohort

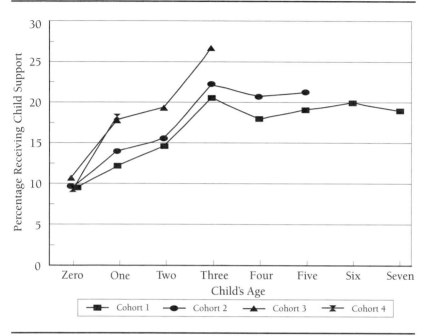

Source: Authors' compilation.
Note: Cohorts 1 through 4 represent never-married mothers who first became mothers in 1988 to 1989, in 1990 to 1991, in 1992 to 1993, and in 1994 to 1995, respectively.

have different child support patterns from those who remain. Like-wise, we are unable to determine whether cross-cohort differences reflect differential characteristics across cohorts or a differential environment faced by different cohorts.

DETERMINANTS OF CHILD SUPPORT RECEIPT: A MULTIVARIATE APPROACH

We use a multivariate approach to disentangle the role of the policy environment from the role of the child's age as determinants of child support receipt. This approach also allows us to control for measurable characteristics that could vary either across cohorts or across ages within a cohort (owing to differential patterns of fertility and marriage). As described earlier, we begin by estimating a probit model, with the dependent variable the receipt of any child

Table 8.1 Mean Child Support Received by Never-Married Mothers When Positive, by Cohort and Age of Children (1997 dollars)

	Zero	One	Two	Three	Four	Five	Six	Seven
Cohort 1	$1,618	$1,242	$1,365	$1,483	$2,002	$2,808	$1,527	$2,272
Cohort 2	$2,350	$2,288	$2,321	$1,620	$2,245	$2,070		
Cohort 3	$1,607	$1,837	$1,719	$2,083				
Cohort 4	$1,716	$2,076						

Source: Authors' compilation.

support. For this analysis, we use a somewhat broader sample: all never-married mothers identified in the 1990 to 1998 March CPS who have an oldest child age seven or younger. We thus pull in earlier cohorts and include a comparable range of child ages from each panel. Our sample for this analysis includes 9,671 cases.

Results are shown in table 8.2. The first panel shows coefficients on the year dummy variables (1989 omitted). Coefficients are positive, increase in magnitude through 1994, and remain roughly stable from 1994 to 1997, with coefficients for 1993 to 1997 statistically significant. All else equal, then, mothers became increasingly likely to receive child support during the mid-1990s, a gain that is maintained over the years considered here. As indicated in the second panel, the age of the child is also a significant predictor of whether mothers will receive support. Specifically, results suggest that mothers are increasingly likely to receive support over the first few years of their child's life, stabilizing at around age three. Taken together, the coefficients for the year and age variables imply that the patterns we saw earlier, in terms of higher rates of support within a cohort over the first few years of a child's life, reflect both a greater tendency to receive support on behalf of somewhat older children and an increasing likelihood of receiving support over the time period in question. Furthermore, these results suggest that the differences in the likelihood of receiving support across cohorts are not merely a reflection of observable differences in the characteristics of different cohorts. Likewise, they suggest that changes in support receipt as children age are not merely a result of changes in the characteristics of never-married mothers of older versus younger children.[7]

Table 8.2 also confirms the importance of a variety of demographic variables that previous studies have found to be predictors of support. In particular, results suggest that mothers age twenty to twenty-four at the birth of their child are more likely to receive support than are mothers who gave birth as teens; that blacks, Hispanics, and other minorities are less likely than are whites to receive support; that the likelihood of receiving support increases with mother's education; that support is less likely to be received by mothers in cities versus rural areas; and that support is somewhat less prevalent in the West and more prevalent in the Midwest. Having an additional child does not alter the probability of receiving support. Finally, we find that mothers who are cohabiting with a

Table 8.2 Probit Model of Receipt by Never-Married Mothers of Child Support Income

	Coefficient	Standard Error	Variable Mean
Year			
1989 (omitted)			
1990	.054	.073	.107
1991	.028	.073	.111
1992	.101	.072	.115
1993	.158*	.070	.124
1994	.250**	.070	.116
1995	.247**	.072	.106
1996	.258**	.071	.113
1997	.246**	.071	.108
Age of child			
Zero (omitted)			
One	.245**	.061	.154
Two	.321**	.063	.137
Three	.447**	.062	.130
Four	.498**	.064	.117
Five	.465**	.066	.110
Six	.437**	.068	.101
Seven	.478**	.071	.085
Age at birth			
Less than twenty (omitted)			
Twenty to twenty-four	.092*	.036	.379
Twenty-five to twenty-nine	.051	.053	.118
Thirty or older	.078	.064	.076
Race			
White (omitted)			
Black	−.395**	.041	.397
Hispanic	−.427**	.050	.204
Other	−.379**	.084	.043
Education			
Less than high school (omitted)			
High school	.265**	.043	.431
College	.354**	.047	.284
Number of children			
One (omitted)			
Two or more	.042	.037	.368
Cohabiting			
No (omitted)			
As household head	−.236**	.061	.131
With household head	.011	.073	.083

Table 8.2 *Continued*

	Coefficient	Standard Error	Variable Mean
Location			
Rural (omitted)			
Central city	−.320**	.046	.425
Other metropolitan area	−.164**	.047	.244
Missing	−.027	.052	.149
Region			
Northeast (omitted)			
Midwest	.083	.045	.217
South	−.002	.050	.321
West	−.140**	.088	.225
N	9,671	—	—
Log-likelihood	−4,001.2	—	—

Source: Authors' compilation.
*p < .05.
**p < .01.

partner are as likely to receive support as are other mothers, but that the subset who are cohabiting as well as household heads is significantly less likely to receive support. Recall that this group includes those who are living with the child's father and thus would not be expected to receive support. These findings are broadly consistent with prior research.[8]

To illustrate the importance of our key variables, we use our model to calculate predicted probabilities of receiving child support for various prototypical mothers. Table 8.3 shows predicted probabilities of support receipt for mothers who vary on a number of dimensions, but who have in common the following characteristics: one child, not cohabiting with a partner, living in the Northeast in a metropolitan area, and not living in a central city.

The first panel illustrates the changing probability of receiving support over time, for a prototypical mother whose first child was born in 1988. The mother in this example is black, has a high school education, and was in her early twenties when her child was born, in addition to the other characteristics noted earlier.[9] She is highly unlikely to receive support in the first year (age zero). However, her predicted probability of receiving support more than triples over the next seven years—from .061 to .209. These predicted probabilities illustrate the changing likelihood of receiving support

Table 8.3 Predicted Probability of Receiving Child
Support for Various Prototypical Mothers,
Based on Probit Model

Year	Child Age	Education	Age at Birth	Race	Predicted Probability
		Follow Mother Over Time			
1989	0	High school	20 to 24	Black	.061
1990	1	High school	20 to 24	Black	.106
1991	2	High school	20 to 24	Black	.115
1992	3	High school	20 to 24	Black	.159
1993	4	High school	20 to 24	Black	.186
1994	5	High school	20 to 24	Black	.203
1995	6	High school	20 to 24	Black	.193
1996	7	High school	20 to 24	Black	.209
		Change Age; Year Constant			
1989	1	High school	20 to 24	Black	.096
1989	2	High school	20 to 24	Black	.110
1989	3	High school	20 to 24	Black	.136
1989	4	High school	20 to 24	Black	.147
1989	5	High school	20 to 24	Black	.140
1989	6	High school	20 to 24	Black	.133
1989	7	High school	20 to 24	Black	.142
		Change Year; Age Constant			
1990	0	High school	20 to 24	Black	.068
1993	0	High school	20 to 24	Black	.082
1997	0	High school	20 to 24	Black	.097
		Change Characteristics; Age and Year Constant			
1997	3	High school	20 to 24	Black	.196
1997	3	High school	Under 20	Black	.172
1997	3	Less than high school	Under 20	Black	.113
1997	3	High school	20 to 24	White	.323
1991	3	College	20 to 24	White	.360

Source: Authors' compilation.
Note: In addition to the characteristics noted, predictions are for mothers with one child, not cohabiting with a partner, living in the Northeast in a metropolitan area, and not in a central city.

while holding demographic variables constant. Note that these predicted probabilities are quite similar to the actual rates of support receipt for cohort 1 in figure 8.1, where we did not control for the mother's characteristics.

The changing probabilities of support receipt documented here reflect an increase in the likelihood of receiving support over the first few years of a child's life, coupled with an increased likelihood of receiving support over the 1990s. To illustrate the magnitude of these separate influences, we calculate the predicted probability of receiving support for a mother with the same characteristics just described, in 1989, on behalf of children of varying ages. Conceptually, this indicates how the likelihood of receiving support would have changed over the first years of a child's life absent changes in policy and opportunity over the 1990s. The next panel indicates that the predicted probability of receiving support more than doubles over the first five years of the child's life, from .061 to .147, after which it declines slightly. We use a similar approach to assess how the likelihood of receiving child support during the first year of a child's life changes over the 1990s. As illustrated in the third panel, the likelihood increases only modestly, from .061 in 1989 to .097 in 1997.

Finally, we demonstrate how the likelihood of receiving support differs among mothers with varying characteristics. We use as an example a mother of a three-year-old, in 1997, for whom we make varying assumptions about race, age at birth, and education. With the same characteristics as our earlier examples, the fourth panel shows that such a mother has a predicted probability of receipt of .196. If she had her child as a teen rather than in her early twenties, the likelihood of receiving support declines by a small amount, to .172. If we also assume she has less than a high school education, her likelihood of receiving support falls to .113. On the other hand, for such a mother who is white and has a high school education, the likelihood of receiving support increases dramatically, to .323. With a college education this increases still further, to .360.

CHILD SUPPORT RELATIVE TO OTHER INCOME SOURCES

Our results thus far have shown that the amount of child support received increases as children age as well as across cohorts. Further, we have seen that this reflects an increase in the share of mothers who receive child support income rather than an increase in the amount of support among recipients. Our multivariate results confirm that the changes across cohorts and ages are not merely reflections of changing sample characteristics.

To place these results in context, we broaden our focus to examine patterns in the receipt of two other forms of income—public assistance and earnings. Figure 8.3 shows the percentage of never-married mothers receiving income from public assistance, again looking separately by cohort and age of child. Not surprisingly, public assistance is a far more prevalent income source than is private child support. Looking across ages and cohorts, between 31 percent and 56 percent of mothers report receipt of public assistance. The most notable patterns here are the cross-cohort differences. In each successive cohort, with only minor exceptions, the share of mothers with children of a given age reporting public assistance receipt declines. For mothers of one-year-olds, the likelihood of reporting public assistance is 52 percent in cohort 1, 51 percent in cohort 2, 42 percent in cohort 3, and 31 percent in cohort 4. The relationship between public assistance receipt and age of child differs across cohorts. For the earliest cohort, public assistance receipt peaks at age two, followed by a decline to roughly initial levels. For the second cohort, the decline among older children is more dramatic. By the time children in this cohort reach age five—the latest point for which we have data—only 36 percent of mothers report public assistance receipt, as compared to 47 percent of mothers of one-year-olds. By the later cohorts, we no longer observe the increase in receipt during the first years of the child's life. This pattern of results strongly suggests that all cohorts are influenced by common underlying factors that reduce the likelihood of public assistance receipt across never-married mothers.

It is notable that the rates of child support and public assistance receipt move in opposite directions, both across cohorts and, in the later cohorts, over the first years of a child's life. Mothers are more likely to receive public assistance than child support at all cohorts and ages considered (note that some receive both), but the growth in the share of mothers receiving at least some child support relative to those receiving at least some welfare is nonetheless noteworthy. For a mother in cohort 1, the likelihood of receiving public assistance in the first year of her child's life is almost five times the likelihood of receiving child support; by the seventh year, the ratio declines to roughly two-to-one. Mothers of one-year-olds in cohort 1 are more than four times as likely to receive public assistance as child support, while mothers in cohort 4 are only 1.6 times as likely to receive public assistance.

Figure 8.3 Percentage of Never-Married Mothers
            Receiving Public Assistance, by Cohort

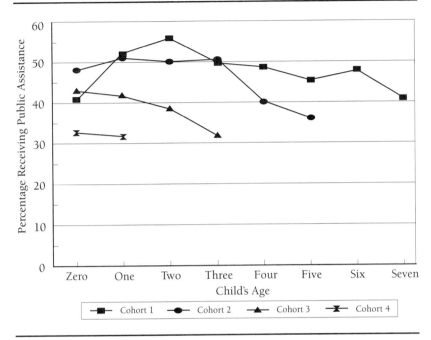

Source: Authors' compilation.
Note: Cohorts 1 through 4 represent never-married mothers who first became mothers in
1988 to 1989, in 1990 to 1991, in 1992 to 1993, and in 1994 to 1995, respectively.

We also examine patterns in the receipt of earned income. The
share of mothers receiving earned income is shown in figure 8.4.
Several findings are apparent. First, the prevalence of earned income supersedes that of either public assistance or private child support, with one-half to three-quarters of mothers reporting earned
income. Second, the likelihood of receiving earned income increases as children age. Among cohort 1, the share with earned
income increases from 50 percent to 72 percent as children age.
Finally, the likelihood of receiving earned income increases across
cohorts. Among mothers of one-year-olds, the share with earnings
increases from 57 percent to 71 percent. The large increase in never-
married mothers with earned income is consistent with the increase
in employment among all single mothers recently reported by Meyer
and Rosenbaum (1998).

Figure 8.4   Percentage of Never-Married Mothers with Earnings, by Cohort

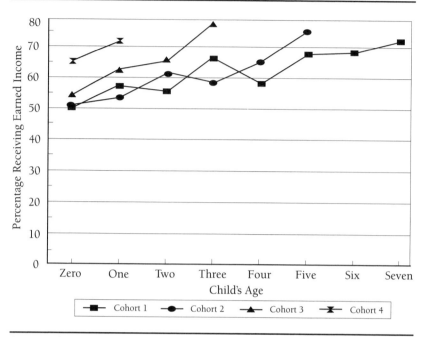

Source: Authors' compilation.
Note: Cohorts 1 through 4 represent never-married mothers who first became mothers in 1988 to 1989, in 1990 to 1991, in 1992 to 1993, and in 1994 to 1995, respectively.

What do these various income patterns mean for the relative importance of child support vis-à-vis other income sources? Here we consider the changing role of child support as a component of mothers' total income packages. We divide total income into five categories: child support, public assistance, earnings, other transfers, and other income. Figure 8.5 shows how these sources contribute to total income among mothers in cohort 1. Focusing first on the totals, it is evident that income (in 1997 dollars) increases considerably as children grow older—from $7,289 at age zero to $12,455 at age seven. Although the magnitude of child support receipts increases over this period, this increase plays a negligible role in the mothers' overall income gains. Earnings, on the other hand, show a marked rise over this period and are the dominant component of the overall income change. Public assistance increases and

Figure 8.5 Income Composition of Never-Married Mothers, Cohort 1

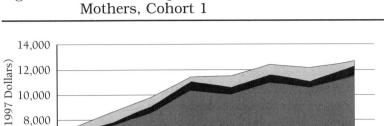

Source: Authors' compilation.
Note: Cohort 1 represents never-married mothers who first became mothers in 1988 to 1989.

then decreases over this period. Because of the increase in earnings, the importance of public assistance as an income component declines.

Figure 8.6 shows a similar analysis, this time looking at mothers of one-year-olds over the four cohorts. We again see a similar pattern. Total income increases somewhat, from $8,508 to $10,052. Child support increases in importance, yet plays an extremely limited role relative to total income. Public assistance dramatically declines across cohorts. As a result of these opposing trends, the ratio of child support to public assistance income increases fivefold, from .08 in cohort 1 to .39 in cohort 4. The gain in child support does not offset the loss in public assistance, however, with the combined value of these income sources considerably lower in cohort 4 than cohort 1. Earnings go up substantially and are again the driving force behind the overall income gain.

These analyses suggest that child support plays a very small role

Figure 8.6 Income Composition of Never-Married Mothers, Child Age One

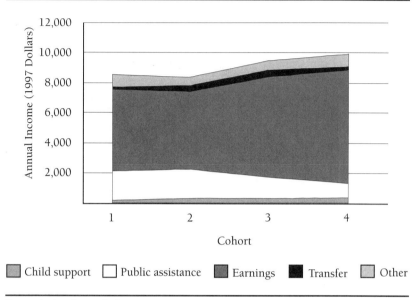

Source: Authors' compilation.
Note: Cohorts 1 through 4 represent never-married mothers who first became mothers in 1988 to 1989, in 1990 to 1991, in 1992 to 1993, and in 1994 to 1995, respectively.

when considered in conjunction with other income sources. This is somewhat deceptive, however. Among child support recipients, income from child support constitutes 13 to 28 percent of total income over the various cohort-age groups (not shown). Although there are no particular trends either by age or across cohorts, it is apparent that child support is a nontrivial income source to the subset of mothers who receive it. The limiting factor in the importance of child support for never-married mothers as a group is that so few actually receive any.

CONCLUSIONS

The past decade has been a period of profound change in the availability of public and private forms of support to single-parent families. There have been major changes in both the welfare system and the private child support system during this period, beginning with the Family Support Act of 1988 and culminating in the 1996 welfare reform legislation. A growing emphasis on child support, coupled with an increasingly stringent welfare system, suggests a potentially important role for child support as an income source to single-parent families.

This chapter has focused on the changing role of child support as an income source for never-married mothers during the 1990s. Our emphasis has been on change in two dimensions—across cohorts, and over time within cohorts. We find that child support has become increasingly common among successive cohorts of never-married mothers, and that within cohorts the likelihood of receiving child support increases over the first several years of a child's life.

Despite gains in support receipt over the 1990s, however, child support continues to be uncommon among never-married mothers. In the most recent cohort considered here—mothers who gave birth in 1994 or 1995—only 17 percent of mothers of one-year-olds received any support. Among all the cohort-age groups considered, the rate of support receipt never exceeded 27 percent. As a result, mean child support across never-married mothers continues to be quite low. On the other hand, child support is clearly not an inconsequential income source among those who do receive something. Average support when positive ranged from $1,200 to $2,800 per year across the cohort-age groups.

The changes we observe in child support receipts occurred in tandem with widespread changes in income from other sources, notably public assistance and earnings. The rate at which never-married mothers received public assistance declined strikingly across cohorts, consistent with the policy changes that were implemented during this time. Within most of the cohorts, public assistance also became less prevalent over the early years of a child's life. Earnings, on the other hand, increased considerably, both across cohorts and as children grew older. The net result of these offsetting changes in the various income components has been an increase in total income across cohorts, and a more sizable increase within cohorts as children age. Note, however, that despite income gains across cohorts and ages, incomes remain quite low throughout the period. Analyses not shown here reveal that the majority of never-married mothers continue to have incomes below the poverty line at all cohort-age points examined.

In the aggregate, child support trends have not had a large impact on overall income patterns, either across or within cohorts. On the other hand, for those who receive such support, it constitutes 12 percent to 28 percent of income, suggesting an important role for a relatively small share of mothers. The finding that most never-married mothers do not benefit from child support should not detract from the finding that for a minority of mothers child support provides an important supplement to other income.

Despite low rates of child support receipt, the apparent growth and subsequent stability in such receipts over the early years of a child's life is quite encouraging. It suggests that child support does not deteriorate as an income source for never-married mothers as their children age, at least for the time period considered here. The likelihood of receiving support over the medium and long term is particularly important in a world in which eligibility for welfare is time-limited.

There remain important questions about child support patterns as children age that we do not address here. Most important, we are able to examine child support receipts only over a relatively short portion of children's lives, for the cohorts included in this analysis. In future work, we hope to examine earlier cohorts of mothers, yielding a longer follow-up period. Longer-term analyses for recent cohorts, however, will not be possible for some time. Note also that the patterns reported here are based on aggregate data and tell us nothing about how child support receipt changes over time at the case level.

From a policy standpoint, the gain in child support receipt across cohorts suggests that efforts to strengthen the child support system have had a measure of success, at least from the standpoint of never-married mothers. Furthermore, our analysis includes only minimal information on outcomes after 1996, a year in which important legislation of relevance to unmarried mothers was enacted. We expect that child support outcomes will continue to improve as a result of this legislation. Note, however, that comparisons over time are a crude way to measure policy impacts. In future work, we hope to include state and time-specific variables describing both the policy environment and the economic context.

Table 8A.1 Sample Sizes for Analysis of Child Support
           Among Never-Married Mothers, by Cohort
           and Age of Child

Cohort	Zero	One	Two	Three	Four	Five	Six	Seven
1	339	336	307	330	291	232	212	197
2	371	346	314	291	241	259	—	—
3	377	350	279	255	—	—	—	—
4	369	307	—	—	—	—	—	—

Source: Authors' compilation.

We are grateful to Mei-Chen Hu for expert research assistance on this project.

NOTES

1. Authors' calculations from the 1998 Current Population Survey (CPS).
2. We use the term "cohort of mothers" to refer to women who first become mothers in a particular year.
3. We follow both years in a cohort for the same length of time. We thus ignore one potential year of data for the earlier year in each cohort. For instance, we follow 1988 births only through the March 1996 CPS because doing so provides us with the eighth year of data—the maximum years available for 1989 births, which are grouped in the same cohort.
4. We use two variables to capture cohabitation: one for mothers who are cohabiting with the head of household, and one for mothers who are cohabiting and are themselves the household head. As we explain later, we expect the latter to include some mothers who are cohabiting with the father of their child; we expect less frequent child support in this group.
5. The number of mothers in our sample who are designated as household head and are cohabiting with a partner serves as an outer limit to the number of mothers remaining in our sample who are cohabiting with the child's father. This ranges from 4 to 14 percent of the sample. We assume that in some of these cases the mother is cohabiting instead with a new partner. The implication is that fewer than 4 to 14 percent of our sample at a given cohort-age group consists of cohabiting parents. This does not include all cohabiting mothers in our sample, because there are also some who are cohabiting with a household head who is not the child's father.

6. The increasing likelihood of child support over time could reflect the fact that mothers of younger children are more likely to be cohabiting with the father of their child. However, we observe the same pattern when we exclude all cohabiting mothers from our analysis (not shown).

7. It is possible, of course, that the changing policy environment—captured here by the year coefficients—differentially affects the likelihood of child support receipt on behalf of children of particular ages. In particular, it seems likely that certain policies (such as those related to paternity establishment) would primarily benefit mothers of the youngest children. However, we ran a variety of models to assess interaction affects between year and child age, with no indication that such differences occur.

   Another reason that the mother of an older child may have a higher probability of receiving support is as follows: as the oldest child ages, the likelihood of the mother having another child increases, perhaps with a different partner, and then the possibility of child support may increase because there are two fathers involved. However, this hypothesis is not supported by our analyses: having an additional child does not significantly affect the probability of receiving support.

8. We did experiment with a variety of models allowing for differential affects of demographic variables over time, with no evidence that such differences existed.

9. We use a black mother because this is the modal race in our sample.

REFERENCES

Bartfeld, Judi, and Daniel R. Meyer. 1994. "Are There Really Dead-beat Dads?: The Relationship Between Enforcement, Ability to Pay, and Compliance in Nonmarital Child Support Cases." *Social Service Review* 68: 219–35.

Beller, Andrea H., and John W. Graham. 1993. *Small Change: The Economics of Child Support.* New Haven, Conn.: Yale University Press.

Bumpass, Larry L., and Hsien-Hen Lu. 1998. *Trends in Cohabitation and Implications for Children's Family Contexts.* Working paper 98–15. Madison, Wis.: Center for Demography and Ecology.

Bumpass, Larry L., and R. Kelly Raley. 1995. "Redefining Single-Parent Families: Cohabitation and Changing Family Reality." *Demography* 32: 97–109.

Dalaker, Joseph, and Mary Naifeh. 1998. *Poverty in the United States: 1997.* U.S. Bureau of the Census Current Population Reports, series P60–201. Washington: U.S. Government Printing Office.

Edin, Kathryn, and Laura Lein. 1997. *Making Ends Meet: How Single*

Mothers Survive Welfare and Low-Wage Work. New York: Russell Sage Foundation.

Garfinkel, Irwin, Daniel R. Meyer, and Sara S. McLanahan. 1998. "A Brief History of Child Support Policies in the United States." In *Fathers Under Fire: The Revolution in Child Support Enforcement,* Irwin Garfinkel, Sara McLanahan, Daniel R. Meyer, and Judith A. Seltzer. New York: Russell Sage Foundation.

Garfinkel, Irwin, and Philip K. Robins. 1994. "The Relationship Between Child Support Enforcement Tools and Child Support Outcomes." In *Child Support and Child Well-being,* edited by Irwin Garfinkel, Sara S. McLanahan, and Philip K. Robins. Washington, D.C.: Urban Institute Press.

Meyer, Bruce D., and Dan T. Rosenbaum. 1998. *Welfare, the Earned Income Tax Credit, and the Employment of Single Mothers.* Working paper. Chicago: Northwestern University and University of Chicago Joint Center for Poverty Research.

Meyer, Daniel R. 1995. "Supporting Children Born Outside of Marriage: Do Child Support Awards Keep Pace with Changes in Fathers' Incomes?" *Social Science Quarterly* 76: 577–93.

Meyer, Daniel R., and Judi Bartfeld. 1998. "Patterns of Child Support Compliance in Wisconsin." *Journal of Marriage and the Family* 60: 309–18.

Meyer, Daniel R., and Pedro M. Hernandez. 1999. "Long-term Patterns of Child Support Payments in Wisconsin." Paper presented at the annual meeting of the Population Association of America, New York (March).

Phillips, Elizabeth, and Irvin Garfinkel. 1993. "Income Growth Among Nonresident Fathers: Evidence from Wisconsin." *Demography* 30: 719–35.

Scoon-Rogers, Lydia. 1999. *Child Support for Custodial Mothers and Fathers: 1995.* U.S. Bureau of the Census Current Population Reports, series P60–196. Washington: U.S. Government Printing Office.

Scoon-Rogers, Lydia, and Gordon H. Lester. 1995. *Child Support for Custodial Mothers and Fathers: 1991.* U.S. Bureau of the Census Current Population Reports, series P60–187. Washington: U.S. Government Printing Office.

Seltzer, Judith A. 1991. "Relationships Between Fathers and Children Who Live Apart: The Father's Role After Separation." *Journal of Marriage and the Family* 53: 79–101.

Sorensen, Elaine, and Ariel Halpern. 1999. "Child Support Enforcement Is Working Better Than We Think." In Urban Institute series "New Federalism: Issues and Options for States" (A-31). Available at: newfederalism.urban.org/html/anf—31.html (extracted April 7, 1999).

U.S. House of Representatives, Committee on Ways and Means. 1998. *1998 Green Book.* Washington: U.S. Government Printing Office.

PART III

Consequences for Children and Adults

CHAPTER 9

Unintended Pregnancy and the Consequences of Nonmarital Childbearing

Sanders Korenman, Robert Kaestner, and Theodore J. Joyce

The consequences of unintended pregnancy are serious, imposing appreciable burdens on children, women, men and families.

> Institute of Medicine, *The Best Intention: Unintended Pregnancy and the Well-being of Children and Families* (1995, 1)

The research to date indicates that, given current economic and social realities, nonmarital childbearing has negative consequences for children, women, and for taxpayers.

> U.S. Department of Health and Human Services, *Report to Congress on Out-of-Wedlock Childbearing* (1995, xiii)

The consequences of nonmarital childbearing and unintended childbearing are thought to be substantial, as clearly illustrated by the conclusions of two major reports quoted in the epigraphs. Despite this similarity in research findings and the fact that nonmarital births are far more likely to be unintended than marital births, analyses of the consequences of unintended childbearing and nonmarital childbearing remain largely distinct.[1] In this chapter, we incorporate information on pregnancy intention into the study of the consequences of nonmarital childbearing for infant health and child development.

By now it is widely recognized that estimates of the effects of nonmarital births may be biased by background factors that give rise to such births.[2] The *Report to Congress on Out-of-Wedlock Childbearing* (Moore 1995, xii) provides a succinct summary of the key analytical challenge:

The central, and very difficult, task in identifying consequences of non-marital childbearing is to disentangle the effects of a person's marital status at childbirth from the effects of the person's other characteristics. The men and the women who become parents outside of marriage tend to be disadvantaged even before pregnancy occurs. If their children have problems or they receive public assistance, researchers must distinguish whether these negative consequences occur because the child was born outside of marriage or because of the parents' preexisting disadvantages.

Women who have nonmarital births tend to have grown up in more disadvantaged circumstances than those who have births within marriage. Their children are likely to be less healthy regardless of their parents' marital status at the time of their birth. Research on the consequences of nonmarital fertility has only recently begun to tackle the problem of bias from heterogeneity in family background (Bronars and Grogger 1994; Angrist and Evans 1998). And we are aware of no research that has investigated the possibility that effects of nonmarital childbearing are confounded by unmeasured pregnancy intentions.

In this chapter, we take four approaches to estimating the consequences of nonmarital childbearing that take into account the confounding influences of family background or pregnancy intention. First, we control for pregnancy intention in models that relate child well-being to the marital status of the mother at the birth of the child. Second, we use differences between and among siblings and first cousins to eliminate heterogeneity bias related to unmeasured family background. In these analyses, the effect of nonmarital childbearing is estimated by comparing outcomes for a child born out of wedlock to those for his or her sibling or first cousin born within marriage. Third, we explore the implications of the assumption that births resulting from unintended pregnancies represent fertility "shocks" in either the timing or number of children. We hypothesize that some women who have nonmarital births as a consequence of an unintended pregnancy would, in the absence of the unintended pregnancy, have had the birth within marriage. Under this assumption, a comparison of outcomes for "unintended" children born to married and unmarried women yields estimates of the effects of nonmarital childbearing.

The assumption that nonmarital births that result from an unintended pregnancy are exogenous is questionable, for a variety of reasons that we discuss later. Therefore, to strengthen the case for exogeneity, our fourth approach is to estimate models in which measures of child support enforcement and the cost and availability of abortion services are used as instruments for pregnancy intention and marital status. In these models, the effect of a nonmarital birth is identified from births that would have been aborted or would have taken place within marriage had abortion services been more readily available or had child support enforcement been more stringent. Indeed, Irwin Garfinkel and his colleagues (1998, 5) explicitly link child support enforcement, unintended pregnancy, and nonmarital births when they predict that

> stronger child support enforcement may have an important deterrent effect on nonmarital fertility. Once young men realize that fathering a child incurs a financial obligation, lasting for up to eighteen years, they may take more precautions to avoid an unintended pregnancy. We know that the vast majority of nonmarital births are unintended (Brown and Eisenberg 1995). We also know that women bear most of the responsibility for contraception. Thus, if fathers were to change their behaviors in this regard, the number of unintended pregnancies would probably decline, as would the number of non-marital births.

Although none of these methods alone is convincing, we hope that, taken together, these approaches will allow a firmer assessment of the consequences of nonmarital childbearing for infant health and child development. The formulation and design of effective social policies depends on identifying the causes of the disadvantages experienced by children born out-of-wedlock. If adverse outcomes associated with nonmarital births are largely the result of *unintended* nonmarital births, it may be appropriate to emphasize family planning more than changing incentives for nonmarital childbearing.

LITERATURE ON THE CONSEQUENCES FOR CHILDREN OF OUT-OF-WEDLOCK CHILDBEARING

In this section, we review the literature that has attempted to estimate the effects of nonmarital childbearing on children. The first point to be made about this literature is that, although much has been written about closely related issues (single parenthood, teen childbearing, divorce), there has been little study of nonmarital childbearing. Thus, Sara McLanahan (1995, 229) begins her review with the following observation: "What are the consequences of nonmarital fertility for children, women, and society? Surprisingly, given the strong interest and concern over the increase in nonmarital births, this question has rarely been examined directly."

The literature on the effects of single parenthood on children also tends to examine outcomes in later childhood, such as high school completion or early fertility, rather than effects in early childhood, when one might expect to find evidence of the more temporally proximate impacts of the mother's marital status at the time of the child's birth. With respect to child well-being, McLanahan (1995) concludes that the effects of single parenthood appear to be larger in adolescence than earlier in childhood, and that they also appear to be larger when the outcome is behavioral rather than cognitive. For example, single parenthood has larger effects on "acting out" and skipping school, but smaller effects on cognitive test scores or marks in school. She also reports that remarriage does not diminish but in fact can exacerbate effects. This finding suggests that heterogeneity may explain some of the disadvantages among children in single-parent families, although there are certainly other interpretations of this result, such as conflict with the stepparent. When researchers have used statistical techniques to adjust for unmeasured differences between single-parent and two-parent families (for example, selectivity corrections), they have found "ambiguous results. . . . On the one hand, there is evidence that unobserved factors are associated with both family disruptions and poor outcomes in children. On the other hand, the disadvantages associated with single motherhood persist to some degree even after taking this correlation into account" (McLanahan 1995, 233). McLanahan also notes that while there is some evidence that children in single-parent families do worse than those who live in two-parent families until age eighteen, there is no evidence that children whose parents divorce do better than children born out-of-wedlock.

Since McLanahan's review, a handful of papers have examined more directly the consequences of nonmarital childbearing for children. Duncan and Brooks-Gunn (1997) guided and compiled a set of longitudinal studies of the effect of income in childhood and other family characteristics, including family structure, on well-being. However, family structure histories are classified in a way that makes it difficult to determine the effects of nonmarital childbearing. Specifically, the various contributing authors interacted family structure at birth with family structure in some follow-up period. Duncan and Brooks-Gunn (1997, 601) conclude that, as a group, the papers "found the effects of family structure to be small and, on most of the ability and achievement measures, nonsignificant." Family structure was found to have substantial and significant effects, however, on some measures of behavior problems and mental health.

Two recent papers (Bronars and Grogger 1994; Angrist and Evans 1998) that estimate the effects of nonmarital fertility pay particular attention to the problem of causal inference. Both focus on consequences for mothers, not children, although Bronars and Grogger do examine one child outcome (educational progress).

Bronars and Grogger (1994) use exogenous variation in fertility generated by the birth of twins. The effect of an unplanned nonmarital birth is estimated by comparing outcomes for women who had a nonmarital twin first birth to those who had a nonmarital singleton first birth. Although they find that nonmarital fertility affects mother's educational status, marital status, completed fertility, and income (largely among black women), they find no effect on the educational progress of children and thus conclude that there is "no evidence that the deleterious effects experienced by the mothers of unplanned children are transmitted to their children" (Bronars and Grogger 1994, 1154).

In a related paper, Angrist and Evans (1998) estimate the effects of the 1970 state abortion reforms on teen and nonmarital childbearing. Focusing on the results related to nonmarital fertility, they find that the state abortion reforms reduce "the probability of having an out-of-wedlock teen birth by roughly 12 percent" among black women, whereas white women experience sharp reductions in teen marriage rates, with little change in teen or out-of-wedlock fertility (Angrist and Evans 1998, 25–26). The resulting policy-induced reduction in marriage among whites had little effect on their schooling or labor market outcomes. The policy-induced reduction in teen and nonmarital fertility among blacks appears to have increased their educational attainment and employment but had little effect on earnings or poverty status. Because the results on the consequences of nonmarital childbearing were mixed, Angrist and Evans recommend that "future work should focus on isolating new sources of exogenous variation in fertility, as well as new sources of data, that can be combined to generate more precise estimates of the effect of teen and out-of-wedlock childbearing" (26). That is the goal of this chapter.

METHODS

As noted earlier, we take several approaches to estimating the effects of nonmarital childbearing on infant health and child well-being. First, we estimate a set of regression models that are standard in the literature. We regress health and developmental outcomes (such as an indicator of low birthweight) on the marital status of the mother at the time of birth. As noted, women who have nonmarital births have grown up in more disadvantaged circumstances, on average, than those who have marital births. Therefore, we include a detailed set of family background controls, such as whether the mother, at age fourteen, lived with both of her parents, and whether her family regularly received newspapers and magazines or had a library card; we also control for her mother's education level.

Second, we add controls for pregnancy intention (unwanted or mistimed) to these models in order to gauge whether the higher incidence of unintended births among unmarried women in the sample accounts for the adverse effects of nonmarital fertility.

Third, we use information on siblings and cousins to control more completely for family background in estimating the effects of nonmarital childbearing. Specifically, we estimate models with fixed effects for each baseline (1979) household. The effects of nonmarital childbearing on child health and development are identified by differences between or among siblings or first cousins in the sample. There is greater within-family variation in mother's marital status among first cousins and siblings than among siblings alone. For example, in our samples of siblings or first cousins, approximately 17 percent of the variation in "never-married" is between siblings, whereas just over 25 percent of the variation in "never-married" is between siblings or first cousins. The proportion of variance within families in other key explanatory variables is much larger. For example, 48 percent of the variation in "unintended" is between siblings, and about 54 percent is between siblings or first cousins.

Our fourth approach is based on the assumption that some unintended nonmarital births result from random events such as contraceptive failures. In this case, the difference between the health of an unintended nonmarital birth and an unintended marital birth provides an estimate of the effect of marital status on infant health and child development. We assume that some nonmarital births would have occurred within marriage were it not for the unintended fertility shock. To make this comparison, we add interaction terms between marital status and pregnancy intention to the models described here. We recognize, however, that pregnancy intention may be determined endogenously with child well-being. The threat of endogeneity bias looms largest when pregnancy intention is reported retrospectively—after the birth of the child—as is most often the case (Rosenzweig and Wolpin 1993; Westoff and Ryder 1977; Joyce, Kaestner, and Korenman 2000b). Even if unintended *pregnancies* result from exogenous "shocks," abortion of unintended pregnancies may be selected in a variety of ways related to child health and development.

To address the possibility that unintended births may not be exogenously determined, therefore, we use instrumental variables to estimate the effects of nonmarital births that result from limited availability of abortion services or weak child support (including paternity establishment) policies or enforcement. Specifically, instruments for pregnancy intention and marital status include those related to abortion availability: whether there was an abortion provider in the county of residence in the year prior to the birth of the child, whether the state had parental notification laws, whether the state provided Medicaid funding of abortions, and state child support enforcement provisions based on Case (1998) and Plotnick et al. (1999).

Although this approach is not new, the validity of some of these instruments has been questioned (Case 1998). As it turns out, the instruments are rather weak predictors of pregnancy intention. Therefore, we regard these estimates as a promising if ultimately unsatisfying attempt at the instrumental variable approach.

DATA

Data are taken from the National Longitudinal Survey of Youth (NLSY), 1979 to 1992. The NLSY collects detailed information on the outcomes and controls needed for this study, including marital status at birth and pregnancy intention for each child, as well as health and developmental outcomes for infants and children (for example, prenatal care utilization, low birthweight, and scores on tests of cognitive and socio-emotional development).

The NLSY includes sizable samples of siblings and first cousins (whose mothers are sisters) that permit examination of differences among siblings (children of a sample mother) and among first cousins (children of sample mothers who are sisters). For example, the health or development of a child born out-of-wedlock can be compared to that of his sibling or first cousin born within marriage. In the NLSY, all household members age fourteen to twenty-one were eligible for inclusion in the sample. Beginning in 1986, children of female sample members were included in biennial child assessments. The mothers of the children in our sibling analyses either had more than one birth after 1978 or had one birth and had a sister in the sample (also age fourteen to twenty-one, and with whom she co-resided in 1979) who had at least one birth after 1978. The children of these women are the child siblings or first cousins who form our sample of births.

Sample sizes vary according to the outcome under consideration. For outcomes related to infant health, sample sizes range from 7,400 to 7,800 children. About 75 percent of these children have at least one sibling who is also in the sample, and about 80 percent have at least one sibling or first cousin who is also in the sample. Sample sizes are smaller for the indicators of child development primarily because of age restrictions for assessments. The sample size is about 3,700 children for the PIAT (Peabody Individual Achievement Test) math and reading assessments, 4,300 for the Behavior Problems Index, and 4,800 for the Peabody Picture Vocabulary Test.

NLSY "geocodes" allow linkage to geographic-based information related to the price of fertility control (for example, abortion providers and state laws governing access to abortion) and state child support enforcement characteristics. Information on the county and state of residence is used to link NLSY records to information on the number of abortion providers in the county of residence, state-level information about abortion funding and regulation, and paternity establishment and child support enforcement.

To measure abortion availability, we use a dichotomous indicator of whether the mother lives in a county with an abortion provider.

For example, in 1992, 84 percent of counties in the United States had no identified abortion provider, and 31 percent of women of reproductive age lived in a county with no provider (Henshaw and Van Vort 1994). Information on abortion providers is from the periodic survey of the Alan Guttmacher Institute (AGI) of all known providers. Data on abortion providers are available annually from 1978 to 1992 except for 1983, 1989, and 1990. For years in which provider data are missing, we use information on providers from the preceding year.

We use two other measures of access to abortion services. We use a dichotomous indicator for whether a woman lived in a state that provided Medicaid funding for therapeutic abortions—in essence, abortion on demand. In 1992, for example, thirteen states funded therapeutic abortions for women on Medicaid (Merz, Jackson, and Klerman 1996). State-level abortion rates appear sensitive to the availability of Medicaid funding (Blank, George, and London 1996; Levine, Trainor, and Zimmerman 1996; Cook et al. 1999). Our second measure of access to abortion is a dichotomous indicator of whether a women lives in a state that requires parental consent or notification before an unemancipated minor can obtain an abortion. Although some studies have found that parental involvement laws reduce teen abortion rates, more recent work has challenged this conclusion (Haas-Wilson 1996; Henshaw 1995; Joyce and Kaestner 1996; Ellertson 1997). Twenty states required either parental consent or notification in 1992 (Merz et al. 1996).

We relied on Case (1998) and Plotnick et al. (1999) for the selection of child support enforcement measures thought to be related to nonmarital fertility. The measures we used include a dichotomous indicator for whether the state provided genetic testing to determine paternity; whether it had "long-arm" statutes to pursue men in other states; whether paternity could be established until the child was eighteen years old; whether presumptive child support guidelines were in use; whether wage withholding was "immediate" when support payments were in arrears; whether wage withholding was mandatory; and the ratio of paternity establishments to the number of nonmarital births (Case 1998; Plotnick et al. 1999). Following Case (1998), we use child support variables two years prior to the birth of the child to account for time to conception and birth and to allow time for fertility and marital behavior to adjust to policy changes.

RESULTS

DESCRIPTIVE STATISTICS

Table 9.1 shows the distribution of sample births by pregnancy intention and mother's marital status at the time of the first interview following the birth. Although we were able to determine the marital status of mothers for all but four births out of the sample of more than 8,000, we were unable to determine pregnancy intention for 11 percent of births.[3]

Pregnancy intention and marital status are clearly associated. About two-thirds of births to married women result from intended pregnancies—neither mistimed nor unwanted at conception—compared to about one-third of births to never-married women. Only 4.4 percent of births to married women in the sample result from unwanted pregnancies, compared to 16.4 percent of births to never-married women. Figures for children born to women who are divorced or separated tend to fall between those for children born to never-married women and those born to married women. If we condition on having nonmissing pregnancy intention, differences in pregnancy intention between married and unmarried women increase (not shown). For example, the percentage of unwanted pregnancies rises to 4.9 percent for births to married women and 18.9 percent for births to never-married women. These figures highlight the strong association between unintended births and nonmarital births.

Table 9.1 Pregnancy Intention by Mother's Marital Status at Birth of Child

Pregnancy Intention	Married	Divorced or Separated	Never Married
Unintended			
Unwanted	4.4%	14.9%	16.4%
Mistimed	20.8	30.9	37.5
Intended	64.5	40.8	32.8
Not determined	10.3	13.4	13.3
Total	100.0	100.0	100.0
Number of observations	5,514	786	1,828

Source: Authors' calculations based on data from the National Longitudinal Survey of Youth, 1979 Cohort.

In tables 9.2 and 9.3, we present descriptive statistics by marital status and pregnancy intention. Table 9.2 presents means for outcomes related to parental behaviors and infant health, as well as demographic and socioeconomic characteristics. Table 9.3 presents means of indicators of cognitive and social development in early childhood. Both marital status and pregnancy intention are correlated with adverse parenting behaviors, poor infant health, and slowed cognitive and social development in early childhood. Looking across the first row of table 9.2, children born to married women as the result of an unwanted pregnancy are twice as likely as those born to married women who intended to become pregnant to receive late prenatal care, and 25 percent more likely to be born low-birthweight. The mothers are more than 50 percent more likely to smoke heavily during pregnancy, and nearly 30 percent less likely to breast-feed. Unintended births are also associated with diminished child well-being for children born to women who are divorced or separated. The relationship between pregnancy intention and parental behavior appears weaker among never-married women.

Within pregnancy intention categories, children born within marriage are generally, though not uniformly, advantaged relative to children born out-of-wedlock. Intended marital births are associated with lower chances of smoking during pregnancy, lower incidence of low birthweight, and higher prevalence of breast-feeding than intended nonmarital births. Unwanted marital births fare better than unwanted nonmarital births according to all indicators except late prenatal care initiation.

Another implication of the figures presented in table 9.2 is that women who carry nonmarital or unintended pregnancies to term differ in many respects from those who do not have nonmarital or unintended pregnancies, or who do not carry such pregnancies to term. Both unintended childbearing and nonmarital childbearing are associated with the mother having grown up in a family of low SES (socioeconomic status). For example, among children born following intended pregnancies, mothers of children born within marriage are less likely than mothers of children born outside of marriage to be black, are more likely to have lived with both parents at age fourteen, and have higher Armed Forces Qualifying Test (AFQT) scores (a measure of academic achievement and ability). Similarly, within marital status categories, women who have intended births have grown up in more advantaged circumstances, on average, than those who have unintended births. Racial identification, family struc-

Table 9.2 Unweighted Sample Means, by Marital Status of Mother and Pregnancy Intention

	Married			Divorced or Separated			Never Married		
	Intended	Mistimed	Unwanted	Intended	Mistimed	Unwanted	Intended	Mistimed	Unwanted
Birthweight and pregnancy behaviors									
Late prenatal care	4.7%	5.2%	10.3%	4.6%	6.8%	9.1%	6.0%	7.9%	6.1%
Heavy smoking	6.8	8.7	10.4	15.5	17.5	23.0	10.3	9.2	11.2
Low birth-weight	6.5	4.3	8.2	9.7	7.8	11.8	11.3	11.9	14.0
Ever breast-fed	55.6	49.3	39.6	40.8	37.8	28.8	26.1	23.7	20.4
Characteristics of child									
Male	51.3	51.1	52.7	57.3	49.4	44.4	50.3	50.2	49.2
First-born	47.7	40.3	17.8	34.6	27.6	5.1	50.4	54.9	42.5
Prospectively reported pregnancy intention	35.2	36.1	35.3	34.0	32.1	24.8	32.6	29.3	30.2

Selected characteristics of mother									
Black	11.7	19.1	24.5	31.5	28.8	41.9	55.3	62.9	68.8
Hispanic	19.6	18.5	28.2	22.7	16.9	17.0	19.0	13.9	11.2
Lived with both parents, age fourteen	73.7	66.8	63.1	54.2	60.1	46.2	41.1	44.5	43.5
Age at birth of child (years)	24.8	23.7	24.7	24.4	24.1	25.6	22.4	21.7	22.3
	(3.7)	(3.7)	(4.2)	(3.8)	(3.8)	(3.6)	(3.8)	(3.8)	(4.2)
Education at birth of child (years)	12.5	12.2	11.4	11.4	11.6	11.0	11.2	11.5	11.1
	(2.4)	(2.1)	(2.3)	(1.9)	(1.9)	(2.1)	(1.9)	(1.8)	(1.9)
AFQT score (percentiles)	43.1	39.9	32.3	26.9	30.9	23.2	17.8	21.4	18.2
	(27.5)	(26.4)	(25.0)	(21.6)	(23.0)	(19.3)	(18.3)	(19.5)	(16.5)
Receiving AFDC at birth of child	3.4	7.1	9.6	34.7	35.4	43.6	45.1	38.2	47.2
Sample size (maximum)	3,556	1,149	241	321	243	117	599	685	301

Source: Authors' calculations based on data from the National Longitudinal Survey of Youth, 1979 Cohort.

Table 9.3 Unweighted Sample Means, by Marital Status of Mother and Pregnancy Intention (Percentiles)

Indicators of Child Development	Married			Divorced or Separated			Never Married		
	Intended	Mistimed	Unwanted	Intended	Mistimed	Unwanted	Intended	Mistimed	Unwanted
Math PIAT	49.8	50.4	43.0	45.4	45.1	38.7	38.1	41.6	39.3
	(26.3)	(26.6)	(26.7)	(26.5)	(25.5)	(26.1)	(24.7)	(25.2)	(24.3)
Reading PIAT	58.3	59.6	53.2	53.4	55.4	45.9	47.5	50.8	49.7
	(26.8)	(26.1)	(27.1)	(29.0)	(28.0)	(25.9)	(27.1)	(26.7)	(27.4)
Behavior Problems Index[a]	60.7	62.8	63.7	68.7	67.4	68.7	66.1	67.1	64.0
	(27.0)	(26.0)	(27.5)	(26.2)	(25.6)	(26.5)	(27.5)	(26.1)	(25.9)
Peabody Picture Vocabulary Test	39.0	37.6	27.0	28.4	27.7	19.5	19.4	21.5	19.5
	(29.4)	(30.0)	(26.5)	(26.8)	(26.0)	(24.3)	(22.0)	(23.6)	(22.6)
Sample size (maximum)	4,244	1,653	297	365	314	94	936	1,300	514

Source: Authors' calculations based on data from the National Longitudinal Survey of Youth, 1979 Cohort.
[a] Higher score indicates more problems.

ture, and AFQT scores vary somewhat less by pregnancy intention than by marital status. Differences by pregnancy intention in family background are rather small among never-married women.

In short, background characteristics of mothers vary substantially by marital status and pregnancy intention, and therefore family background and pregnancy intentions must be controlled in estimating the effects of nonmarital childbearing on infant health and child development. That is the purpose of the multivariate analyses to which we now turn.

BASIC REGRESSION ANALYSES

Table 9.4 reports results from multivariate regressions of the effects of marital status and pregnancy intention on indicators of parental behavior and infant health. Table 9.5 presents results from models of development in early childhood. All models contain controls for basic demographic characteristics, as well as the socioeconomic background of the mother's family when she was fourteen. The controls are listed in the table footnotes. For each outcome (dependent variable), we present five models. Aside from controls for demographic characteristics and family background of the mother, the first model includes only marital status variables. In the second model, we add controls for pregnancy intention in order to determine whether pregnancy intention accounts for the adverse outcomes associated with nonmarital births. In the third model, to control more completely for family background, we add fixed effects for the mother's family of origin. Here the effects of nonmarital and unintended births are identified by differences among siblings or first cousins. The fourth and fifth models present marital status effects estimated from unintended fertility "shocks." Specifically, in these models the effect of a nonmarital birth is estimated as the difference in outcomes between a nonmarital unintended birth and a marital unintended birth.

In cross-section estimates, nonmarital births are significantly associated with late initiation of prenatal care, increased smoking during pregnancy, low birthweight, reduced breast-feeding (table 9.4, column 1), lower scores on tests of math, reading, and vocabulary skills, and more behavior problems (table 9.5, column 1). In these estimates, births following unintended pregnancies (especially unwanted pregnancies) are also associated with late prenatal care, ma-

Table 9.4 Effects of Nonmarital Childbearing on Outcomes Related to Infant Health: OLS Coefficients (Robust Standard Errors)

Outcome/Marital Status	(1)[a]	(2)[b]	(3)[c]	Estimates Based on Unintended Fertility Shocks	
				(4)[d]	(5)[c]
Late prenatal care					
Never married	.022*	.018*	−.006	.018	.010
	(.008)	(.008)	(.019)	(.012)	(.022)
Divorced or separated	.009	.006	−.002	.010	.014
	(.010)	(.010)	(.020)	(.017)	(.027)
Heavy smoking					
Never married	.058*	.052*	.028	.040*	.012
	(.011)	(.011)	(.018)	(.015)	(.020)
Divorced or separated	.111*	.106*	.051*	.106*	.047**
	(.016)	(.015)	(.021)	(.023)	(.027)
Low birthweight					
Never married	.047*	.048*	.015	.060*	.003
	(.010)	(.012)	(.021)	(.013)	(.025)
Divorced or separated	.028*	.028*	−.004	.035*	−.007
	(.012)	(.012)	(.022)	(.017)	(.031)

Ever breast-fed

Never married	−.146*	−.102*	−.048**	−.113*	−.052**
	(.017)	(.021)	(.025)	(.023)	(.030)
Divorced or separated	−.102*	−.094*	−.014	−.079*	−.001
	(.021)	(.021)	(.026)	(.031)	(.034)
Controls for pregnancy intention?	No	Yes	Yes	Yes	Yes
Family fixed effects?	No	No	Yes	No	Yes

Source: Authors' calculations based on data from the National Longitudinal Survey of Youth, 1979 Cohort.

Note: OLS estimates, with standard errors adjusted for heteroskedasticity and clustering among siblings using Stata 5.0's algorithm for robust estimations (Stata Corporation 1997).

[a] Controls include, in addition to the variables listed in the table, dummy variables for year of birth of child (13), region (3), and urban residence (2) in the year following the birth of the child; dummy variables for black and Hispanic origin of mother; and characteristics of the mother's household when she was fourteen: two-parent family, whether the household received newspapers and magazines, whether someone had a library card, and the educational attainment of the mother's mother (in years). The model also includes a dummy variable for whether the mother reported pregnancy intention during pregnancy or after delivery.

[b] Adds to model 1 controls for pregnancy intention (dummy variables for "unwanted" and "mistimed").

[c] Adds to model 2 fixed effects (dummy variable) for the family of the child's maternal grandparent, and therefore effects are identified by variation among children who are siblings (same mother) or first cousins (their mothers are sisters). Standard errors are adjusted for clustering among siblings. Effects of variables that do not vary among first cousins or siblings cannot be estimated.

[d] Same as model 2 except that it includes an interaction between pregnancy intention and marital status. In addition, the control for pregnancy intention is a single dummy variable for "unintended," which is the aggregation of the categories "unwanted" and "mistimed." The indicator variable for "unintended" is interacted with the "never-married" and "divorced" indicator variables. The effect of marital status reported in the table is, for example, the sum of the "never-married" main effect and the "never-married*unintended" interaction; it is therefore the difference between the outcome for an unintended child born to a never-married woman and an unintended child born to a married woman.

[e] Adds family fixed effects to model 4 (see model 3 description).

*p ≤ .05.
**.05 < p ≤ .10.

Table 9.5 Effects of Nonmarital Childbearing on Child Development: OLS Coefficients (Robust Standard Errors) (Percentiles)

Outcome-Marital Status	(1)[a]	(2)[b]	(3)[c]	Estimates Based on Unintended Fertility Shocks	
				(4)[d]	(5)[e]
Math (PIAT)					
Never married	−3.43*	−3.17*	−2.41	−1.36	−2.02
	(1.21)	(1.24)	(2.71)	(1.55)	(3.16)
Divorced or separated	−2.51	−2.34	1.55	−1.91	0.56
	(1.66)	(1.67)	(3.35)	(2.23)	(4.23)
Reading (PIAT)					
Never married	−5.27*	−5.24*	−3.55	−4.17*	−3.05
	(1.19)	(1.22)	(2.62)	(1.51)	(3.11)
Divorced or separated	−3.61*	−3.59*	0.70	−2.68*	1.66
	(1.57)	(1.59)	(3.17)	(2.16)	(4.03)
Behavior Problems Index[f]					
Never married	3.95*	3.34*	3.81	2.41	3.03
	(1.20)	(1.23)	(2.47)	(1.49)	(2.82)
Divorced or separated	6.53*	6.07*	3.24	4.43*	1.43
	(1.49)	(1.49)	(2.81)	(2.11)	(3.79)

Peabody Picture Vocabulary Test

Never married	−6.19*	−5.55*	−2.20	−4.32*	−2.70
	(0.99)	(1.02)	(1.92)	(1.29)	(2.28)
Divorced or separated	−4.78*	−4.34*	1.61	−4.48*	2.22
	(1.28)	(1.30)	(2.18)	(1.81)	(2.86)
Controls for pregnancy intention?	No	Yes	Yes	Yes	Yes
Family fixed effects?	No	No	Yes	No	Yes

Source: Authors' calculations based on data from the National Longitudinal Survey of Youth, 1979 Cohort.

Note: OLS estimates, with standard errors adjusted for heteroskedasticity and clustering among siblings using Stata 5.0's algorithm for robust estimations (Stata Corporation 1997). Outcomes are age-normed percentile scores for the assessment (e.g., test). See Baker et al. 1993 for a complete description and discussion. When children were assessed at more than one age, we selected the first available assessment.

[a] Controls include, in addition to the variables listed in the table, dummy variables for year of birth of child (13), region (3), and urban residence (2) in the year following the birth of the child; dummy variables for black and Hispanic origin of mother; and characteristics of the mother's household when she was fourteen: two-parent family, whether the household received newspapers and magazines, whether someone had a library card, and the educational attainment of the mother's mother (in years). The model also includes a dummy variable for whether the mother reported pregnancy intention during pregnancy or after delivery.

[b] Adds control for pregnancy intention (dummy variables for "unwanted" and "mistimed") to model 1.

[c] Adds to model 2 fixed effects (dummy variable) for the family of the child's maternal grandparent, and therefore effects are identified by variation among children who are siblings (same mother) or first cousins (their mothers are sisters). Standard errors are adjusted for clustering among siblings. Effects of variables that do not vary among first cousins or siblings cannot be estimated.

[d] Same as model 2 except that it includes an interaction between pregnancy intention and marital status. In addition, the control for pregnancy intention is a single dummy variable for "unintended," which is the aggregation of the categories "unwanted" and "mistimed." The indicator variable for "unintended" is interacted with the "never-married" and "divorced" indicator variables. The effect of marital status reported in the table is, for example, the sum of the "never-married" main effect and the "never-married*unintended" interaction; it is therefore the difference between the outcome for an unintended child born to a never-married woman and an unintended child born to a married woman.

[e] Adds family fixed effects to model 4 (see model 3 description).

[f] A higher score on the Behavior Problems Index indicates more behavior problems.

*p ≤ .05.

ternal smoking during pregnancy, reduced breast-feeding, and lower vocabulary test scores (results not shown; see also Joyce, Kaestner, and Korenman 2000a). However, despite the fact that nonmarital births are far more likely than marital births to be unintended (table 9.1), and even though unintended births are associated with adverse health-related outcomes for infants, pregnancy intention accounts for essentially none of the adverse effects of marital status on parenting behaviors, infant health, or child development. (Compare marital status effects in the first and second columns of tables 9.4 and 9.5.)

Controlling for family background through comparisons of siblings or first cousins appears to reduce substantially the estimated effects of nonmarital births.[4] Remaining, however, are a few substantial and significant differences by marital status. In models with family fixed effects, there appears to be more smoking during pregnancy among divorced women, and less breast-feeding of children born to never-married women (table 9.4, column 3).

The results in table 9.5 are less clear-cut. On the one hand, adding family fixed effects to the models (column 3) substantially reduces the estimated adverse effects of divorce on child development, renders them insignificant, and in some cases reverses their signs. The possible exception to this pattern is the Behavior Problems Index, for which the effect of divorce remains sizable although not significant in models with family fixed effects. On the other hand, the effects of being born to a never-married woman remain sizable in models with family fixed effects but are not statistically significant. In sum, results reported in the first three columns of tables 9.4 and 9.5 indicate that standard cross-sectional (as compared to family fixed-effects) estimates of the effects of nonmarital childbearing probably overstate the adverse effects of nonmarital births. There is little evidence of adverse effects of nonmarital childbearing on infant health and pregnancy behaviors related to infant health. There is also little evidence for an effect of divorce on child development. Evidence for an effect of being born to a never-married woman on child development is mixed.

We next turn to a set of models that include interactions between marital status and pregnancy intention (columns 4 and 5 of tables 9.4 and 9.5). If unintended births are interpreted literally to be exogenous shocks to fertility timing or completed family size, then comparisons of unintended births born outside of marriage to those born within marriage provide estimates of the effects of out-of-wed-lock births on child health and development. We compare out-comes for unintended nonmarital births to those for unintended marital births in order to control for unintended status as we isolate the effects of marital status. Columns 5 and 6 of tables 9.4 and 9.5 summarize the results of these analyses. Here we have collapsed unwanted and mistimed births into a single category for unin-tended birth. The models underlying the estimates reported in col-umn 4 include only exogenous family background controls such as race and characteristics of the mother's family when she was four-teen. The model underlying the estimates reported in column 5 include fixed effects for family of origin. (That is, estimates are derived from differences between siblings or first cousins.)

The estimates of the effect of out-of-wedlock childbearing on in-fant health and related parenting behaviors based on unintended fertility shocks are comparable to standard estimates. (Compare es-timates in columns 4 and 2 in table 9.4.) The figures in column 5 are similar to those in column 3, both of which summarize the results of models that include family fixed effects.

In table 9.5, however, using unintended fertility to estimate the effect of a nonmarital birth makes more of a difference to the esti-mates and, in fact, produces smaller effects of nonmarital births on child development. (Compare column 2 with column 4.) Adding family fixed effects to these models weakens the effects further still, so that there is less evidence of an adverse effect of nonmarital childbearing in column 5 than in column 3. This result suggests that some bias from endogenous marital status may persist even in models that control for family background with family fixed effects. This finding is consistent with the hypothesis that some of the ad-verse effects attributed to marital status are instead due to changes in mothers' circumstances that are correlated with both marital sta-tus and child welfare. Using the random nature of unintended fer-tility appears to reduce this source of bias.[5]

DISCUSSION AND
ADDITIONAL ESTIMATES

The main result from tables 9.4 and 9.5 is that, although there are sizable and significant effects of nonmarital childbearing in "cross-sectional" models, once family background is controlled with family fixed effects, there is little evidence of an adverse effect of non-marital fertility on outcomes related to infant health or child development. Two exceptions and some qualifications, however, should be noted. First, being divorced appears to increase heavy smoking during pregnancy, and never having been married appears to reduce breast-feeding, both by about five percentage points. The five-per-centage-point effect of divorce on heavy smoking during pregnancy is large since this behavior is rare. Fewer than 10 percent of pregnant married women report smoking one or more packs of cigarettes per day, so this effect amounts to a more than 50 percent increase in the proportion who smoke. Since about half of married women in the sample (ever) breast-feed their infants, however, the five-percentage-point effect of never-married status represents a modest 10 percent decrease in breast-feeding.

Estimates based on comparisons of the effects of unintended fertility between married and unmarried women suggest that unintended children born into marriage do about as well (or as poorly) as their unintended siblings or cousins born outside of marriage. Marital status per se does not make much difference. A critic might respond that the disadvantages of nonmarital births could therefore derive from the fact that they are more likely to be unintended, especially unwanted. But this hypothesis is clearly refuted by the estimates presented in the first and second columns of tables 9.4 and 9.5. Pregnancy intention accounts for essentially none of the association between out-of-wedlock births and infant health or child development.

We conducted a number of additional analyses to explore the robustness of the results and to address a number of potential weaknesses. First, we estimated models with detailed controls for the SES of the mother in the year of the child's birth (for example, her income, education, AFQT score, welfare use). These models produced estimates that were slightly smaller (in absolute value) than those reported in column 1 of tables 9.4 and 9.5, but larger than those in column 3. However, the SES of the mother in the year of the child's birth may be an important mediator of the effect of a nonmarital or unintended birth on child health and development. The advantage of the fixed-effects model is that it controls for family background (that is, factors common to siblings or first cousins who share maternal grandparents) without including controls for potentially endogenous SES variables.

Second, we estimated models in which we restricted the sample to women who reported pregnancy intention prospectively (during pregnancy). This restriction is intended to address the concern that women might rationalize pregnancy intention after the birth of the child (see, for example, Westoff and Ryder 1977), and therefore that pregnancy intention might be determined endogenously with infant health or development. For example, a woman who has an infant with health or developmental problems might be more likely after the birth of the child to report that the pregnancy was unintended (Rosenzweig and Wolpin 1993).[6] In the present analysis, the effects of nonmarital childbearing on infant health and related parenting behaviors estimated from unintended fertility shocks were unchanged when the sample was restricted to women who reported pregnancy intentions during pregnancy. On the other hand, the effects of nonmarital childbearing on child development were somewhat larger (in absolute value) for this sample, although statistical inferences did not change.

Third, we estimated models in which we distinguished between unwanted and mistimed births and their interactions with marital status. In these models, the effects of marital status estimated from unintended "fertility shocks" were generally similar to those reported in columns 4 and 5 of tables 9.4 and 9.5. Where we found evidence for an adverse effect of a nonmarital birth using unintended fertility shocks (for example, reduced breast-feeding among never-married women and elevated smoking among divorced women), the effects of marital status were slightly larger when the birth was reported to be unwanted as compared to unintended (which includes mistimed births).

A limitation of the estimates of the effects of nonmarital fertility based on unintended births presented in tables 9.4 and 9.5 is the maintained assumption that unintended pregnancies result from random events (for example, contraceptive failures). To bolster the case for exogeneity of unintended and nonmarital fertility, we estimated models in which we used measures related to the cost and availability of abortion services at the county and state level and measures of child support enforcement at the state level as instruments for pregnancy intention (and their interactions with marital status). Unintended pregnancies are more likely to be brought to term if abortion services are more expensive or less readily available; nonmarital childbearing may be more likely when child support enforcement is lax (Plotnick et al. 1999; Case 1998).[7]

The results of the instrumental variable (IV) estimates are easily summarized. The IV estimates are most often very imprecise and implausibly large, and therefore not informative. First-stage F-statistics suggest that state and county abortion availability and state child support enforcement variables were at best marginally valid instruments for unintended births. (In other words, first-stage F-statistics for the joint significance of the instrumental variables were generally no larger than 2.0; see Bound, Jaeger, and Baker 1995.) One possible explanation of the weak results is that, as noted by Trussell and Vaughan (1999), unintended pregnancy is far from synonymous with contraceptive failure. In particular, many unintended pregnancies result from unprotected sexual intercourse rather than contraceptive failures, and many pregnancies that appear to result from contraceptive failures are not reported to be unintended. Although we believe this "experiment" is conceptually appropriate, more precise estimates will require the identification of better sources of exogenous variation in nonmarital fertility. One possibility is to explore definitions of unintended fertility that are more closely linked to contraceptive failure.

An early version of this paper was presented at the meetings of the Population Association of America, Los Angeles (March 2000). The research is supported by a grant from the National Institute of Child Health and Human Development. We thank James Walker and participants in the conference on nonmarital fertility at the University of Wisconsin at Madison for comments, and we thank Sara McLanahan for the data on child support policies and enforcement.

NOTES

1. The Institute of Medicine (1995) report treats marital status as a mediating factor in the statistical relation between unintended fertility and child well-being. In other words, one of the reasons unintended births are thought to be harmful to children is that they are more likely to be nonmarital.

2. The literature on the consequences of teenage childbearing has demonstrated that the failure to control adequately for family socio-

economic background leads to exaggerated estimates of the consequences of teenage childbearing for child health and development
(Geronimus 1987; Geronimus and Korenman 1993; Geronimus, Korenman, and Hillemeier 1994; and Hotz, McElroy, and Sanders 1997).

3. We independently developed an algorithm for determining pregnancy
   intention in the NLSY. We cross-checked our assignment of pregnancy
   intention with independent assignments by Baydar (1995) and Rosenzweig and Wolpin (1993). There was agreement in over 90 percent of
   cases. When we could not assign pregnancy intention, we used the
   assignment of Baydar (1995) if available.

4. It also reduces substantially the effects of unintended births (not
   shown).

5. Another finding from models with interactions that is not apparent in
   the tables is that the effect of being born following an unwanted pregnancy is often significant, but only for children of married women;
   the effect of a mistimed birth is most often not significant.

6. Joyce, Kaestner, and Korenman (2000b) conclude, however, that retrospective reporting of pregnancy intention does not bias estimates of
   either the number of unintended births or their consequences for infant health.

7. Of course, the availability of abortion services also affects sexual behavior and hence the risk of an unintended pregnancy. See Klerman
   (1998) for a discussion of these issues.

REFERENCES

Angrist, Joshua D., and William N. Evans. 1998. "Schooling and Labor
Market Consequences of the 1970 State Abortion Reforms." College
Park: University of Maryland, Department of Economics (May). Un-
published paper.

Baker, Paula C., Canada K. Keck, Frank L. Mott, and Stephen V. Quinlan.
1993. *NLSY Child Handbook*. Columbus, Ohio: Center for Human Resource Research.

Baydar, Nazli. 1995. "Consequences for Children of Their Birth Planning
Status." *Family Planning Perspectives* 27(6): 228–34.

Blank, Rebecca, Christine C. George, and Rebecca London. 1996. "State
Abortion Rates: The Impact of Policies, Providers, Politics, Demographics, and Economic Environment." *Journal of Health Economics* 15: 513–
53.

Bound, John, David Jaeger, and Regina Baker. 1995. "Problems with Instrumental Variables When the Correlation Between the Instruments
and the Explanatory Variable Is Weak." *Journal of the American Statistical Association* 90: 443–50.

Bronars, Stephen G., and Jeff Grogger. 1994. "The Economic Consequences of Unwed Motherhood: Using Twin Births as a Natural Experiment." *American Economic Review* 84(5): 1141–56.

Brown, Sarah S., and Leon Eisenberg, eds. 1995. *The Best Intentions: Unintended Pregnancy and the Well-Being of Children and Families.* Washington, D.C.:National Academy Press.

Case, Anne. 1998. "The Effect of Stronger Child Support Enforcement on Nonmarital Fertility." In *Fathers Under Fire: The Revolution in Child Support Enforcement,* edited by Irwin Garfinkel, Sara S. McLanahan, Daniel R. Meyer, and Judith Seltzer. New York: Russell Sage Foundation.

Cook, Philip J., Alan Parnell, Michael Moore, and Deanna Pagnini. 1999. "The Effects of Short-term Variation in Abortion Funding on Pregnancy Outcomes." *Journal of Health Economics* 18(2): 241–57.

Duncan, Greg J., and Jeanne Brooks-Gunn, eds. 1997. *Consequences of Growing Up Poor.* New York: Russell Sage Foundation.

Ellertson, Charlotte. 1997. "Mandatory Parental Involvement in Minors' Abortions: Effects of the Laws in Minnesota, Missouri, and Indiana." *American Journal of Public Health* 87: 1367–74.

Garfinkel, Irwin, Sara S. McLanahan, Daniel R. Meyer, and Judith Seltzer, eds. 1998. *Fathers Under Fire: The Revolution in Child Support Enforcement.* New York. Russell Sage Foundation.

Geronimus, Arline T. 1987. "On Teenage Childbearing and Neonatal Mortality in the United States." *Population and Development Review* 13(2): 245–80.

Geronimus, Arline T., and Sanders Korenman. 1993. "Maternal Youth or Family Background?: On the Health Disadvantages of Infants with Teenage Mothers." *American Journal of Epidemiology* 137(2): 213–25.

Geronimus, Arline T., Sanders Korenman, and Marianne M. Hillemeier. 1994. "Does Young Maternal Age Adversely Affect Child Development?: Evidence from Cousin Comparisons in the United States." *Population and Development Review* 20(3): 585–609.

Haas-Wilson, Deborah. 1996. "The Impact of State Abortion Restrictions on Minors' Demand for Abortions." *Journal of Human Resources* 31: 140–58.

Henshaw, Stanley. 1995. "Impact of Requirements for Parental Consent on Minors' Abortions in Mississippi." *Family Planning Perspectives* 27: 120–22.

Henshaw, Stanley, and Jennifer Van Vort. 1994. "Abortion Services in the United States, 1991 and 1992." *Family Planning Perspectives* 26(3): 100–6.

Hotz, V. Joseph, Susan W. McElroy, and Seth Sanders. 1997. "The Impacts of Teenage Childbearing on the Mothers and the Consequences of Those Impacts for Government." In *Kids Having Kids: Economic Costs and Social Consequences of Teen Pregnancy,* edited by Rebecca Maynard. Washington, D.C.: Urban Institute Press.

Institute of Medicine. 1995. *The Best Intentions: Unintended Pregnancy and the Well-being of Children and Families.* Washington, D.C.: National Academy Press.

Joyce, Theodore, and Robert Kaestner. 1996. "State Reproductive Policies and Adolescent Pregnancy Resolution: The Case of Parental Involvement Laws." *Journal of Health Economics* 15: 579–607.

Joyce, Theodore, Robert Kaestner, and Sanders Korenman. 2000a. "The Effect of Pregnancy Intention on Child Development." *Demography* 37(1): 83–94.

———. 2000b. "On the Validity of Retrospective Assessments of Pregnancy Intention." New York: Baruch College CUNY, School of Public Affairs. Unpublished paper.

Klerman, Jacob A. 1998. "Welfare Reform and Abortion." In *Welfare, the Family, and Reproductive Behavior,* edited by Robert A. Moffitt. Washington, D.C.: National Academy Press.

Levine, Phillip, A. Trainor, and David Zimmerman. 1996. "The Effect of Medicaid Abortion Funding Restrictions on Abortions, Pregnancies, and Births." *Journal of Health Economics* 15: 555–77.

McLanahan, Sara S. 1995. "The Consequences of Nonmarital Childbearing for Women, Children, and Society." In U.S. Department of Health and Human Services, *Report to Congress on Out-of-Wedlock Childbearing.* DHHS publication (PHS) 95–1257. Washington: U.S. Government Printing Office (September).

Merz, Jon F., Catherine A. Jackson, and Jacob A. Klerman. 1996. "A Review of Abortion Policy: Legality, Medicaid Funding, and Parental Involvement, 1967–1994." *Women's Rights Law Reporter* 17(1): 1–61.

Moore, Kristen A. 1995. "Nonmarital Childbearing in the United States." In U.S. Department of Health and Human Services. *Report to Congress on Out-of-Wedlock Childbearing.* DHHS publication (PHS) 95–1257. Washington: U.S. Government Printing Office (September).

Plotnick, Robert D., Irwin Garfinkel, Daniel Gaylin, Sara S. McLanahan, and Inhoe Ku. 1999. "Better Child Support Enforcement: Can It Reduce Teenage Premarital Childbearing?" Unpublished working paper #99–01. Center for Research on Child Wellbeing, Princeton University.

Rosenzweig, Mark, and Kenneth Wolpin. 1993. "Maternal Expectations and *Ex Post* Rationalizations: The Usefulness of Survey Information on the Wantedness of Children." *Journal of Human Resources* 28(2): 205–30.

Stata Corporation. 1997. *Stata Statistical Software: Release 5.0.* College Station, Tex.: Stata Corporation.

Trussell, James, and Barbara Vaughan. 1999. "Contraceptive Failure, Contraceptive Discontinuation, and Resumption of Contraceptive Use: Results from the 1995 National Survey of Family Growth." *Family Planning Perspectives* 13(2): 64–72, 93.

U.S. Department of Health and Human Services. 1995. *Report to Congress on Out-of-Wedlock Childbearing.* DHHS publication (PHS) 95–1257. Washington: U.S. Government Printing Office (September).

Westoff, Charles F., and Norman B. Ryder. 1977. "The Predictive Validity of Reproductive Intentions." *Demography* 14(4): 431–53.

CHAPTER 10

Intergenerational Effects of Nonmarital and Early Childbearing

Robert Haveman, Barbara Wolfe, and Karen Pence

Concurrent with the upward trend in the average age at which women experience their first birth is the seemingly perverse increasing trend in the birth rate among unmarried women. This nonmarital birth rate (the number of nonmarital births per 1,000 unmarried women) increased from 29.4 in 1980 to 46.9 in 1994, declining slightly to 44.8 by 1996.[1] As a share of all births, births to unmarried women rose from 18.4 percent in 1980 to nearly one-third (32.4 percent) in 1996. In that year, nonmarital births accounted for more than one-quarter of births to white women, nearly 70 percent of births to black women, and more than 40 percent of births to Hispanic women. Births to unmarried women as a share of all births vary substantially across states, from 16.2 in Utah to 45 in Mississippi and 66.1 in Washington, D.C., reflecting differences in both the race and ethnic structure of regional populations and differences in the rates of marital births across groups. The increase in the birth rate to unmarried women (that is, births per 1,000 unmarried women) from 1980 to 1996 also occurred across all age groups (see table 10.1).

Of these changes, the rapid increase in the number of births to unmarried teenagers has attracted the most attention. From 1970 to 1994, the proportion of all teenage births accounted for by unmarried women increased from 30 to 79 percent; currently nonmarital births to teenagers account for 30 percent of all nonmarital births. Several adverse consequences are thought to be associated with teen nonmarital childbearing. For one thing, teen mothers often appear to be harmed by the experience. More than one-quarter of teenage mothers receive welfare within a year of giving birth, and a much smaller percentage of teen mothers finish high school than do their peers who do not give birth. For teenagers, motherhood clearly hampers the economic and, in many cases, marriage oppor-

Table 10.1 Birth Rates for Unmarried Women, 1980 and 1996, by Age

Age	1980	1996
Fifteen to nineteen	28	43
Twenty to twenty-four	41	71
Twenty-five to twenty-nine	34	57
Thirty to thirty-four	21	41
Thirty-five to thirty-nine	10	20
Forty to forty-four	3	5

Source: Authors' compilation.

tunities they might otherwise have had, and they experience a sudden end to their own childhood.[2] There is also evidence that children who are born to an unmarried teen experience less favorable outcomes when they become young adults, relative to outcomes for children born to older unmarried women or married women (see Haveman, Wolfe, and Peterson 1996).

The impact of being born to an unmarried mother more generally has not received the attention afforded the teen out-of-wedlock birth issue. Yet single mothers, irrespective of age, may also be disadvantaged by the birth, because they often serve as the sole source of economic and emotional support for their children. As with unmarried teen women, the birth of a child may limit the future economic and marriage opportunities of unmarried mothers more generally.

In addition to the implications of nonmarital childbearing for unmarried mothers, there is equal cause to be concerned about future opportunities for their children, who may experience disadvantages that impede their development and ultimate attainments. They are more likely to grow up in a poor and mother-only family, to live in a family dependent on welfare income, to live in a poor or underclass neighborhood, and to have poorer health and lower school performance than children born to married mothers.

Although these adverse implications of unmarried childbearing are troublesome, the nonmarital birth event itself may not be responsible for the observed patterns of poverty and welfare recipiency among unmarried mothers, or of low attainments among their offspring. Indeed, women who give birth while single may have family backgrounds or personal characteristics that account for, or at least contribute to, their own and their children's lack of success; giving birth may be just another manifestation of an unmarried mother's low-income background or adverse childhood experiences.

A number of researchers have put forward this explanation for the relatively poor attainments of teen unmarried mothers (Luker 1991; Nathanson 1991; Hotz et al. 1995). One recent study that controlled for family background by comparing sisters who became mothers at different ages found only negligible differences in a variety of outcomes between teen and nonteen unmarried mothers (see Geronimus and Korenman 1992), but these results do not appear robust. A subsequent critique (and reanalysis of their model) concludes that "the socio-economic effects of teen motherhood do not disappear, nor, indeed, are they small" (Hoffman, Foster, and Furstenberg 1993, 2).

In this study, we seek to measure the adverse effect of nonmarital (versus marital) childbearing on the likely success of a woman's offspring. We conjecture that women who give birth while unmarried experience lower levels of human capital investment (through schooling and work experience), fewer marriage options, and reduced labor supply and income. Because of the mother's lower human capital and economic well-being and the higher probability that she will remain a single parent, her children are more likely to grow up with fewer family resources and less adult supervision, and hence lower attainments (acquiring less education, for example, or experiencing a higher probability of having a teen nonmarital birth). We further hypothesize that giving birth while an unmarried teenager has a larger adverse effect on children's outcomes than giving birth as an unmarried adult.

Hence, we study two questions: Does a child born to an unmarried mother have lower attainments as a young adult owing to the lower life trajectory of the mother (relative to her circumstances had she been married)? Are these adverse effects of unmarried childbearing larger for the children of teen unmarried mothers than for those of older unmarried mothers?

In the following sections, we present several models designed to reveal the impact on a child's success as a young adult of being born to an unmarried mother. We study two attainment indicators: whether a child graduates from high school, and whether a daughter gives birth as an unmarried teen. Using the estimates from these models, we simulate the expected changes in these outcomes if the mother had been married, and if a teen unmarried mother had postponed childbearing from her teenage years to her twenties.

MODELS OF THE EFFECTS OF NONMARITAL CHILDBEARING ON CHILDREN'S OUTCOMES

We present three models designed to estimate the effect on children of being born to an unmarried mother, adjusting for the age at which she gives birth. We estimate these three models for children's educational and (for daughters) teen nonmarital childbearing outcomes. For each model, we distinguish four age categories for the unmarried mothers—under eighteen, eighteen to twenty, twenty-one to twenty-four, and twenty-five or older.

The first model presumes that, prior to giving birth, unmarried mothers are identical to married mothers in their characteristics. We posit that becoming an unmarried mother reduces a woman's human capital investment, probability of marriage, and expected income after giving birth, and that an unmarried mother's lifetime trajectory of resources and level of living falls short of the trajectory she would have experienced had she been married. Under these conditions, the *postbirth* circumstances of unmarried mothers would fall below those of married mothers even though their *prebirth* characteristics are similar, a shortfall attributable to giving birth while unmarried. These poorer postbirth circumstances due to nonmarital childbearing are likely to have adverse effects on the lives of the resulting offspring. Hence, in this specification, we estimate the intergenerational effect of giving birth when unmarried as a simple equation relating the child's outcome to a dummy variable indicating whether the mother was unmarried when the child was born. Because the mother's age at the child's birth may also have an effect on the child's attainments, we also explore the consequences for children's attainments of being born to a teen unmarried mother versus an older unmarried mother.

Our second model reflects the view that, even in prebirth years, there are differences between unmarried and married mothers (and between early- and later-unmarried mothers) that are likely to influence the development and attainments of their children. To the extent that such *prebirth* differences are accurately described by measured characteristics of these mothers, the total effect of non-marital childbearing on children's outcomes can be measured by statistically controlling for these characteristics. Hence, we estimate equations relating children's outcomes to a dummy variable indicating whether the child was born to an unmarried mother, plus variables to control for relevant prebirth differences in the mother's choices and background. This specification again accounts for the consequences for children's attainments of being born to a teen unmarried mother rather than an older unmarried mother.

In addition, in our estimates of this model for the teen nonmarital childbearing outcome (but not the high school graduation outcome), we entertain the possibility that not only do unmarried and married mothers differ in some important *prebirth* ways, but also that their children experience different policy environments during their youth and adolescent years. Hence, in addition to controlling for differences in the observed prebirth characteristics between unmarried younger and older mothers, we also estimate a model that controls for differences in selected aspects of the "policy environment" in which their children live. If the coefficients on the variables describing this policy environment affect only the teen daughter's nonmarital birth outcome, the coefficients on the unmarried (and early-fertility) dummy variables in this model should not differ significantly from those of the prior model (which contained variables describing the prebirth characteristics of the mother, but not these policy variables). However, if these policy variables also proxy for the environment during the mother's prebirth years, they may have affected her choices as well as those of the daughter. In this case, the coefficients on the unmarried (and early-fertility) variables are likely to change from those in the prior model and are preferred to them. In either case, however, if the coefficients on these policy environment variables are economically and statistically significant, changes in these instruments could reduce the probability of the teen nonmarital outcome.

In our final model, we add a set of variables that interact the mother's marital status at the child's birth with the mother's age at the time of birth. This allows us to determine whether the effect of mother's marital status on children's outcomes is similar across maternal age at time of birth. If the effects of being unmarried at the time of birth are due only to that status, the interaction variables would be statistically insignificant, and the estimated effect of marital status would not change from that estimated in prior models. However, if these effects differ by the age of the mother, implying that conditions specific to the mother's age at time of birth (for example, maturity, self-confidence, parental support) are relevant in assessing the effect of nonmarital maternal status on children's outcomes, the coefficients on the interaction variables would be statistically significant.[3]

DATA USED IN ESTIMATION

In our estimation, we use information on 1,899 children from the Panel Study of Income Dynamics (PSID) who were born from 1965 through 1972 and then surveyed for each of twenty-one subsequent years (ending with the 1992 survey year).[4] The data include background information such as age and marital status of the child's mother when the child was born and a sentence completion test measure of the IQ of the head of household (in 1972).[5] In some of our specifications, we included retrospective information on the mother's parents that is available in the PSID, such as education level, whether they were married when the mother grew up, and income level.

We merged on to our data set an extensive array of year- and state-specific policy information to describe the public and neighborhood resources available to the child while growing up. These variables, most of which relate to fertility behavior (sexual activity, birth control, abortion), include:

- State-specific welfare generosity[6]

- Per capita state expenditures on family planning[7]

- Whether the state required parental consent for abortions

- Whether the state Medicaid program funded abortions

- State teen birth rate

- Percentage of out-of-wedlock births in the state

- Ratio of abortions to pregnancies among teens in the state

- Whether the state allowed abortions pre–*Roe v. Wade*

These jurisdiction-based policy variables are matched to individuals during each of a number of teenage years depending on the jurisdiction of the girl's residence in each year.

Table 10.2 presents the means and standard deviations of the variables that we use, for both the total sample and the 929 females in the sample used to estimate the nonmarital birth equations.

ESTIMATING INTERGENERATIONAL EFFECTS OF NONMARITAL CHILDBEARING

We present estimates of the effects of being born to an unmarried mother on the probability that the child will graduate from high school and (for girls) on the probability that a daughter will have an out-of-wedlock birth while a teenager. Whether a child graduated from high school is measured as of age twenty; whether a daughter gave birth out-of-wedlock as a teen is measured over ages fifteen to eighteen. We fit the models using maximum-likelihood probit estimation.

SPECIFICATION OF THE MODELS

We provide estimates from three specifications for the high school graduation outcome, and from four specifications for the teen nonmarital childbearing outcome. Each estimate reflects a particular view of the *prebirth* characteristics of mothers (and/or the policy environment in which the children grew up). We estimate each model using two alternative definitions of an unmarried mother: a mother who had never been married at the time of the child's birth, and more broadly, a mother who was not married at the time of this child's birth. We report only one set—those for the latter definition—because the results are similar across the estimates.[8]

Our first specification presumes that there are no prebirth differences in family background and policy environments between unmarried and married mothers that might affect children's outcomes. In addition to the variable describing the mother's marital status, we include dummy variables for the gender and race of the child, as well as a set of variables that measure the mother's age when the child was born.[9]

Table 10.2 Means and Standard Deviations of Variables Used in Estimation

Variable	Full Sample Statistics (N = 1,899)		Female Sample Statistics (N = 929)	
	Mean	Standard Deviation	Mean	Standard Deviation
Child graduated from high school	.755	.430	NA	NA
Child had out-of-wedlock birth at eighteen	NA	NA	.165	.371
Mother not married at time of birth	.236	.425	.227	.419
Mother lived with both her parents	.645	.479	.640	.480
Mother gave birth at seventeen or younger	.096	.295	.101	.302
Mother gave birth at eighteen to twenty	.217	.413	.207	.405
Mother gave birth at twenty-one to twenty-four	.288	.453	.296	.457
Mother gave birth at twenty-five or older	.398	.490	.396	.489
Firstborn child	.367	.482	.364	.481
Female child	.489	.500	NA	NA
Maternal grandfather had a high school education or more	.290	.454	.288	.453
Maternal grandmother had a high school education or more	.366	.482	.361	.480
Head's sentence completion score (on a thirteen-point scale)	9.053	2.311	8.980	2.337
Child is African American	.431	.495	.438	.496
Mother is Catholic	.154	.361	.157	.364
Mother grew up poor	.433	.496	.420	.494
Proportion of years child lived in Standard Metropolitan Statistical Area from ages six to fifteen	.657	.440	.636	.448
Average real annual public family planning expenditures per capita in states child lived from ages thirteen to nineteen (dollars)	NA	NA	.891	.263

Table 10.2 *Continued*

Variable	Full Sample Statistics (N = 1,899)		Female Sample Statistics (N = 929)	
	Mean	Standard Deviation	Mean	Standard Deviation
Average teen birth rate in states child lived between ages thirteen and eighteen (rate per 1,000 teens)	NA	NA	54.906	13.574
Average percentage of births out-of-wedlock in states child lived between ages thirteen and eighteen	NA	NA	19.918	6.727
Average ratio of teen abortions to pregnancies in states child lived between ages thirteen and eighteen	NA	NA	.375	.108
Proportion of years that abortions were not permitted prior to the *Roe v. Wade* decision in states child lived between ages thirteen and eighteen	NA	NA	.048	.211
Proportion of years child lived in states requiring parental consent for abortion between ages thirteen and eighteen	NA	NA	.131	.313
Proportion of years child lived in states that funded abortion through Medicaid between ages thirteen and eighteen	NA	NA	.397	.460
Real average maximum state welfare benefits when child was fifteen to eighteen (measured in dollars)	NA	NA	197.703	83.015

Source: Authors' compilation.

The second specification tests the hypothesis that unmarried and married mothers have different observed pre-childbirth characteristics that might influence both their decision to give birth out-of-wedlock and their children's attainments. In addition to the non-marital childbearing dummy variable (and the variables describing race, the child's gender, and the mother's age), this specification also adds variables that describe a variety of the mother's characteristics prior to the child's birth, including:

- A dummy variable indicating whether the mother lived with both her parents when she was growing up

- A dummy variable indicating whether the mother's father and mother had a high school education or more

- The score of the head of household on a sentence completion test given in 1972

- A dummy variable indicating whether the mother was a Catholic

- A dummy variable indicating whether the mother grew up in a poor family

- A dummy variable indicating whether the child was a firstborn

- A dummy variable for whether the child lived in an urban area during his or her childhood (designed to capture a component of the child's environment while growing up)

This specification is expanded in the case of the teen nonmarital childbearing outcome by adding to the prior specification a series of variables that describe the policy environment that influenced children's choices in their adolescent years. These policy variables include:

- Average real maximum monthly state welfare benefits in the state where the daughter lived between the ages of fifteen and eighteen

- Average annual real public per capita family planning expenditure in the state where the daughter lived between the ages of thirteen and nineteen, and the proportion of years that abortions were funded by Medicaid in the state where the daughter lived between the ages of thirteen and eighteen

- Average state teen birth rate, average percentage of state births that were out-of-wedlock, and the average ratio of abortions to pregnancies among teens in the state where the daughter lived between the ages of thirteen and eighteen

- Two indicators of the legal climate regarding abortions: average number of years that parental consent was required for a teen to obtain an abortion, and the proportion of years that abortions were not permitted prior to the *Roe v. Wade* decision in the state where the daughter lived between the ages of thirteen and eighteen

A final specification estimates the extent to which the processes by which the schooling and teen nonmarital childbearing outcomes are determined (including the effect of the mother's marital status on these outcomes) vary with the mother's age when the child is born. In this specification, dummy variables capturing the mother's age when she gave birth are interacted with the unmarried mother dummy variable.

Since our sample includes multiple children in the same family in a number of instances, we adjust our methodology to take into account correlations in outcomes among children from the same family.[10] We do this by estimating our models as random-effects probit models. In this specification, part of the error term is unique to each individual, and part of the error term is common to all members of the same family. The model is estimated by maximum-likelihood estimation using Gauss-Hermite quadrature.[11]

ESTIMATION RESULTS

Our results on the intergenerational effects of early childbearing are presented in table 10.3 for the high school graduation outcome, and in table 10.4 for the daughter's teen nonmarital childbearing outcome. The education specifications are estimated over the full sample of mother-child pairs; those for teen adolescent motherhood are estimated over the sample of mother-daughter pairs. Three specifications are presented for the high school graduation outcome, while an additional specification including the policy variables is presented for the teen nonmarital birth outcome.

Our results for the simple model of the high school graduation outcome are in column 1 (model 1) of table 10.3. The coefficient on the unmarried dummy variable is negative and statistically significant at the 1 percent level. In this parsimonious specification, being a male and being African American are negatively related to the probability of graduating from high school. A likelihood ratio

Table 10.3 Effects of Nonmarital Childbearing on Probability That Child Graduated from High School (Standard Error)

	Model 1 Coefficient	Model 2 Coefficient	Model 3 Coefficient
Mother not married at birth of child	−.524*** (.111)	−.458*** (.109)	−.154 (.248)
Mother age eighteen to twenty at birth	.014 (.146)	.086 (.146)	.292 (.222)
Mother age twenty-one to twenty-four at birth	.090 (.148)	.236 (.156)	.421* (.220)
Mother age twenty-five or older at birth	.143 (.147)	.394** (.164)	.620*** (.223)
Mother age eighteen to twenty at birth and not married	—	—	−.321 (.293)
Mother age twenty-one to twenty-four at birth and not married	—	—	−.255 (.300)
Mother age twenty-five or older at birth and not married	—	—	−.490* (.301)
Child is African American	−.309*** (.099)	.080 (.107)	.080 (.107)
Female child	.238*** (.080)	.244*** (.079)	.245*** (.079)
Firstborn child	—	.329*** (.101)	.322*** (.101)
Mother lived with both her parents	—	.275*** (.086)	.279*** (.086)
Maternal grandfather has a high school education or more	—	.259** (.114)	.260** (.114)
Maternal grandmother has a high school education or more	—	.149 (.106)	.146* (.106)
Head of household's sentence completion score	—	.094*** (.020)	.096*** (.020)
Mother is Catholic	—	.128 (.131)	.126 (.131)
Mother grew up poor	—	−.010 (.088)	−.003 (.088)
Proportion of years child lived in Standard Metropolitan Statistical Area between ages six and fifteen	—	−.156* (.102)	−.161* (.102)

Table 10.3 *Continued*

	Model 1 Coefficient	Model 2 Coefficient	Model 3 Coefficient
Constant	.736***	−.815***	−1.027***
	(.191)	(.297)	(.332)
Log-likelihood	−993.4	−957.73	−956.36
Chi-square	68.67***	114.89***	116.76***
Rho	.367***	.309***	.306***
	(.060)	(.064)	(.064)

Source: Authors' compilation.
Note: N = 1,899.
* = .10 level.
** = .05 level.
*** = .01 level.

test indicates that the age at which the mother gives birth is not statistically significant, even though the pattern of coefficients suggests that the probability that the child will graduate is positively related to the mother's age at the time the child was born.[12]

Model 2 in table 10.3 controls for a variety of prebirth characteristics of the mother, in addition to the unmarried, male, African American, and mother's age dummy variables. The magnitude of the negative-signed probit coefficient on the unmarried variable is slightly reduced, though it remains statistically significant. Although only the oldest category of mother's-age-at-time-of-birth variables is statistically significant, the pattern suggesting that the children of younger mothers are less likely to complete high school is more marked than in model 1. A number of the prebirth characteristics of the mother are related to the high school graduation outcome. Children with grandfathers who are high school graduates, with mothers who grew up with both parents, and with a head of household who has high measured IQ scores are more likely to graduate from high school than children whose mothers do not have these characteristics. When these prebirth variables are included in the specification, the gender of the child is still statistically significant, but the child's race is not. If the child is the firstborn, the probability that he or she will graduate from high school is increased, and this effect is statistically significant.

In model 3, we allow the effect of mother's age on the child's schooling attainment to vary by her marital status when the child was born. The results suggest that children born to unmarried mothers are less likely to graduate from high school than are children born to mothers of the same age who are married. For the children of married mothers, the probability that the child will graduate from high school increases sharply with the age of the mother. This pattern can be seen from the mother's age-at-time-of-birth coefficients, which are also jointly statistically significant at the 10 percent level according to a likelihood ratio test.[13]

This pattern is dampened substantially for the children of unmarried mothers. For example, the cumulative coefficient for the children of unmarried twenty-one- to twenty-four-year-old mothers is a very small .01.[14] Therefore, unlike the children of married mothers, the children of unmarried mothers are not more likely to graduate from high school as the age of the mother increases. These results suggest that being born to a mother who was not married at the time of birth is more closely associated with a poorer schooling outcome for a child than is the mother's age at time of birth. The pattern of relationships for the other variables are unchanged from those of model 2.

In all three models, we reject the standard probit specification against the random-effects probit specification, the results of which are reported in table 10.3. The test for this is whether rho, which is the estimated correlation of the error terms for members of the same family, is significantly different from zero. Our estimate of rho is statistically significant at the 1 percent level, justifying the random-effects specification for the high school graduation outcome.

Table 10.4 presents our estimates of the effect of having an unmarried mother on the probability that a daughter will give birth as an unmarried teenager. In model 1, the coefficient on the not-married dummy variable is positive but not at all statistically significant. As the additional prebirth characteristics of the mother and the state-specific, fertility-related policy variables are added in models 2, 3 and 4, the probit coefficients on the unmarried mother variable fall in magnitude (or change sign) and remain statistically insignificant. The dummy variables for the mother's age at the child's birth indicate that daughters born when their mothers were older than eighteen are significantly less likely to have an unmarried birth than are the daughters of teen mothers.

The mother's age-not-married interaction dummy variables introduced in model 4 are consistent with this pattern. For the daughters of both married and unmarried mothers, being born to an older mother decreases the probability that the daughter will have a teen nonmarital birth. In contrast, the effect of marital status is small. Only for the oldest group of mothers is there statistically significant evidence that being born to an unmarried mother increases the probability that her teen daughter will give birth out-of-wedlock.

Across the models in table 10.4, being firstborn is negatively related to the probability of having a teen unmarried birth and is statistically significant. Unlike the results for educational attainment, African American daughters are more likely than non-African Americans to give birth as an unmarried teenager, even when statistical controls for the mother's prebirth characteristics and the fertility-related variables in the state where the girl lived are included in the specification.[15]

The control variables indicating the mother's prebirth characteristics generally have the signs that one would expect, a priori, and in most cases are statistically significant. Daughters with a grandfather who is a high school graduate and with a mother who grew up with both of her parents are less likely to have a teen nonmarital birth than daughters without these characteristics, and these patterns are statistically significant. Unlike the education results, the head of household's IQ score is not related to the probability of having an unmarried teen birth. Coefficients on the variables indicating the mother's religious affiliation (being a Catholic) indicate that this factor is unrelated to this outcome.

Of the fertility-related state policy variables introduced in models 3 and 4, only the level of per-capita family planning expenditures in the state in which the girl grew up is statistically significant. This variable is negatively related to the probability of having a teen nonmarital birth in both of these models. None of the other state variables, including the generosity of state welfare spending, are related to this outcome.[16] Living in an urban area is associated with a negative outcome in both the high school graduation and teen nonmarital birth outcomes, but in both cases the variable is significant at most at the 10 percent level. Unlike the high school graduation results, rho is statistically significant for only two of the specifications, suggesting that a random-effects model is not necessarily a better fit in terms of capturing factors that increase the probability of a teen pregnancy outcome.

Table 10.4 Effects of Nonmarital Childbearing on Probability That Child Had an Out-of-Wedlock Birth at Age Nineteen or Younger: Female Sample (Standard Error)

	Model 1 Coefficient	Model 2 Coefficient	Model 3 Coefficient	Model 4 Coefficient
Mother not married at birth	.076 (.153)	.070 (.163)	.009 (.157)	-.495 (.333)
Mother age eighteen to twenty at birth	-.602*** (.205)	-.699*** (.222)	-.703*** (.214)	-.995*** (.314)
Mother age twenty-one to twenty-four at birth	-.708*** (.206)	-.943*** (.245)	-1.014*** (.240)	-1.292*** (.320)
Mother age twenty-five or older at birth	-.844*** (.204)	-1.176*** (.258)	-1.198*** (.253)	-1.594*** (.335)
Mother age eighteen to twenty at birth and not married	—	—	—	.446 (.415)
Mother age twenty-one to twenty-four at birth and not married	—	—	—	.411 (.421)
Mother age twenty-five or older at birth and not married	—	—	—	.965** (.429)
Child is African American	1.13*** (.175)	.922*** (.189)	1.05*** (.192)	1.06*** (.198)
Firstborn child	—	-.440*** (.175)	-.478*** (.172)	-.450*** (.174)
Mother lived with both her parents	—	-.247* (.134)	-.263** (.130)	-.281** (.133)
Maternal grandfather has a high school education or more	—	-.332* (.192)	-.424** (.189)	-.436** (.192)
Maternal grandmother has a high school education or more	—	.060 (.166)	.120 (.163)	.135 (.165)
Head of household's sentence completion score	—	-.021 (.032)	-.020 (.030)	-.025 (.031)

	(1)	(2)	(3)	(4)
Mother is Catholic	—	−.047	−.038	−.021
		(.235)	(.227)	(.230)
Mother grew up poor	—	.088	.080	.060
		(.137)	(.133)	(.134)
Proportion of years child lived in SMSA during ages six to fifteen	—	.314*	.283	.294*
		(.170)	(.171)	(.174)
Average public family planning expenditures per capita in states child lived at ages thirteen to nineteen	—	—	−1.349***	−1.311***
			(.357)	(.353)
Average teen birth rate in states child lived at ages thirteen to eighteen	—	—	.007	.007
			(.010)	(.010)
Average proportion of births out of wedlock in states child lived at ages thirteen to eighteen	—	—	.003	.002
			(.014)	(.014)
Average ratio of teen abortions to pregnancies in states child lived at ages thirteen to eighteen	—	—	−.280	−.254
			(1.367)	(1.380)
Proportion of years that abortions were not permitted prior to the *Roe v. Wade* decision in states child lived at ages thirteen to eighteen	—	—	.266	.284
			(.428)	(.430)
Proportion of years child lived in states requiring parental consent for abortion at ages thirteen to eighteen	—	—	.016	−.000
			(.239)	(.242)
Proportion of years child lived in states that funded abortion through Medicaid at ages thirteen to eighteen	—	—	.056	.110
			(.201)	(.205)
Real average maximum state welfare benefits at child's ages fifteen to eighteen	—	—	.001	.000
			(.001)	(.001)
Constant	−1.15***	−.570	.157	.446
	(.224)	(.429)	(.773)	(.794)
Log-likelihood	−348.45	−338.28	−327.93	−325.18
Chi-square	63.72***	59.01***	175.36***	180.86***
Rho	.231*	.269*	.181	.188
	(.134)	(.139)	(.147)	(.153)

Source: Authors' compilation.
Note: N = 929.
* = .10 level.
** = .05 level.
*** = .01 level.

SIMULATION RESULTS

In tables 10.5 and 10.6, we report the predicted effects of being born to an unmarried (relative to a married) mother on the probability that a child will graduate from high school and (for daughters) have a teen nonmarital birth. The simulated effects of the age of the mother on these probabilities are also reported.[17]

Table 10.5 presents simulation results for the high school graduation outcome. The weighted base probability of graduating from high school by age twenty is .82 for the youths in our sample. The table indicates that, holding only mother's age and race and child's gender constant (table 10.3, model 1), the probability that the average youth in our sample will graduate from high school if born to an unmarried mother is .67, but it is .83 if the mother had been married.[18] Hence, being an unmarried mother reduces the probability that the child will graduate from high school by .16, or by 19 percent. Employing the estimates that account for the mother's prebirth characteristics (table 10.3, model 2) indicates a minimally smaller change (.14) in this effect of mother's marital status at the time of birth. When the estimated coefficients from the model that accounts for the interaction of mother's age and marital status at time of birth are used (table 10.3, model 3), the estimate is also .14.

The second panel of table 10.5 indicates the effect of an unmarried mother's age at the time of birth on the child's probability of graduating from high school. For unmarried mothers, the probability that the child will graduate from high school rises with the mother's age at the child's birth. For example, if an unmarried mother who is seventeen or younger had delayed birth until she was twenty-one to twenty-four (and no other variable had changed), the probability that her child would graduate from high school would increase by .04 (model 1) or .09 (model 2), depending on the estimates used in the simulation (see numbers in bold italics). The effect of this delay is estimated to be .06 when the coefficients from model 3, which includes age-marital status interaction terms, are used.

The final panel of table 10.5 indicates the expected probability that a child will graduate from high school by age twenty if a mother with the average prebirth characteristics of unmarried mothers were to give birth at various ages.[19] These results suggest that the impact of marriage (obtained from age-specific compari-

Table 10.5 Simulated Effects of Mother's Marital Status and Age at Child's Birth on the Probability of Child's High School Graduation

	Effect of Mother's Marital Status	
	Unmarried	Married
Model 1	.67	.83
Model 2	.65	.79
Model 3	.64	.78

Effect of Mother's Age at Child's Birth for an Unmarried Mother				
	Under Eighteen	Eighteen to Twenty	Twenty-One to Twenty-Four	Twenty-Five or Older
Model 1				
Under eighteen	*.64*	.65	*.68*	.69
Eighteen to twenty	—	.64	.67	.69
Twenty-one to twenty-four	—	—	.70	.71
Twenty-five or older	—	—	—	.71
Model 2				
Under eighteen	*.59*	.63	*.68*	.73
Eighteen to twenty	—	.62	.67	.72
Twenty-one to twenty-four	—	—	.67	.72
Twenty-five or older	—	—	—	.70
Model 3				
Under eighteen	*.63*	.62	*.69*	.68
Eighteen to twenty	—	.62	.68	.67
Twenty-one to twenty-four	—	—	.68	.67
Twenty-five or older	—	—	—	.64

Effect of Mother's Age at Child's Birth for a Married Mother (With Prebirth Characteristics of an Unmarried Mother)				
Model 1				
Under eighteen	*.81*	.81	*.83*	.85
Eighteen to twenty	—	.81	.83	.84

(Table continues on p. 306.)

Table 10.5 *Continued*

	Under Eighteen	Eighteen to Twenty	Twenty-One to Twenty-Four	Twenty-Five or Older
Twenty-one to twenty-four	—	—	.85	.86
Twenty-five or older	—	—	—	.86
Model 2				
Under eighteen	.75	.78	.82	.86
Eighteen to twenty	—	.77	.81	.85
Twenty-one to twenty-four	—	—	.81	.85
Twenty-five or older	—	—	—	.83
Model 3				
Under eighteen	.69	.78	.81	.86
Eighteen to twenty	—	.77	.81	.85
Twenty-one to twenty-four	—	—	.80	.85
Twenty-five or older	—	—	—	.83

Source: Authors' compilation.
Note: Since some children leave our sample after 1985, we use 1985 weights to maximize sample size. The base probability that the child will graduate from high school is .82.

sons between the second and third panels) is larger than the impact of the mother's age at the time of birth. For example, using the coefficients from model 1, we predict that the probability of graduating from high school for the child of a teen unmarried mother would increase by about .15 to .17 if the mother had been married.[20] However, if we simulate the effect of delaying childbearing (for the unmarried mother simulated to be married) from less than eighteen years to ages twenty-one to twenty-four, the probability increases by .02 (model 1) to .12 (model 3). The effect of an unmarried mother less than eighteen years old both becoming married and delaying childbearing to ages twenty-one to twenty-four is simulated to increase from .64 to .83 (by .19) in model 1, from .59 to .82 (by .23) in model 2, and from .63 to .81 (by .18) in model 3. Hence, the effect of changes in the mother's marital status on the probability of the child graduating from high school dominates that of her age at the child's birth.

Table 10.6 presents analogous simulated estimates of the probability that a daughter will give birth as an unmarried teenager depending on the mother's marital status and age at time of birth.[21] Again, the other variables in the estimated models are held constant in the simulations. The overall weighted base probability that a girl will have a teen out-of-wedlock birth is .11. Based on the estimates from model 1 (table 10.4), the probability that a girl born to an unmarried mother will have an unmarried birth is .19, compared to a probability of .18 if she had been married.[22] In models 3 and 4, the effect of mother's marital status is similarly minuscule. If the unmarried mother was seventeen or younger, our estimates indicate that the probability that the daughter would have a teen nonmarital birth ranges from .30 (model 4) to .36 (model 3). If these young unmarried mothers had delayed childbearing until they were twenty-one to twenty-four, the probability of their daughters having a teen out-of-wedlock birth would drop by more than two-thirds in models 3 and 4, to .10 and .11, respectively.

Hence, consistent with the coefficients in table 10.4, the effect of the mother's age at the time of her daughter's birth on the probability that her daughter will have a teen nonmarital birth is substantially larger than the effect of her marital status on this outcome. This age effect is very large in moving from the youngest age-at-birth category (giving birth at seventeen or younger) to older ages, irrespective of the marital status of the mother. In sum, the mother's age when she gave birth seems far more important than her marital status as a predictor of whether her daughter is likely to give birth as an unmarried teenager.

CONCLUSION

Our results suggest that very different family dynamics may lie behind the educational and teen fertility outcomes of children born to young unmarried mothers. Children of unmarried mothers are substantially less likely to graduate from high school than the children of married mothers, regardless of the mother's age at the time of birth. Therefore, the mother's marital status is a more important factor than her age in predicting the probability of high school

Table 10.6 Simulated Effects of Mother's Marital Status and Age at Child's Birth on the Probability of Daughter Having a Teen Nonmarital Birth

	Effect of Mother's Marital Status	
	Unmarried	Married
Model 1	.19	.18
Model 2	.22	.21
Model 3	.22	.24

Effect of Mother's Age at Child's Birth for an Unmarried Mother				
	Under Eighteen	Eighteen to Twenty	Twenty-One to Twenty-Four	Twenty-Five or Older
Model 1				
Under eighteen	*.35*	.18	*.16*	.13
Eighteen to twenty	—	.22	.19	.16
Twenty-one to twenty-four	—	—	.14	.11
Twenty-five or older	—	—	—	.12
Model 3				
Under eighteen	*.36*	.16	*.10*	.08
Eighteen to twenty	—	.26	.18	.15
Twenty-one to twenty-four	—	—	.18	.14
Twenty-five or older	—	—	—	.13
Model 4				
Under eighteen	*.30*	.16	*.10*	.14
Eighteen to twenty	—	.24	.17	.23
Twenty-one to twenty-four	—	—	.16	.21
Twenty-five or older	—	—	—	.19

Effect of Mother's Age at Child's Birth for a Married Mother (With Prebirth Characteristics of an Unmarried Mother)				
Model 1				
Under eighteen	*.33*	.16	*.14*	.12
Eighteen to twenty	—	.20	.17	.14

Table 10.6 *Continued*

	Under Eighteen	Eighteen to Twenty	Twenty-One to Twenty-Four	Twenty-Five or Older
Twenty-one to twenty-four	—	—	.12	.10
Twenty-five or older	—	—	—	.11
Model 3				
Under eighteen	.35	.16	.10	.08
Eighteen to twenty	—	.25	.18	.15
Twenty-one to twenty-four	—	—	.18	.14
Twenty-five or older	—	—	—	.12
Model 4				
Under eighteen	.47	.17	.11	.07
Eighteen to twenty	—	.26	.19	.13
Twenty-one to twenty-four	—	—	.18	.12
Twenty-five or older	—	—	—	.11

Source: Authors' compilation.
Note: Since some children leave our sample after 1985, we use 1985 weights to maximize sample size. The base probability that the daughter will have a teen nonmarital birth is .11.

graduation for her child. In contrast, the daughters of very young mothers are substantially more likely to have a teen nonmarital birth than the daughters of older mothers, regardless of the mother's marital status. For this outcome, the mother's age is a far more important factor.

Although these results suggest that the dynamics behind these outcomes may differ, the underlying message is clear: when a mother gives birth while unmarried or at a very young age, her children—and hence society—bear a substantial cost. This is so even after taking into account the differences we observe in the prebirth backgrounds of these mothers compared to later-fertility mothers, or in the policy environment when the child is growing up (in the case of teen nonmarital childbearing).

So far, our estimates of these "costs" of mother's nonmarital or early childbearing (or, conversely, the benefits of being married when giving birth or of delaying childbearing) have been stated in terms of levels of the child's schooling and (for daughters) teen nonmarital childbearing. For policy purposes, it would be helpful if the burden on either the children or society (or the benefit to them) implied by changes in these childbearing patterns could be stated in dollar terms. If this were done, policymakers could compare the reductions in costs (or increases in benefits) in these dimensions with the costs of policies that might be able to secure a reduction in the incidence of nonmarital or early childbearing.

We would emphasize that we have estimated only a few of the intergenerational effects of nonmarital and early childbearing. Were it possible to ensure that young women would postpone childbearing until they were older or married, their own educational and employment opportunities would probably expand in ways that we do not capture in our estimates; such changes could have additional positive impacts on the well-being of their children. Thus, even after taking into account the characteristics and experiences that separate unmarried mothers from mothers who give birth while married, there is substantial evidence that the children of unmarried mothers do worse than the children of their married counterparts. Postponing childbearing among teens and encouraging childbearing in marriage is likely to contribute to the well-being of their children, as well as to society's.

APPENDIX

Table 10A.1 Robustness Tests for Teen Nonmarital Childbearing Outcome (Standard Error)

	Race-Age, Race-Marital Status Interactions		State Fixed Effects	
	Table 3, Model 2: Coefficient	With Interactions: Coefficient	Table 3, Model 3: Coefficient	With Fixed Effects: Coefficient[a]
Mother not married at birth	.070 (.163)	−.995 (.653)	.009 (.157)	.034 (.166)
Mother age eighteen to twenty at birth	−.699*** (.222)	−1.134*** (.432)	−.703*** (.214)	−.735*** (.225)
Mother age twenty-one to twenty-four at birth	−.943*** (.245)	−1.478*** (.426)	−1.014*** (.240)	−1.076*** (.252)
Mother age twenty-five or older at birth	−1.176*** (.258)	−1.870*** (.457)	−1.198*** (.253)	−1.340*** (.273)

Table 10A.1 *Continued*

	Race-Age, Race-Marital Status Interactions		State Fixed Effects	
	Table 3, Model 2: Coefficient	With Interactions: Coefficient	Table 3, Model 3: Coefficient	With Fixed Effects: Coefficient[a]
Black	.922***	.145	1.05***	1.199***
	(.189)	(.414)	(.192)	(.228)
Black; mother not married at birth	—	1.22*	—	—
		(.676)		
Black; mother age eighteen to twenty years at birth	—	.559	—	—
		(.484)		
Black; mother age twenty-one to twenty-four years at birth	—	.681	—	—
		(.469)		
Black; mother age twenty-five or older at birth	—	.938**	—	—
		(.478)		
Average public family planning expenditures per capita in states child lived at ages thirteen to nineteen	—	—	−1.349***	−.811
			(.544)	(.353)
Proportion of years child lived in states requiring parental consent for abortion at ages thirteen to eighteen	—	—	.016	1.816**
			(.239)	(.887)
Constant	−.570	.007	.157	−4.180
	(.429)	(.510)	(.773)	(7.787)
Log-likelihood	−338.28	−334.82	−327.93	−303.47
Chi-square	59.01***	56.13***	175.36***	68.46**
Rho	.269*	.277*	.181	.150
	(.139)	(.143)	(.147)	(.149)

Source: Authors' compilation.
Note: [a] N = 838.
* = .10 level.
** = .05 level.
*** = .01 level.

NOTES

1. These rates and those on nonmarital fertility discussed later in the chapter are from Ventura et al. (1998).
2. Hotz, McElroy, and Sanders (1995) suggest that the earnings loss attributable to early childbearing is largely offset by an increase in welfare and other transfer income for the mothers, at least in the years immediately following the birth.

3. Note that the "effect" is not indicated by individual coefficients, but rather by the combination of the coefficients on the interaction variables with those on the base-level variables.

4. There were 6,507 members of the PSID born between 1965 and 1972. We exclude from the sample all of the observations that were missing: (a) the mother's identification number, (b) whether the mother graduated from high school by age twenty, (c) whether a teen nonmarital birth had occurred by age eighteen, and (d) the mother's marital status when the child was born. Also excluded were observations for those (e) who were incarcerated or had died before reaching age twenty and (f) who did not respond for two consecutive years. For the included observations, we assigned the mean of prior and subsequent year values when data were missing. Some children left the sample after 1985 but are retained in our sample because they meet all other criteria for inclusion. See Becketti, Gould, Lillard, and Welch (1988), Lillard and Panis (1994), and Fitzgerald, Gottschalk, and Moffitt (1998) on attrition in the PSID. These studies find little reason for concern that attrition, which accounts for the bulk of our omitted observations, has reduced the representativeness of the sample.

5. We assume that, when the head of household is not the mother, because of assortative mating the score of the head of the house is a reliable proxy for that of the mother of the child.

6. For each state, we have annual data from 1968 to 1992 on the state maximum monthly benefits for the Aid to Families with Dependent Children (AFDC) program, the maximum food stamps benefit, and the average Medicaid expenditures for AFDC families. In incorporating this information into our basic data set, we match maximum benefits (the maximum amount paid by the state as of July of that year to a family of four with no other income) in 1976 dollars (deflated by the personal consumption expenditure deflator) for the years when the child is six to twenty-one. For food stamps, the benefit is the amount of the allotment (or the allotment minus the purchase requirement) for a family of four with no other income—again measured as of July of that year. Finally, average Medicaid expenditures for each state equal three times the state-specific, fiscal-year-per-child Medicaid expenditures for dependent children under twenty-one who are in categorically needy families plus the state-specific, average-per-person annual Medicaid payments for adults in categorically needy families. These are deflated into 1976 dollars using the current price index for medical care.

7. 1984 values are an average of 1983 and 1985 values for each observation; 1986 values are an average of 1985 and 1987 values. Again, these have been converted to 1976 dollars.

8. Estimates for the narrower, never-married variable are available from the authors.

9. As indicated earlier, these latter variables are included to measure the effect on children's outcomes of early versus late nonmarital childbearing.

10. We thank Lee Lillard for suggesting this to us.

11. This is standard with STATA's xtprobit command. For more background on this technique, see Butler and Moffitt (1982).

   As a robustness test, we also estimated a probit model with Eicker-White ("robust") standard errors. These standard errors incorporate heterogeneity of an unknown form. (Our specific estimation technique also controlled explicitly for the stratification and clustering of the PSID sample design.) The coefficients and standard errors are essentially unchanged. These results are available from the authors on request.

12. The likelihood ratio test statistic, 1.68, is distributed chi-squared with three degrees of freedom.

13. The test statistic is 10.82 with six degrees of freedom, which is statistically significant at the 10 percent level of significance.

14. The independent effect of mother's age when the child was born is the sum of the coefficients on the mother's age, her marital status, and the interaction variable for nonmarital mothers.

15. Given the significant coefficient on the race variable in the table 10.4 models, we estimated a model that interacts the variables of interest—mother's marital status and age at the time of the child's birth—with the African American dummy variable to test for structural differences in the determinants of children's attainments across racial groups. These robustness results are presented in the appendix; the first column of table 10A.1 repeats the coefficients from table 10.4, model 2, and the second column adds the interaction variables to this specification. The coefficient on the African American not-married interaction is large, positive, and statistically significant at the 10 percent level. The African-American-times-age coefficients are all large and positive, and the oldest age-race coefficient is statistically significant at the 5 percent level. We conclude that the effects of the mother's age and marital status at the time the child is born on the probability that the daughter will have a teen nonmarital birth are greater for African Americans than for the remainder of the sample.

16. It is possible that these policy variables reflect the effect of state-based preferences, economic status, or other factors rather than the policies themselves. To test the robustness of these estimates interpreted as effects of policy differences, we estimated a state fixed-effects model (retaining the family random-effects specification in

table 10.4). The results are shown in table 10A.1, columns 3 and 4. Column 3 repeats the coefficients from table 10.4, model 3; column 4 presents the coefficients with state fixed effects added. (The fixed-effects specification is fit over 838 daughters, while the table 10.4 models are estimated over 929 daughters. Observations in 15 of the 30 states represented in the full sample had no teen nonmarital birth, and hence had to be dropped. Owing to collinearity, the variable indicating the percentage of years the daughter lived between the ages of thirteen and eighteen in states that did not permit abortions prior to the *Roe v. Wade* decision was dropped in the fixed-effects specification.) The fixed-effects specification does not alter the sign or significance of the mother's prebirth characteristics. However, the coefficient on the family planning policy variable changes from −1.35 to −.81, and the t-statistic falls from 3.82 to 1.49. Moreover, the coefficient on the variable describing the proportion of years that the daughter lived in states requiring parental consent for abortion at ages thirteen to eighteen becomes large and statistically significant in the fixed-effects specification. In the table 10.4 specification, the t-statistic on this variable is .07; in the fixed-effects specification, the t-statistic increases to 2.05. We conclude that state policy variables are related to teen daughters' nonmarital childbearing choices, but that the relationships are interrelated with other state characteristics. Note, however, that if the size of a state is correlated with any of the variables, the coefficients in the fixed-effects model are biased.

17. In these simulations, children are placed into groups corresponding to the marital status (and age) of their mothers when they gave birth. For each observation, we hold constant the values of the control variables in each of the relevant models in tables 10.3 and 10.4. Then we change the values of the variables that indicate the mother's age and marital status at birth. Using this new set of coefficients, for each observation we calculate the probability of the relevant outcome (high school graduation, teen nonmarital birth). The probabilities displayed in the simulation are the weighted averages of the newly predicted probabilities for each case. Even though some of the coefficients are not statistically significant, they are our best predictor of the likely impact on children of the mother's marital status and age at birth. Although an extensive set of mother's prebirth and policy environment variables is included in some of the models, unobserved factors may nevertheless cause error in our simulated effects.

18. These simulated changes in probabilities are estimated only over girls born to unmarried mothers.

19. Note that these simulated effects do not indicate the effects of alternative ages at the time of the child's birth for a woman with the

characteristics of a married mother. Estimates of the effect of an un-married mother becoming married are obtained by comparing the age-specific probabilities in the second and third panels of the table.

20. For example, the probabilities in the second panel of table 10.5 for unmarried and under-eighteen range from .64 to .69 in model 1; the probabilities in the third panel for married and under-eighteen range from .81 to .85.

21. We report the simulations for models 1, 3, and 4. The simulation results using model 2 are available from the authors.

22. These simulated probabilities are estimated only over girls born to unmarried mothers. These girls are more likely than the daughters of married mothers to have background characteristics that are associated with having a teen birth. Since we hold these background characteristics constant in the simulations, both of these probabilities are higher than the overall weighted probability of 0.11.

REFERENCES

Becketti, Sean, William Gould, Lee Lillard, and Finis Welch. 1988. "The PSID After Fourteen Years: An Evaluation." *Journal of Labor Economics* 6(4): 472–92.

Butler, John S., and Robert Moffitt. 1982. "A Computationally Efficient Quadrature Procedure for the One-Factor Multinomial Probit Model." *Econometrica* 50(May): 761–64.

Fitzgerald, John, Peter Gottschalk, and Robert Moffitt. 1998. "An Analysis of Sample Attrition in Panel Data: The Michigan Panel Study of Income Dynamics." *Journal of Human Resources* 33(2): 251–99.

Geronimus, Arline, and Sanders Korenman. 1992. "The Socioeconomic Consequences of Teen Childbearing Reconsidered." *Quarterly Journal of Economics* 107(November): 1187–1214.

Haveman, Robert, Barbara Wolfe, and Elaine Peterson. 1996. "How Do the Children of Early Childbearers Fare as Young Adults?" In *Kids Having Kids: Economic Costs and Social Consequences of Teen Pregnancy,* edited by Rebecca Maynard. Washington: Urban Institute Press.

Hoffman, Saul, Michael Foster, and Frank Furstenberg. 1993. "Reevaluating the Costs of Teenage Childbearing." *Demography* 30(February): 1–13.

Hotz, V. Joseph, Susan W. McElroy, and Seth G. Sanders. 1995. "The Costs and Consequences of Teenage Childbearing for Mothers." Chicago: University of Chicago, Harris Graduate School of Public Policy Studies. Unpublished paper.

Lillard, Lee A., and Constantijn W. A. Panis. 1994. *Attrition from the PSID:*

Household Income, Marital Status, and Mortality. Santa Monica, Calif.: Rand Corporation.

Luker, Kristen. 1991. "Dubious Conceptions: The Controversy over Teen Pregnancy." *American Prospect* 5(Spring): 73–83.

Nathanson, Constance A. 1991. *Dangerous Passage: The Social Control of Women's Adolescence.* Philadelphia: Temple University Press.

Ventura, Stephanie, Joyce A. Martin, Sally Curtin, and T. J. Matthews. 1998. "Report of Final Natality Statistics, 1996." *Monthly Vital Statistics Report* 46(11, June 30 supplement).

CHAPTER 11

Finding a Mate? The Marital and Cohabitation Histories of Unwed Mothers

Daniel T. Lichter and Deborah Roempke Graefe

A voluminous literature documents the correlates and consequences of transitions to first marriage among American women and men (see, for example, Goldscheider and Waite 1986; Lichter, LeClere, and McLaughlin 1991; Oppenheimer 1994). Marriage is linked with adult economic, physical, and psychological well-being, especially for men (Waite 1995; Nock 1998). For women, the transition to marriage is associated with exits from poverty, while marital disruption has negative economic consequences for women and children (Holden and Smock 1991; Peterson 1996; Haveman, Wolfe, and Pence, this volume). For the most part, studies of unwed teen motherhood center on its short- and long-term economic consequences (or lack thereof); our understanding of the subsequent marital histories of unmarried mothers, especially teen mothers, is virtually nonexistent (Geronimus and Korenman 1992; Hoffman, Foster, and Furstenberg 1993). This omission is unfortunate. The "end of welfare as we know it," especially time limits on welfare receipt, may create new incentives for unmarried mothers to enter marital and nonmarital unions as an adaptation to economic hardship and to cutbacks in the welfare safety net (Edin and Lein 1997; Lichter and Gardner 1996–1997).

In this chapter, we use retrospective family life history data from the 1995 National Survey of Family Growth (NSFG95) to examine transitions into marital and cohabiting unions among women age fifteen to forty-four. Specifically, we compare the marital histories of teen mothers with those of older unmarried mothers, as well as with unmarried women without nonmarital births. Given the relative lack of information on this topic, we are interested in several basic questions. What proportion of unwed mothers (including teen mothers) eventually form marital or nonmarital unions? Which factors (such as race, socioeconomic background, and cohabitation status) are associated with differences in union transitions between unmarried mothers and unmarried women without children? Does the observed negative association between unmarried childbearing and subsequent union formation reflect processes of "selection" (for example, women with low "marriageability" are also more likely to be unwed mothers) or other causal processes? Our life table analysis and estimated hazard models provide a first step toward a better understanding of how nonmarital childbearing shapes the subsequent marital and cohabitation histories of young women.

In general, our study is designed to document the process of entry into first marriage among unmarried mothers, including teen mothers. Our study bridges a large literature on "the retreat from marriage" and recent work on welfare incentive effects on family formation (South and Lloyd 1992; Lichter, McLaughlin, and Ribar 1997; Moffitt 1995). Indeed, there has been surprisingly little empirical research on the marital and cohabitation experiences of young women following a nonmarital birth. For unmarried teen mothers, the presence of young children undoubtedly creates a new and uncertain set of marital incentives and constraints. Our study provides a point of departure for better understanding the union formation process of young mothers during a period in the United States when marriage and childbearing are being uncoupled (Cherlin 1988).

UNION FORMATION AMONG
AMERICAN MOTHERS

The "retreat from marriage" has continued apace in the United States over the past three decades. Between 1970 and 1993, the U.S. marriage rate declined from 140 to 87 per 1,000 unmarried women (age fifteen to forty-four)—a decline of almost 40 percent (U.S. Department of Health and Human Services 1995). In 1996, 68.5 percent of women age twenty to twenty-four had never been married, compared with only 35.8 percent in 1970 (Saluter and Lugaila 1998). Delayed marriage is also evident in the rise in median age at first marriage, from 20.3 to 24.8 among U.S. women over the 1950 to 1996 period. For many women, delayed marriage often means never marrying; indeed, the first-marriage rate is 41.1 among never-married women age thirty-five to thirty-nine, compared with 109.4 among women age twenty-five to twenty-nine (U.S. Department of Health and Human Services 1995). Moreover, life table estimates indicate that only 86.6 percent of young women would eventually marry if current age-specific marriage rates continued indefinitely, a drop from 94.1 percent observed in 1970 (Schoen and Weinick 1993). Clearly, the retreat from marriage is reflected in continuing declines in marriage rates, increases in average age at marriage, and the rise in the proportions of those who have never married.

Most explanations of declining U.S. marriage rates center on the declining pool of "marriageable" or economically attractive men (Tucker and Mitchell-Kernan 1995; Oppenheimer 1997), on the growing economic independence of women (McLanahan and Casper 1995), and on cultural shifts that emphasize individualism over familialism (Bumpass 1990). None has provided a completely satisfactory explanation, however, of temporal shifts or subgroup differentials in union formation (for example, between African Americans and whites) (Mare and Winship 1991; Brien 1997). At the same time, relatively few empirical studies have examined the complex link between union formation and unwed childbearing, a situation we propose to remedy here. We argue that changes in union formation are inextricably linked to recent trends in nonmarital and teen fertility (Lichter 1995; Ventura et al. 1995), especially as nonmarriage among unwed mothers has become more common.

Our guiding hypothesis is that nonmarital childbearing is negatively associated with subsequent union formation—marriage and cohabitation. But the nature of this association is ambiguous. Indeed, any observed statistical association may reflect the alternative processes of *social causation* or *social selection,* or perhaps both. For example, one causal argument stresses that declines in marriage contributed to the rise in unwed childbearing (Lichter 1995; Smith et al. 1996). Smith and his colleagues (1996) showed, for black women, that virtually all of the rise in the nonmarital fertility ratio (between 1968 and 1985) was due to increases in the percentage of women "at risk" of a nonmarital birth (that is, increasing percentages unmarried). At the population level, the substantive implication is clear: the rise in the nonmarital fertility ratio is largely a consequence of the changing marital status composition of the population; that is, it results from delayed marriage or rising nonmarriage (rather than from the rise of nonmarital fertility rates or declines in marital birth rates). At the individual level, nonmarriage places more young women "at risk" of an unwanted nonmarital birth (even in the absence of changes in nonmarital fertility rates). Some observers also claim that the absence of good marital opportunities, coupled with women's greater economic independence and the declining stigma of unwed childbearing, have elevated nonmarital childbearing (rather than marriage) as a key marker of adult status for young women (South 1996; Hogan and Kitagawa 1985). Nonmarital fertility may thus be a behavioral manifestation of difficulties in finding a suitable marriage partner.

An alternative view holds that the rise in nonmarital fertility has instead "caused" the retreat from marriage. Unwed childbearing presumably reduces the attractiveness or "marriageability" of young mothers in the marriage market. For male suitors, the additional emotional and social costs of marrying a mother (as opposed to a childless woman) are reflected in the burden of sharing the mother's time and attention with her child and in the obligations associated with the newly acquired parental role. The economic costs also increase for potential suitors, who, with marriage, bear the obligation of supporting or sharing in household expenses, which include those directed toward the mother's children. It also is an empirical question whether the stigma associated with marriage to an unwed mother may be greater than the stigma from marriage to a divorced mother.

Unwed childbearing also affects mothers' marital search activities. To be sure, children place obvious time constraints on mothers, but they also engender economic and social constraints that limit mothers' exposure to potential marital partners. For example, children absorb resources that might otherwise be directed toward the purchase of personal items (clothes, for example) or leisure activities (such as joining a health club) that might enhance the mother's attractiveness in the marriage market. Early nonmarital childbearing may also alter mothers' life course trajectories in negative ways, at least from the perspective of providing opportunities to form intimate relationships. For example, a nonmarital birth may reduce women's attractiveness for marriage by preventing them from achieving educational goals, increasing their poverty and keeping their earnings low, and making them newly dependent on extended kin and government transfers, while at the same time reducing their access to economically attractive men in school, in the workplace, or in "good" neighborhoods. The substantive implication is clear: unwed childbearing is expected to reduce the probability of marriage. Indeed, evidence from studies of remarriage indicate that nuptiality rates are lowest among divorced women with the largest number of co-resident children, especially preschool children (who are likely to require especially time-intensive parenting).

Whether unwed childbearing "causes" delayed marriage or non-marriage or vice versa is unclear. Indeed, it remains ambiguous whether any statistical association, if observed, is causal or due to the failure to control other measured and unmeasured factors (Geronimus and Korenman 1992; Upchurch, Lillard, and Panis, this volume); this is the social selection argument. For example, it may well be that young women who bear children outside of marriage are "bad marriage material" because they have characteristics, such as poor emotional adjustment, interpersonal problems, and economic difficulties, that reduce the likelihood that they will marry *regardless of whether they give birth out-of-wedlock or not*. In many ways, the analytic issue here parallels those contained in a contentious literature about the longer-term consequences of adolescent fertility on education and economic well-being (Geronimus and Korenman 1992; Hotz, McElroy, and Sanders 1997). Does early unwed childbearing lead to a disadvantaged later life, or would these young mothers, because of their personal and family circumstances, experience these disadvantages regardless of their childbearing experiences? Several innovative studies have attempted to control for unobserved traits by comparing the socioeconomic achievement of sisters who did and did not have a nonmarital birth, or by comparing the later well-being of teen mothers with that of teenage women who miscarried a pregnancy (who are assumed to be a random selection from the same population). Such studies generally show that the deleterious effects of teen childbearing are substantially reduced when unmeasured variables are taken into account (Geronimus and Korenman 1992), although other studies indicate that effects on schooling and nonmarital childbearing remain large (Upchurch, Lillard, and Panis, this volume).

In this study, we examine the postbirth marital and cohabitation histories of young women. Our multivariate analysis follows closely the recent study by Bennett, Bloom, and Miller (1995) on the influence of nonmarital childbearing on subsequent union formation, including cohabitation and marriage as competing outcomes, controlling for observed family background characteristics (for example, parental education and race). Unlike these authors, however, we evaluate in our study whether this influence differs by prior cohabitation, and our life table analyses document differences by the age of the mother at first birth. We also acknowledge that the effects of nonmarital childbearing and subsequent unstable relationships may well be endogenous; both may "select" on the same observed (grades, family background, and so on) and unobserved (such as temperament) characteristics. Lacking data on siblings in the NSFG95, we nevertheless can compare the prospective marital histories of teens whose pregnancies were brought to term with those of teens whose pregnancies were terminated (through either abortion or miscarriage).

DATA AND METHODS

Cycle 5 of the National Survey of Family Growth (NSFG95) provides detailed retrospective life history information, including family background, marital and nonmarital relationship histories, and fertility experiences, for 10,847 women age fifteen to forty-four in 1995. We use this information to create event history files for 10,804 never-married women at age fourteen. These files permit prospective analysis of the consequences of nonmarital fertility for subsequent union formation that takes into account both time-invariant background characteristics of the woman and time-varying factors, including her age and non-union and nonmarital fertility. This analysis of the transition to marriage also takes into account nonmarital cohabitation immediately preceding the episode of risk.

Our multivariate discrete-time analysis follows that of Bennett, Bloom, and Miller (1995). Models of first-union transitions include race ("African American" coded 1 versus all others), mother's education ("less than a high school education" serves as the reference group in all models), rural residence (coded 1 versus "nonrural residence"), and age at first sexual intercourse (a set of dummy variables indicating first intercourse at age sixteen to eighteen, at nineteen to twenty-two, or at twenty-three or older, with "younger than 16" as the reference group). Our empirical analysis estimates the effects of out-of-union childbearing, a time-varying covariate in multivariate models, and a subsample delimiter in life table comparisons.

Distributions for these variables are shown in table 11.1 for all person-year records of women age fourteen and over in the NSFG data. These data are right-censored by marriage (or, in some instances, cohabitation) or by the date of the survey in 1995. These data reveal that 36.3 percent of the person-year records were marked by a nonmarital pregnancy (at the beginning of the "risk" period). About 17 percent had a nonmarital birth. Almost one-third

Table 11.1 Descriptive Statistics for NSFG95 Never-Married Women at Age Fourteen

Variable	Weighted Percentage/Mean (Standard Deviation)
Had nonmarital pregnancy	36.3%
Had nonmarital birth	17.4
Had a teen pregnancy	23.6
Had a teen birth	12.9
Married within six months of birth (among women with a nonmarital birth)	7.8
Pregnancy ended with induced abortion (among women with a nonmarital pregnancy)	29.9
Pregnancy ended with miscarriage (among women with a nonmarital pregnancy)	11.5
First child lives with mother (among women with a nonmarital first birth)	79.8
First child relinquished for adoption (among women with a nonmarital first birth)	0.43
Woman's mother has a high school degree	42.4
Woman's mother has more than a high school degree	27.3
Woman's race is African American	13.7
Woman's age in 1995	30.6 years (8.3 years)
Rural residence	14.0
Woman's age at first sexual intercourse	
Less than sixteen	22.9
Sixteen to eighteen	40.7
Nineteen to twenty-two	19.8
Twenty-three or older	16.5

Source: Authors' compilation.
Note: N = 10,804.

of pregnancies ended in abortion, and another 11.5 percent ended in miscarriage. The large majority of premaritally born children (about 80 percent) lived with their mother at the end of the risk period. Nearly 8 percent of unwed mothers were married within six months of the birth of their children, presumably to the biological father.

Preliminary descriptive analysis of the probability of marrying by age thirty-five is based on observed proportions of women at each age who either did or did not have a nonmarital birth in the following year. Discrete-time event-history modeling evaluates the risk of transition to marriage or cohabitation associated with characteristics described by covariates included in the model. All models control for the woman's age during the period of observation or, for cohort analysis of the consequence of a nonmarital birth, the duration of the period of risk of marriage following that birth. For multivariate analyses, age is collapsed into these categories: younger than eighteen, eighteen to nineteen, twenty to twenty-four, twenty-five to twenty-nine, thirty to thirty-four, and thirty-five or older. This strategy approximates Cox regression in a continuous-time framework (Blossfeld, Hamerle, and Ulrich-Mayer 1989), where time-dependent covariates are treated as step functions and bias in the estimated effects of covariates is minimized by specifying a semi-parametric form of the baseline hazard function.

Separate life table estimates are then provided for all women: those who had a nonmarital birth, those who had a first birth as a teenager, and those who had a nonmarital first birth as a teenager. For women who experienced a nonmarital first birth, life tables are created that consider their child's living arrangement, and for those who experienced a nonmarital first pregnancy, whether the pregnancy ended with miscarriage or abortion. All other analyses take advantage of an event-history analytical approach. All life table analyses are based on data in person-years, and most begin with age fourteen and censor with a transition to marriage or the date of interview. Life tables for evaluating cohort effects and the influence of the child's living arrangement begin with the nonmarital birth. Logistic regression models yield transition hazards—conditional probabilities of experiencing the event of interest during a time interval, given that the event was not experienced prior to the interval in question—according to the method described by Guilkey and Rindfuss (1987).

FINDINGS

NONMARITAL CHILDBEARING AND UNION FORMATION

We begin in table 11.2 by establishing the relationship between nonmarital childbearing and the likelihood of not marrying by age thirty-five (for a similar analysis with the NSFG88, see Bennett et al. 1995). Women are classified by whether they remain unmarried and childless at age x and either (1) had a nonmarital birth in the following year (column 2) or (2) did not have a nonmarital birth (column 1). Our results have a straightforward interpretation: a nonmarital birth reduces the likelihood of being married at age thirty-five. For example, girls who had a nonmarital birth at age fourteen were 58 percent more likely to have never married by age thirty-five than girls who did not have a nonmarital birth (20.56 percent versus 12.99 percent). Similarly, unmarried mothers at age nineteen were 59 percent more likely not to have married by age thirty-five. For twenty- to twenty-four-year-olds, the relationship between nonmarital fertility and subsequent marriage is even stronger. Indeed, 38 percent of unmarried mothers age twenty to twenty-four had not married by age thirty-five, compared with 19 percent of women without a nonmarital birth.

The transition to first marriage is associated with many factors (see, for example, Bennett et al. 1995; Lichter et al. 1991), including nonmarital fertility. Table 11.3 presents the results from hazards models that include other conventional variables as controls, replicating the analyses of Bennett and his colleagues (1995) for women in the 1980s. The first four columns include all women; columns 4

Table 11.2 Women Never Married by Age Thirty-Five

Age	No Nonmarital Birth	Nonmarital Birth Within a Year of Age x
Fourteen	12.99%	20.56%
Fifteen	13.14	16.28
Sixteen	13.45	19.50
Seventeen	14.17	23.97
Eighteen	15.54	34.74
Nineteen	17.96	28.71
Twenty to twenty-four	18.87	38.12

Source: Authors' compilation.

Table 11.3 The Relationship between Nonmarital Childbearing and the Risk of First Marriage, Controlling for Age

	Including Women Who Married Within Six Months of Their Nonmarital Birth				Excluding Women Who Married Within Six Months of Their Nonmarital Birth			
Variables	Bivariate Models	Bennett et al. (1995, Table 2, Panel 1)	Model 1	Model 2	Bivariate Models	Bennett et al. (1995, Table 2, Panel 2)	Model 3	Model 4
Nonmarital birth (time-varying)	.25** [1.29]	-.121*	-.02 [.97]	-.46** [.63]	.07* [1.08]	-.316*	-.23** [.80]	-.67** [.51]
Black	-.64** [.53]	-.695*	-.77** [.46]	-.65** [.53]	-.67** [.51]	-.669*	-.74** [.48]	-.63** [.54]
Mother's education:								
High school	.10** [1.11]	-.144*	-.13** [.88]	-.12** [.88]	.11** [1.11]	-.150*	-.14** [.87]	-.14** [.87]
More than high school	-.32** [.73]	-.479*	-.47** [.63]	-.42** [.66]	-.31** [.73]	-.496*	-.48** [.62]	-.45** [.64]
Rural residence	.32** [1.38]	.385*	.37** [1.44]	.34** [1.40]	.33** [1.39]	.388*	.37** [1.45]	.35** [1.41]
Cohabiting in prior month (time-varying)	1.77** [5.89]	—	—	1.48** [4.39]	1.76** [5.81]	—	—	1.49** [4.45]
-LogL	—	32,993	—	—	—	32,171	—	—
-2LogL	—	—	—	—	—	—	—	—
Intercept model	—	—	85,051.786	—	—	—	83,310.048	—
Full model	—	—	81,111.5**	78,612.6**	—	—	79,365.8**	76,872.7**
Number in sample	1,202,459 person-months	8,345 observations	1,202,459 person-months	1,202,459 person-months	1,190,437 person-months	8,234 observations	1,190,437 person-months	1,190,437 person-months

Source: Authors' compilation.
Note: Odds ratios in brackets.
*p ≤ .05.
**p ≤ .01.

through 8 include results from analyses that exclude women who married within six months of their nonmarital birth. This distinction is important, since nonmarital fertility may accelerate the transition to first marriage to the biological father but not to other men. Although we cannot establish paternity or determine whether mothers marry their children's father, following Bennett and his colleagues (1995), we can reasonably assume that marriages that occur within six months of the birth of a child involve the biological father. By eliminating these rapid postbirth marriages, we are able to evaluate whether a nonmarital birth reduces the likelihood of marriage to someone else, that is, a man who is not the father of the mother's child.

We begin in model 1 by noting that the odds of marriage among African American women are only 46 percent of the odds among nonblack women. The lower marriage rates among black women clearly are not due to the lower marriageability associated with high rates of nonmarital fertility (see also Lichter et al. 1991). Women from higher education backgrounds have a lower risk of marriage than women whose mothers have less than a high school education. And rural women are 44 percent more likely to marry than nonrural women, a result clearly consistent with past research (McLaughlin, Lichter, and Johnston 1993). The positive zero-order effect (.25) of a nonmarital birth on subsequent marriage is eliminated when these variables are controlled in model 1.

When women who married within six months of their nonmarital birth are excluded from the analyses (model 3), the negative effect of a nonmarital birth indicates that unmarried mothers tend to marry their child's father rapidly and other mothers have slow transitions to marriage. A nonmarital birth reduces the likelihood of marriage to a man other than the child's father by one-fifth (the odds ratio is .80), confirming that Bennett's findings, first observed for the 1980s (reproduced here in columns 2 and 6 of table 11.3), continued to apply, albeit less strongly, in the 1990s (Bennett et al. 1995).

Nonmarital childbearing among cohabiting couples is associated with subsequent transitions to marriage (Manning 1993), and Upchurch, Lillard, and Panis (this volume) have shown that a nonmarital pregnancy hastens transitions to marriage. To address this issue, we include a variable for cohabitation in model 2, which takes into account the fact that roughly 40 percent of all nonmarital

Table 11.4 The Influence of Out-of-Union Childbearing on the Probability of a First Union, First Formal Union, and First Informal Union, Controlling for Age (Thirty and Older)

	First Union		First Formal Union (Marriage)			First Informal Union (Nonmarital Cohabitation)	
Variables	Model 1	Bennett et al. (1995, Table 4)	Model 2: All Women	Bennett et al. (1995, Table 4)	Model 3: Cohabiting Women	Model 4	Bennett et al. (1995, Table 4)
Out-of-union birth	−.25** [.77]	−.151*	−.38** [.69]	−.343*	−.16* [.85]	−.01 [.99]	.249*
African American	−.75** [.47]	−.507*	−.82** [.44]	−.644*	−.58** [.56]	−.62** [.54]	−.216*
Mother's education:							
High school	−.22** [.80]	−.159*	−.15** [.86]	−.104*	.30** [1.35]	−.16** [.85]	−.121#
More than high school	−.47** [.63]	−.364*	−.41** [.66]	−.370*	.21** [1.23]	−.26** [.77]	.063
Rural residence	.24** [1.27]	.237*	.31** [1.36]	−.322*	.15** [1.16]	.08 [1.08]	−.309*
Age sixteen to eighteen at first intercourse	−.45** [.64]	.065	−.19** [.83]	.117	.18** [1.19]	−.65** [.52]	−.013
Age nineteen to twenty-two at first intercourse	−.90** [.41]	−.471*	−.44** [.64]	−.295*	.29** [1.34]	−1.37** [.25]	−.732*
Age twenty-three or older at first intercourse	−1.86** [.16]	−1.114*	−1.28** [.28]	−.864*	.63** [1.88]	−2.67** [.07]	−1.768*
−LogL	—	23,755	—	22,631	—	—	6,415
−2LogL							
Intercept model	66,411.4	—	63,948.3	—	24,014.7	29,642.6	—
Full model	62,300.5**	—	60,990.9**	—	23,052.9**	27,514.9**	—
Number in sample	667,090 person-months	4,221	796,390 person-months	4,221	129,794 person-months	663,110 person-months	4,221

Source: Authors' compilation.
#p ≤ .10.
*p ≤ .05.
**p ≤ .01.

births occur to cohabiting couples (Bumpass and Lu 1999). The results indicate that nonmarital childbearing is an important negative predictor of marriage (b = −.46). The likelihood of marriage among unwed mothers is only .63 of that of other women, and it is even lower if we exclude marriages that occurred within six months of childbirth (.51). Clearly, these results reinforce the view that nonmarital childbearing is a major impediment to subsequent marriage among American women (see Upchurch, Lillard, and Panis, this volume).

The negative effect of nonmarital childbearing on union formation—both formal and informal—is further revealed in the results presented in table 11.4. Here we fit hazards models to first union (either marital or nonmarital), first formal union (marriage), and first informal or cohabiting union. The models include out-of-union births, as well as several standard control variables, including age at first intercourse as a control for sexual development. Bennett and his colleagues (1995) reported that out-of-union births were negatively associated with first-union formation (either marriage or cohabitation), but that the effect was negative for first marriage and positive for first informal union. The substantive implication is that nonmarital childbearing is associated with cohabitation at the expense of marriage. This also implies that nonmarital fertility places unwed mothers on a track of subsequent family instability, given the currently observed high dissolution rates and short durations of most cohabiting unions (Bumpass and Lu 1999; Graefe and Lichter 1999).

Indeed, the results in table 11.4 generally corroborate the previous results of Bennett and his colleagues (1995). Our results show that nonmarital fertility has a statistically significant negative effect (b = −.25) on first-union formation. But this finding is due entirely to its effects on marriage rather than cohabitation. Like Bennett and his colleagues (1995), we find at the bivariate level (model not shown) that nonmarital fertility increases the risk of transitions into cohabiting unions.[1] However, unlike those authors, we show an inconsequential net effect of nonmarital childbearing on informal union formation (model 4). Our results corroborate findings from a recent study by Clarkberg (1999), which examined transitions from singlehood to cohabitation using data from the National Longitudinal Study of the High School Class of 1972. More specifically, bivariate results (not shown) indicate that unwed

Table 11.5 Women Not Married at Age Fourteen Who Ever Marry, by Nonmarital Childbearing Status (Cumulative Percentage)

Childbearing Status	Married by Age x										
	Eighteen	Twenty	Twenty-One	Twenty-Two	Twenty-Three	Twenty-Four	Twenty-Five	Twenty-Six	Thirty	Thirty-Five	Forty
All women (N = 109,179 person-years)	15.4%	28.9%	36.7%	44.8%	52.6%	59.7%	65.9%	71.2%	82.9%	86.7%	87.2%
Women with no nonmarital birth (N = 76,498 person-years)	15.9	30.0	38.1	46.4	54.2	61.4	67.5	72.6	84.2	87.9	88.3
Women with a nonmarital birth (N = 32,681 person-years)	10.6	18.6	23.2	28.1	33.2	38.2	43.1	47.6	61.5	69.5	71.7
Women with a teen birth (N = 15,072 person-years)	41.5	55.9	61.8	66.7	70.8	74.1	76.8	78.9	83.3	84.7	84.8
Women with a nonmarital teen birth (N = 12,603 person-years)	17.3	28.5	34.4	40.2	45.7	50.7	55.2	59.0	68.7	72.5	73.0

Source: Authors' compilation.

mothers are 1.55 times more likely to form informal co-residential unions than are other women, but this effect is explained entirely by antecedent background characteristics of the mother. When the analysis is restricted to cohabiting women (model 3), a nonmarital birth has a significant negative effect on marriage transitions; cohabiting women are 15 percent less likely to marry if they have a child out-of-wedlock than if they delay fertility. Clearly, nonmarital childbearing alters the postbirth marital histories of young women.

LIFE TABLE ESTIMATES OF MARRIAGE

In table 11.5, our life tables estimates, based on the entire NSFG95 sample of women age fourteen to forty-four, indicate that 87.2 percent will marry by age forty. Most (82.9 percent) of these women, given current age-specific first-marriage rates, are expected to be married by age thirty. If the sample is restricted to women with no nonmarital birth, 88.3 percent are expected to marry by age forty. Obviously, these estimates are confounded by cohort trends in marriage and nonfertility, but they nevertheless reflect the lived experiences of women who were age fourteen to forty-four in 1995.

In contrast, only 71.7 percent of women who have had a nonmarital birth will marry by age forty. Women with nonmarital births have cumulative marriage rates at age forty that are roughly 20 percent lower than those for women who did not have a nonmarital birth. Although at every age the cumulative percentage of women who have ever been married is lower for unwed mothers than for women without out-of-wedlock children, differences seem greatest at younger ages. For example, unwed mothers were 38 percent less likely to be married at age twenty-five than their counterparts who delayed childbearing until after marriage (67.5 percent versus 43.1 percent). At the age of twenty, women with nonmarital births are about 40 percent less likely to have ever married than women who bear a first child after marriage. Such results are consistent with earlier results reported in tables 11.2, 11.3, and 11.4.

The bottom two rows of table 11.5 provide life table estimates of the cumulative percentages of those who marry among women with teen births and with teen nonmarital births. Not surprisingly, the marriage rates of women with any teen birth (both marital and nonmarital) are quite high—56 percent are married by age twenty, and 85 percent are expected to be married by age forty. When the sample is restricted to women with nonmarital teen births (bottom row, table 11.5), only about 28 percent are married by age twenty, 69 percent by age thirty, and 73 percent by age forty. As before, the marriage rates among unmarried mothers—including teen mothers—are very low in comparison to all women and women without unwed births.

These cumulative marriage rates (based on the entire sample of NSFG95 women) may misrepresent current marriage experiences of young women in light of observed marriage trends among more recent cohorts of young mothers. Bumpass and Lu (1999), for example, report a decline in the proportion of women who legitimize nonmarital births through marriage from the 1960 to 1964 nonmarital birth cohort to the 1985 to 1989 cohort. Table 11.6 provides life table estimates of the cumulative percentages of women experiencing first marriage, by nonmarital birth cohort. Column 1

Table 11.6 Women Experiencing a Nonmarital First Birth Who Marry by 1995, by Nonmarital Birth Cohort

Nonmarital Birth Cohort (Person-Years)	Married within Year x of Birth						
	1	2	3	4	5	6	7
1964 to 1969 (863)	16.5%	29.0%	38.7%	46.2%	52.2%	57.0%	60.9%
1970 to 1974 (3,249)	12.4	22.6	31.2	38.5	44.6	49.8	54.3
Twenty or older at birth	14.0	25.4	34.7	42.5	49.0	54.5	59.1
Less than twenty at birth[a]	12.0	22.0	30.4	37.5	43.5	48.7	51.1
1975 to 1979 (3,976)	9.0	16.6	23.2	28.9	33.9	38.2	42.0
Twenty or older at birth	8.9	16.6	23.2	29.0	33.9	38.3	42.1
Less than twenty at birth[a]	6.0	16.6	23.2	28.9	33.9	38.2	42.0
1980 to 1984 (4,780)	9.5	17.6	24.6	30.7	35.9	40.5	44.5
Twenty or older at birth	10.5	19.3	26.9	33.3	38.9	43.7	47.9
Less than twenty at birth[b]	8.8	16.4	23.0	28.7	33.7	38.1	42.0
1985 to 1989 (4,105)	5.7	12.3	19.4	26.6	33.5	39.6	44.8
Twenty or older at birth	5.3	11.5	18.2	25.1	31.6	37.5	42.6
Less than twenty at birth[c]	6.1	13.2	20.8	28.5	35.7	42.0	47.4
1990 to 1995 (1,924)	6.0	14.6	21.7	27.0	30.2	—	—
Twenty or older at birth	6.5	13.9	20.7	25.8	28.9	—	—
Less than twenty at birth[a]	7.2	15.3	22.7	28.2	31.6	—	—

Source: Authors' compilation.
[a] Difference between this group and women who were twenty or older at the birth is not statistically significant.
[b] Difference between this group and women who were twenty or older at the birth is significant at p = .09.
[c] Difference between this group and women who were twenty or older at the birth is significant at p = .19.

shows the percentages of unmarried mothers (for successive non-marital birth cohorts) who married within one year of a nonmarital birth. These results corroborate those of Bumpass and Lu (1999). Older cohorts of unwed mothers were more likely to marry during the child's first year than is the case among today's younger cohorts. For example, among unwed mothers in the 1970 to 1974 period, 12.4 percent married within one year of the birth of the child. Among the most recent cohort (1990 to 1995), only 6.0 percent married within one year. Moreover, 44.6 percent of the older cohort (1970 to 1974) married within five years, compared with 30.2 percent among the most recent cohort (1990 to 1995).

We also observe rather large differences between pre-1975 cohorts and post-1975 cohorts in the proportions of unwed mothers who ultimately married. Such differences are not altogether surprising; these cohorts are distinguished by rather dramatic shifts in fertility and in the stigma associated with unwed childbearing and single motherhood. For example, for pre-1975 cohorts, 75 percent

8	9	10	11	12	13	14	15	20	25	30
64.7%	66.7%	68.9%	70.7%	72.3%	73.6%	74.7%	75.7%	78.8%	80.5%	81.3%
58.2	61.5	64.4	66.9	69.2	71.1	72.9	74.4	80.0	83.4	—
63.1	66.4	69.3	71.8	74.0	75.9	77.6	79.1	84.3	87.3	—
57.0	60.3	63.2	65.8	68.0	70.0	71.8	73.4	79.0	82.5	—
45.4	48.3	50.9	53.3	55.4	57.2	58.9	60.4	66.1	—	—
45.4	48.4	51.0	53.3	55.4	57.3	59.0	60.5	66.1	—	—
45.4	48.3	50.9	53.3	55.4	57.2	58.9	60.4	66.1	—	—
48.1	51.2	54.0	56.4	58.6	60.6	62.4	63.9	—	—	—
51.6	54.8	57.6	60.1	62.4	64.3	66.1	67.7	—	—	—
45.4	48.5	51.2	53.6	55.7	57.7	59.4	61.0	—	—	—
49.0	52.2	54.6	—	—	—	—	—	—	—	—
46.6	49.8	52.1	—	—	—	—	—	—	—	—
51.7	55.0	57.4	—	—	—	—	—	—	—	—
—	—	—	—	—	—	—	—	—	—	—
—	—	—	—	—	—	—	—	—	—	—
—	—	—	—	—	—	—	—	—	—	—

married within fifteen years after a nonmarital birth (in other words, before most children leave home). For the 1975 to 1979 and the 1980 to 1984 cohorts, less than two-thirds were married within fifteen years of a nonmarital birth. The implication is clear: nonmarital childbearing is becoming more strongly associated over time with persistent nonmarriage.

One common argument is that nonmarital fertility—especially for older women—may increasingly be viewed as a "marker" of adult status, especially if opportunities to marry are limited by shortages of potential marital partners or other barriers to marriage. Most nonmarital fertility in the United States occurs among women over the age of twenty (Ventura et al. 1995). It is therefore reasonable to argue that older unwed mothers are less likely to subsequently marry than younger unwed mothers. On the other hand, teen mothers (compared with older unmarried mothers) may have other personal or economic problems that reduce their attractiveness in the marriage market (such as lower education or neighborhood dislocations). Our results are ambiguous on this issue. For older cohorts (pre-1975), older unwed mothers tended to have higher rates of marriage than young unwed mothers, but this pattern has reversed among more recent cohorts. For example, for the 1985 to 1989 cohort of unwed mothers, 35.7 percent of teen mothers married within five years, compared with 31.6 percent among mothers age twenty or older.

Moreover, if these data are reevaluated in terms of cumulative marriage rates by a particular age (say, age thirty), then teen unwed mothers are substantially more likely to marry than their older counterparts. As a simple illustration, younger unwed mothers in the 1985 to 1989 cohort after ten years can be compared with older unwed mothers after five years (when they are roughly the same age). This comparison indicates that 57.4 percent of teen mothers marry by age twenty-five to twenty-nine, compared with only 31.6 percent of the older women. Clearly, in this comparison, the impediments to marriage are substantially higher among older unwed mothers than among younger unwed mothers. Or, alternatively, unwed motherhood *results* from the limited prospects for marriage or other unmeasured traits, an issue of endogeneity to which we now turn.

ISSUES OF ENDOGENEITY

Our results suggest a strong association between unwed childbearing and union formation, but it is difficult to make strong causal assertions. Unmarried mothers may have many observed and unobserved characteristics that are associated with both nonmarital fertility and nonmarriage (for example, women who have difficulty maintaining interpersonal relationships). Obviously, we cannot observe the counterfactual case, that is, whether mothers who stayed unmarried would have become married had they not had a child out-of-wedlock.

We approach this analytical problem in two ways. First, we compare our life table marriage estimates for women with a nonmarital birth with those of women who became pregnant but either miscarried or aborted the pregnancy. For our purposes here, we make the reasonable assumption that pregnant women (regardless of how the pregnancy is resolved) are drawn from the same population of women. This "random assignment" of pregnant women to experimental (childbearing women) and control groups (women who miscarry) controls for unmeasured confounding variables (Hotz et al. 1997). Thus, any observed marriage differences between unwed mothers and women whose pregnancies ended in miscarriage are due to unwed childbearing. Obviously, this is not true in the case of abortion, which is highly selective of some groups and also may be seriously underreported (Saul 1998). We nevertheless include life table estimates for this population subgroup for purposes of comparison.

Second, we compare unwed mothers who keep their children—the children live in the mother's home—with unwed mothers whose children do not live at home. Previous research on remarriage (Sweeney 1997) shows that divorced women with children are much less likely to remarry than childless divorced women. The usual inference is that children create disincentives (including financial and child-rearing costs) for prospective male partners, and that children restrict a mother's search activities for partners, although Bennett and his colleagues (1995) conclude that this is not the case. We therefore expect that unwed mothers who maintain custody of their children will have significantly lower marriage rates than mothers who relinquish custody.

Table 11.7 provides life table–based cumulative ever-married rates for women who lost a nonmarital pregnancy (row 1), miscar-

Table 11.7 Women with a Nonmarital First Pregnancy Who Ever Marry, by Pregnancy Loss and Age at Pregnancy

Characteristics of Nonmarital First Pregnancy	Married by Age x										
	Eighteen	Twenty	Twenty-One	Twenty-Two	Twenty-Three	Twenty-Four	Twenty-Five	Twenty-Six	Thirty	Thirty-Five	Forty
All women, pregnancy lost (N = 20,593 person-years)	9.7%	19.1%	24.7%	30.9%	37.5%	44.0%	50.3%	56.2%	72.8%	80.9%	82.7%
All women, pregnancy miscarried (N = 5,914)	12.8	26.6	30.0	36.7	43.4	49.8	55.8	61.1	75.2	81.4	82.5
All women, pregnancy aborted (N = 14,679 person-years)	8.8	17.5	23.0	29.2	35.8	42.5	49.1	55.1	72.7	81.4	83.4
Teenage women, pregnancy miscarried (N = 2,506 person-years)	20.9	38.0	47.0	55.4	62.8	69.0	74.0	77.7	85.0	86.5	86.5
Teenage women, pregnancy aborted (N = 6,498 person-years)	13.6	25.6	32.6	39.9	47.1	53.9	60.0	65.2	78.2	83.0	83.7

Source: Authors' compilation.

ried the nonmarital pregnancy (row 2), or aborted a nonmarital pregnancy (row 3). For these three subpopulations of pregnant women, the percentages marrying by a given age are remarkably similar; roughly 83 percent can expect to marry by age forty. The more interesting comparison, however, is with cumulative marriage rates at age forty, previously reported in table 11.5, for women *with* (71.7 percent) and *without* a nonmarital birth (88.3 percent). These results suggest that "selection" into unwed childbearing accounts for only a small fraction of the large marriage difference between unwed mothers and women without nonmarital births. In fact, women with unwed pregnancies that are terminated (by miscarriage or abortion) are more similar to women without a nonmarital birth than to women with a nonmarital birth, regardless of age at first conception. The substantive implication is that causal arguments regarding the effect of nonmarital childbearing on subsequent marriage cannot be rejected.

At the same time, the causal mechanisms for such effects are unclear. Does the child itself create new costs or barriers to marriage for the mother? In table 11.8, we provide life table estimates of marriage for unwed mothers, distinguishing between those who retain custody of their child and those who are not custodial parents. The results indicate that cumulative marriage rates are higher among mothers who give up their out-of-wedlock children than among those who maintain custody. For unwed mothers who give up custody, 63 percent are married within ten years. For unwed custodial mothers, the corresponding figure is lower at 53 percent. These differences are intriguing and consistent with our causal hypothesis, but they are not conclusive. Mothers who retain custody may be different in uncertain ways from mothers who give up custody of their children (Meyers and Garansky 1993). Fortunately, any differences are likely to *reinforce* rather than negate our causal conclusions. From previous research on child custody orders, we know that mothers without custody exhibit certain traits (for example, mental health or economic problems) that would arguably reduce rather than enhance their attractiveness in the marriage market.

DISCUSSION AND CONCLUSION

Our goal of evaluating the relationship between unwed childbearing and subsequent union formation is increasingly important from a

Table 11.8 Women Who Ever Marry Following a Nonmarital Birth, by Child's Living Arrangement

| Child's Living Arrangement | Percentage Marrying Within Year x of Birth | | | | | | | |
	One	Five	Ten	Fifteen	Twenty	Twenty-Five	Thirty
Not in mother's home (adopted, deceased, or whereabouts unknown)	10.4%	41.7%	63.1%	71.8%	77.8%	79.6%	80.3%
In mother's home	7.9	33.3	52.6	62.7	67.5	69.5	70.2

Source: Authors' compilation.
Note: N = 18,897 person-years.

policy standpoint. The new welfare reform bill and resulting public assistance program, Temporary Assistance for Needy Families (TANF), are targeted at welfare-dependent and nonemployed single mothers. An explicit goal of the new policy is to discourage non-marital fertility (for example, through abstinence programs and re-wards to states for reducing unwed childbearing) while supporting childbearing and child-rearing within two-parent, married-couple families. Faced with time limits on welfare receipt, unmarried mothers must adapt economically to the new welfare environment in many ways; indeed, in the absence of welfare income, incentives to marry or cohabit may increase among single mothers with minor children. Yet our understanding of union formation processes among unwed mothers is limited.

Our chapter addresses this void. Retrospective family life history data from the 1995 National Survey of Family Growth indicate that nonmarital childbearing is associated with significant reductions in the likelihood of being married at age thirty-five. At age fourteen, for example, girls who had a nonmarital birth were 58 percent more likely to have never been married by age thirty-five than girls who did not have a nonmarital birth (20.6 percent versus 13.0 percent). Nonmarital childbearing is positively associated with the subse-quent formation of informal or cohabitating unions, but this is due entirely to family background characteristics. Our life table analysis also indicates that only 72 percent of women who had a nonmarital birth can expect to be married by age forty, a figure that is roughly 20 percent lower than it is for women who did not have a nonmari-tal birth. Moreover, the lower marriage rate among unwed mothers evidently is not due to selection alone. The cumulative marriage rates of women with unwed pregnancies that are terminated (by miscarriage or abortion) are more similar to those of women with-out nonmarital births than to women with nonmarital births. The substantive implication is that causal arguments regarding the long-term negative effect of nonmarital childbearing on subsequent mar-riage cannot be rejected (see Upchurch, Lillard, and Panis, this vol-ume).

To be sure, our study has been largely descriptive. As such, fu-ture work must identify and evaluate the specific potential causal mechanisms through which nonmarital childbearing may diminish subsequent prospects for marriage. From the perspective of single mothers, for example, nonmarital childbearing and child-rearing may reduce marital search activities, limit "exposure" to economically attractive prospective partners (if childbearing cuts short women's educational or occupational achievement), or serve as an alternative route to family formation and reduce the incentive to form traditional husband-wife families (for example, women with children are less likely than childless women to "desire to marry"). Any incentive to marry may also be discouraged by the resulting loss of welfare income available to single mothers with children (McLaughlin and Lichter 1997). From the perspective of the potential male partner of the mother, the presence of another man's children in the home may represent a financial and emotional cost that discourages marriage. Knowing that the children will also compete for the mother's time and attention may also affect his incentive to marry. Clearly, if marriage is to be a major adaptive response of unwed mothers to the new welfare environment and to low income, our attention should now be focused on the specific constraints faced by unwed mothers in the marriage market.

Whether marriage should be encouraged or not as a specific policy tool has a contentious history (for example, "wed-fare" programs). On the one hand, marriage may contribute positively to the economic and emotional well-being of children of single mothers, who may benefit themselves emotionally from marriage to a supportive spouse (for example, married women report better mental health than single women). On the other hand, marriage may create new economic and emotional dependencies on men that are ultimately unhealthy for both women and children (for example, abusive relationships). We cannot adjudicate these competing concerns here. Our goal has been more modest—to evaluate the prospective marital histories of unwed mothers in a policy environment that increasingly views marriage as a potential panacea.

This research was supported in part by grants from the National Science Foundation and the Russell Sage Foundation, and by a Population Research Center Core Grant (P30 HD28263-01) from the National Institute of Child Health and Human Development to the Population Research Institute, Pennsylvania State University. The helpful comments of Michael Rendall are gratefully appreciated.

NOTE

1. The risk set for analyses excludes women who were cohabiting at the time of the birth of their first child.

REFERENCES

Bennett, Neil G., David E. Bloom, and Cynthia K. Miller. 1995. "The Influence of Nonmarital Childbearing on the Formation of First Marriages." *Demography* 32: 47–62.

Blossfeld, Hans-Peter, Alfred Hamerle, and Karl Ulrich-Mayer. 1989. *Event History Analysis: Statistical Theory and Application in the Social Sciences.* Hillsdale, N.J.: Erlbaum.

Brien, Michael J. 1997. "Racial Differences in Marriage and the Role of Marriage Markets." *Journal of Human Resources* 32: 741–78.

Bumpass, Larry L. 1990. "What's Happening to the Family?: Interactions Between Demographic and Institutional Change." *Demography* 27: 483–98.

Bumpass, Larry L., and Hsien-Hen Lu. 1999. "Trends in Cohabitation and Implications for Children's Family Contexts in the United States." *Population Studies* 54: 29–41.

Cherlin, Andrew J. 1988. "The Weakening Link Between Marriage and the Care of Children." *Family Planning Perspectives* 20: 302–6.

Clarkberg, Marin. 1999. "The Price of Partnering: The Role of Economic Well-Being in Young Adults' First Union Experience." *Social Forces* 77: 94–68.

Edin, Kathryn, and Laura Lein. 1997. *Making Ends Meet: How Single Mothers Survive Welfare and Low-Wage Work.* New York: Russell Sage Foundation.

Geronimus, Arline T., and Sanders Korenman. 1992. "The Socioeconomic Consequences of Teen Childbearing Reconsidered." *Quarterly Journal of Economics* 52: 1187–1214.

Goldscheider, Francis, and Linda Waite. 1986. "Sex Differences in the Entry into Marriage." *American Journal of Sociology* 92: 91–109.

Graefe, Deborah Roempke, and Daniel T. Lichter. 1999. "Life Course Transitions of American Children: Parental Cohabitation, Marriage, and Single Motherhood." *Demography* 36: 205–17.

Guilkey, David K., and Ronald R. Rindfuss. 1987. "Logistic Regression Multivariate Life Tables: A Communicable Approach." *Sociological Methods and Research* 16: 276–300.

Hoffman, Saul D., E. Michael Foster, and Frank F. Furstenberg Jr. 1993. "Reevaluating the Costs of Teenage Childbearing." *Demography* 30: 1–13.

Hogan, Dennis P., and Evelyn M. Kitagawa. 1985. "The Impact of Social Status, Family Structure, and Neighborhood on the Fertility of Black Adolescents." *American Journal of Sociology* 90: 825–52.

Holden, Karin, and Pamela Smock. 1991. "The Economic Costs of Marital Dissolution: Why Do Women Bear a Disproportionate Cost?" *Annual Review of Sociology* 17: 51–78.

Hotz, V. Joseph, Susan W. McElroy, and Seth G. Sanders. 1997. "The Impacts of Teenage Childbearing on the Mothers and the Consequences of Those Impacts for Government." In *Kids Having Kids: Economic Costs and Social Consequences of Teen Pregnancy,* edited by Rebecca Maynard. Washington, D.C.: Urban Institute Press.

Lichter, Daniel T. 1995. "The Retreat from Marriage and the Rise in Nonmarital Fertility." In *Report to Congress on Nonmarital Fertility.* Washington: U.S. Department of Health and Human Resources.

Lichter, Daniel T., and Erica Gardner. 1996–1997. "Welfare Reform and the Poor Children of Working Parents." *Focus* 18(2): 65–70.

Lichter, Daniel T., Felicia B. LeClere, and Diane K. McLaughlin. 1991. "Local Marriage Markets and the Marital Behavior of Black and White Women." *American Journal of Sociology* 96: 843–67.

Lichter, Daniel T., Diane K. McLaughlin, and David C. Ribar. 1997. "Welfare and the Rise in Female-Headed Families." *American Journal of Sociology* 103: 112–43.

Manning, Wendy. 1993. "Marriage and Cohabitation Following Premarital Conception." *Journal of Marriage and the Family* 55: 839–50.

Mare, Robert D., and Christopher Winship. 1991. "Socioeconomic Change and the Decline of Marriage for Blacks and Whites." In *The Urban Underclass,* edited by Christopher Jencks and Paul E. Peterson. Washington, D.C.: Brookings Institution.

McLanahan, Sara, and Lynne Casper. 1995. "Growing Diversity and Inequality in the American Family." In *State of the Union,* edited by Reynolds Farley, vol. 2. New York: Russell Sage Foundation.

McLaughlin, Diane K., and Daniel T. Lichter. 1997. "Poverty and the Marital Behavior of Young Women." *Journal of Marriage and the Family* 59: 582–94.

McLaughlin, Diane K., Daniel T. Lichter, and Gail M. Johnston. 1993. "Some Women Marry Young: Transitions to First Marriage in Metropolitan and Nonmetropolitan Areas." *Journal of Marriage and the Family* 55: 827–38.

Meyers, Daniel, and Steven Garansky. 1993. "Custodial Fathers: Myths, Realities, and Child Support Policy." *Journal of Marriage and the Family* 55: 73–89.

Moffitt, Robert. 1995. "The Effect of the U.S. Welfare System on Nonmarital Childbearing." In *Report to Congress on Out-of-Wedlock Childbearing.* Washington: U.S. Department of Health and Human Services.

Nock, Stephen L. 1998. *Marriage in Men's Lives.* Cambridge: Oxford University Press.

Oppenheimer, Valerie K. 1994. "Women's Rising Employment and the Future of the Family in Industrial Societies." *Population and Development Review* 20: 293–342.

———. 1997. "Women's Employment and the Gains to Marriage: The Specialization and Trading Model." *Annual Review of Sociology* 23: 431–53.

Peterson, Richard R. 1996. "A Re-evaluation of the Economic Consequences of Divorce." *American Sociological Review* 61: 528–36.

Saluter, Arlen F., and Terry A. Lugaila. 1998. "Marital Status and Living Arrangements: March 1996." *Current Population Reports* P20–496. Washington: U.S. Bureau of the Census.

Saul, Rebekah. 1998. "Abortion Reporting in the United States: An Examination of the Federal-State Partnership." *Family Planning Perspectives* 30(September-October): 244–47.

Schoen, Robert, and Robin M. Weinick. 1993. "The Slowing Metabolism of Marriage: Figures from 1988 U.S Marital Status Life Tables. *Demography* 30: 737–46.

Smith, Herbert L., S. Philip Morgan, and Tanya Koropeckyj-Cox. 1996. "A Decomposition of Trends in the Nonmarital Fertility Ratios of Blacks and Whites in the United States, 1960–92." *Demography* 33: 141–52.

South, Scott. 1996. "Mate Availability and the Transition to Unwed Motherhood: A Paradox of Population Structure." *Journal of Marriage and the Family* 58: 265–79.

South, Scott, and Kim M. Lloyd. 1992. "Marriage Markets and Nonmarital Fertility in the United States." *Demography* 29: 247–64.

Sweeney, Megan M. 1997. "Remarriage of Women and Men After Divorce: The Role of Economic Prospects." *Journal of Family Issues* 18: 479–502.

Tucker, M. Belinda, and Claudia Mitchell-Kernan. 1995. *The Decline in Marriage Among African Americans.* New York: Russell Sage Foundation.

U.S. Department of Health and Human Services. 1995. "Advance Report of Final Marriage Statistics, 1989 and 1990." *Monthly Vital Statistics Report* 43(12, July 14 supplement).

Ventura, Stephanie, Christine A. Bachrach, Laura Hill, Kelleen Kaye, Pamela Holcomb, and Elisa Koff. 1995. "The Demography of Out-of-Wedlock Childbearing." In *Report on Out-of-Wedlock Childbearing.* Washington: U.S. Department of Health and Human Services.

Waite, Linda. 1995. "Does Marriage Matter?" *Demography* 32: 483–507.

CHAPTER 12

The Impact of Nonmarital Childbearing on Subsequent Marital Formation and Dissolution

Dawn M. Upchurch, Lee A. Lillard, and Constantijn W. A. Panis

Economic and social theories point to the detrimental influences of nonmarital childbearing on marriage formation and stability (Becker 1973; Becker, Landes, and Michael 1977; Morgan, Lye, and Condran 1988), and recent empirical findings support these perspectives (for example, Bennett, Bloom, and Craig 1989; Bennett, Bloom, and Miller 1995; Martin and Bumpass 1989). Explanations for the reduced likelihood of marriage among women with non-marital children propose that these children may be viewed as economic and psychic burdens to a future spouse and that they may also hinder the search process for the woman (Bennett, Bloom, and Miller 1995; Lichter and Graefe, this volume; Waite and Lillard 1991). Explanations for the increased likelihood of divorce stem from arguments of marriage-specific capital: these children may be a source of marital stress because they belong to only one partner (Becker et al. 1977; Cherlin 1978; Morgan et al. 1988; Waite and Lillard 1991). Recent conceptualizations of family-building behaviors also suggest that childbearing, marriage, and divorce decisions are often interrelated in complex ways (Bumpass 1990; Pagnini and Rindfuss 1993), although the link between nonmarital pregnancy and marriage has weakened in recent years (Akerlof, Yellen, and Katz 1996; Bumpass 1990; Casterline, Lee, and Foote 1996; Pagnini and Rindfuss 1993).

The purpose of this chapter is to examine the impact of nonmarital childbearing on subsequent marriage formation and dissolution.[1] In particular, we are concerned with distinguishing the potential consequences of nonmarital childbearing (that is, the direct effects) from spurious association due to joint determination (selection).

Data from the National Longitudinal Survey of Youth (NLSY) are analyzed, and we jointly model five separate life course processes—nonmarital fertility, marriage formation, marital dissolution, marital fertility, and educational progression—using econometric innovations developed by Lillard (1993).

We find that white, Hispanic, and black women with nonmarital children have significantly lower risks of marrying than childless women. For white and Hispanic women, children from a previous marriage also reduce their risk of remarriage. However, women who are nonmaritally pregnant have significantly higher risk of marrying. We find no direct effect of nonmarital children on the risk of marital dissolution after accounting for the endogeneity of these processes. Rather, our findings suggest that there are unmeasured characteristics that predispose women to both nonmarital childbearing and marital instability. Married women who are currently pregnant or who have children from that marriage have significantly lower risk of dissolution. In contrast, white and Hispanic women who were pregnant on their wedding date have a significantly higher risk of dissolution. Thus, nonmarital children appear to slow down women's marital search, but once married, the nonmarital children do not directly contribute to the risk of separating. And though a nonmarital pregnancy hastens the marital search process, there are continuing direct effects for whites and Hispanics that increase their risk of subsequent marital dissolution.

THEORETICAL BACKGROUND AND HYPOTHESES

The conceptual framework developed for this work integrates key aspects from economic and sociological theories of family-building behaviors and incorporates the dynamic and interrelated approach offered by the life course perspective (Becker 1991; Becker et al. 1977; Cherlin 1978; Elder 1995, 1997; Willis and Haaga 1996). Specifically, we view family-building behaviors as dynamic, sequential, and mutually influencing (Casterline et al. 1996; Yamaguchi and Ferguson 1995) and posit that women's childbearing decisions are interrelated with other life experiences, in particular, decisions regarding marital formation and dissolution (Brien, Lillard, and Waite 1999; Elder 1997).

Nonmarital childbearing may be viewed as a family-building behavior that occurs under particular economic and social conditions where the benefits of marriage are minimal (Willis 1999; Willis and Haaga 1996). This is the case in marriage markets where there is an excess of women who are economically self-sufficient, and so non-marital childbearing is a more common family formation strategy among economically disadvantaged groups and where marriageable men are relatively scarce (McLaughlin and Lichter 1997; Willis 1999; Willis and Haaga 1996; Wilson 1987; Wilson and Neckerman 1986). Thus, childbearing and marriage, although related, are par-tially separable family-building behaviors (Bumpass 1990; Cherlin 1990; Pagnini and Rindfuss 1993; Willis and Haaga 1996).

Economic models of fertility assume that childbearing decisions are static, occurring once for a unified couple (Becker 1960, 1991). However, childbearing decisions may be modified as women gain experience and additional information once they become mothers (Yamaguchi and Ferguson 1995). We propose that childbearing de-cisions are rational choices made among alternatives and contingent on constraints (Becker 1960, 1991) and posit that the transition to motherhood (with emphasis on nonmarital motherhood) is the re-sult of a sequence of fertility-related decisions that are purposive (Elder 1997). A nonmarital birth is the result of several decisions: a woman chooses to not use an effective contraception; upon becom-ing pregnant, she chooses not to abort; and finally, she chooses to not marry.

EFFECTS OF CHILDBEARING ON SUBSEQUENT MARRIAGE FORMATION

The timing of marriage can be seen as a search process in which women meet potential spouses, each having different levels of match quality (Mortensen 1988; Oppenheimer 1988). Nonmarital children affect this search process because they pose social and eco-nomic constraints and time limitations for mothers, such that the opportunities for meeting potential spouses are reduced. For exam-ple, social networks and interactions centered on child-related ac-tivities, such as child-care sharing and increased contacts with ex-tended kin and family members, limit women's interaction with possible partners. Also, nonmarital children may be viewed as eco-nomic and psychic burdens to potential spouses (Bennett, Bloom, and Miller 1995). That is, a prospective partner may believe that the additional costs of sharing a mother's tie, child-care responsibilities, household expenses, and other responsibilities are untenable. Thus, we hypothesize that single women with a nonmarital child (or children) will have longer durations of searching and thus a lower risk of marrying than single women who are childless. Similarly, the number of nonmarital children may affect marriage prospects because of the heightened obstacles associated with additional children, including attractiveness to future partners and increased time constraints.

In contrast, a nonmarital pregnancy would shorten the marital search in an effort to legitimate the birth (Goldscheider and Waite 1986; Parnell, Swicegood, and Stevens 1994). The propensity to legitimate a pregnancy is influenced by the social norms governing the acceptability of nonmarital childbearing as well as the availability of "marriageable" partners (Anderson 1991; East 1998; St. John and Rowe 1990; Wilson 1987). Thus, we hypothesize that women who conceive nonmaritally will have an increased risk of marrying, and we expect black women who conceive nonmaritally to have a lower risk of marrying than their white counterparts (Manning and Smock 1995; Parnell et al. 1994).

The impact of prior marital children on subsequent remarriage is also examined since we analyze both first- and higher-order marriages. The general arguments developed with respect to nonmarital children and marriage search are applicable here; women with children from a previous marriage, however, may be at an additional disadvantage because these children are part of marriage-specific capital. As before, children may discourage prospective spouses who are not interested in raising children from a prior relationship. Also, marital children may spend time with both parents in joint custody arrangements, and the involvement of the children's father after divorce and the additional time constraints brought on by these arrangements could impede a woman's search, reducing her risk of marriage (Koo and Suchindran 1980; Teachman and Heckert 1985; Weiss and Willis 1985). We hypothesize, therefore, that women with children from a previous marriage incur a longer search period and therefore have a lower risk of remarrying than childless women. We also compare and contrast the effects of prior marital children with those of nonmarital children on marrying.

In addition to these direct influences of the presence of children on the risk of marrying, there may also be unobserved characteristics of the woman that predispose her to both having children and marrying. For example, becoming a mother and a wife may hold a similar attraction for women who want to start the family-building process, and alternately, women who choose to defer family building may forgo both motherhood and marriage. That is, we propose that individual women have an unmeasured underlying propensity toward family-building behaviors that varies across women. This unmeasured trait is characterized by a woman-specific unobserved heterogeneity term in our modeling efforts. The assumption, however, does not necessarily presume that women's desires are fixed; rather, we allow for possible changes by taking into account women's prior experiences (previous births and marriages, for instance) and the potential endogeneity of those experiences. Consequently, women's decisionmaking is allowed to change as experience is gained during their early life course.

EFFECTS OF CHILDBEARING ON MARITAL DISSOLUTION

Theoretical models of marriage and childbearing have conceptualized children born within a marriage as part of marriage-specific capital (Becker 1973; Becker et al. 1977). The accumulation of marriage-specific capital reduces the likelihood that a married couple will dissolve their marriage because of the high costs of leaving and the increased benefits of the relationship. The presence of marital children increases the gains of family life and provides nonsubstitutable pleasure to the parents (Morgan et al. 1988). Additionally, couples with children may experience more normative disapproval regarding divorce than childless couples (Thornton 1977) and therefore be more likely to stay together. Thus, children born in a marriage provide a stabilizing influence and would therefore reduce the risk of divorce relative to that of childless couples. This protective effect, however, occurs only when the children are young (Cherlin 1977; Waite and Lillard 1991). Additionally, a current pregnancy may signal an increased commitment to the relationship and would decrease the likelihood that a couple will dissolve a marriage.

Stepchildren, in contrast, may destabilize a new marriage because they belong to only one spouse and also are a source of ties outside the relationship, such as the child's other biological parent and his or her extended family (Becker et al. 1977; Cherlin 1978; White and Booth 1985). We hypothesize that children from prior marriages weaken the current marriage and thus increase the woman's risk of separation. The influence of nonmarital children on marital dissolution would operate in a similar manner. Nonmarital children, though not the product of a formal marital union, are children from a relationship outside of the current marriage. Therefore, these children would also be a source of conflict within a marriage (Cherlin 1978; Heaton 1991; Waite and Lillard 1991), and so we hypothesize that the presence of nonmarital children increases the risk that a marriage will dissolve.

There may also be unobserved characteristics that influence the woman's decisions about both childbearing and separation. Although there is theoretical and empirical support for the idea that family-building strategies may be interchangeable for some women (Brien, Lillard, and Waite 1999; Bumpass 1990), we are somewhat more circumspect in our hypotheses regarding childbearing and separation. In the case of nonmarital fertility, it might be that the woman places less value on marriage per se, and thus, should a subsequent marriage become problematic, she would be more inclined to dissolve the union (positive correlation). Alternately, a woman who places a high value on motherhood may also highly value being a wife and thus be disinclined to separate (negative correlation). Once again, our model assumes that individual women have some unmeasured propensity for these behaviors, but we allow women's subsequent decisions regarding childbearing and marriage to be influenced by their prior behaviors and experiences.

DATA

The data used for the analysis are from the National Longitudinal Survey of Youth (NLSY). The NLSY has several unique features that make it ideally suited for our work. First, it includes detailed information on the timing of events related to all of the life course processes considered. Second, individuals are surveyed approximately annually so that concurrent information is available at the time (before and after) when the events and transitions under study are occurring. Third, the sample is young enough so that the behaviors we are studying are occurring within the sample panel period for most individuals.

The NLSY is a nationally representative sample of more than 12,600 youths age fourteen to twenty-one in 1979 who have been reinterviewed annually through 1991 (Center for Human Resource Research 1991). The original sample design consisted of three independent probability samples: a cross-sectional sample to represent all non-institutionalized youths age fourteen to twenty-one; a supplemental sample that oversamples blacks, Hispanics, and economically disadvantaged whites; and a military sample (discontinued in 1985). Attrition rates have been low over the study period; over 90 percent of the original sample was reinterviewed in 1991. The sample used in our analysis consists of 5,825 women originally interviewed in 1979, omitting the military sample, 848 disadvantaged white women (discontinued in 1991), and women for whom no accurate event history could be constructed.[2] We use information obtained through the 1991 panel, when the women were age twenty-six to thirty-three. Thus, the analysis considers those life course experiences occurring through young adulthood, observed over a period of approximately twenty years.

To analyze the interrelationships of the life course processes we consider here, it was necessary to construct detailed event histories for each individual woman. To do this, information obtained annually regarding women's childbearing, marriage, and educational experiences is utilized. The NLSY records whether a particular event occurred (for example, marriage) as well as the date (month and year) when the event happened. We measure all births starting at an approximate conception date (nine months prior to the date of birth), and by comparing these dates with the start and end dates of marriages, we are able to assess whether the conception is nonmarital, marital, or nonmaritally conceived and maritally born. Only formal marriages are considered, starting at the reported wedding date and ending at the reported date of separation (rather than the date of legal divorce). (One important limitation of the NLSY is that detailed cohabitation histories were not collected. We are therefore able to analyze only formal marital unions. Other chapters in this volume, using other data sources, explicitly investigate the importance of cohabitation.) To construct educational histories, we consider enrollment status, grade (in year intervals for high school), and level (for high school, college, and beyond). By comparing dates of enrollment (and level) with dates of conceptions and marriages, we are able to establish the relative timing of all of these events for each woman. Thus, for each woman, we construct a life course event-history "timeline," where the risk period begins at (exact) age ten and extends through her current age in 1991.

In the remainder of this section, all fractions and percentages reported have been computed using sampling weights. Table 12.1 shows the number of nonmarital and marital conceptions (leading to live birth) per woman, stratified by race-ethnicity. There are up to seven nonmarital conceptions per woman in the data. The fraction of all women having one or more nonmarital conceptions is 28.1 percent, with large race-ethnic differences: 36.5 percent among Hispanic women, 62.0 percent among black women, and 21.4 percent among white women. Blacks are also more likely to have higher-order nonmarital conceptions than both Hispanic and white women. The data also contain information regarding nonmarital conceptions between marriages (not shown here). Over all women, 23.9 percent have a nonmarital conception prior to a first marriage, and 6.5 percent have a nonmarital conception after the first marriage (that is, between marriages). A total of 19.0 percent of all nonmarital conceptions ended in a marital birth.

The last four columns of table 12.1 show the distribution of marital conceptions. There are up to seven marital conceptions (leading to a live birth) in this sample, with 51.5 percent of women having at least one marital conception—56.7 percent of Hispanic women, 33.1 percent of black women, and 54.4 percent of white women. Black women are less likely to have higher-order marital conceptions than either Hispanic or white women. Combining both nonmarital and marital conceptions provides a picture of the overall fertility of the women in the sample (not shown). Of all pregnancies (leading to live births) in the sample, 25.2 percent led to a nonmarital birth, 66.4 percent took place within a marriage, and 8.4 percent started nonmaritally but led to a marital birth. There are large ethnic differences with respect to the fraction of births that are nonmarital: among black women, 67.1 percent of births are nonmarital, compared with 14.6 percent for white women and 27.8 percent for Hispanic women.

Table 12.2 shows the number of marriages per woman, for all women and by race-ethnicity. There are up to five marriages in this sample. We see that 74.6 percent of the sample of women marry at least once, with substantial race-ethnic differences. By the time of the last interview, Hispanic women (73.2 percent) and white

Table 12.1 Nonmarital and Marital Conceptions per Woman, by Race-Ethnicity and for All Women

Number	While Unmarried				While Married			
	Hispanic	Black	White	Total	Hispanic	Black	White	Total
Zero	63.50%	38.03%	78.58%	71.95%	43.29%	66.93%	45.62%	48.46%
One	24.11	27.14	16.52	18.49	19.40	18.12	21.54	20.92
Two	7.18	20.96	4.03	6.60	23.13	10.08	22.79	21.03
Three	3.64	8.75	0.68	2.00	9.67	3.97	8.26	7.75
Four	1.00	3.31	0.13	0.63	3.33	0.70	1.25	1.30
Five	0.56	1.50	0.01	0.25	0.71	0.20	0.49	0.46
Six	0.00	0.24	0.05	0.07	0.27	0.00	0.05	0.06
Seven	0.00	0.07	0.00	0.01	0.21	0.00	0.01	0.02
Number in sample	977	1,471	3,377	5,825	977	1,471	3,377	5,825

Source: Authors' compilation.
Note: Weighted percentages.

Table 12.2 Marriages per Woman, by Race-Ethnicity and
for All Women

Number	Hispanic	Black	White	Total
Zero	26.79%	48.86%	21.48%	25.37%
One	63.48	47.74	65.79	63.12
Two	8.83	4.59	11.17	10.10
Three	0.61	0.74	1.22	1.11
Four	0.29	0.00	0.32	0.28
Five	0.00	0.07	0.02	0.02
Number in sample	977	1,471	3,377	5,825

Source: Authors' compilation.
Note: Weighted percentages.

women (78.5 percent) are much more likely to have experienced at least one marriage than blacks (51.1 percent). Additionally, 11.5 percent of the total sample have second- or higher-order marriages: 12.7 percent of whites, 5.4 percent of blacks, and 9.7 percent of Hispanics. Thus, the results in these tables demonstrate that there are substantial numbers of repeated events of all behaviors we are considering: nonmarital and marital conceptions, and marriages and marital dissolutions.

Table 12.3 illustrates the diversity in early life course transitions in the NLSY sample. The "traditional" life course pattern (ending school, marrying, and then having a first child) is followed by only 33.1 percent of white and Hispanic ("nonblack" in the table) women and 10.5 percent of black women. Among high school dropouts, the difference is even larger, with many black women not yet married at the end of the period for which we observe them. In general, black women exhibit a somewhat larger diversity in their early life course transitions than do white and Hispanic women. Across education categories, black women are more likely to have a child before leaving school than white and Hispanic women.

EMPIRICAL MODEL

In this section, we describe empirical equations for (re)marriage and for marital dissolution, emphasizing the estimated effects of the potentially endogenous nonmarital and marital fertility measures. Although the equations include other potentially endogenous variables that are dealt with empirically, those are not discussed explic-

Table 12.3 Life Course Pattern Distribution and Sample Sizes

	All	All Education		Less Than High School		High School Graduate		College Graduate	
		Black	Nonblack	Black	Nonblack	Black	Nonblack	Black	Nonblack
Stop school, first baby, married	4.0%	8.4%	3.3%	12.0%	9.8%	7.6%	2.1%	2.7%	0.3%
Stop school, first baby, never married	3.6	13.4	2.0	19.3	4.2	12.3	1.7	2.2	0.5
Stop school, married, first baby	30.0	10.5	33.1	3.5	35.7	13.0	35.2	11.4	18.1
Stop school, married, no first baby	11.5	5.9	12.5	3.2	8.1	6.8	13.3	6.5	14.8
Stop school, never married, no baby	18.6	17.4	18.8	10.3	11.1	17.9	19.6	39.9	26.4
First baby, stop school, married	2.3	7.7	1.5	9.3	3.0	7.6	1.2	2.1	0.0
First baby, stop school, never married	3.1	16.1	1.0	25.8	2.2	13.0	0.9	10.1	0.1
First baby, married, stop school	2.6	8.0	1.7	9.7	3.5	7.9	1.5	2.7	0.3
Married, stop school, first baby	7.1	3.9	7.6	2.5	6.9	4.2	7.2	6.9	10.5
Married, stop school, no first baby	6.4	2.8	7.0	0.7	2.9	2.9	6.8	9.1	14.3
Married, first baby, stop school	10.7	6.0	11.5	3.7	12.7	6.8	10.5	6.5	14.7
Number in sample	5,825	1,471	4,354	373	1,153	1,006	2,684	92	517

Source: Authors' compilation.
Note: Weighted percentages. "Nonblack" includes both whites and Hispanics.

itly here. The focus is on the effects of measures of nonmarital fertility and of marital fertility on marriage and marriage dissolution after accounting for spurious or indirect relationships such as self-selection or reverse effect (simultaneous feedback).

However, these relationships are part of a larger model on the interrelationships between nonmarital childbearing, schooling (continuing in school), marriage, marital childbearing, and marital dissolution. The fuller model is represented by the set of equations in table 12.4.[3] Although not all of the interrelationships are discussed here, it should be kept in mind that they are part of the fuller model where appropriate.

We begin with a discussion of the outcomes of primary interest—marriage and dissolution—followed by a discussion of the primary explanatory variables: nonmarital and marital fertility.

MARRIAGE AND REMARRIAGE

The empirical model of remarriage is developed to study the hazard rate for transitions from the unmarried to the married state for all spells of time a woman was unmarried from age ten to the date of the last interview date. Each period of risk of marriage begins at age ten or the date of separation of the last marriage, as appropriate, and either end at the next reported marriage date (month and year) or is censored at the last survey date.

The marriage model specifies the continuous-time log-hazard of getting married as a function of time-varying covariates, duration dependencies, and unobserved heterogeneity. For individual j at time t, the log hazard of marrying for the l–th time at time t is given by

$$\ln h_1{}^m(t) = \beta_0 + \beta_1' X_1(t) + \beta_2' PCur_1(t) + \beta_3' NMKid_1(t) + \beta_4' MarKid_1(t) + \beta_5' Pmar_1 + \varepsilon^m$$

where $1 = 1,...,N_m$ for a woman with N_m unmarried spells. The person subscript j is suppressed throughout for notational simplicity. The vector $X_1(t)$ includes all covariates that are not listed in the equation but appear in table 12.4. These include both exogenous and other endogenous time-varying covariates and durations. All of the covariates explicitly listed are potentially endogenous and are the focus for this analysis. The variable $PCur_1(t)$ indicates "cur-

Table 12.4 Processes and Model Specifications

	Processes				
Explanatory Variables	Nonmarital Fertility	Education	Marriage	Marital Fertility	Marriage Dissolution
Potentially endogenous					
Education					
Completed level	X	—	X	X	X
Duration since enrolled	X	—	X	X	X
Out of school by level	X	—	X	X	X
Children					
Currently pregnant	—	X	X	—	X
Presence, number, type[a]	X	X	X	X	X
Duration since last	X	—	—	X	X
Marital status					
Married: status, duration	—	X	—	X	X
Separated, divorced, widowed	X	X	X	—	—

Exogenous						
Race-ethnicity	X	X	X	X	X	X
Time-dependent variables						
Age (t)	X	X	X	—	X	X
Calendar time (t)	X	X	X	X	X	X
Net family income (t) (log)	X	X	X	X	X	X
Family background (age fourteen)						
Education of parents	X	X	X	—	—	—
Religion	X	—	—	X	X	X
Family structure	X	X	X	X	—	X
Macrolevel variables (state or county by year)						
Education						
Education expenditures per 1,000 population	—	X	—	—	—	—
Fertility						
Family planning clinics per 1,000 population	X	—	—	—	X	—
Number of abortions per 1,000 population	X	—	—	—	X	—
Marriage markets						
sex ratio, by race	—	—	X	—	—	—
Dissolution						
Divorce laws	—	—	—	—	—	X

Source: Authors' compilation.

[a] Types include marital and nonmarital. In addition to a woman's own earned income, which may be endogenous, family income included non-earned income and income from other family members. We treat family income as exogenous.

rently pregnant." The variables $NMKid_1(t)$ and $MarKid_1(t)$ are the number of children born outside of marriage and the number of children born to previous marriages as of time t, respectively. $PMar_1$ is the number of prior marriages, representing a form of occurrence dependence.

The stochastic term ε^m is a woman-specific residual (heterogeneity) affecting both the first marriage and all remarriages and is assumed normally distributed, $\varepsilon^m \sim N(0, \sigma^2_{\varepsilon m})$. The number of replications of marriage spells provides strong identification of the woman-specific heterogeneity component.[4]

MARRIAGE DISSOLUTION

The empirical model of marriage dissolution is developed to study the hazard rate for transitions from the married to the unmarried state for all spells of time a woman was married from age ten to the date of the last interview. Each period of risk of marital dissolution begins at the date of marriage and either ends at the date of dissolution (separation) of the marriage or is censored at the last survey date (month and year), as appropriate.

The model of dissolution specifies the continuous-time log-hazard of marriage dissolution as a function of time-varying covariates, duration dependencies, and unobserved heterogeneity. For individual j at time t, the log-hazard of the dissolution of marriage m is given by:

$$\ln h_m^{\ d}(t) = \theta_0 + \theta_1'X_m(t) + \theta_2'NMKid_m(t) + \theta_3'PMarKid_m(t)$$
$$+ \theta_4'PCur_m(t) + \theta_5'MarKid_m(t)$$
$$+ \theta_6'MarDur_m(t) + \theta_7'PMarDate_m + \theta_8'PMar_m + \varepsilon^d$$

where $m = 1,...,N_d$ for a woman with N_d marriages. The vector $X_m(t)$ includes all covariates not explicitly listed in the equation but appearing in table 12.4. These include both exogenous and other endogenous time-varying covariates and durations. All of the covariates explicitly listed are potentially endogenous and are the focus for this analysis. The variables $NMKid_m(t)$ and $PMarKid_m(t)$ are the number of children born outside of marriage and the number of children born to previous marriages as of time t, respectively. The variable $PCur_m(t)$ indicates "currently pregnant," and the variable $MarKid_m(t)$ is the number of marital children born to the current marriage. We also include PMarDate$_m$ to indicate whether the woman was pregnant at the time of her wedding date (that is, whether she conceived nonmaritally). MarDur$_m$(t) is the duration of the current marriage, measured as three piece-wise linear segments (a spline) of zero to one year, one to seven years, and seven years or more, respectively. PMar$_m$ is the number of prior marriages, a form of occurrence dependence.

The stochastic term ε^d is a woman-specific residual term (heterogeneity) affecting the hazard of dissolution in all marriages and is assumed normally distributed, $\varepsilon^d \sim N(0,\sigma^2_{\varepsilon d})$. Again, the number of replications provides strong identification of the woman-specific heterogeneity component.

ENDOGENEITY OF THE FERTILITY OUTCOMES AND SELF-SELECTION INTO AND OUT OF MARRIAGE

The relationships represented in the marriage and dissolution hazard equations make the usual assumption (impose the restriction) that the effect of a time-varying explanatory variable is based on only its value as of the current instantaneous time t. No future values of the variable matter for the current instantaneous hazard of occurrence, although the variable itself may reflect the past occurrence of or outcome of the same or other processes—analogous to Granger causality in time series. This is assumed whether the time-varying variable is exogenous or is the endogenous outcome of a related (jointly modeled) process. It is in fact the joint modeling of the related processes that is the basis of our modeling strategy.

Why might the joint modeling strategy be beneficial? First, if there are lagged outcomes of the same process (for example, number of previous marriages), then those measures will not be independent of the current hazard if there is heterogeneity in the hazard process, ε^m or ε^d. Failure to account for heterogeneity will bias the estimated effect of lagged occurrences as well as other covariates. Conditional on the heterogeneity vector, the lagged occurrence variable is independent of the current hazard because the heterogeneity vector is assumed constant for the person but varies among women.

Second, if the heterogeneity term in a related marital status process is correlated with the one under consideration, then, in the aggregate, there will be nonrandom self-selection into the current marital state. For example, currently married women, at risk of separation and of marital conception, must have married at least once. Women with a high hazard of marriage (ε^m) are more likely to be in the married state (at each point in time) than women with a low marriage hazard, so that if ε^m and ε^d are correlated, then there will be nonrandom selection into the risk pool. If the correlation is nonzero, then married women will have higher (lower) risk of marital dissolution than a randomly selected woman. If the correlation is positive (negative) the expected value of ε^d, conditional on being married, will be positive (negative).

Third, the heterogeneity terms of related processes determining the current or lagged values of explanatory variables may be correlated with the one in the process under consideration. If so, the explanatory variables that are based on the current status, past occurrence, or functions of past outcomes of those processes will not, in the aggregate, be independent of the heterogeneity term of the process under consideration. This is the source of the potential endogeneity of the pregnancy and prior nonmarital and marital fertility variables in the marriage and dissolution hazard equations.

In addition, there may be "simultaneity feedback" from one or more related processes if the outcomes of those processes are also dependent on the outcome of the process under consideration, even if the heterogeneity terms are not correlated. For example, having been married affects the hazard of nonmarital fertility, and having had a nonmarital birth affects the hazard of marriage. This may generate what might alternatively be termed reverse-causality bias.

Next we consider the processes determining the primary explanatory variables that may be endogenous.

Nonmarital and Marital Fertility

To account fully for the endogeneity of the measures of nonmarital and marital fertility, we specify our model for each of them. A woman is at risk of nonmarital conception while unmarried, beginning at age ten, the date of separation from the last marriage, or the birth of the last nonmarital child, as appropriate, and ending at the time of conception (dated from the birth) or censored at the last survey date. A woman is at risk of marital conception while married, beginning at the date of marriage or the birth of the last child, as appropriate, and ending at the time of conception (dated from the birth) or censored at the last survey date.

The log-hazard of nonmarital conception k at time t for individual j is given by

$$
\begin{aligned}
\ln h_k^{cu}(t) = {} & \gamma_0 + \gamma_1' X_k(t) + \gamma_2' \text{Parity2p}_k + \gamma_3' \text{TimeKid2p}_k(t) \\
& + \gamma_4' \text{NMKid}_k + \gamma_5' \text{PMar}_k + \gamma_6' \text{MarKid}_k + \varepsilon^{cu}
\end{aligned}
$$

where $k = 1,...,N_{cu}$ for a woman with N_{cu} at-risk spells. We explicitly measure nonmarital conceptions, which may lead to a marital birth if the woman marries while pregnant. The log-hazard of marital conception c at time t for individual j is given by

$$
\begin{aligned}
\ln h_c^{cm}(t) = {} & \gamma_0 + \gamma_1' X_c(t) + \gamma_2' \text{Parity2p}_c + \gamma_3' \text{TimeKid2p}_c(t) \\
& + \gamma_4' \text{NMKid}_c + \gamma_5' \text{Pmar}_c + \gamma_6' \text{MarKid}_c + \varepsilon^{cm}
\end{aligned}
$$

where $c = 1,...,N_{cm}$ for a woman with N_{cm} at-risk spells. The variable Parity2p_k indicates second- and higher-order conception intervals (already having had a child), $\text{TimeKid2p}_k(t)$ measures the duration since the last child was born, and $\text{NMKid}_k(t)$, PMar_k, and $\text{MarKid}_k(t)$ have already been defined.

There will be simultaneity feedback to the marriage and dissolution processes if the variable PMar_k is significant, since it implies having been previously married and separated or divorced.

The stochastic terms ε^{cu} and ε^{cm} are woman-specific residual terms (heterogeneity) affecting the hazard of nonmarital and marital conceptions, respectively, and are each assumed normally distributed. There will be a spurious relationship between nonmarital and marital fertility outcomes and marriage formation and/or dissolution if the correlations between $(\varepsilon^{cu}, \varepsilon^{cm})$ and $(\varepsilon^m, \varepsilon^d)$ are not all zero (even without PMar_k in the fertility equations), that is, $\underline{\varepsilon} \sim N(0, \Sigma_{\varepsilon\varepsilon})$ where $\Sigma_{\varepsilon\varepsilon}$ is not diagonal. That is, if there are unmeasured factors represented by these stochastic terms that affect more than one outcome or are correlated across outcomes, the estimated relationship will be biased unless the unmeasured factors are taken into account.

ESTIMATION

We take a full information maximum likelihood (FIML) approach to estimation that provides an efficient solution to the potential problems discussed earlier, given the assumptions of the model. First, we provide a fully specified system of equations that describes all the relationships in the model.[5] Table 12.4 summarizes all variables included in the full joint model, including the potentially endogenous variables, exogenous and time-dependent variables, and macrolevel variables.

Second, we derive the probability of the observed sequence of outcomes for each woman over her period of observation (approximately twenty years), which is represented by the marginal likelihood function. Conditional on the vector of heterogeneity terms in the full model, the outcomes of all the replications of the various processes are independent, and the joint conditional probability is the product of the conditional probabilities of the individual occurrences of the outcomes. The joint marginal likelihood of the observed outcomes is then obtained by multiplying the joint conditional likelihood by the joint distribution of heterogeneity components and integrating the result over the full range of the heterogeneity components. Details of the formation of the likelihood function are provided in Lillard, Panis, and Upchurch (1994) and described in a technical appendix available from the authors.

IDENTIFICATION

Each of the five behavioral processes involves an explanatory variable that is some function of an outcome of one or more of the other behavioral process. Those outcomes may be characterized as the current state of another process or a current measurement based on prior outcomes of other processes. These include being currently married, being currently unmarried, having been married previously, being currently nonmaritally pregnant, being currently maritally pregnant, the presence and number of nonmarital children, and the presence and number of marital children. Each equation is a function of measures based only on prior transitions or outcomes. All sources of correlation between processes are assumed to be fully represented by the woman-specific heterogeneity terms $\underline{\varepsilon}$ that are constant across replications of each process.[6] Conditional on the woman-specific heterogeneity terms $\underline{\varepsilon}$, the measures based on past outcomes (own or others) are effectively exogenous, and thus their effects are identified if the model is estimated appropriately. The aggregate correlation in outcomes due to variation among women in $\underline{\varepsilon}$ is accounted for by integrating (or summing) over the range of values that these stochastic terms may take, weighted by their density function.

In addition, the model in this chapter assumes joint normality of the vector of heterogeneity random-effect terms $\underline{\varepsilon}$. As noted, there are multiple replications of each outcome, so that there is identification of the distribution of each heterogeneity term, whether or not normality is assumed.[7] Even though not all processes are repeated for every woman (or even observed at all), the observation of repeated behavior for a subset of women with some overlap across processes will identify the heterogeneity in each process and the correlations between them.[8]

RESULTS

The top panels of tables 12.5 and 12.6 present the results for the log-hazard of marrying and the log-hazard of marital separation, respectively. To explicitly show parameter estimate biases due to ignoring heterogeneity and/or endogeneity, we build and estimate the model in three steps. Each equation is modeled without unmeasured heterogeneity ($\sigma^2 = 0$) in model 1 (first column). Model 2 (column 2) accounts for unmeasured heterogeneity but ignores the cross-process endogeneity of education, marriage, and prior fertility (under the restriction that all correlations of the unobservables across processes are zero). Model 3 (the preferred specification, in column 3) is the jointly estimated full model, including heterogeneity and allowing the unmeasured factors to be correlated across processes. A comparison of the three columns in tables 12.5 and 12.6 reveals the extent to which parameter estimates are biased when heterogeneity and/or endogeneity are ignored. The results below focus on model 3 (joint model), making comparisons in findings across models as relevant. Since this chapter focuses on the effects of nonmarital fertility, marital fertility, and pregnancy status on marriage and dissolution, these results are highlighted in tables 12.5 and 12.6. Results for the complete set of covariates included in the models may be found in the appendix. The bottom panels of tables 12.5 and 12.6 show the error structure for the relevant models.

EFFECTS OF NONMARITAL AND PRIOR MARITAL
FERTILITY ON MARRIAGE FORMATION

The first set of research questions concerns the potential direct effects of a woman's prior fertility history and pregnancy status on

Table 12.5 Marriage Formation Hazard Estimates: Effects of Nonmarital (and Other) Childbearing

Covariates: Fertility History and Pregnancy Status	Model 1: No Heterogeneity	Model 2: No Endogeneity	Model 3: Joint
White and Hispanic women			
Currently pregnant	1.8586***	1.9220***	1.5766***
	(0.0483)	(0.0558)	(0.0705)
Prior nonmarital child(ren)	−0.0205	0.0730*	−0.1630***
	(0.0338)	(0.0424)	(0.0583)
Prior marital child(ren)	−0.0118	−0.0836	−0.2584***
	(0.0436)	(0.0540)	(0.0693)
Black women			
Currently pregnant	0.9976***	1.0092***	0.6831***
	(0.1263)	(0.1304)	(0.1374)
Prior nonmarital child(ren)	0.0607	0.0678	−0.2483***
	(0.0516)	(0.0559)	(0.0714)
Prior marital child(ren)	0.1886	0.1408	−0.0426
	(0.1678)	(0.1913)	(0.2190)

Error Structure			
Heterogeneity			
Marriage formation			0.9820***
			(0.0670)
Nonmarital fertility			1.1129***
			(0.0617)
Marital fertility			0.4951***
			(0.0697)
Correlations			
Marriage formation— nonmarital fertility			0.6997***
			(0.0574)
Marriage formation— marital fertility			−0.0661
			(0.1614)
Nonmarital fertility— marital fertility			0.1269
			(0.1421)

Source: Table 12A.1 (for covariates) and table 12A.3 (for error structure).
Note: Asymptotic standard errors in parentheses.
* = .10 level.
** = .05 level.
*** = .01 level.

Table 12.6 Marital Dissolution Hazard Estimates: Effects of Nonmarital (and Other) Childbearing

Covariates: Fertility History and Pregnancy Status	Model 1: No Heterogeneity	Model 2: No Endogeneity	Model 3: Joint
White and Hispanic women			
Currently pregnant	−1.0194***	−1.1148***	−1.3509***
	(0.1215)	(0.1260)	(0.1317)
Pregnant at marriage date	0.3911***	0.5130***	0.5040***
	(0.0863)	(0.1133)	(0.1465)
Child(ren) current marriage	−0.4534***	−0.6335***	−0.9427***
	(0.0423)	(0.0553)	(0.0879)
Prior nonmarital child(ren)	0.3099***	0.3993***	0.1565
	(0.0555)	(0.0837)	(0.1127)
Prior marital child(ren)	−0.1651*	−0.1526	−0.4651***
	(0.0917)	(0.1116)	(0.1242)
Black women			
Currently pregnant	−0.4236*	−0.4814*	−0.7378***
	(0.2533)	(0.2711)	(0.2750)
Pregnant at marriage date	0.2106	0.2501	0.2774
	(0.1773)	(0.2537)	(0.2694)
Child(ren) current marriage	−0.2138**	−0.2851**	−0.6028***
	(0.0900)	(0.1151)	(0.1359)
Prior nonmarital child(ren)	0.2044***	0.2561**	0.0053
	(0.0709)	(0.1019)	(0.1217)
Prior marital child(ren)	−0.0024	0.1849	−0.1908
	(0.1828)	(0.2408)	(0.2620)
Error Structure			
Heterogeneity			
Dissolution			1.1317***
			(0.1041)
Correlations			
Dissolution—nonmarital fertility			0.3248***
			(0.1068)
Dissolution—marital fertility			0.6116***
			(0.1572)
Dissolution—marriage formation			0.2579**
			(0.1125)

Source: Table 12A.2 (covariates) and table 12A.3 (error structure).
Note: Asymptotic standard errors in parentheses.
* = .10 level.
** = .05 level.
*** = .01 level.

her chances of marrying. Table 12.5 shows these results, separately for black women and for white and Hispanic women.[9] As hypothesized, white, Hispanic, and black women with a nonmarital child have a significantly lower risk of marrying than childless women, and the risk decreases with each additional nonmarital child.[10] In contrast, women who are nonmaritally pregnant have significantly *higher* risks of marrying than women who are not pregnant. And though the risk of marrying increases for all nonmaritally pregnant women, the magnitude is greater for white and Hispanic women than for black women. Lastly, we find that women with children from prior marriages also have a lower risk of remarrying than women who are childless; these effects are significant only for white and Hispanic women.[11]

Thus, our findings demonstrate that, for white and Hispanic women, children born nonmaritally or born in prior marriages significantly hinder their chances of remarrying. For black women, only children born nonmaritally significantly reduce their risk of marrying. These findings generally confirm our hypotheses regarding the impact of nonmarital and marital children on marriage. Also as expected, women who are nonmaritally pregnant are much more likely to marry than women who are not pregnant.

The second set of questions is concerned with issues of selection, that is, to what extent are childbearing and marriage decisions jointly determined? A comparison of the coefficients of model 2 (no endogeneity) and model 3 (joint model), and the error structure results in table 12.5, shed light on that issue. For all women, the coefficient for nonmarital fertility goes from insignificantly positive in model 2 to negative and highly significant in model 3. This is due to the positive and significant correlation of the unobserved heterogeneity components in the nonmarital fertility and marriage formation equations ($\rho_{\varepsilon^c u_{\varepsilon^m}} = 0.6997$): women with a high (low) propensity for conceiving nonmaritally also have a high (low) propensity to marry. This positive correlation leads to a positive bias in the parameter estimates, as demonstrated in model 2. Thus, failure to account for this correlation leads to substantively different and incorrect conclusions.

Similarly, the effect of current pregnancy is positively biased (overstated) when we do not account for the positive correlation between nonmarital fertility and marriage. For white and Hispanic women, the coefficient for marital children becomes more negative across models and is significant in model 3. For blacks, the coefficient changes direction but remains insignificant. The correlation between marriage formation and marital fertility is negative but not significant.

In summary, we find both direct and selection effects of nonmarital fertility on the risk of getting married (and remarried). We find that a premarital pregnancy accelerates wedding plans, presumably because the father of the child and the prospective spouse are the same individual. However, women with children from prior relationships experience much lower risk of marrying than childless women, and the risk depends on whether the children are from prior marriages or were born outside of marriage. For white and Hispanic women, we find that children from previous marriages reduce women's hazard of remarrying somewhat more so than the presence of nonmarital children (-0.2584 versus -0.1630). In contrast, the hazard of remarriage for black women with children from a prior marriage is not significantly different than for childless women, while black women with nonmarital children have a substantial reduction in risk of marrying.

EFFECTS OF NONMARITAL AND MARITAL FERTILITY ON MARITAL DISSOLUTION

We now turn to the results for marital dissolution, first focusing on the direct effects of women's fertility history and current pregnancy status. Table 12.6 shows the estimates for white and Hispanic women and for black women.

The first three fertility history and pregnancy status variables pertain to those experiences that occurred in the current marriage. Married women who are currently pregnant have significantly lower risk of ending their marriages, and the effect is almost twice as great for white and Hispanic than for black women. Additionally, women with children from their current marriage have significantly lower risk of separating than women who are childless, and the effect is stronger for white and Hispanic women than for black women. However, if the woman was pregnant at the time she married (that is, the couple conceived nonmaritally), the child's effect on reducing the separation risk is partially offset (by about half). This effect is significant only for white and Hispanic women.

The last two fertility history variables pertain to childbearing experiences that occurred prior to the current marriage. In contrast to our hypotheses, we find no significant effect of having nonmarital children on the risk of dissolving a marriage, for either white and Hispanic women or black women. That is, we find no direct effect of the presence of nonmarital children on the risk of marital dissolution. We do see, however, that married women with children from a prior marriage are less likely to separate than their childless counterparts. This effect is significant for white and Hispanic women, but not for blacks.

We next consider the extent to which selection is operating with respect to these fertility behaviors and marital dissolution. The second panel of table 12.6 summarizes the error structure and correlations across the processes we consider. The table shows a positive and significant correlation of the unmeasured heterogeneity components for nonmarital fertility and dissolution ($\rho_{\varepsilon^{cu}\varepsilon^d} = 0.3248$). In other words, women with a high propensity to have nonmarital children also tend to have a high propensity to dissolve their marriage. This positive correlation results in a positive bias of the coefficient on prior nonmarital children. Failure to account for the selection would lead to the conclusion that prior nonmarital children are disruptive (model 2), but that association is in fact purely due to selection (model 3).

The correlation of the unobserved heterogeneity components of marital dissolution and marital fertility is positive and significant ($\rho_{\varepsilon^d\varepsilon^{cm}} = 0.6116$). That is, women who have an increased propensity to have marital children also have higher propensities to dissolve their marriages. Comparing the results in model 2 and model 3 in table 12.6, we see that the protective effect of having marital children on the risk of separating would be underestimated if the endogeneity of marital fertility in the marital separation equation is not taken into account.

DISCUSSION AND CONCLUSIONS

In this chapter, we examined the influences of nonmarital childbearing on the risks of marrying and separation. We jointly modeled five life course processes to account for their potential endogeneity, separating out direct effects from spurious correlation. Although this chapter focuses on the impact of nonmarital fertility, we also examined the influences of prior marital fertility and pregnancy status on the risks of marrying and separating. In so doing, our analysis provides a more comprehensive picture of ways in which childbearing histories influence family-building activities, and our dynamic approach demonstrates the importance of the timing of events on these outcomes.

As expected, we find that having a child nonmaritally reduces a woman's risk of subsequently marrying. If, however, a woman is nonmaritally pregnant, her risk of marrying substantially increases. Additionally, for white and Hispanic women, having children from a previous marriage substantially reduces the risk of remarriage. In contrast to our expectations, having nonmarital children does not directly increase the risk of separating; the association in the data is purely due to selection. Having children from the current marriage reduces the risk of that marriage dissolving, as does a current pregnancy. For white and Hispanic women, having children from a prior marriage also reduces the risk of separation. However, for whites and Hispanics, having been pregnant at the marriage date increases the risk of separation. In other words, while a premarital pregnancy hastens marriage, it also destabilizes it.

Lastly, our findings demonstrate important selection effects operating across fertility and family-building behaviors. We find significantly positive correlations between marriage and separation, on the one hand, and nonmarital and marital fertility, on the other. Failure to account for these selections leads to positive biases in commensurate parameter estimates. In some cases, the effects are under- or overstated; in other cases, substantively different conclusions arise when we control for selection.

Our finding that nonmarital childbearing significantly decreases a woman's chance of marrying is supported by work that analyzed the effect of a first nonmarital birth on first marriage (Bennett, Bloom, and Craig 1989; Bennett, Bloom, and Miller 1995; Lichter and Graefe, this volume). The work presented here expands on this previous research by including first- and higher-order nonmarital children as well as marriages. With each additional nonmarital child, the risk of marrying continues to decline. For white and Hispanic women, having children from a previous marriage also significantly reduces their prospects for remarrying, and this has been confirmed by prior work (Koo and Suchindran 1980; Teachman and Heckert 1985). Only nonmarital children have this effect among black women.

In contrast, a nonmarital pregnancy (leading to a live birth) significantly increases the risk that a woman will marry, a finding that underscores the importance of considering the relative timing of fertility-related events. Nonmaritally pregnant women may be particularly motivated to marry in order to legitimate the birth (Goldscheider and Waite 1986; Parnell, Swicegood, and Stevens 1994), and we find that effects are stronger among Hispanic and white women than blacks (Manning and Landale 1996). There is also a carryover effect of nonmarital pregnancy on the risk of dissolving a marriage—white and Hispanic women who were pregnant at their marriage date are significantly more likely to separate than those who were childless and not pregnant. The shorter marital search may lead to a less suitable partner match and hence a higher propensity for the marriage to end (Oppenheimer 1988).

We also find strong support for the idea that women make joint decisions about nonmarital childbearing and marriage. Women who have a high propensity to have a nonmarital child also have a high propensity to marry, suggesting that these types of family formation strategies are interrelated and perhaps interchangeable (Axinn and Barber 1997; Brien, Lillard, and Waite 1999; Bumpass 1990).

With respect to marital dissolution, we find no *direct* effect of having nonmarital children, in contrast to our expectations. Although the coefficients for all women are in the expected direction (positive), they are not significant. These findings are in contrast to previous work that did find a significant disruptive effect (for example, Heaton 1991; Lillard and Waite 1993). An explanation for this discrepancy is provided by comparing models 2 and 3 in table 12.6. When the endogeneity of nonmarital fertility and marital dissolution is ignored, we do see positive and significant effects of nonmarital childbearing on the hazard of separating. However, this observed effect is entirely due to selection—women with a high propensity to have a nonmarital birth also tend to be more likely to separate. Women with a nonmarital child may be disinclined to stay in a problematic marriage because they have prior experience caring for their child as a single mother. Also, if family-building behaviors are somewhat interchangeable, then a woman with a nonmarital child might be more willing to leave a marriage because she is willing to redefine her "family" as herself and her child.

We find that married women who are currently pregnant or who have children from their current marriage are significantly less likely to separate than their childless counterparts. Although others have found that the protective effect of children on separation is present only when the children are young (Cherlin 1977; Waite and Lillard 1991), we did not include age of children in our analysis (primarily because our focus is on the effects of nonmarital fertility). We also find a significantly positive correlation between marital fertility and marital dissolution, suggesting selection in operating across these family processes as well.

In conclusion, we find direct negative effects of nonmarital childbearing on the likelihood of marriage, but no direct effects of those children on dissolving a marriage. Nonmarital children appear to delay women's marriage formation, but once married, the nonmarital children do not contribute to the risk of separating. We also find that marital fertility plays an important role in the risks of marrying and separating. Lastly, our work demonstrates that failure to account for the endogeneity of nonmarital fertility and marriage as well as nonmarital fertility and separation leads to incorrect substantive conclusions regarding the nature of these family-building behaviors.

APPENDIX: FULL SET OF PARAMETER ESTIMATES BY EQUATION

Table 12A.1 Marriage Formation Hazard Estimates

Covariates	Model 1: No Heterogeneity	Model 2: No Endogeneity	Model 3: Joint
Fertility history			
Nonblack, currently pregnant	1.8586*** (0.0483)	1.9220*** (0.0558)	1.5766*** (0.0705)
Nonblack, prior nonmarital child(ren)	−0.0205 (0.0338)	0.0730* (0.0424)	−0.1630*** (0.0583)
Nonblack, prior marital child(ren)	−0.0118 (0.0436)	−0.0836 (0.0540)	−0.2584*** (0.0693)
Black, currently pregnant	0.9976*** (0.1263)	1.0092*** (0.1304)	0.6831*** (0.1374)
Black, prior nonmarital child(ren)	0.0607 (0.0516)	0.0678 (0.0559)	−0.2483*** (0.0714)
Black, prior marital child(ren)	0.1886 (0.1678)	0.1408 (0.1913)	−0.0426 (0.2190)

(Table continues on p. 372.)

Table 12A.1 *Continued*

Covariates	Model 1: No Heterogeneity	Model 2: No Endogeneity	Model 3: Joint
Marriage history			
Nonblack, previously married	0.2305*** (0.0398)	−0.1009 (0.0935)	−0.5963*** (0.1021)
Black, previously married	0.4900*** (0.1829)	0.1370 (0.2213)	−0.3207 (0.2397)
Education			
Nonblack, out of school, high school dropout	1.3183*** (0.0649)	1.3735*** (0.0716)	1.1448*** (0.0830)
Nonblack, out of school, high school graduate	1.0964*** (0.0577)	1.0957*** (0.0605)	1.0349*** (0.0627)
Nonblack, out of school, less than high school	1.1041*** (0.0773)	1.0967*** (0.0837)	1.1555*** (0.0903)
Black, out of school, high school dropout	0.3919** (0.1610)	0.2728 (0.1724)	0.1000 (0.1837)
Black, out of school, high school graduate	0.6705*** (0.1129)	0.5836*** (0.1204)	0.5472*** (0.1255)
Black, out of school, less than high school	0.5451** (0.2566)	0.4259 (0.2788)	0.4463 (0.2933)
Out of school zero to two years	−0.1416*** (0.0322)	−0.0939*** (0.0347)	−0.0544 (0.0352)
Out of school more than two years	−0.0249*** (0.0087)	−0.0139 (0.0097)	−0.0038 (0.0103)
Demographics and family background			
Black	0.0161 (0.0929)	−0.0029 (0.1008)	0.0505 (0.1096)
Hispanic	−0.0816 (0.0553)	−0.0740 (0.0665)	0.0528 (0.0806)
Age ten to eighteen	0.8635*** (0.0403)	0.8859*** (0.0414)	0.9457*** (0.0444)
Age eighteen to twenty-five	−0.1109*** (0.0148)	−0.0750*** (0.0179)	−0.0173 (0.0193)
Age twenty-five or older	−0.0471*** (0.0133)	−0.0276* (0.0153)	−0.0018 (0.0166)
Non-intact family at age fourteen	0.1064*** (0.0332)	0.1326*** (0.0401)	0.2615*** (0.0483)
Family income	0.2879*** (0.0143)	0.3077*** (0.0155)	0.3280*** (0.0162)
Family income missing	0.0994*** (0.0337)	0.0950*** (0.0352)	0.0907** (0.0361)

Table 12A.1 Continued

Covariates	Model 1: No Heterogeneity	Model 2: No Endogeneity	Model 3: Joint
Macrolevel variables and calendar time			
Male/female ratio	0.8942***	0.9138***	0.9601***
	(0.0501)	(0.0515)	(0.0522)
Calendar time (relative to 1980)	−0.0384***	−0.0464***	−0.0494***
	(0.0067)	(0.0081)	(0.0095)
Intercept	−4.3724***	−4.6340***	−4.8122***
	(0.1547)	(0.1708)	(0.1767)

Source: Authors' compilation.
Note: Asymptotic standard errors in parentheses.
* = .10 level.
** = .05 level.
*** = .01 level.

Table 12A.2 Marital Dissolution Hazard Estimates

Covariates	Model 1: No Heterogeneity	Model 2: No Endogeneity	Model 3: Joint
Fertility history			
Nonblack, currently pregnant	−1.0194***	−1.1148***	−1.3509***
	(0.1215)	(0.1260)	(0.1317)
Nonblack, pregnant at marriage date	0.3911***	0.5130***	0.5040***
	(0.0863)	(0.1133)	(0.1465)
Nonblack, child(ren) current marriage	−0.4534***	−0.6335***	−0.9427***
	(0.0423)	(0.0553)	(0.0879)
Nonblack, prior nonmarital child(ren)	0.3099***	0.3993***	0.1565
	(0.0555)	(0.0837)	(0.1127)
Nonblack, prior marital child(ren)	−0.1651*	−0.1526	−0.4651***
	(0.0917)	(0.1116)	(0.1242)
Black, currently pregnant	−0.4236*	−0.4814*	−0.7378***
	(0.2533)	(0.2711)	(0.2750)
Black, pregnant at marriage date	0.2106	0.2501	0.2774
	(0.1773)	(0.2537)	(0.2694)
Black, child(ren) current marriage	−0.2138**	−0.2851**	−0.6028***
	(0.0900)	(0.1151)	(0.1359)
Black, prior nonmarital child(ren)	0.2044***	0.2561**	0.0053
	(0.0709)	(0.1019)	(0.1217)
Black, prior marital child(ren)	−0.0024	0.1849	−0.1908
	(0.1828)	(0.2408)	(0.2620)

(Table continues on p. 374.)

Table 12A.2 *Continued*

Covariates	Model 1: No Heterogeneity	Model 2: No Endogeneity	Model 3: Joint
Marriage Duration and history			
Marriage duration zero to	0.5328***	0.8002***	0.8490***
one year (spline)	(0.1418)	(0.1588)	(0.1598)
Marriage duration one to	0.0690***	0.1874***	0.2092***
seven years (spline)	(0.0201)	(0.0275)	(0.0338)
Marriage duration seven	0.0633**	0.1342***	0.1231***
years or more (spline)	(0.0296)	(0.0333)	(0.0362)
Previously married	0.6772***	0.0443	0.0062
	(0.0895)	(0.1386)	(0.1849)
Education			
High school dropout	0.0390	0.1486*	0.2085*
	(0.0625)	(0.0874)	(0.1170)
Some college or more	0.0087	−0.0190	−0.1087
	(0.0909)	(0.1171)	(0.1358)
Demographics and family background			
Black	0.2365*	0.3072	0.3655*
	(0.1342)	(0.1882)	(0.1912)
Hispanic	−0.1097	−0.0953	−0.0175
	(0.0916)	(0.1434)	(0.1484)
Age ten to eighteen	−0.2029*	−0.2587**	−0.1997
	(0.1055)	(0.1180)	(0.1290)
Age eighteen to twenty-five	−0.0453**	−0.0434*	−0.0168
	(0.0211)	(0.0257)	(0.0323)
Age twenty-five or older	−0.1118***	−0.1311***	−0.0855***
	(0.0193)	(0.0233)	(0.0282)
Nonblack* non-intact	0.2550***	0.3407***	0.3798***
family at age fourteen	(0.0596)	(0.0865)	(0.0909)
Black* non-intact family at	0.0384	0.0430	0.1351
age fourteen	(0.1328)	(0.1920)	(0.1919)
Catholic	0.0703	0.0615	0.0672
	(0.0588)	(0.0816)	(0.0822)
Jewish	−0.1246	−0.1251	−0.1763
	(0.4902)	(0.5605)	(0.5752)
Family income	−0.2957***	−0.3782***	−0.3768***
	(0.0087)	(0.0130)	(0.0134)
Family income missing	−0.2152***	−0.2515***	−0.2375***
	(0.0587)	(0.0641)	(0.0638)

Table 12A.2 *Continued*

Covariates	Model 1: No Heterogeneity	Model 2: No Endogeneity	Model 3: Joint
Macrolevel variables and calendar time			
Easy divorce state	0.1807***	0.2152***	0.2033***
	(0.0542)	(0.0697)	(0.0687)
Calendar time (relative to 1980)	−0.0014	−0.0098	−0.0258
	(0.0117)	(0.0158)	(0.0163)
Intercept	−0.4000**	−0.3406*	−0.4319**
	(0.1579)	(0.2005)	(0.2156)

Source: Authors' compilation.
Note: Asymptotic standard errors in parentheses.
* = .10 level.
** = .05 level.
*** = .01 level.

Table 12A.3 Heterogeneity: Variance-Covariance Structure

		Nonmarital Fertility ϵ^{cu}	Marriage Formation ϵ^{m}	Marital Fertility ϵ^{cm}	Marriage Dissolution ϵ^{d}
Nonmarital fertility	ϵ^{cu}	1.1129*** (0.0617)	—	—	—
Marriage formation	ϵ^{m}	0.6997*** (0.574)	0.9820*** (0.0670)	—	—
Marital fertility	ϵ^{cm}	0.1269 (0.1421)	−0.0661 (0.1614)	0.4951*** (0.0697)	—
Marriage dissolution	ϵ^{d}	0.3248*** (0.1068)	0.2579** (0.1125)	0.6116*** (0.1572)	1.1317*** (0.1041)
Education	λ	−0.4426*** (0.0898)	0.1147 (0.0964)	0.0992 (0.2546)	0.0731 (0.1059)

Source: Authors' compilation.
Note: Asymptotic standard errors in parentheses.
* = .10 level.
** = .05 level.
*** = .01 level.

This research is supported by grant R01 HD 30856 from the Population Research Center of the National Institute of Child Health and Human Development. The software for this application, aML, was developed by Lillard and Panis. We recognize Patricia St. Clair for her exceptional diligence in preparation of the event histories. We thank James Walker for his helpful critique and the conference participants for their comments and suggestions. The authors dedicate this chapter to the memory of their senior colleague, Lee A. Lillard.

NOTES

1. For ease of presentation, we use the term "nonmarital childbearing" (or "births" or "fertility"). However, the measurement is from the time of conception. We consider only those conceptions that lead to a live birth (either marital or nonmarital), not all conceptions, in accordance with most of the prior research on this topic.

2. We censored 4.0 percent of women at some point during the panels because of survey responses that were inconsistent with previously reported event histories, or because the respondent missed two or more consecutive survey interviews.

3. The full model, described in a technical appendix available from the authors, is discussed more fully in Lillard, Panis, and Upchurch (1994).

4. One might be concerned that the number of spells observed is determined by the same parameters being estimated and thus endogenous. This is correct, but there is no bias imparted to estimated parameters when using the full information maximum likelihood (FIML) estimation procedures in this study. This is confirmed in a Monte Carlo simulation of this and related issues by Lillard and Cottet (1998). Their results also indicate that coefficient estimates are quite robust to departures from normality in the single-outcome setting with several replications. These simulation results apply to multiple replications of a single-outcome process, but they do not explore the multidimensional heterogeneity case considered here.

5. The full model includes, in addition to the four processes described earlier, equations for continuing in school from one grade to the next until schooling is completed. We do not present the estimates of the parameters of the schooling progression or of the fertility processes in this chapter since the focus is on the consequences (rather than the determinants) of nonmarital fertility (for additional detail,

see Lillard, Panis, and Upchurch 1994; and Upchurch, Lillard, and Panis 2001).

6. This assumes, for example, that there is no additional source of correlation between nonmarital fertility and marriage in the never-married spell that does not carry over into unmarried spells after marriage. Similarly, it assumes no correlation between the risk of dissolution and marital fertility specific to a marriage. These are in principle testable assumptions not addressed in this chapter.

7. If normality is not assumed, then an alternative multivariate distributional assumption is required. One might use, for example, a multivariate finite mixture. We do not pursue these alternatives here.

8. Lillard and Cottet (1998) demonstrate the consistency of the parameters in normal-based, qualitative, dependent-variable models in which the number of replications depends on the heterogeneity component.

9. We found no significant differences between white and Hispanic women and therefore combined them into one category.

10. In an alternative model specification, we examined whether the child's age influenced the risk of marrying, but this effect was not significant.

11. We also tested for age effects of marital children and found they were not significant.

REFERENCES

Akerlof, George A., Janet L. Yellen, and Michael L. Katz. 1996. "An Analysis of Out-of-Wedlock Childbearing in the United States." *Quarterly Journal of Economics* 61(2): 277–317.

Anderson, Elijah. 1991. *Streetwise: Race, Class, and Change in an Urban Community.* Chicago: University of Chicago Press.

Axinn, William G., and Jennifer S. Barber. 1997. "Living Arrangements and Family Formation Attitudes in Early Adulthood." *Journal of Marriage and the Family* 59: 595–611.

Becker, Gary S. 1960. "An Economic Analysis Fertility." In *Demographic and Economic Change in Developed Countries,* edited by the Universities-National Bureau Committee for Economic Research. Princeton, N.J.: Princeton University Press.

———. 1973. "A Theory of the Allocation of Time." *Economic Journal* 81: 813–47.

———. 1991. *A Treatise on the Family.* Cambridge, Mass.: Harvard University Press.

Becker, Gary S., Elisabeth Landes, and Robert T. Michael. 1977. "An Economic Analysis of Marital Instability." *Journal of Political Economy* 85: 1141–87.

Bennett, Neil G., David E. Bloom, and Patricia H. Craig. 1989. "The Divergence of Black and White Marriage Patterns." *American Journal of Sociology* 95(3): 692–722.

Bennett, Neil G., David E. Bloom, and Cynthia K. Miller. 1995. "The Influence of Nonmarital Childbearing on the Formation of First Marriages." *Demography* 32(1): 47–62.

Brien, Michael J., Lee A. Lillard, and Linda J. Waite. 1999. "Interrelated Family-Building Behaviors: Cohabitation, Marriage, and Nonmarital Conception." *Demography* 36(4): 535–52.

Bumpass, Larry L. 1990. "What's Happening to the Family?: Interactions Between Demographic and Institutional Change." *Demography* 27(4): 483–98.

Casterline, John B., Ronald D. Lee, and Karen A. Foote. 1996. "Fertility in the United States: New Patterns, New Theories." *Population and Development Review,* vol. 22(supplement).

Center for Human Resource Research. 1991. *The NLS Handbook—1991: The National Longitudinal Surveys of Labor Market Experience.* Columbus: Ohio State University.

Cherlin, Andrew. 1977. "The Effect of Children on Marital Dissolution." *Demography* 14: 265–72.

———. 1978. "Remarriage as an Incomplete Institution." *American Journal of Sociology* 84: 634–50.

———. 1990. "Recent Changes in American Fertility, Marriage, and Divorce." *Annals of the American Academy of Political and Social Sciences* 510: 145–54.

East, Patricia L. 1998. "Racial and Ethnic Differences in Girls' Sexual, Marital, and Birth Expectations." *Journal of Marriage and the Family* 60: 150–62.

Elder, Glen H., Jr. 1995. "The Life Course Paradigm: Social Change and Individual Development." In *Examining Lives in Context: Perspectives on the Ecology of Human Development,* edited by Phyllis Moen, Glen H. Elder Jr., and Kurt Lüsher. Washington, D.C.: American Psychological Association.

———. 1997. "The Life Course and Human Development." In *Handbook of Child Psychology,* vol. 1, *Theoretical Models of Human Development,* edited by Richard M. Lerner. New York: Wiley.

Goldscheider, Francis K., and Linda J. Waite. 1986. "Sex Differences in Entry into Marriage." *American Journal of Sociology* 92: 91–109.

Heaton, Tim B. 1991. "Time-Related Determinants of Marital Dissolution." *Journal of Marriage and the Family* 53: 285–95.

Koo, Helen P., and C. M. Suchindran. 1980. "Effects of Children on Women's Remarriage Prospects." *Journal of Family Issues* 1: 497–515.

Lillard, Lee A. 1993. "Simultaneous Equations for Hazards: Marriage Duration and Fertility Timing." *Journal of Econometrics* 56: 189–217.

Lillard, Lee A., and Thiery Cottet. 1998. "Some Monte-Carlo Results on the Impact of Heterogeneity Distributional Assumptions in Panel Data: Continuous, Censored, and Qualitative Dependent Variables." Unpublished paper, RAND (March).

Lillard, Lee A., Constantijn W. A. Panis, and Dawn M. Upchurch. 1994. "Interdependencies over the Life Course: Women's Fertility, Marital, and Educational Experiences." Working paper. Santa Monica, Calif.: Rand Corporation.

Lillard, Lee A., and Linda J. Waite. 1993. "A Joint Model of Childbearing and Marital Disruption." *Demography* 30(4): 653–81.

Manning, Wendy D., and Nancy S. Landale. 1996. "Racial and Ethnic Differences in the Roles of Cohabitation in Premarital Childbearing." *Journal of Marriage and the Family* 58: 63–77.

Manning, Wendy D., and Pamela J. Smock. 1995. "Why Marry?: Race and the Transition to Marriage Among Cohabitors." *Demography* 32: 509–20.

Martin, Teresa C., and Larry L. Bumpass. 1989. "Recent Trends in Marital Disruption." *Demography* 26: 37–51.

McLaughlin, Diane K., and Daniel T. Lichter. 1997. "Poverty and the Marital Behavior of Young Women." *Journal of Marriage and the Family* 59: 582–94.

Morgan, S. Philip, Diane N. Lye, and Gretchen A. Condran. 1988. "Sons, Daughters, and the Risk of Marital Disruption." *American Journal of Sociology* 94: 110–29.

Mortensen, Dale T. 1988. "Matching: Finding a Partner or Otherwise." *American Journal of Sociology* 94: S215–40.

Oppenheimer, Valerie K. 1988. "A Theory of Marriage Timing." *American Journal of Sociology* 94: 563–91.

Pagnini, Deanna L., and Ronald R. Rindfuss. 1993. "The Divorce of Marriage and Childbearing: Changing Attitudes and Behavior in the United States." *Population and Development Review* 19(2): 331–47.

Parnell, Allan M., Gray Swicegood, and Gillian Stevens. 1994. "Nonmarital Pregnancies and Marriage in the United States." *Social Forces* 73(1): 263–87.

St. John, Craig, and David Rowe. 1990. "Adolescent Background and Fertility Norms: Implications for Racial Differences in Early Childbearing." *Social Science Quarterly* 71: 152–62.

Teachman, Jay D., and Daniel A. Heckert. 1985. "The Impact of Age and Children on Remarriage." *Journal of Family Issues* 6: 185–203.

Thornton, Arland. 1977. "Children and Marital Stability." *Journal of Marriage and the Family* 39: 531–40.

Upchurch, Dawn M., Lee A. Lillard, and Constantijn W. A. Panis. 2001. "Nonmarital Childbearing: Influences of Education, Marriage and Fertility." Under review.

Waite, Linda J., and Lee A. Lillard. 1991. "Children and Marital Disruption." *American Journal of Sociology* 96: 930–53.

Weiss, Yoram, and Robert J. Willis. 1985. "Children as Collective Goods in Divorce Settlements." *Journal of Labor Economics* 3: 268–92.

White, Linda K., and Alan Booth. 1985. "The Quality and Stability of Remarriages: The Role of Stepchildren." *American Sociological Review* 50: 689–98.

Willis, Robert J. 1999. "A Theory of Out-of-Wedlock Childbearing." *Journal of Political Economy* 107(6): S33–64.

Willis, Robert J., and John G. Haaga. 1996. "Economic Approaches to Understanding Nonmarital Fertility." In *Fertility in the United States: New Patterns, New Theories*, edited by John B. Casterline, Ronald D. Lee, and Karen A. Foote. *Population and Development Review* 22 (supplement).

Wilson, William J. 1987. *The Truly Disadvantaged: The Inner City, the Underclass, and Public Policy.* Chicago: University of Chicago Press.

Wilson, William J., and K. M. Neckerman. 1986. "Poverty and Family Structure: The Widening Gap Between Evidence and Public Policy Issues." In *Fighting Poverty: What Works and What Doesn't*, edited by Sheldon Danziger and Daniel Weinberg. Cambridge: Cambridge University Press.

Yamaguchi, Kazuo, and Linda R. Ferguson. 1995. "The Stopping and Spacing of Childbirths and Their Birth-History Predictors: Rational Choice Theory and Event-History Analysis." *American Sociological Review* 60: 272–98.

PART IV

Summary

CHAPTER 13

Nonmarital Fertility: Lessons for Family Economics

Shelly Lundberg

The chapters of this book provide a wealth of information on the correlates of, and changes in, nonmarital childbearing in the United States and Europe. A number of methodological advances have been made, and some progress in sorting out causal relationships from selection is evident. Several disciplinary perspectives are represented, and the studies use many different sources of data—some familiar and some unfamiliar to the average researcher in this area. What have we learned? The studies based on U.S. data focus on the causes and effects of nonmarital fertility, and a few general observations can sum up most of the new evidence, though they cannot capture the richness of the individual studies:

- Nonmarital childbearing reduces subsequent union formation, and much of this association seems to be causal (Wu, Bumpass, and Musick; Upchurch, Lillard, and Panis; Lichter and Graefe).

- A nonmarital birth is associated with negative outcomes for children, but it is not yet clear how much of this relationship is causal (Haveman, Wolfe, and Pence; Korenman, Kaestner, and Joyce).

- The role of fathers following a nonmarital birth varies, and different measures of paternal commitment are positively correlated (Bartfeld and Meyer).

- The generosity of welfare programs does appear to affect rates of nonmarital childbearing. This dependence is more apparent when we look at the childbearing of women in their twenties rather than teenagers (Foster and Hoffman). Male and female wages are also important and can help to explain the recent time-series pattern of increasing nonmarital births and declining welfare benefits (Moffitt).

• State policymakers will have considerable difficulty designing targeted policies to reduce the "illegitimacy ratio," given the variability in the demographic composition of nonmarital births across states (Kaye).

The studies based on data from western Europe (Kiernan; Ermisch) are particularly valuable for the broader perspective they provide. The American studies are concerned with the choice between legal marriage and a composite alternative. The European studies show that the increase in nonmarital childbearing has been principally due to a substitution of cohabiting unions for marriage. As Kiernan's cross-country comparison notes, the growth of cohabitation focuses our attention on changes and differences in laws and institutions concerning parental rights and responsibilities that may affect choices between alternative parenting arrangements.

Three themes that I find particularly interesting emerge from this evidence. First, we have learned that the behavior of older (non-teen) mothers is important for explaining nonmarital childbearing in the United States, since mothers age twenty and over account for 70 percent of all nonmarital births. This fact has implications for methods of analysis, since the economist's assumption of a rational decisionmaker is more plausible when adults are the agents of interest. It also shifts the policy focus from the prevention of pregnancy, the main goal of program response to teen childbearing, to the promotion of marriage among young adults. Marriage behavior and recent changes in marriage behavior become the interesting dimension of evolving family structure.

Second, we have seen that the partnership context of nonmarital births is heterogeneous and that this heterogeneity is important for child outcomes. Since more than 40 percent of nonmarital births now occur within a cohabiting union, the marriage–sole parent dichotomy is no longer adequate for either theory or empirical analysis. We need to extend our analysis, at a minimum, to the question of what determines the decision to cohabit rather than marry, and to how cohabitation might affect the impact of nonmarriage on children. Cohabitation clearly has different implications for poverty, welfare dependence, and paternal involvement in child-rearing than does sole motherhood. In the United States, it may be necessary to extend this framework further and recognize significant paternal involvement by noncohabiting fathers, as in the "visiting" relationships more common in African American communities.

Finally, it is apparent that family researchers need to move beyond a static decisionmaking framework and allow for dynamic aspects of marriage and fertility decisions. Behavioral responses to welfare are likely to depend on the expected persistence of benefits, and similarly, decisions to marry or cohabit will depend on the expected duration of those relationships. Young women are forward-looking agents, and their nonmarital childbearing decisions will reflect the expected consequences of motherhood for future marriage and the expected extent and duration of father involvement and support.

Economists and other social scientists should avoid the temptation to regard childbearing outside of marriage as simply a problem or a pathology. The legal context in which childbearing occurs will affect investments in children, and marriage may well be the arrangement most conducive to the efficient provision of that preeminent public good, children.[1] But fundamental to an economic approach is the recognition that nonmarital childbearing is a choice, and that the increase in nonmarital fertility is likely to be an adaptive response of individuals, not only to changes in labor markets and public assistance policies but also to fundamental changes in the long-term contract represented by marriage.

When a child is born outside of marriage, it is likely that nonmarital birth was a more desirable outcome for the parents than the feasible alternatives. For the young woman at least, single motherhood must be preferable to being single and childless (though restrictions on the availability of contraception and abortion must qualify this statement), and the young parents must have been unable to negotiate an agreement involving legal marriage that would have left both better off. The gains to marriage for the young parents depend on both the potential surplus available in the marriage and on the ability of the couple to enforce a long-term contract that will support the generation of that surplus. Marital surplus that arises from specialization and gains from trade requires a long-term contract in which the partner who specializes in home production does not suffer from the erosion of her outside earnings opportunities. The gains to specialization, and thus to marriage, have been eroded both by the convergence of male and female wages and by the increased probability of divorce. Other sources of marital surplus, such as the joint consumption of public goods, are available in alternative arrangements such as cohabitation.

It is important to specify what the relevant alternatives are for the men and women making decisions about marriage and parenthood. The marginal impact of changes in welfare policies or conditions in the marriage market will depend on which options the agents at the margin are choosing between. Within this choice framework, the heterogeneity of nonmarital regimes becomes interesting: unmarried parents can choose from among a variety of arrangements in partnership (cohabitation, visiting, separate), paternal provision of time and money, and the division of parental authority. The relative attractiveness of marriage will depend on the value of the best alternative arrangement, given the characteristics of the available partner, family support, welfare programs, and labor market conditions.

For individuals who face this choice, what are the important differences between cohabiting relationships and marriage? In both arrangements, the partners can enjoy the benefits of household economies of scale and the consumption of household public goods, including children. There would appear to be two main distinctions, apart from tax and employer benefit considerations: the degree of long-term commitment implied by the relationship and the division of parental rights. Marriage involves the announcement of a permanent commitment that, if plausible, may support more specialization and thus greater surplus than cohabitation, and marriage is more costly to dissolve. It also confers paternal custody rights that cohabitation does not.

If there is substantial uncertainty about the future benefits of the relationship, owing to a high probability of dissolution, employment instability, and low wages, the parents may prefer to defer or avoid marriage, and the mother may be reluctant to share permanent parental rights with the father. This uncertainty, when combined with the erosion of marital surplus implied by reduced specialization, may argue for a period of extended search for a long-term marital partner. A young mother may have little incentive to "settle" rather than to wait longer for Prince Charming to arrive, despite the costs associated with a nonmarital birth. The high rates of eventual marriage documented by Lichter and Graefe support the notion that marriage is being deferred rather than rejected. Upchurch, Lillard, and Panis present a related, provocative finding. A woman who has a high propensity to have a nonmarital birth also has a high propensity to marry, and they note that "family-building behaviors may be interchangeable." It is clear that variability in preferences is important, and this result raises the possibility that, for women with a high propensity for "family building," children and husband may be substitutes.

McLanahan and Garfinkel emphasize that early reports from the Fragile Families study find fathers to be very much present at the time of a nonmarital birth. This is a surprise, and it suggests that choices are still to be made about the future of this new family. How can we describe the objectives of young men and young women who are making decisions about marriage and childbearing? There does not seem to be an obvious answer to this question, particularly with respect to their relationships with each other and with their child, and economists have pursued disparate modeling approaches. In Willis's (1999) model of nonmarital childbearing, men receive utility from knowing that they have children, whether or not they have any contact with them. In more conventional models (including, in this respect, Neal's [1999]), men enjoy children as a public good, but only within marriage.

I would suggest an alternative theoretical approach in which unmarried parents are in continuous negotiation over a variety of issues: child support, father's involvement with and mother's treatment of the child, obligations to other romantic partners and children, and recognition (formal or informal) of the father's rights and authority with respect to the child. It seems likely that many young fathers value the social recognition of their paternal role and the exercise of decisionmaking power, while the mothers, though they value the father's involvement with the child, may find any diminution of their sole authority over the child costly or risky. This process of negotiation (combined, perhaps, with information-gathering and the development of trust) may lead to a transition to cohabitation or marriage, or to the end of the relationship. Institutional rules concerning child support, the establishment of paternity, or the rights of fathers can affect the terms of this exchange and, therefore, the equilibrium levels of parental inputs to children and the actual consequences of the nonmarital birth. For example, an increase in paternal rights may increase child well-being by increasing the father's incentive to invest in his child, or it may reduce children's welfare by devaluing the mother's primary bargaining chip. At the moment, given the endogeneity of observed establishment of legal paternity, we do not know which of these effects will dominate.

Where do we go from here? Among the interesting questions that remain are these: What determines the choice of a partnership arrangement between mother and father at birth? And what are the consequences of this choice for the child?

The first research priority, it seems to me, is more extensive modeling of parenting and partnership choices. We need both more theory and more information, perhaps nonquantitative, about what unmarried parents do and what they care about. We need to specify individual objectives and the range of options available inside and outside of marriage, including the implications of different living arrangements for both budget constraints and property rights in children. Only in the context of this complete choice set can we consider the effects of policy levers. For example, we have a great deal of evidence concerning the effect of welfare on the marriage/ nonmarriage choice, but no evidence on the effects of policy on the tripartite sole parenthood/cohabitation/marriage choice.

With respect to the effects of nonmarital births on child outcomes, a production function approach would seem to have much to offer. There is no strong reason to believe that marital status per se affects children, but rather that marital status may be associated with parental inputs that do, in turn, affect child outcomes. The heterogeneity in nonmarital living arrangements and paternal involvement require that these inputs be measured directly. Though the data requirements of this approach are daunting, this is essentially the path that has been taken by the literature on the effects of divorce, and the problems are analogous.

It is also important to continue to focus on the dynamic aspects of marriage and fertility choices, moving away from treating a nonmarital birth as an event with causes and consequences and toward a model of the marital and fertility history of an individual as a set of interdependent decisions in a life cycle context.

The past few years have presented researchers with rapid changes in marital and fertility behavior—in particular, the increase in cohabitation—combined with a dramatic revision of policies affecting low-income single parents. There is tremendous inertia in our analytical frameworks in the social sciences, and on this topic we are having to run very fast to keep up with events. This volume steps up the pace and shows that a constrained choice framework, combined with more flexibility in defining the behavior of interest and greater concern for dynamic effects, has great promise for increasing our understanding of the changing family.

NOTE

1. This observation forms the basis of the Weiss and Willis (1985) analysis of divorce settlements and child support payments.

REFERENCES

Neal, Derek. 1999. "The Economics of Family Structure." Madison: University of Wisconsin. Unpublished paper.

Weiss, Yoram, and Robert Willis. 1985. "Children as Collective Goods and Divorce Settlements." *Journal of Labor Economics* 11(4): 629–79.

Willis, Robert. 1999. "A Theory of Out-of-Wedlock Childbearing." *Journal of Political Economy* 197(6), part 2: S33–64.

CHAPTER 14

New Developments in the Study of Nonmarital Childbearing

Andrew J. Cherlin

This volume on nonmarital fertility marks a transition in the demographic and economic analyses of childbearing outside of marriage. It brings together three research domains that, until recently, have existed more or less independently but can no longer remain so: union formation and dissolution; adolescent fertility; and welfare policy. All are concerned with nonmarital fertility, but most researchers in these traditions have stayed within the boundaries of their subfield. The sheer fact of bringing them together is significant. Whether the three will coalesce into a coherent research domain remains to be seen, but the editors of this volume clearly believe that the new domain is coming of age.

Why are these research domains converging now? One important reason is the rise of cohabitation in the Western developed countries, a trend that has important implications for the study of adolescent fertility and welfare policy. The basic facts are well known to most readers: since the 1970s, cohabitation outside of marriage has become common and acceptable behavior among the working and middle classes. In the United States, about half of all young adults live with a partner before marrying for the first time, and perhaps two-thirds of all previously married individuals live with a partner before remarrying (Bumpass and Sweet 1989). At first, relatively few middle-class cohabitors had children (outside of the Scandinavian countries), but the proportion has increased: in the United States, about 40 percent of all cohabiting unions include children from current or former unions (Bumpass, Sweet, and Cherlin 1991).

As this change took hold, marriage lost its near-exclusive status as the only accepted context for bearing and raising children. In 1950 only about 4 percent of children were born outside of marriage; as of 1997, 32 percent were born outside of marriage (U.S. National Center for Health Statistics 1998a). As the percentage rose, observers became concerned about childbearing outside of marriage, assuming that most of it occurred to single women not living with a partner. That was a good assumption in the 1960s and 1970s, but it has become increasingly inaccurate, as I discuss later in this chapter. Analysts of childbearing outside of marriage must now consider two types: the familiar single mother, and the less familiar cohabiting couple.

COHABITATION AS A CONTEXT FOR BIRTH

The past decade or so has been a period of striking increases in the prevalence and importance of childbearing in cohabiting unions in the United States. Bumpass and Lu (1999) estimated that, as of 1995, 40 percent of nonmarital births in the United States occurred to women who were cohabiting. Furthermore, they concluded, nearly all of the increase in the percentage of children born outside of marriage between 1988 and 1995 was due to increases in births to cohabiting couples. These facts have not been digested by policymakers and social commentators, nearly all of whom write and speak as if the "out-of-wedlock birth problem" were entirely an issue of single women, many of them young, giving birth.

The recent growth in the number of births to cohabiting couples has occurred not so much among the poor as among the working and middle classes. Kelleen Kaye shows in this volume that women with high school degrees have been an important source of the overall increase in nonmarital births (an increase that includes births to cohabitors). It is these women, not high school dropouts, who have been responsible for the upward trend in nonmarital births of late. We can infer that many working- and middle-class women who, two decades ago, would have married prior to giving birth are now finding cohabitation to be an acceptable alternative setting in which to bear children.

Many western European countries have also experienced an increase in cohabiting couples, as Kathleen Kiernan's chapter in this volume shows. The Scandinavian countries have the highest percentages, and a second tier of countries with a high percentage is led by France. The percentages are somewhat lower in the United Kingdom, and substantially lower in southern European countries such as Spain and Italy. Where does the United States fall on this continuum? Its percentage of cohabiting couples is similar to the

Table 14.1 Nonmarital Births in the United States and
the United Kingdom, by Union Status

	United States	United Kingdom
Births to married women	67%	63%
Births to cohabiting women	14	22
Births to single women	19	15

Source: Author's compilation.

United Kingdom's (see table 14.1). John Ermisch's chapter on the United Kingdom presents a distribution of births by union status that is comparable to that of the United States (Bumpass and Lu 1999; Ermisch, this volume). Ermisch reports that 70 percent of the recent increase in nonmarital births in the United Kingdom is due to births to cohabiting couples; as I noted, the figure in the United States is closer to 100 percent.

The increasing share of births to cohabiting women suggests that having children in a cohabiting union has become mainstream behavior in most of Western society. It is no longer a marginal, frowned-upon lifestyle of the poor and the unconventional. To be sure, there is evidence that, in the United States at least, marriage is still the preferred context for raising children. The average duration of cohabiting unions remains relatively short in the United States—only about half last more than eighteen months (Bumpass, Sweet, and Cherlin 1991). But behavior could continue to change, and it is possible that in twenty years the percentage of births to cohabiting women will approach the percentage of births to married women. If this were to occur, then the characteristics of unmarried women giving birth would be more similar to those of married women giving birth.

Already about one in four American children will spend time in a cohabiting union while growing up (Graefe and Lichter 1999). If the percentage of births within cohabiting unions further increases at the expense of births within marriages, there will be even less family stability for children because cohabiting unions break up at a higher rate than do marital unions (Bumpass and Sweet 1989). Indeed, Wu, Bumpass, and Musick (this volume) find that cohabiting unions are about twice as likely to dissolve as marital unions following a first birth. Consequently, children in cohabiting unions experience rapid transitions into either single-parent families or marriage-based families (Graefe and Lichter 1999). In part, this instability could be due to the self-selected nature of cohabitors (they may be less likely to remain in any kind of union), and over time, if the shift continues, the self-selection could decrease. Indeed, in the Scandinavian countries, where cohabitation is most common, the difference in dissolution rates between marital unions and cohabiting unions is smaller than elsewhere in Europe (Kiernan, this volume). But the barriers to ending a cohabitation are lower than the barriers to ending a marriage: there are fewer legal entanglements to ending a cohabiting union, and friends and family generally do not take as negative a view of the breakup. It seems likely, therefore, that the dissolution rate for cohabiting couples will continue to be somewhat higher than it is for married couples. Some recent articles have suggested that the stability of children's family lives is an important predictor of their adjustment as adults (Wu and Martinson 1993). And we also might expect that, after a breakup, formerly cohabiting fathers would be even less involved in their children's lives than divorced fathers. On the other hand, cohabitation may allow some couples to quickly end unions that, if continued, would lead to prolonged conflict that would be harmful to the child.

ADOLESCENT CHILDBEARING

In the mind of the public—and until recently, in the minds of researchers as well—births to unmarried teenagers have been at the center of the nonmarital fertility picture. Much more concern has been expressed about teenage single mothers than about older single mothers, for important reasons—the former are perceived to be at risk of not finishing school, not being self-sufficient adults, and perhaps not being as competent at caring for their children. Of late, given the increasing visibility of nonmarital births to older women, some observers have been arguing that too much attention is paid to teenagers. They note that only one-third of nonmarital births occur to teenagers. Yet teenagers remain an important part of the picture. One-half of all nonmarital *first* births occur to teenagers, many of whom have subsequent nonmarital births when they are older.[1] Much of the story of nonmarital childbearing, then, starts with teenagers (see Wu, Bumpass, and Musick, this volume). From a policy perspective, adolescent nonmarital childbearing—and 76 percent of births to teenagers occur outside of marriage (U.S. National Center for Health Statistics 1998b)—is important because giving birth outside of marriage may set in motion an undesired life path and also because it may be easier to influence a sixteen-year-old than a twenty-five-year-old as she makes fertility decisions.

Nevertheless, the academic literature on adolescent childbearing has changed dramatically over the past decade or so. According to the old wisdom, young women who have a child as a teenager, in the oft-cited phrase, "have 90 percent of their life's script written for them" (Campbell 1968, 238), and the script is full of negative events, such as not graduating from high school. The chapter by Robert Haveman, Barbara Wolfe, and Karen Pence, who show that a woman's probability of graduating from high school is lower if she is unmarried at first birth, fits within this tradition.

However, revisionist researchers have argued that many of the problems exhibited by teenage mothers are due, not to having a child, but to the deprived environment in which they often live or hard-to-measure personal characteristics. The implication is that teenage mothers would experience many negative life events even if they postponed childbearing. Sanders Korenman, a leading revisionist scholar, continues that mode of thinking in the chapter he co-authored with Robert Kaestner and Theodore J. Joyce. They compare teenagers who are related, either as siblings or as cousins, and who therefore have more similar environments (and genetic endowments) than do a group of teenagers selected at random for a survey. In each set of relatives, some had given birth as teenagers and some had given birth at older ages. The authors find only modest differences in the health and development of the children born to teenage mothers and the children born to older mothers. Other contributors to this volume find suggestions in the national survey data that even before giving birth women who will later give birth as single parents are different from women who will later give birth within a marriage.

In the jargon of the literature, a *selection effect* is occurring: young women whose life chances are limited are more likely to self-select into the group of women who give birth. If so, then it is an error to attribute their limited life chances to the birth itself; many of the negative outcomes might have occurred even had no birth occurred. Most scholars in the field now agree that a substantial selection effect does exist. A recent study by Hotz, McElroy, and Sanders

(1997) uses a "natural experiment"—the fact that, more or less randomly, some pregnant women miscarry—to investigate the selection effect. The authors compared young women who had become pregnant and miscarried with women who gave birth in their teens. Ten years later the teenage mothers were doing as well as, or better than, the women who miscarried as teens. The latter group had their first children, on average, at age twenty. In other words, Hotz, McElroy, and Sanders essentially found that delaying childbirth until the end of the teenage years seemed not to produce better adult outcomes than having a child as a teenager.

This is not to say that there is no effect at all of having a birth as a teenager. Two chapters in this volume make the case that even after attempts to control for selectivity, some negative consequences can be found. Daniel T. Lichter and Deborah Roempke Graefe, in an analysis modeled after Hotz, McElroy and Sanders, also use the "natural experiment" of miscarriages. They first confirm the well-known finding that teenage mothers marry at lower rates than do women who did not have children as teenagers. If a selection effect explains this finding, they reason, then women who miscarry as teenagers should marry at rates similar to those for the teenage mothers because teenage pregnancy, whatever the birth outcome, would be a marker for unobserved characteristics that affect the likelihood of marrying. They report, however, that women who miscarried marry at rates that are closer to the higher rates they find for women who did not give birth or miscarry as teens than to the lower rates they find for teenage mothers. They also find that single mothers whose children did not live with them married at rates more similar to those for childless women than those for single mothers whose children lived with them. The implication is that selection effects cannot explain all differences and that it is plausible that a true cause-and-effect relationship exists between giving birth outside of marriage and having a lower likelihood of subsequently marrying.

This implication is also supported by the findings in the chapter by Dawn M. Upchurch, Lee A. Lillard, and Constantijn W. A. Panis. They attempt to adjust their statistical model of the effects of nonmarital childbearing on the rate of marriage for unobserved factors that may be correlated with both the likelihood of having a child nonmaritally and having a lower likelihood of marriage. Even after the adjustments are made, women with children born nonmaritally have lower rates of marriage than do women without children born nonmaritally.

A recent analysis of data from the Woodlawn Project (Jacobsen 1998a, 1998b) may help us reconcile some of these findings. The project is a longitudinal study of individuals who were first studied when they were in first grade in the Woodlawn neighborhood, which was then one of the poorest neighborhoods of Chicago. Almost all were African Americans from low-income families, and by design, all lived in the same neighborhood. They were given an extensive battery of tests and assessments, and their parents were interviewed. As a result, the Woodlawn study tries to control for typically unobservable variation by holding neighborhood constant and measuring an unusually broad set of cognitive, behavioral, and emotional characteristics. Jacobsen (1998a, 1998b) reports on outcomes for women in the Woodlawn sample who were reinterviewed at age thirty-two. She found that women who had postponed birth to age twenty or twenty-one were faring no better than women who gave birth as teenagers. However, women who gave birth after age twenty-two did have better life outcomes at age thirty-two.

So one interpretation of the Hotz, McElroy, and Sanders (1997) study and of Jacobsen's analysis of the Woodlawn data is that (1) the benefits of postponing childbearing from the teenage years to age twenty or twenty-one are not nearly as great as most writers on teenage childbearing two decades ago (and many today) thought, but (2) women who postpone childbirth to around age twenty-two do show better life outcomes. (See also the discussion later in this chapter of Foster and Hoffman's chapter in this volume.) This formulation raises a question: What factors are responsible for the better outcomes of those who did not give birth until twenty-two? When the research literature was suggesting that a postponement from age fifteen to seventeen made a difference, the inference was that girls needed to finish high school and that teenagers were sometimes not ready to become parents. But it is harder to argue that nineteen- and twenty-year-olds are not yet ready to parent; after all, a large number of first-time mothers in the 1950s were nineteen- and twenty-year-olds. It seems likely that many of those who waited until twenty-two also completed high school and either continued on to college or obtained job experience.

The policy implication of this recent body of research, then, may be that, other things being equal, postponing a birth from age fifteen to eighteen makes little difference in a woman's life, but postponing a birth from fifteen to twenty-two might make a difference. The problem with this policy statement is that it's far easier to encourage young women to postpone childbearing from fifteen to eighteen than from fifteen to twenty-two. Accomplishing the latter goal requires that young women at high risk of early childbearing be given the opportunity and the resources not only to finish high school but also to further develop their human capital by attending college or developing a career, all the while using contraception effectively and resisting pressure to bear a child. This is a tall order. It suggests that campaigns and programs focused on the young and mid-teen will not be sufficient to make a difference in the life outcomes of girls who are at high risk of pregnancy and childbearing.

NONMARITAL CHILDBEARING AND WELFARE POLICY

Nonmarital childbearing has long been a central topic in research on welfare policy. The main cash assistance program for the poor, first titled Aid to Dependent Children, was established as part of the Social Security Act of 1935. It was intended to provide support to widowed mothers whose husbands died before qualifying for social security benefits. But starting in the 1950s, the percentage of unmarried mothers who were separated, divorced, or never-married rose steadily. Correspondingly, the bulk of the caseload of the program renamed Aid to Families with Dependent Children (AFDC) consisted of dependent children and their mothers who had given birth outside of marriage or were divorced or separated from their husbands. As this transformation progressed, public support for the AFDC program fell. Its critics charged that AFDC encouraged childbearing outside of marriage and fostered dependence on public assistance rather than individual initiative.

Moreover, these same years saw a great increase in the percentage of married mothers who worked outside of the home. At the end of the century, about two-thirds of married women with preschool-aged children were working for pay, including about half of mothers with children under age one. With increasing acceptance of middle-class mothers with young children working for pay, the justification eroded for providing cash assistance to poor mothers so that they could stay home with their young children. A series of modifications of AFDC during the 1970s and 1980s were intended to encourage work effort. This trend culminated in 1996, when Congress passed a landmark bill restructuring welfare, the Personal Responsibility and Work Opportunity Reconciliation Act (PRWORA). This law placed a five-year lifetime limit on the use of federal funds to provide welfare payments to a family. It also required most adults receiving welfare to work by the end of two years. States were free to set shorter time limits, and many did.

Supporters of PRWORA shared the longtime concern about childbearing outside of marriage; the legislation even includes federal bonuses to states that lower their rate of out-of-wedlock births the most. Underlying this concern is the widespread belief that welfare benefits encourage childbearing outside of marriage because they offer support for single mothers. However, until recently at least, the evidence has not suggested a strong effect. A review of the evidence by Robert Moffitt (1995, this volume) found that the effect was moderate at best (although it may have been increasing in the years before publication of the 1995 article). A more recent article by Rosenzweig (1999) using data from the National Longitudinal Survey of Youth found larger effects of AFDC payments on nonmarital childbearing by adolescents and young adults.

Foster and Hoffman (this volume) replicate Rosenzweig's analysis using the data from the Panel Study of Income Dynamics. They confirm his findings, with two caveats. First, the finding is sensitive to the exact specification of the model. Second, they find that the effect is no longer statistically significant when they restrict the analysis to teenagers. (Rosenzweig had included young women through age twenty-two.) This finding suggests that the fertility of adolescents is less responsive to variations in welfare benefits.

For most of its history, AFDC was largely restricted to women who were not married or living with a man. As recently as the 1960s, some welfare departments were making nighttime visits to families to make sure there was no man in the house. But those days are gone. Many welfare offices allow women to live with men who are not the fathers of their children and, under certain circumstances, to live with the fathers themselves. Moffitt, Reville, and

Winkler (1998) estimated that, as of the late 1980s, 8 to 9 percent of all AFDC recipients were living with a male partner in the household. And since 1996, PRWORA has liberalized the rules for supporting two-parent families. As a result, welfare policymakers and researchers must now be mindful of cohabitation; it is likely that a growing proportion of welfare-receiving families will consist of a mother and her cohabiting partner. Observers of welfare can no longer assume that "unmarried parent" means "single parent."

Fathers are the overlooked actors in the research literature and the policy debates about welfare. Certainly, the demographic literature has focused largely on mothers. And the welfare system was organized in a way that excluded most men from receiving cash benefits, either individually or as members of a two-parent family. This situation is beginning to change. Researchers are paying more attention to issues involving fathers (see McLanahan and Garfinkel, this volume; Bartfeld and Meyer, this volume). PRWORA, as noted, incorporates some two-parent families, although these families are still a small minority of all recipients. In the policy debates, the focus has been not on father presence but rather on father absence—and specifically, on how nonresident fathers can be encouraged to provide more support to children whose mothers are receiving welfare. PRWORA requires mothers to empower the state to obtain child support from nonresident fathers. States are attempting to increase the number of nonmaritally born children for whom paternity is legally established. It appears that nonresident fathers are more involved in their children's lives if they legally acknowledge paternity, but this is not necessarily a cause-and-effect relationship, because unmeasured factors may make some fathers both acknowledge paternity and stay involved with their children.

CONCLUSION

Nonmarital childbearing is a much more complex phenomenon than it was a few decades ago, and the research in this volume reflects that change. Because of the rise of cohabitation, unmarried childbearing is no longer synonymous with single parenthood; a substantial and growing share of nonmarital births—currently about 40 percent in the United State—occur to cohabiting women (although this is less true for blacks than for whites; see Wu, Bumpass, and Musick, this volume). These cohabiting unions are, in general, less stable than marital unions, so a great deal of movement in and out of cohabiting status is to be expected. Moreover, nonmarital childbearing is no longer a phenomenon of the poor. To be sure, it remains substantially more common among the poor, but recent increases have occurred among nonpoor, better-educated individuals. The focus of the research literature on nonmarital childbearing, however, has remained on the poor, young, minority, single mother. It is time to broaden that focus, and doing so is one achievement of this volume. The authors are cognizant of the social changes that have occurred. They provide a perspective on cohabiting unions as well as on single parents. They pay attention to young adults and adults as well as teenagers. They examine the roles of fathers as well as mothers.

What of the future? If current trends continue, a growing proportion of children will be born to cohabiting couples. Under one scenario, we could become similar to the Scandinavian countries, where there are few births to single mothers but as many births to cohabiting mothers as to married mothers. In that case, the study of nonmarital fertility would become more and more similar to the study of marital fertility. It might even cease to exist as a separate subfield. I consider that outcome, however, to be unlikely. For one thing, middle-class cohabitation has been common in the United States for three decades now, and Americans still do not show the pattern of prolonged cohabitation that has been prevalent in the Scandinavian countries. Marriage still seems to be the preferred status; its persistence indicates that it is unlikely to be supplanted by cohabitation anytime soon. Second, it is very likely that, whatever adult women do, many adolescent mothers will give birth outside of marital or cohabiting unions. As long as the rate of adolescent childbearing in the United States remains substantially higher than in other Western countries, there will be many more young, unpartnered women giving birth here than elsewhere. And the study of nonmarital fertility will remain a mixture of single parents and cohabiting couples, adolescents having a first birth and adults a later birth, absent fathers who sometimes have little to do with their children and cohabiting fathers who are more involved, and poor mothers on welfare and working- and middle-class mothers who choose not to, or believe they cannot afford to, marry. This is the varied landscape that researchers are likely to view in the years ahead.

NOTE

1. From unpublished tabulations provided by the U.S. National Center for Health Statistics.

REFERENCES

Bumpass, Larry L., and Hsien-Hen Lu. 1999. "Trends in Cohabitation and Implications for Children's Family Contexts in the United States." *Population Studies* 54: 29–41.

Bumpass, Larry L., and James A. Sweet. 1989. "National Estimates of Cohabitation: Cohort Levels and Union Stability." *Demography* 26: 615–25.

Bumpass, Larry L., James A. Sweet, and Andrew J. Cherlin. 1991. "The Role of Cohabitation in Declining Rates of Marriage." *Journal of Marriage and the Family* 53: 913–27.

Campbell, Arthur A. 1968. "The Role of Family Planning in the Reduction of Poverty." *Journal of Marriage and the Family* 30: 236–45.

Graefe, Deborah Roempke, and Daniel T. Lichter. 1999. "Life Course Transitions of American Children: Parental Cohabitation, Marriage, and Single Motherhood." *Demography* 36: 205–17.

Hotz, V. Joseph, Susan Williams McElroy, and Seth G. Sanders. 1997. "The Impacts of Teenage Childbearing on the Mothers and the Consequences of Those Impacts for Government." In *Kids Having Kids: Economic Costs and Social Consequences of Teen Pregnancy,* edited by Rebecca A. Maynard. Washington: Urban Institute Press.

Jacobsen, Jill Marie. 1998a. "Does Timing of First Birth Affect Young Adult Outcomes in a Population of At-Risk African American Women?" Paper presented at the annual meeting of the American Sociological Association, San Francisco (August 23).

———. 1998b. "Does Timing of First Birth Affect Young Adult Outcomes in a Population of At-Risk African American Women?" Ph.D. diss., Johns Hopkins University.

Moffitt, Robert A. 1995. "The Effect of the Welfare System on Nonmarital Childbearing." In U.S. National Center for Health Statistics, *Report to Congress on Out-of-Wedlock Childbearing*. Washington: U.S. Government Printing Office.

Moffitt, Robert A., Robert Reville, and Anne E. Winkler. 1998. "Beyond Single Mothers: Cohabitation and Marriage in the AFDC Program." *Demography* 35: 259–78.

Rosenzweig, Mark. 1999. "Welfare, Marital Prospects, and Nonmarital Childbearing." *Journal of Political Economy* 107: S33–64.

U.S. National Center for Health Statistics. 1998a. "Birth and Deaths: Preliminary Data for 1997." *National Vital Statistics Reports* 47(4). Washington: U.S. Government Printing Office.

————. 1998b. "Report of Final Natality Statistics, 1996." *Monthly Vital Statistics Reports* 46(11, supplement). Washington: U.S. Government Printing Office.

Wu, Lawrence L., and Brian C. Martinson. 1993. "Family Structure and the Risk of a Premarital Birth." *American Sociological Review* 58: 210–32.

Index

Numbers in **boldface** refer to figure or tables.

403